AF361385

THE GASTRONOMICAL ARTS IN SPAIN

Food and Etiquette

EDITED BY FREDERICK A. DE ARMAS
AND JAMES MANDRELL

The Gastronomical Arts in Spain

Food and Etiquette

UNIVERSITY OF TORONTO PRESS
Toronto Buffalo London

© University of Toronto Press 2022
Toronto Buffalo London
utorontopress.com
Printed in the U.S.A.

ISBN 978-1-4875-4052-4 (cloth)   ISBN 978-1-4875-4054-8 (EPUB)
                                 ISBN 978-1-4875-4053-1 (PDF)

Library and Archives Canada Cataloguing in Publication

Title: The gastronomical arts in Spain : food and etiquette / edited by
    Frederick A. de Armas and James Mandrell.
Names: De Armas, Frederick A., 1945– editor. | Mandrell, James, editor.
Series: Toronto Iberic ; 65.
Description: Series statement: Toronto Iberic ; 65 | Includes bibliographical
    references and index.
Identifiers: Canadiana (print) 20220137625 | Canadiana (ebook) 20220137684 |
    ISBN 9781487540524 (cloth) | ISBN 9781487540548 (EPUB) |
    ISBN 9781487540531 (PDF)
Subjects: LCSH: Food habits – Spain – History. | LCSH: Gastronomy –
    Spain – History. | LCSH: Food – Spain – History. | LCSH: Food in literature. |
    LCSH: Spain – Social life and customs.
Classification: LCC GT2853.S7 G37 2022 | DDC 394.1/20946–dc23

We wish to acknowledge the land on which the University of Toronto Press
operates. This land is the traditional territory of the Wendat, the Anishnaabeg,
the Haudenosaunee, the Métis, and the Mississaugas of the Credit First
Nation.

University of Toronto Press acknowledges the financial support of the
Government of Canada, the Canada Council for the Arts, and the Ontario Arts
Council, an agency of the Government of Ontario, for its publishing activities.

Contents

Illustrations

THE GASTRONOMICAL ARTS IN SPAIN

Food and Etiquette

Introduction

In late 2010, the Spanish National Library in Madrid opened an exhibit dedicated to the history of gastronomy with the title "La cocina en su tinta." A clever play on words – literally "Cooking in its ink" or "Cooking in print" – the phrase "en su tinta" immediately references the popular preparation of squid, *calamares* or *chipirones en su tinta*, or squid in its ink. As such, the emphasis in the various displays was on manuscripts and books, magazines, photographs, and ephemera drawn from the library's extensive collections. But there were also additional materials, including works of art from the Museo del Prado and utensils and other objects from the Museo de Artes Decorativas [The Museum of Decorative Arts] and the Museo del Traje [Clothing Museum]. The exhibition offered a rich overview of the many ways that what is in fact a basic need becomes a matter of cultural interest.[1]

The exhibition was organized by world-renowned chef Ferran Adrià, who in 2011 would close his award-winning restaurant El Bulli; noted scholar María del Carmen Simón Palmer, of the Consejo Superior de Investigaciones Científicas [Spanish National Research Council] and the Real Academia de Gastronomía [Spanish Royal Academy of Gastronomy]; and Isabel Moyano Andrés, a senior member of the library staff. Not coincidentally, these three important figures represent distinct communities that have propelled recent interest in food and foodways, cooking, and gastronomy: the popular, including the worlds of formal and informal restaurants and of modern print culture; the academic, with a broad interest in the history and traditions of food and its consumption; and the institutional, which safeguards and, as in the case of this exhibition, shares artifacts from different times and places.

As exciting as the exhibition was, it only confirmed what cultural observers already recognized: that food had been having and was continuing to have a moment. In the popular domain, television programs, even entire channels, have been devoted to food and its preparation; print culture, including food magazines of all stripes, has dealt with everything from the humble to the traditional to *haute cuisine*, from local and regional cuisines to national traditions. Academic communities have paid increasing attention to food as an object of study from a variety of perspectives and have ranged widely in terms of chronology and geography. And institutions charged with cultural preservation have become increasingly aware of the treasures in their possession.

Spain is no exception in this regard. The study of food – or *alimento*, *alimentación* – in Spain is possessed of a long and venerable tradition. From the earliest collections of recipes to the most recent studies of the discourse on food in literary and other kinds of texts, questions of *alimentación* have attracted popular and erudite commentary alike. But, as the words *alimento* and *alimentación* suggest, studies of food are not limited to specific foods or preparations, but to a host of concerns related to the production, presentation, and consumption of food for reasons of hunger, sustenance, health, and even gluttony, on the one hand, and of etiquette and ostentation, on the other. These concerns include a broad set of ideas related to subsistence and nutrition, diet and well-being, the foodstuffs and dishes characteristic of Spain as a whole as well as of specific regions, and matters of food cultivation and distribution as well as foodways and the influence of other national traditions.

In fact, as María del Carmen Simón Palmer notes, in Spain, prior to the early 1800s, "bajo el amplio concepto de 'alimentación', se englobaban textos médicos, técnicos, didácticos, recetarios, etc." [under the broad notion of "food" were included medical, technical, didactic texts, recipe books, etc.] (2003, 13). She notes that these works are as much a part of the discourse on food writ large as the more traditional and familiar cookbook.[2] Thus, the range of texts involving considerations of food gives a good sense of the different topics taken up here for discussion. Numerous sources, dating back to the fifteenth century and through the nineteenth century, address a variety of topics such as carving meat, serving meals, food hygiene, the medicinal use of food, questions of etiquette and social conduct, and harvesting, among others. In an early essay, from 1423, the *Arte cisoria* [The Art of Carving], Enrique de Villena addresses the carving and serving of food at the royal table, from descriptions of different serving pieces to matters of protocol and the need for cleanliness. Cristóbal Acosta's 1578 *Tractado de las drogas y medicinas de las Indias Orientales con sus plantas debuxadas* [Treatise on drugs and medicines in the East Indies, with sketches of plants from life] deals with the medicinal uses of plants, herbs, and spices with chapters devoted to cinnamon, cloves, and coconut as an antidote to poisons. By the nineteenth century, the subject of carving is joined to questions of etiquette and social mobility in conduct manuals such as Mariano Rementería y Fica's *Manual del cocinero, cocinera, repostero, pastelero, confitero y botillero, con el método para trinchar y servir toda clase de viandas, y la cortesanía y urbanidad que se debe usar en la mesa* [Manual for the cook, female cook, pastrycook, confectioner, and beverage maker, with the method for carving and serving all kinds of foods, and the courtesy and urbanity that one ought to use at the table] (1828).[3]

But what we might refer to as the modern study of Spanish food culture probably could be said to date from the late nineteenth century and would include texts as diverse as the 1888 *La mesa moderna. Cartas sobre el comedor y la cocina cambiadas entre el doctor Thebussem y Un cocinero de S.M.* [The modern table. Letters about the dining room and the kitchen exchanged by Dr Thebussem and one of His Majesty's cooks] and Ángel Muro's *El practicón. Tratado completo de cocina* (1884) [The skilful one: Complete treatise on cooking]. In the first instance, Mariano Pardo y Figueroa and José de Castro y Serrano write under the pseudonym of el Dr Thebussem and behind the mask of a chef in the royal household, respectively, and debate the nature of Spanish cuisine, especially that of the court. The letters, first published in the newspaper *La Ilustración Española y Americana* in 1876, are by turns humorous and insightful, exploring a variety of issues but always returning to the matter of what is Spanish about Spanish food. Similar issues attend Muro's lengthy cookbook, but here we get a good sense of the way that Spanish culinary tradition has, in fact, yielded to the hegemony of French cuisine. In this regard, Emilia Pardo Bazán's 1913 *La cocina española antigua* [Old (traditional) Spanish cuisine] and 1917 *La cocina española moderna* [Modern Spanish cuisine], both in the series she founded, Biblioteca de la Mujer [The woman's library], pursue the question of what is Spanish against the backdrop of tradition and modernity.[4]

As for more scholarly approaches to the matter of Spanish cuisine, the topic has been approached generally as well as from the perspective of period, place, and institution, and in terms of literature. More general studies range from Dionisio Pérez's 1929 *Guía del buen comer español* [Guide to good Spanish food] to *El libro de la cocina española* (1970) [The book of Spanish cuisine], by Nestor Luján and Juan Perucho.[5] Lorenzo Díaz has done much for discussions of Spanish food in the context of literature, with a series of suggestively titled books involving different periods and authors,[6] restaurants,[7] and places.[8] However, the recent scholarly impulse towards the study of food, whether or not it was recognized as such, came from María del Carmen Simón Palmer, who, over a series of publications, showed just how rich the field could be.

As early as 1977 she began laying the foundation for a more complex understanding of food and sustenance in Spain with the publication of *Bibliografía de la gastronomía española: notas para su realización* [Bibliography of Spanish gastronomy: Notes for its realization]. This overview of the vast number of texts comprising discourse in Spain on topics related to food writ large is bookended twenty-five years later, in 2003, by the definitive *Bibliografía de la gastronomía y la alimentación en España* [Bibliography of the gastronomy and food culture of Spain]. In between these two substantial volumes, Simón Palmer added studies and books that demonstrated a special interest in the Spanish court, with *La alimentación y sus circunstancias en el Real Alcázar de Madrid* [Food culture and its circumstances in the Real Alcázar of Madrid] and *La cocina de Palacio 1561–1931* [The royal kitchen 1561–1931], and the documentation of *Libros antiguos de cultura alimentaria (siglo XV–1900)* [Antiquarian books devoted to food culture (from the fifteenth century to 1900)]. Of course, Simón Palmer was not the only one to explore these topics.[9] All of these – and many other studies – give a sense of the richness of the conversation around the topic of food in Spain, as well as suggest the vast areas to be explored.

Yet, to speak of food in Spain, of Spanish gastronomy, without qualification, is to overlook, perhaps occlude, the effects of Spain's multicultural past and its imperial reach. Centuries of Semitic presence in the Iberian Peninsula, including Muslim rule, brought to Spain foodstuffs and terminology that shape Spanish cuisine to this day. Rice, for example, including its cultivation, arrives in Spain with the Muslims, and *arroz*, the Spanish word for the grain, follows a similar etymological route, which is distinct from other Romance languages. Where Italian (*riso*) – and French (*riz*), through Italian – draw on Latin, Greek, and beyond, the Spanish *arroz* travels back in time to the Greek through classical Arabic. Similar stories could be told about oil (*aceite*), apricots (*albaricoques*), almonds (*almendras*), saffron (*azafrán*), eggplant (*berenjena*), spinach (*espinaca*), and myriad other foods as well as herbs and spices. Jewish culture contributes distinct preparations such as the *adafina*, a *hamin* or slowly cooked savoury stew, served on *shabat*, the Jewish sabbath day, in a preparation like that of many Spanish stews, such as the *olla podrida*, or rotten pot, which can contain a hodgepodge of meats and vegetables (Cantera Montenegro 2003, 32–4). And America also contributed to the Spanish diet by sending to Europe what are now foundational foods and spices, such as potatoes, tomatoes, and paprika, which is made from peppers.

While Muslim and Jewish traditions contributed much to the varieties of foods, with the conversion of these groups to Christianity at a time when numerous prohibitions were in place, the display or the concealment of food and food preparation became key elements. In a recent book, Jillian Williams explains, for example, how recent converts from Judaism would at times preserve their Jewish identity through the purchase and preparation of food, buying ritually slaughtered meats and cooking unleavened bread. On the other hand, it was important to display the drinking of wine and the consumption of pork to assert one's Christian identity: "In fifteenth and sixteenth-century Spain it was common to display a leg of ham or a rasher of bacon in *morisco* homes as a symbol of assimilation into the Christian religion" (Williams 2017, 28). Old-Christian homes, on the other hand, featured female cooks who often embodied or evoked Martha in the story of Jesus' visit to the two sisters. Jennifer S. Wyant explains: "Mary and Martha stood at the centre of a number of debates about the nature of Christian discipleship, and they have proven to be lively characters. Martha left the kitchen to preach the gospel and slay dragons, only to return to the kitchen, while Mary remarkably has encompassed all of the other Mary's in the New Testament" (2019, 265). The active and the contemplative life are thus juxtaposed, and Martha became the image of the mystical cook in Spanish cooking manuals and even in early modern art.

It is important to study the cooks and the works they produced. In this regard, Carolyn Nadeau points to early modern palace cooks in Spain, showing that they are no longer anonymous. Some acquire reputations that go well beyond the borders of the peninsula, as Spanish food becomes known throughout Europe and national identities are tied to specific recipes. Daniela Gutierrez Flores, in a ground-breaking dissertation, looks not just at famous and courtly cooks but also to the presence of these figures in different social classes and groups. Her study ranges from palace chefs to servants of African descent, and from low-ranked nuns to Spanish picaresque figures, taking up not only the study of these cooks but also the preparation of different foods from both sides of the Atlantic (Gutiérrez Flores, manuscript).

In ways small and large, then, Spanish gastronomy was influenced by a number of important encounters, a coming and going of foodstuffs and ideas about food and its preparation. This can be seen in two examples, an ingredient and a book: sugar, on the one hand, and, on the other, the Spanish translation of Jules Gouffé's *Le Livre de Cuisine* [Cookbook]. Sugar is particularly interesting, as it has a complex history and uncertain origins in East India or Southeast Asia, perhaps New Guinea, perhaps China, an uncertainty that speaks of various cultural encounters (Satō 2015, 15). The cultivation of sugar cane is carried to the West in large part by Muslims, who introduce it to the Islamic Mediterranean, including Sicily and Andalucía. Over time, the cultivation of sugar cane and production of sugar shifts, first, in the fifteenth century, to the Madeira Islands and the Azores, with the Portuguese, and the Canary Islands, courtesy of the Spanish, and from there with Columbus to the Americas (Mintz 1985, 23–32; Satō 2015, 30–2). Eventually sugar production is taken over by other European powers (Mintz 1985, 35), but it's clear that, through sugar, Spain, and Portugal, served as a point of contact between the Muslims, the Americas, and the rest of Europe.

For the Europeans, sugar was a luxury good, a foodstuff, a spice, and a medicine (Mintz 1985, 30). But as Joseph Imorde notes, sugar has a spiritual corollary, as in the metaphor of *dulcedo Dei*, or the sweetness of God,[10] of which mention is found in the Bible (Psalm 33:9) as well as in the writings of early modern theologians, and which figures prominently in Augustine's *Confessions*: "The Confessions are – so to speak – sugar coated with the divine delicacies of the *dulcedo Dei*. Augustine calls God 'my sweetness,' 'my holy sweetness,' 'never delusive sweetness,' 'good and steady sweetness,' the 'truest and highest sweetness,' even 'the sum of all sweetnesses.' To enjoy the infinite sweetness of the *dulcedo Dei* it was necessary to have a very refined palate, the so-called 'palate of the heart' (*palatum cordis*)" (Imorde 2014, 3, 5). But the rhetoric of sweetness common in religious discourse, up into the nineteenth century according to Imorde, comes to be looked at unfavourably, when sugar is no longer seen as a luxury because it is commonly available thanks to cultivation of the sugar beet. Instead, it came to be understood that sugar was a health nightmare, initially creating problems, like halitosis and dental cavities, for the wealthiest of people as early as the seventeenth century, for figures such as Elizabeth I of England and Louis XIV of France,[11] and much later for the common folk, when, because so inexpensive, it was consumed in ever greater amounts (Imorde 2014, 9).

Another significant encounter arises from Spain's pronounced curiosity about the world around it, a curiosity that manifests itself not only in the traces of other places and times but also through the translation of texts and traditions from elsewhere. The 1885 translation of Gouffé's *Le Livre de Cuisine*, first published in Paris by Hachette in 1867, with revised editions in 1870, 1874, 1877, 1881, and 1884, offers a case in point, representing the authoritative introduction of French cuisine to a broad Spanish public and perhaps an acknowledgment of its hegemony.[12] In fact, Gouffé's *Libro de cocina* was one of the few French cookbooks translated into Spanish: of the important contributions to French cuisine authored by La Varenne, Menon, Alexandre Viard, Carême, and Louis-Eustache Audot, none was translated into Spanish prior to 1885.[13]

Divided into two parts, *Le Livre de Cuisine* first explores, in nineteen chapters over almost 330 pages, *la cuisine de ménage*, or home-style cooking, and, in the second part, *la grande cuisine*, which occupies seventeen chapters and, with appendices, over 450 pages. Gouffé notes in the preface that this division, which is indeed innovative, serves as a correction to a general confusion:

On confond ordinairement dans les ouvrages culinaires la petite et la grande cuisine, les mets les plus simples avec ceux du genre le plus compliqué; de là, un amalgame des plus fâcheux, et qui explique comment l'étude et la pratique de l'art culinaire ont fait si peu de progrès jusque'à ce jour. (1867, ii)[14]

[One tends to confuse domestic cooking and *haute cuisine* in culinary works, the simplest dishes with those of the most complicated kind, resulting in a most unfortunate amalgamation that explains how we have made so little progress to this day in the study and practice of the culinary art.]

We would, however, be mistaken to think that Gouffé was acknowledging the importance of domestic cooking. Instead, as Stephen Mennell comments, "What may appear unusual respect and attention paid to domestic cookery by one of the élite of French professional chefs is better understood … as an attempt to establish domestic and professional cuisines as two quite distinct disciplines and distinct conceptions of good cooking" (1985, 150). Yet the book isn't simply divided into two parts. It's written for two distinct types of readers and cooks, the home cook and the chef, who are understood in terms of sex and class, where "la cuisinière bougeoise" [the middle-class cook], a woman, is not to be confused with "un chef de grande maison" [a chef of a great home], a man who is given a professional title (Gouffé 1867, ii), notions that are, not surprisingly, easily translated to Spanish circumstances.

It's difficult to give a sense of the sheer impact of Gouffé's *Le Livre de Cuisine* and the Spanish translation, *El libro de cocina*, without having a copy of either book at hand. It's not just the length, 846 pages in the Spanish translation, but the ingenious wood engravings and the spectacular colour plates by Etienne Antoine Eugène Ronjat. In French or Spanish, the book is a feast for the eyes. The engravings detail foodstuffs, cooking utensils, and techniques, such as in the thirty-second figure (Gouffé 1867, 87; Gouffé 1885, 93), which shows the position of the hands when adding thickening agents to a sauce (fig. 0.1). The colour plates range, in the first part of the book, from cuts of meat to trussed fowl as well as from some simple appetizers to, in the second

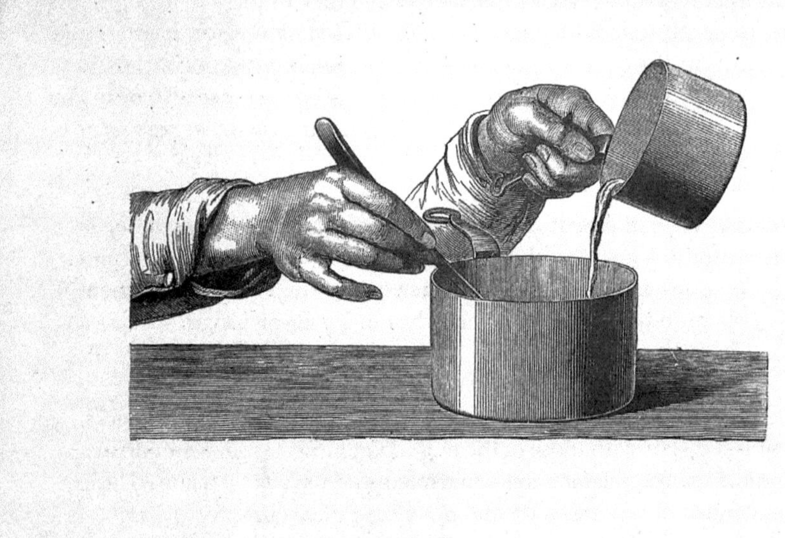

Figure 0.1. Figure 32 from Jules Gouffé's *El libro de cocina*: the position of the hands while adding a thickening agent to a sauce. Madrid: Librerías de A. de San Martín, 1885.

part, stunningly beautiful tableaux of almost unimaginable complexity, such as, in the twelfth plate, "Téte de veau en tortue"/"Cabeza de ternera con salsa à la tortuga" [Calf's head with turtle sauce] (Gouffé 1867, 498; Gouffé 1885, 498), where the calf's head is concealed under an extravagant decoration involving crayfish, olives, and truffles, among other garnishes (fig. 0.2), or, in the twenty-third plate (Gouffé 1867, 692; Gouffé 1885, 696), a display of two dishes, a lobster salad and a *mayonesa de filetes de lenguado*, a gelatin mould of sole filets garnished with crayfish tails and hearts of lettuce (fig. 0.3).

We would be justified at this point to recall Roland Barthes's "mythology" entitled "Ornamental Cookery," where he draws a distinction between the presentation of food as seen in two very different magazines popular in France in the 1950s, *Elle* and *L'Express*, which are addressed, respectively, to the middle class and the working classes (1991, 79). According to Barthes, *Elle* offers every week a "fine colour photograph of a prepared dish" such as "a mould of crayfish surrounded by their red shells," the effect of which is to create a "smooth coating," a fiction, that "belongs to a visual category, and cooking according to *Elle* is meant for the eye alone, since sight is a genteel sense" (1991, 78).

Figure 0.2. Plate 12 from Jules Gouffé's *El libro de cocina*: calf's head with turtle sauce. Madrid: Librerías de A. de San Martín, 1885.

Barthes concludes that readers of *Elle* get only fiction, while readers of *L'Express* get recipes for real dishes that they will be able to prepare. The mythology invoked is one of economics and social class, in which the food seen in *Elle* "is an openly dream-like cookery ... objects at once near and inaccessible, whose consumption can perfectly well be accomplished simply by looking. It is, in the fullest meaning of the word, a cuisine of advertisement, totally magical" (1991, 79). In terms of the world portrayed in Gouffé's *Le Livre de Cuisine* and *El libro de cocina*, there's no expectation that a middle-class cook will necessarily essay, much less master, through practice, the nuances of *haute cuisine*. The images in the second half of the book serve instead as aspirations, or, in Barthes's words, as representations of "an openly dream-like cookery"; they are, quite literally, "a cuisine of advertisement, totally magical" (1991, 79). To reframe the *Libro de cocina* in Barthes's terms, the book is like neither *Elle* nor *L'Express*, but both in one: the first part of the book is more like *L'Express*, possible, and the second, like *Elle*, a fiction. And

Figure 0.3. Plate 23 from Jules Gouffé's *El libro de cocina*: lobster salad and *mayonnaise de filets de sole*. Madrid: Librerías de A. de San Martín, 1885.

the images depict victuals that are, if not as glazed or shiny as Barthes's description of the foods photographed for *Elle*, what we might now refer to as a kind of gastro- or food porn that obscures rather than reveals the primary ingredient being featured and that appeals, at least in some instances, more to the eyes than to the tastebuds.[15]

Still and all, the translation of French cuisine to Spanish is somewhat less than ideal. The translation of the prose narration tends to be accurate. But the recipes suffer from numerous errors and omissions: quantities are switched, ingredients are left out, and there are numerous errors in the French, as we see in the twentieth plate, showing what should be "Chaud froid de pollo a la gelatina" and "Aspic a la Bellevue, where "chaud" is rendered as "chuad" (fig. 0.4). This suggests how fraught with peril the process of translation of one culinary tradition into another is, not merely in a practical sense, but as a process of accuracy, accommodation, and assimilation, where attention may flag or a pen may slip; where ingredients may not be known, easily found, or even named in a new language; where tastes and preferences

Figure 0.4. Plate 20 from Jules Gouffé's *El libro de cocina*: chaud-froid sauce of chicken in gelatin and aspic à la Bellevue. Madrid: Librerías de A. de San Martín, 1885.

vary; and where different preparations may bear meaning in distinct ways. Some of this can be seen in another plate from *El libro de cocina*, the twenty-fourth (Gouffé 1885, 730), which portrays two spectacular presentations of fruit, "Manzanas a la parisien" and a "Macedonia de frutas," or a cake crowned with apples and other fruits in a sweet syrup and an elaborate timbale with fruit salad (fig. 0.5). Among other issues, "Macedonia de frutas," for "Macédoine de fruits," represents a failure of translation, since this particular use of "macedonia," referring to a fruit salad, is not documented in Spanish until well into the twentieth century. The result is a collision of cuisines and languages in a rendering that misfires even as it attests to inherent, almost reflexive, resistance to the importation of a foreign culture.

This is by way of suggesting that any discussion of Spanish cuisine engages, implicitly or explicitly, with other food traditions, which, in turn, hints at the many difficult choices it was necessary to make in compiling the essays found here. There were questions of geography

Figure 0.5. Plate 24 from Jules Gouffé's *El libro de cocina*: apples à la parisienne and fruit salad. Madrid: Librerías de A. de San Martín, 1885.

and time period, of scope and disciplinary approach. There was also the question of the medium of expression, of words or images, the latter as in Spanish *bodegones* or still lifes, paintings involving all things associated with food, which have been well studied by Alfonso E. Pérez Sánchez, William B. Jordan and Peter Cherry, and, particularly, Norman Bryson, among others.[16] In the end, it was important to represent a diversity of viewpoints while recognizing the limitations imposed by the fact of a collection of individual contributions. Of course, were space unlimited, it would be tempting to offer something in the nature of an encyclopedia that would reflect the diversity of disciplines with a stake in the discussion of the history of gastronomy along with food, cooking, foodways, and the impact that the Spanish Empire had on eating and eating practices in Spain. But even then, there would be oversights and omissions. In the end, taking the written word in its many forms as a point of departure seemed appropriate.

Thus, through a series of essays that focus on texts spanning from the medieval to the contemporary periods, this volume presents a carefully curated overview of the art of gastronomy in Spain. In recent years, and thanks to the pioneering works of Structuralists such as Claude Lévi-Strauss, among others, we have come to understand the value of gastronomy as an essential site of culture. Even cookbooks, once thought to be of little importance, are today viewed as key texts, as they "directly link consumption of food and the consumption of a text as a commodity ... and when studied as a genre, cultural values emerge through the pattern of foodstuffs, cooking methods and presentations that recur" (Nadeau 2016, 189). Text and food come together in this volume, since, as Ronald Tobin asserts: "The cook and the poet both work at *bricolage* – making something new out of something old – and through a process of selection, renovation and imagination, they perform an archetypal, sacred and creative act that produces original, complex products which change the consumer emotionally[,] intellectually and physically (1990, 4). If cookbooks are of such significance, what are we to say of banquets? From Plato's symposium to contemporary feasts, they feature different aspects of this cultural event. Michel Jeanneret notes, "The combination of words and food in a convivial scene gives rise to a special moment when thought and the senses enhance rather than tolerate each other" (1991, 1). Indeed, these two forms of oral satisfaction were central to the transmission of Renaissance ideals. As these words are turned into texts, we can discover the full symbolic range of these festivities, from the "banquet of sense," which, for Frank J. Kermode, stands for the quasi-bestial man, to the Christian sacrament of the Eucharist.

The essays that follow encompass a series of cultural objects and a number of interests, ranging from medicine to science, from banquets to etiquette, and from specific recipes to cookbooks. In this textual banquet of sense, the first course focuses on foodstuffs and includes honey, beeswax, *olla podrida*, and corn. The first essay deals with the production of honey, as well as its by-product, beeswax, in early Christian culture. Ryan Giles focuses on four songs from the *Cantigas de Santa Maria* [Songs to Holy Mary] in order to relate them to the multi-confessional context of thirteenth-century Castile. For Giles, Mary's maternal body parallels the honeycomb, as her followers collect the nectars and return to their hive as a symbol of repentance and reconciliation. Indeed, the *colmena* [hive] becomes a tabernacle that miraculously houses the king bee, Jesus, born of the Virgin, who appears in the churches in the form of the honeyed Eucharist. The *Cantigas* in this way figuratively represent penitents and converts as a swarm of honeybees, following their Christian king to the hive. The second essay moves us from the medieval and religious realms to the secular and early modern world, while focusing on Spanish Stew [*Olla podrida*]. Here, Carolyn Nadeau contributes to the rich ongoing dialogue on Spain's early modern gastronomy by comparing the two most important court cookbooks of the early modern period, the first written by Ruperto de Nola in 1520 and the second by Francisco Martínez Montiño almost a century later (1611). Centring on the Spanish Stew, the essay also examines images of Spanish cuisine from beyond Spain's borders. By using cookbooks and journals from Italy, France, and England, Nadeau seeks to understand how different European cooks and gastronomes identify and describe Spanish cuisine. Curious readers will encounter in an appendix two recipes from the period, which they may wish to replicate. The third essay, by John Slater, takes up three moments in the history of maize's narrative development – Spain in the seventeenth century, France in the nineteenth, and the United States in the twentieth – to illustrate how stories of the origin and dissemination of maize have been deployed as political mythologies. For Slater, tales about the origins of corn are often a way of constructing an identity, telling a story of racial difference, or resisting a dominant narrative. Using a most felicitous analogy, he labels maize an "undocumented traveller." Slater's essay echoes Nadeau's piece in the sense that both relate food to identity. This third essay also serves as "supplement" to Ryan Giles's piece, since Slater turns away from Spanish Christian symbolism of the honeybee moving to the hive and points to American maize moving to Spain, but in a way that sheds its New World Indigenous connections. The first course, then, sensitizes the palate as honey, while the Spanish stew and the ever-changing maize exhibit their many facets and entice the curious reader to experience a second course.

The second course in this collection deals with what to eat, and how, in sixteenth- and seventeenth-century Spain. While in the first course we were able to "consume" three different foodstuffs as they travelled symbolically or physically across lands, here we must pause and make sure that the diet is appropriate for the individual and that the way in which it is consumed aligns with the social class and decorum of the customers. The first of three essays is by Fernando Serrano Larráyoz. He argues that, by the sixteenth century, dietary prescriptions had become individualized, and thus dietetic recommendations were crafted to treat individuals' specific illnesses, in this case Juan Rena and Juan de Alarcón (his servant). These dietetic prescriptions go hand in hand with other recommendations, including the use of unguents, plus bathing and massages (in lieu of exercise). The study of these accounts and their comparison with similar texts already well known allow us to understand better the eating habits and prescriptions of the period. As Rena expresses the desire to eat egg yolks, they would be cooked with cinnamon and sugar (rather than honey). Indeed, no longer is honey to be seen as a religious image as in Giles's essay, nor are the spices linked to identity or origin. More to the point are wine, sleep, and emotions. This chapter is followed by Julio Vélez-Sainz's piece on food and etiquette in Renaissance theatre. This critic seeks to insert Spanish Renaissance drama, a much-neglected field of study even among Hispanists, within the larger context of socio-historical analyses of literature. Utilizing what Norbert Elias has aptly termed the "history of manners," Vélez-Sainz shows how Spanish Renaissance authors, such as Juan del Enzina and Lucas Fernández, project new meanings on how the early modern European self was constructed, through a kind of decorum reflected in table manners, proper utensils used at meals, etc. While medical tracts and treatises on manners exhorted the nobleman to eat in a measured manner, plays of the period include scenes of overeating. Shepherds are contrasted with other characters, showing their rusticity through the types of food they eat and the excesses in which they indulge. Turning to an eclogue by Lucas Fernández, this essay shows that the shepherds' excess of hair, bushy beards and thick eyebrows, contrasts with the highly groomed soldier who also is temperate in terms of food. On the other hand, Enzina's *Eclogue of Fileno, Zambardo and Cardonio* shows how unrequited passion can transform a mannered Fileno into a quasi-savage figure. As he throws away all his possessions, particularly his lute, he descends into a kind of madness, which does not prevent him from enjoying some breadcrumbs he has saved. In a curious turn, the actors in some of these plays were paid with food. Although they enacted figures of rustics and nobles, they would overeat, underlining their place in society. As time went on, and with the publication of these plays, the courtly ideals presented in these works were then taken up by the general public. The savages with unruly hair and customs were transformed. This essay, then, bridges the gap between gastronomy and manners, showing how they depend on each other. This second essay echoes the first course in that it invokes questions of identity, but it belongs here since it is much more about how foods are consumed. The third essay, by Frederick A. de Armas, describes different key repasts in the *comedia*, while seeking to foreground the many dramatic possibilities and the many registers and symbolic significance of these scenes. He divides these gastronomical moments into five general categories: celestial suppers, unholy banquets, rustic repasts, banquets of sense, and demonic feasts. From the sight of the celestial to demonic touch, these feasts provide insights into the purpose, uses, and meanings of these culinary events in the works of Calderón de la Barca, Claramonte,

Lope de Vega, Moreto, Ruiz de Alarcón, Tirso de Molina, and Valdivielso. The banquet emerges as an essential component of the theatre of early modern Spain, with its many dramatic elements, its malleable script, and its metatheatrical and performative nature. This panoramic essay rounds out Vélez's in-depth study of food and manners, pointing to different types of banquets rather than to different forms of etiquette. De Armas's piece serves to balance the dietetic prescriptions of the first essay in this second course with a series of banquets that allow the consumer to end this section fully satiated.

The third course moves us away from the past and allows us to enjoy modern appetites and culinary fashions. The first essay draws on Felipe V's reign in order to discuss food in eighteenth-century Spain. James Mandrell explains that, where the arrival of Felipe V brought with it renewed interest in and emphasis on French customs, including French food, appetite for these plates was tempered both by what they represented and by matters of means and the availability of ingredients. Mandrell demonstrates how food, one of many points of reference, functioned as a site of cultural negotiation and, as such, came to be embedded in different forms of discourse reflecting matters of appetite and hunger as well as traces of memory. Through three vignettes, Mandrell explores the extent to which the discourse on food in the eighteenth century was neither univocal nor possessed of a simple straightforward history. Instead, the vignettes reveal ongoing negotiations relating to appetite and hunger that will remain unresolved throughout the period. The second essay, by Íñigo Sánchez Llama, turns to Mariano José de Larra's periodical writings. He argues that, with a classic formation, an openness to Romantic tendencies, and involvement in the modernizing processes emerging in the heat of Spanish liberalism, Larra postulates not just the adoption of the cultural values associated with European modernity but the establishment of a genuinely modern Spanish literature in accordance with the exigencies of nineteenth-century social and aesthetic changes. Larra's various articles on culinary topics make reference to traditional Spanish gastronomy in order to develop a precise analysis of the factors that prevent the consolidation of modern tendencies in Spain. In the third piece included in this section, Dorota Heneghan examines the symbolic values of meals in Benito Pérez Galdós's *El amigo Manso* [Friend Manso] and the way in which Galdós implicated them in his critique of the conservative and progressive sectors of Restoration society. Informed by Galdós's journalistic works on food as well as the popular cookbooks and culinary manuals that emerged from the writing of social hygienists and commentators in late nineteenth-century Spain, Heneghan explores the ways in which

Galdós entwined references to meals and eating habits with his views on politics, education, and gender. Heneghan argues that, in doing so, Galdós conveyed his preoccupation with the impact of the status quo on the future of Spain.

In the final essay of this section, José Colmeiro traces the gastronomic thought of Catalan author and journalist Manuel Vázquez Montalbán, a central figure to understand the culinary revolution of post-Franco Spain and the emergence of gastronomic literature. Through a thorough examination of the author's vast fictional and journalistic writing, Colmeiro analyses the manifold critiques and satires of the rapidly changing culinary and food cultures of twentieth-century Spain. Colmeiro argues that, through the idea of "the palate of memory," Vázquez Montalbán poses gastronomy as a fundamental cultural space where history, identity, and memory are constructed outside the confines of ideology and nationalism, and where globalization, consumerism, and morality are resisted.

The hearth is a most ancient site, a key to the home and a place that has many connotations. From the humblest of abodes to the most sumptuous of residences, food used to be prepared here, feeding the hungry, satiating the glutton, satisfying even the mind, as the dining area has the potential of becoming a symposium for the most discerning. As the kitchen developed with its myriad smells and ingredients from faraway lands, the well-to-do left it behind as a sensuous but perhaps infernal region, with its fires and shouts, and retired to other parts of the residence. The cook was forgotten. Their banquets, then, like that of Macbeth, had a ghost in their midst. But as time went on, the cook acquired a place of distinction. Already in seventeenth-century Spain, cooks sought fame and fortune with cookbooks and recipes that travelled the known world. In homes of the less fortunate, this was the space for the woman, the wife. In convents, the cook was one of the most important yet least valued members of the community, striving to feed others, while she would be forever hungry for the religious fervour that surrounded her. In the countryside, the rustic shepherd was envisioned holding knife, flint, earth, swivel, and tinder. The more august the space, the more foods intermingled as if they were guests from all over the world: the lowly maize, which many thought of uncertain origin, helped to create new legends; the delightful honey was draped with Christian symbols; wheat came to represent the Eucharist, while a mere sheaf of wheat represented Astraea, goddess of the Golden Age; cinnamon, a sought-after spice from the east, became a remedy for disease. The Spanish Stew came to identify most of Iberia, while French food became a subject of contention in eighteenth-century Spain.

It would be impossible to bring together in one volume the many sights and sounds of the kitchen, the many kinds of cooks, the development of national foods, the importance of food as medicine and as ostentation, and the rise of myriad forms of identity. We only seek to provide a taste of some of the many ways in which food, etiquette, medicine, and taste develop in Spain over time. Since the kitchen is a messy place, we do not wish to fix different periods with labels and years. The Middle Ages, the Renaissance, the Golden Age, and the early modern periods wander through the volume unchecked. With the eighteenth century and then modernity we reach a more stable frame. In all, we encourage investigation through different methods, as if we were bringing together a series of recipes that would require diverse means of preparation.

While for centuries Spain developed its own culinary cultures, over time these became overshadowed by the internationalization of food trends. French cuisine started to exert its influence in the Spanish peninsula as early as the eighteenth century, as James Mandrell explains. It claimed hegemony in Spain by the late nineteenth century, reaching its heights of influence with the "nouvelle cuisine" begun in the 1960s. But, by the 1990s, as Colmeiro asserts in his essay on Vázquez Montalbán, the diverse Spanish offerings ignited a reevaluation of gastronomy in Iberia. This collection, then, echoes the new interest in Spanish foods and seeks to give the reader a taste of its many ingredients and dishes.

We would like to express our appreciation to all who made this volume possible. In particular, we would like to thank Gregory Baum for translating the essays by Colmeiro, Sánchez Llama, and Serrano Larráyoz; and thank you to Daniela Gutiérrez Flores for her help in assembling and editing this volume. We also are grateful for support for this project from the University of Chicago and Brandeis University. Particular mention is due to Anne Walters Robertson, Dean of the Humanities Division at the University of Chicago, and the Theodore and Jane Norman Fund for Faculty Research and Creative Projects at Brandeis University.

NOTES

1   The exhibition opened 22 December 2010 and closed 13 March 2011. A volume of essays touching on a range of topics related to the exhibition – including cookbooks, the publications on and implements on the confection of sweets, and "herramientas curiosas" [cooking gadgets] – was published under the same title, *La cocina en su tinta*. Since the exhibition, the Biblioteca Nacional has developed extensive resources for the study of food, among them a web-based guide, compiled by Lourdes Gutiérrez

Gutiérrez and Antonio Rodríguez Vela, on materials on food in Spain from the fifteenth through the nineteenth centuries. *Gastronomía española: Siglos XV–XIX: guía bibliográfica* is available at the library website, and a digital version of the guide is available for download.

2 Simón Palmer states that these are "obras que de una u otra forma aluden al hecho alimentario, ya sea con dietas especiales para prevenir enfermedades, ya con noticias de nuevos productos hallados en viajes a otros continentes, o bien con mejoras industriales en la elaboración de vinos o aceites" [works that in one way or another allude to the fact of food, either with special diets to prevent diseases, or with news of new products found on trips to other continents, or with industrial improvements in the production of wines or oils] (2003, 13).

3 There are a multitude of instructional books that instruct readers on topics as diverse as how to make beer (Juan Manuel Ballesteros's 1827 *Opúsculo sobre la cerveza: método de elaborarla* [Opuscule on beer: The method of its preparation]), on the mineral waters and baths in Asturias (José Garófalo y Sánchez's 1861 *Monografía de las Aguas y Baños minero-medicinales de Fuente Santa de Buyeres de Nava (Asturias)* [Monograph on the mineral-medicinal waters and baths of Fuente Santa de Buyeres de Nava (Asturias)]), and how to harvest mushrooms safely (Telésforo de Aranzadi's 1897 *Setas ú hongos del País Vasco: guía para la distinción de los comestibles y venenosos, los parásitos de plantas cultivadas y enumeración sistemática de los indiferentes* [Mushrooms or fungi of the Basque Country: A guide for the distinction of the edible and the poisonous, parasites of cultivated plants, and the systematic enumeration of the differences]).

4 See Lara Anderson's informative discussion of Spanish cuisine and national identity (2013).

5 See also Entrambasaguas (1975); Martínez Llopis (1989); and Medina (2005).

6 See Díaz (2003a, 2003b, 2005).

7 See Díaz (1996).

8 See Díaz (1990, 1992).

9 Among many others, María de los Ángeles Pérez Samper (1998, 2011) furthers of the exploration of food culture in Spain, and Fernando Serrano Larráyoz (2002, 2006, 2011) takes the discussion about food culture in Spain into new territory with a focus on medicine and diet in the Kingdom of Navarra. And then there are studies of food in/and literature, such as Marina Domecq (1997), José Esteban (2006), Carolyn Nadeau (2016), and Jodi Campbell (2017).

10 For more on the concept of *dulcedo Dei*, see Chatillon (1957).

11 See David 1887 and Cabanès 1898 for detailed discussions of Louis XIV's dental problems, which appear to have been due at least in part to the consumption of sugar.

12 As the revisions and multiple editions suggest, Gouffé's book was well
    known and popular in France, and, as such, a prime candidate for trans-
    lation. There were five: into English in 1869, German in 1872, Spanish in
    1885, and, in 1895, German and Italian. Correspondence between Hachette
    and Antonio de San Martín, representing the Librería de A. de San Martín,
    the Spanish publisher, indicates that the Spanish translation was most
    likely based on the fourth edition, of 1877.

13 Jules Gouffé (1807–77) was a French chef who worked and wrote in the
    tradition of *grande*, or *haute*, *cuisine* as pioneered by François Pierre de La
    Varenne. Part of a family of pâtissiers that included his brother Alphonse,
    who became the pastry chef in Queen Victoria's court, Jules Gouffé trained
    in his father's pastry shop in Paris, spent seven years under the tutelage of
    Marie-Antoine Carême, and then, in 1840, opened his own establishment
    on the fashionable Rue du Faubourg-Saint-Honoré. He was the author of
    four volumes on cookery, one on preparing meats and fish (*Recettes pour
    préparer et conserver les Viandes et les Poissons salés et fumés, les terrines, les
    galantines, les légumes, les fruits, les confitures, les liqueurs de famille, les sirops,
    les petits fours, etc.* [1869]), another on soups (*Le Livre de Soupes et des Potages*
    [1872]), and yet another on pastry (*Le Livre de pâtisserie* [1873]), as well as,
    of course, his first book, *Le Livre de Cuisine*. All of his books were published
    by Hachette, one of the premier French publishing houses, but only *Le
    Livre de Cuisine* was translated into Spanish.

14 The Spanish translation of this passage, in *El libro de cocina*, reads: "Or-
    dinariamente se confunden en las obras culinarias la pequeña y la gran
    cocina, los platos más sencillos con los del género más complicado, re-
    sultando una deplorable amalgama que explica los escasos progresos que
    han hecho hasta el día el estudio y la práctica del arte culinario" (v–vi).

15 "Gastro-porn" is the term coined by Alexander Cockburn (1977), "food
    porn" the more common usage. See McBride (2010).

16 On the Spanish still-life tradition, in addition to Pérez Sánchez (1983),
    Jordan and Cherry (1995), and Bryson (1990), see the insightful studies
    by Aterido (2002); Bergström (1970); Cavestany (1936 and 1940); Cherry
    (1999); Gállego (1987); Jordan (1992); Luna (1995); and Sánchez López
    (2008).

WORKS CITED

Acosta, Cristóbal. 1578. *Tractado de las drogas y medicinas de las Indias Orientales
    con sus plantas debuxadas al biuo.* Burgos: Martin de Victoria.
Anderson, Lara. 2013. *Cooking Up the Nation: Spanish Culinary Texts and
    Culinary Nationalization in the Late Nineteenth and Early Twentieth Century.*
    Colección Támesis. Serie A, Monografías 321. Woodbridge: Tamesis.

Aterido, Ángel. 2002. *El bodegón en la España del siglo de oro*. Madrid: Edilupa.

Barthes, Roland. 1991. *Mythologies*. Translated by Annette Lavers. New York: Noonday; Farrar, Straus & Giroux.

Bergström, Ingvar. 1970. *Maestros españoles de bodegones y floreros del siglo XVII*. Translated by Matica Goulard de Westberg. Madrid: Insula.

Bryson, Norman. 1990. *Looking at the Overlooked: Four Essays on Still Life Painting*. Cambridge, MA: Harvard University Press.

Cabanès, Agustin. 1898. *Curious bypaths of history being medico-historical studies and observations by Dr. Cabanès*, 27–39. Paris: C. Carrington.

Campbell, Jodi. 2017. *At the First Table: Food and Social Identity in Early Modern Spain*. Lincoln: University of Nebraska Press.

Cantera Montenegro, Enrique. 2003. "La carne y el pescado en el sistema alimentario judío en la España medieval." *Espacio, Tiempo y Forma*, Serie III, H-Medieval, 16: 13–51.

Cavestany, Julio. 1936 and 1940. *Floreros y bodegones en la pintura española: Catálogo ilustrado de la exposión*. Madrid: Palacio de la Biblioteca Nacional.

Chatillion, Jean. 1957. "Dulcedo, Dulcedo Dei." In *Dictionnaire de Spiritualité*, edited by Marcel Viller et al., vol. 3, cols. 1777–95. Paris: Beauchesne.

Cherry, Peter. 1999. *Arte y naturaleza: el bodegón español en el Siglo de Oro*. Translated by Ivars Barzdevics. Madrid: Fundación de Apoyo a la Historia del Arte Hispánico, Doce Calles.

La Cocina en su tinta. 2010. Madrid: Publicaciones de la Biblioteca Nacional de España.

Cockburn, Alexander. 1977. "Gastro-Porn." *New York Review of Books*, 8 December. https://www.nybooks.com/articles/1977/12/08/gastro-porn/

David, Th. 1887. "The Teeth of Louis XIV." *Dental Advertiser* 18: 94–9.

Díaz, Lorenzo. 1990. *Madrid: bodegones, mesones, fondas y restaurantes. Cocina y sociedad, 1412–1990*. Madrid: Espasa Calpe.

Díaz, Lorenzo. 1992. *Madrid: tabernas, botillerías y cafés, 1476 1991*. Madrid: Espasa Calpe.

Díaz, Lorenzo. 1996. *Jockey: Historia de un restaurante*. Los 5 Sentidos 24. Barcelona: Tusquets.

Díaz, Lorenzo. 2003a. *La cocina del barroco: la gastronomía del Siglo de Oro en Lope, Cervantes y Quevedo*. Madrid: Alianza.

Díaz, Lorenzo. 2003b. *La cocina del Quijote*. Madrid: Alianza.

Díaz, Lorenzo. 2005. *Ilustrados y románticos: cocina y sociedad en España, siglos XVIII y XIX*. Madrid: Alianza.

Domecq, Marina. 1997. *Comer con otros ojos*. Huesca: La Val de Onsera.

Dr Thebussem, El [Mariano Pardo y Figueroa]. 1888. *La mesa moderna. Cartas sobre el comedor y la cocina cambiadas entre el doctor Thebussem y Un cocinero de S.M.* Madrid: Librerías de Fernando Fé.

E.J.B. 1887. "Toros en Galicia." *La Lidia* 6.33 (14 November): 4.

Entrambasaguas, Joaquín de. 1975. *Gastronomía española*. 2 vols. Madrid: La Muralla.

Esteban, José. 2006. *La cocina en Galdós y otras noticias literario-gastronómicas.* 2nd ed. Madrid: Editorial Fortunata y Jacinta.

Gállego, Julián. 1987. *Visión y símbolos en la pintura española del Siglo de Oro.* Ensayos Arte Cátedra. Madrid: Cátedra.

García-Tapia Bello, Jose Luís. 2009. "Presencia (y ausencia) española en China hasta 1973." *Boletín Económico de ICE* 2972 (1–15 September): 71–93.

Garófalo y Sánchez, José. 1861. *Monografía de las Aguas y Baños minero-medicinales de Fuente Santa de Buyeres de Nava (Asturias)*. Madrid: Manuel Rojas.

Gouffé, Jules. 1867. *Le Livre de Cuisine*. Paris: Hachette.

Gouffé, Jules. 1885. *El libro de cocina*. Madrid: Librerías de A. de San Martín.

Gutiérrez Flores, Daniela. "The Poetics of the Kitchen: Cooks and the Literary Culture of the Early Modern Spanish Atlantic." Dissertation: University of Chicago (in progress).

Gutiérrez Gutiérrez, Lourdes, and Antonio Rodríguez Vela. N.d. *Gastronomía española: siglos xv–xix: guía bibliográfica.* http://www.bne.es/es/Micrositios/Guias/gastronomia/Comentadas_s_XV-XVII/DetalleImagen5.html?origen=galeria.

Imorde, Joseph. 2014. "Carlo Dolci and the Aesthetics of Sweetness." *Getty Research Journal* 6 (January): 1–12.

"Inutilidad de las academias." 1897. *El Mortero* 4.148 (5 June): 1201.

Jeanneret, Michel. 1991. *A Feast of Words: Banquets and Table Talk in the Renaissance*. Translated by Jeremy Whitely and Emma Hughes. Chicago: University of Chicago Press.

Jordan, William B. 1992. *La imitación de la naturaleza: los bodegones de Sánchez Cotán*. Translated by Ma Jesús Gonzalo. Madrid: Museo Nacional del Prado.

Jordan, William B., and Peter Cherry. 1995. *Spanish Still Life from Velázquez to Goya*. London: National Gallery Publications.

Kermode, J. Frank. 1961. "The Banquet of Sense." *Bulletin of the John Rylands Library* 15: 68–99.

Lévi-Strauss. Claude. 1983. *The Raw and the Cooked. Mythologiques*. Vol. 1. Translated by John and Doreen Weightman. Chicago: University of Chicago Press.

Luján, Nestor, and Juan Perucho. 2003. *El libro de la cocina española: gastronomía e historia*. Los 5 Sentidos 37. Barcelona: Tusquets.

Luna, Juan J. 1995. *Los alimentos de España en la pintura: bodegones de Luis Meléndez*. Madrid: MERCASA.

Martínez Llopis, Manuel M. 1989. *Historia de La Gastronomía Española*. El Libro de Bolsillo. Libros Útiles 1378. Madrid: Alianza.

McBride, Anne E. 2010. "Food Porn." *Gastronomica* 10.1 (Winter): 38–46.

Medina, F. Xavier. 2005. *Food Culture in Spain*. Food Culture around the World. Westport, CT: Greenwood.

Mennell, Stephen. 1985. *All Manners of Food: Eating and Taste in England and France from the Middle Ages to the Present*. Oxford: Basil Blackwell.

Mintz, Sidney W. 1985. *Sweetness and Power: The Place of Sugar in Modern History*. New York: Viking.

Muro, Ángel. 1894. *El practicón. Tratado completo de cocina al alcance de todos y aprovechamiento de sobras*. 5th ed. Madrid: Librería de Miguel Guijarro.

Nadeau, Carolyn A. 2016. *Food Matters: Alonso Quijano's Diet and the Discourse of Food in Early Modern Spain*. Toronto: University of Toronto Press.

Ollé, Manel. 2008. "300 años de relaciones (y percepciones) entre España y China." *Huarte de San Juan. Geografía e Historia* 15: 91–9.

Palacios Bañuelos, Luis. 2013. "Las relaciones entre España y China, una larga historia." *Historia Actual Online* 30: 151–63.

Pérez, Dionisio. 1929. *Guía del buen comer español: inventario y loa de la cocina clásica de España y sus regiones*. Madrid: Patronato Nacional de Turismo / Sucesores de Rivadeneyra.

Pérez Samper, María de los Ángeles. 1998. *La alimentación en la España del Siglo de Oro*. Alifara. Estudios. Huesca: La Val de Onsera.

Pérez Samper, María de los Ángeles. 2011. *Mesas y cocinas en la España del siglo XVIII*. La Comida de La Vida. Somonte-Cenero, Gijón: Trea.

Pérez Sánchez, Alfonso E. 1983. *Pintura española de bodegones y floreros de 1600 a Goya: Museo del Prado, noviembre 1983/enero 1984*. Madrid: Ministerio de Cultura, Dirección General de Bellas Artes y Archivos.

Sánchez López, Andrés. 2008. *La pintura de bodegones y floreros en España en el siglo XVIII*. Madrid: Fundación de Arte Hispánico.

Satō, Tsugitaka. 2015. *Sugar in the Social Life of Medieval Islam*. Islamic Area Studies 1. Leiden: Brill.

Sellés, Eugenio. 1891. "Un millón de recetas." *Almanaque de "Conferencias Culinarias" de Ángel Muro*. Madrid: Librería de Fernando Fé. 75–7.

Serrano Larráyoz, Fernando. 2002. *La mesa del rey: cocina y régimen alimentario en la Corte de Carlos III "El Noble" de Navarra (1411–1425)*. Pamplona: Institución Príncipe de Viana.

Serrano Larráyoz, Fernando. 2006. *La oscuridad de la luz, la dulzura de lo amargo: cerería y confitería en Navarra, siglos XVI–XX*. Colección Historia 19. Pamplona: Universidad Pública de Navarra-Nafarroako Unibertsitate Publikoa.

Serrano Larráyoz, Fernando. 2011. *Un recetario navarro de cocina y repostería (Siglo XIX)*. Somonte-Cenero, Gijón: Trea.

Simón Palmer, María del Carmen. 1977. *Bibliografía de la gastronomía española: notas para su realización*. Biblioteca de La Cocina Clásica Española 2. Madrid: Velázquez.

Simón Palmer, María del Carmen. 1982. *La alimentación y sus circunstancias en el Real Alcázar de Madrid*. El Madrid de Los Austrias. Serie Estudios 2. Madrid: Instituto de Estudios Madrileños.

Simón Palmer, María del Carmen. 1994. *Libros antiguos de cultura alimentaria (Siglo XV–1900)*. Córdoba: Diputación Provincial.

Simón Palmer, María del Carmen. 1997. *La cocina de Palacio 1561–1931*. Madrid: Castalia.

Simón Palmer, María del Carmen. 2003. *Bibliografía de la gastronomía y la alimentación en España*. La Comida de La Vida 1. Somonte-Cenero, Gijón: Trea.

Tobin, Ronald W. 1990. *Tarte à la Crème: Comedy and Gastronomy in Molière's Theater*. Columbus: Ohio State University Press.

Villena, Enrique de. 1984. *Arte Cisoria*. Edited by Russell V. Brown. Biblioteca Humanitas de Textos Inéditos 3. Barcelona: Humanitas.

Williams, Jillian. 2017. *Food and Religious Identities in Spain, 1400–1600*. London and New York: Routledge.

Wyant, Jennifer S. 2019. *Beyond Mary and Martha: Reclaiming Ancient Models of Discipleship*. Emory Studies in Early Christianity. Atlanta: Society for Biblical Studies.

FIRST COURSE

Foodstuffs

1 Divine Food: Making and Tasting Honey in the *Cantigas de Santa Maria*

RYAN D. GILES

One of the most valuable commodities during the Middle Ages was the beehive, since it provided both candle wax and the primary sweetener in the medieval diet until the fifteenth century, when sugar began to be more widely introduced on the Peninsula – although sugar cane was being produced earlier in coastal regions of Valencia and Granada. Honey played a crucial role in premodern Iberian cuisine: one of the earliest cookbooks composed on the Peninsula, the Catalan *Llibre de Sent Sovi* [Book of Sent Sovri] (1324), for example, includes instructions for making a sauce with this ingredient, as well as a recipe for a popular confection. Juan Ruiz's *Libro de buen amor* provides further references to sweetmeats during the same period.[1] Moorish and Sephardic cooking typically included honeyed sauces during the Middle Ages and beyond, as David Gitlitz and Carolyn Nadeau have shown. These often combined the sweetness of the honeycomb with bitter and sour flavours produced from fruits, juices, or vinegar, but also incorporated almond milk, saffron, and other spices, as well as salted broths. The curative qualities of honey were no less valuable, whether it was applied to spider webs in the dressing of wounds (due to honey's antibacterial effects), used to treat ulcers and illnesses believed to be caused by an excess of phlegm, added to disguise the taste of unpleasant medicines or even conceal poisons, uses that are metaphorically referenced in Juan Manuel's early fourteenth-century *Conde Lucanor* and Ruiz's poem, respectively.[2]

In keeping with the "sensory turn" that has characterized recent scholarship in the humanities and social sciences, one might wonder how honey tasted in medieval Spain – compared to familiar, contemporary varietals – before considering how meaning was attached to this food.[3] María Antonia Carmona Ruiz has studied the early history of apiculture in the province of Seville following the region's conquest in the thirteenth century. Her work provides information on the sorts of honey used in medicine and food that would have been served on the table of the most famous Spanish medieval king, Alfonso X "the Wise." The ruler of Castile became increasingly sick in his later years, and spent much of his time in this Andalusian city, dying there in 1284. Surviving correspondence reports that he suffered from sinus infections and congestion, which would have been treated with honey, in addition to fevers, ulcers, and eventually dropsy, finally succumbing to cancer.[4] A number of the king's celebrated *Cantigas de Santa Maria* [Songs of Holy Mary] (c. 1280) relate to food culture and show the king being attended by physicians. Carmona Ruiz finds that beekeeping was practised in isolated provincial highlands deemed unfit for cultivating crops but abounding in aromatic flowering plants, bushes, and trees. Particularly valued were areas where thyme, rosemary, sage, and wild broom grew naturally, beside evergreen oaks, blossoming mastic and strawberry trees known for their fragrant resin, and drupe and unedo fruits. Such sources of pollen and nectar would have imparted a delicate herbal smell and taste, heightened sweetness, and at the same time added a slightly bitter flavour to local honey, which was filtered through cheese-cloth and retained a dark amber colour.[5] The same qualities would have characterized, more broadly, honey produced at higher elevations in other Mediterranean regions.

This context sheds light on the kind of sensory experience that is evoked by melliferous imagery in Alfonso X's collected songs of the Virgin. My purpose in the pages that follow is to examine four songs from the collection, in which Marian meanings are attached to the production and sweetness of honey, as well as its byproduct, beeswax, in medieval Christian culture; and finally to consider how these relate to the multiconfessional context of thirteenth-century Castile.

Song 128, with the refrain "Tan muit' é con Jesú-Cristo Santa María juntada" [So close is Holy Mary to Jesus Christ], relates how a greedy beekeeper, wanting to profit from an increased production of honey and wax, asks an old woman for an incantation or "escantaçôn" (v. 14). Presumably his bees have left in a swarm, or he plans to steal a neighbour's colony by attracting them to one of his hives. A recurrent problem throughout medieval Europe, apian theft would be addressed in later Spanish legislation studied by Carmona Ruiz. The requested incantation no doubt refers to a variation of the medieval "swarm charms" that have been preserved in Latin as well as some vernacular languages. These religious formulas were intended to conjure bees to return to or not abandon the hive, calling specifically on the power of Mary as well as the persons of the Trinity. Evidence from Spain, such as Pedro Ciruelo's early sixteenth-century *Reprovación de las supersticiones y hechizerías* [Reproval of superstitions and sorceries], suggests that such charms were not only recited but also written on paper or parchment and placed inside the hive as amulets ["cédulas"] inscribed with divine words from Scripture (1978, 107). The crone in the song, however, instructs the beekeeper to obtain a consecrated host, consonant with accusations that would be commonly made against witches and villainous infidels later in the Middle Ages. Instead of swallowing the *Corpus Christi* at Mass, she tells him to place it in one of his beehives ["colmẽas"] (v. 23). These objects had openings on the top and bottom, and shelves for the honeycomb. Illuminations from the *Cantigas* depict a cylindrical ceramic hive, which was used instead of wicker to keep the bees cool. When the beekeeper opens this hive, he finds a waxen Virgin holding the infant Jesus (see fig. 1.1).

The sweet-smelling beehive is later brought into the church by a procession of believers, where it once again contains a host consecrated at Mass, which miraculously appears there as the priest again celebrates the Eucharist. One of the witnesses in the manuscript illumination of this scene, interestingly, appears to be a Jewish man wearing a hood.

Kathleen Kulp-Hill, in her study of this song, relates its imagery to other figurative uses in the collection of "sensations of taste and smell … awakened by the names of food – honey, fritters, fresh cheese, or roasting meat," noting that the flavour and attendant "odor of sanctity" is said to transcend mere earthly foods (1980, 6). A striking example of this type of imagery that also involves a host can be found in *cantiga* 4, "A madre do que livrou" [Mother of him who delivered], when a Jewish boy attends Mass, takes communion from a miraculously animate statue of the Virgin holding the Christ child, and finds that it tastes sweeter than honey, "mais doce ca mel" (v. 50). This prompts his father to angrily throw him into an oven, where he is then saved by Mary.

Another host miracle in the *Cantigas* is remarkably similar to that of the greedy beekeeper, number 208: "Aquele que ena Virgen / carne por seer veúdo fillou" [He who took on flesh in the Virgin to be seen]. This tale takes place in Toulouse, where a heretical beekeeper attends Easter Mass and steals the communion wafer in the same way as the peasant in 128. The sinner can be assumed to be a Cathar, or member of the thirteenth-century outlawed sect that denied the mystery of Catholic sacraments, and in particular the Eucharist. Significantly, they also denied that Mary was God's instrument for the Incarnation of his Word. Concealing the uneaten host in his mouth, the heretic intends to deny the real presence of the Body of Christ by feeding it to his bees, in what appears to be an act of desecration and a kind of mock Mass: "abellas

Figure 1.1. *Cantiga* 128 illuminations. Códice Rico (T), fol. 182r. Biblioteca de El Escorial, MS T.I.1.

comed' aquesto ca eu o vinoo bevi" [bees, eat this, because I drank the wine] (v. 31).

The implication seems to be that the bees will eat the host because it is so sweet, as suggested elsewhere in the *Cantigas*, such as the example of the Jewish boy at communion. Jesús Montoya Martínez has pointed out that, like the beekeeper who follows the advice of an old woman in 128, the heretic attempts to draw on magical powers that practitioners of sorcery and witchcraft sinfully attributed to the species of Eucharistic bread (as opposed to partaking in a communion that he apparently disbelieves). Notions of the wafer's sweet flavour recall exegetical readings in which the divine Word and manna of God that were provided to the Israelites in the desert were said to have tasted like honey (Douai-Rheims Version, Exodus 16:31). In song 208, the apparition of the Virgin and child in a hive is described in more detail than in 128, as the sinner expects to find an abundance of valuable honey but instead encounters a miniature chapel with an altar, complete with a Marian statue, all seemingly made of beeswax. The sacred object, like the one in the earlier story, is suggestive of reliquaries from the period that represent the Virgin and child and were sometimes designed to open up like tabernacles and capsules. At the same time, it brings to mind the medieval tradition of producing *exvotos* or votive offerings out of beeswax, which could be purchased by pilgrims and other devotees and were often given to shrines as a means of commemorating and giving thanks for miracles reportedly brought about through the intervention of Mary and other saints. Apart from candles, these could also be created as representational objects, meant to signify some aspect of the purported miracle. The florid, nectarous smell coming from the heretic's hive in the *cantiga*, hinting at the incomparable taste of its honey, is so delicious that he at once decides to confess and return to the true faith, and sings praises to the Virgin. Like the greedy beekeeper, he informs local clergy of the miracle, and a procession is formed to carry the little chapel made of beeswax into the cathedral.

As María Dolores Bollo-Panadero has observed, this song fits in to the ongoing "topic" of "a possible redemption of the heretic," and as part of the collection's overall representation of the "Other," including Jews and Muslims, "in a positive light" so long as they "are suitable for conversion" (2008, 169). More recently, Francisco Prado-Vilar has demonstrated how all of the *Cantigas* draw on the "bio-theological" power of the virginal body of Mary, providing a vessel for the redemption of humankind, though the Incarnation of Christ in her womb (2011, 126). Her body thus becomes a site of transformational potentiality, as when new converts are reborn in parturient, baptismal fonts, or, in the case of the earlier-mentioned song 4, emerge from an oven in a way that alludes to the living bread of Christ.

In spite of the intentions of beekeepers in what might be called hive-host miracles, the bees' home becomes productive and transformative in a spiritual instead of a material sense once it has received the host. Hives enclose a sweet food that is revealed to be Christ, as opposed to a magical substance, just as the incarnation was prepared in the virginal vessel of Mary's body. To more fully understand why this truth should be illustrated by an apian, melliferous tabernacle, it is necessary to first unpack longstanding theological connotations that are inherent in such imagery. The Christian association of male and female chastity with honeybees can be traced back to Ambrose of Milan's third-century *De virginibus* [On virginity]. Intended to promote celibate vows in imitation of Mary, the treatise offers a telling commentary on a verse from the Song of Songs: "Let my beloved come into his garden ... O my sister, my spouse, I have gathered ... aromatic spices: I have eaten the honeycomb with my honey" (1896a, 5.1). Ambrose, whose name would come to be linked to the "sweet food" of his words [Latin *ambrosia*], explains that "virginity is fit to be compared to bees," so that any woman who refuses marriage and instead commits herself to chastity is "an imitator of bees, whose food is flowers, whose offspring is collected and brought together by the mouth ... your words ... have no covering of guile, that they may be pure ... let an eternal succession of merits be brought forth by your mouth" (1896a, 8.40).

Importantly, the buzzing of worker bees as they collect nectar to make honey is likened to prayers and praises of God being sung by religious women. This can be compared to scenes in Alfonso's hive-host songs, when Christians recite the canonical hours, the Mass, and hymns as they bring a "colmêa" in procession to their church: "con procisson e cantando ... as oras todas compridas disseron aquel dia con ssa noite ... outro dia ar disseron sa missa" (no. 128, vv. 58–60, 63); "e con grandes precissões foron e dando loor aa Virgen gloriosa, Madre de Nostro Sennor" (no. 208, vv. 50–1). Implicit is a well-known verse from the Psalms that would be sung as part of the Hours, "how sweet are thy words to my palate! more than honey to my mouth" (Ps. 118:103). In another treatise, *De spiritu sancto* [On the Holy Spirit], Ambrose considers the eating of honey itself, as opposed to bees tasting flowers (1896b, 2.6–9). To illustrate this chaste food, he quotes from a memorable scene in the Book of Judges when Samson (14:9), on his way to an ill-fated marriage proposal, draws on the power of the Holy Ghost to tear open the body of a lion. Later he mysteriously finds a swarm of bees there, and scoops out honey to feed himself and his parents. In her analysis of Ambrose's reading,

Virginia Burrus explains how the Bishop of Milan interprets this as "a sign for the converted virginal soul who drinks in the divine ... gives forth her honey ... If the Virgin is the receptacle of the seed of the Spirit, she is also the honey bee contained within his leonine skin" (2000, 163).

The connection between honeybees and chastity is partly based on an ancient belief – and confusion with flying insects that lay their eggs in carrion – that bees do not procreate through sex, but instead originate from the dead bodies of other organisms, as can be seen in the Greek myths of Melissa and Aristaeus. This idea was repeated by Virgil, Ovid, and Pliny the Elder, as well as theological authorities like Ambrose's influential student, Augustine, and later Isidore of Seville.[6] Needless to say, a notion of new life naturally issuing forth from death would have especially appealed to the symbolic thinking of early Christians. Usually, though not always, the queen bee was misidentified as a male king, and the drones as well as the workers described as females. Exceptions can be found, for instance, in swarm charms that invoke a "mater aviorum" [mother of bees], who could be controlled by "Maria" and her son (Fife 1964, 154–5). A typical example of the signification of the king bee in medieval culture can be found in a widely read thirteenth-century textbook called *De proprietatibus rerum* [On the properties of things]. The author, an English Franciscan named Bartholomew, describes how, among honeybees: "maidenhood ... is common to them all ... for they are not wearied with the service of Venus ... with lechery ... with the sorrow of child birth. And yet they bring forth swarms of children. Bees make among them a king ... and love their king ... honor and worship him" (1905, 12.6).

Medieval Christian writers often likened this apian *rex* to Christ, as can be seen in a thirteenth-century sermon by the Portuguese Franciscan St Anthony of Padua. Noting that bees are beautiful, darkly coloured creatures, he follows Ambrose by likening them to the bride in the Song of Songs, writing: "Penitents ought to do as the bees, who, when their king flies from the hive, fly with him ... Christ, our King, flew to us from the hive, that is to say, from the bosom of the Father, whom we ought to follow like good bees, and to fly with Him" (Neal 1856, 244–5). In another sermon, Anthony describes the hive as a spiritual home of humility and grace, producing comfort and food that are freely given to all who seek them (as opposed to the monetary value of wax and honey): the hive having been prepared by female bees for the "King of Angels to inhabit ... our bee ... has offered to God the Father a honeycomb; that is, the incarnate Word, who is God and man" (Gambero 2005, 204). His interpretation is not unlike that of another thirteenth-century preacher, St Bonaventure, who draws on Bernard of Clairvaux to imagine the conception of Christ as a divine bee flying to Mary, gathering the purest nectar: making his honey from "the sweet smelling flower of thy perpetual virginity, he rested upon it, he embraced it" (1932, 12). Such widespread Eucharistic interpretations help clarify what is meant by Alfonsine songs that show consecrated hosts being placed in beehives. Beekeepers in the Middle Ages sought to predict where and when colonies would swarm in the warm months of spring and early summer, which they assumed was the only time the king left the hive – and which coincided with the Easter season on the liturgical calendar. At stake was the loss of all of their bees, through sickness or the disappearance of workers which might cause an otherwise healthy colony to collapse.

The two *cantigas* that I have been focusing on implicate notions of Christ as the king bee who swarms to his bride, liken the taste of honey to the Word of God, and view Mary as the instrument of spiritual honey making. A similar concept can be found in Gonzalo de Berceo's earlier thirteenth-century miracles, where a redeemed sinner appears as a ghost to report how "la Gloriosa" brought him to the heavenly Jerusalem, complete with "dulz vergel, çerca de dulz colmena" [sweet garden, beside a sweet hive] (Berceo 1987, 298ac). Imagery in these Spanish miracles accords with the writings of Church Fathers – as well as influential theologians and high-profile Marian devotees from the high Middle Ages – who expanded on verses from the Song of Songs and other biblical passages to metaphorically equate honey production to central mysteries of the Christian faith. Greedy and heretical beekeepers in Alfonsine songs wrongly remove the Christological king bee from the hive of his church, or *mater ecclesiae*, in the form of a consecrated host, and place him in their own worldly hives. But the Saviour in both miracles returns, or is flown back – as it were – to his apiary home through the Incarnation and Eucharist, bringing all of his bees with him. Mary's maternal body is made to parallel the honeycomb, and her followers collect the nectars and return to their hive as a symbol of repentance and reconciliation, according not only to St Anthony but also to Alfonso's *cantigas* 128 and 208:

> Un vilão que era d' abellas cobiiçoso, / por aver en mel e cera que lle non custasse nada ... ouve na colmêa de Deus o corp' ensserrado ... E abriu aquela logo u a osti' enserrara, / e viu Santa Maria, mui crara, / con seu Fillo Jhesu-Cristo en seus braços ... Un erege ... disse: "verei que obra feit" an no ostia as abellas' ... *Aquel que ena Virgen carne por seer veudo* ... Abriu muy tost' a colmêa, e hûa capela viu / con seu altar estar dentro, e a omagen cousiu / da Virgen cono seu Fillo sobre ele, e ar sentiu un odor tan sabroso ... grandes precissões ... cataron a colmêa ... e repentiron-sse

muito e choraron assaz, / loando Santa Maria que muitos miragres faz/
con seu Fillo Jhesu-Cristo. (vv. 1–2, 28–34; 1–2, 37–57)

[A peasant who was greedy for bees, to have honey and wax that cost him
nothing … he had enclosed the body of Christ in the hive … opening the
hive in which he had put the host, he saw there Holy Mary, most fair, with
her son Jesus Christ in her arms … A heretic … said: "Now I shall see what
the bees have done with the host" … *He who took on flesh in the Virgin to
be seen* … He hastily opened the hive, and he saw a chapel with its altar
there inside, and he recognized the image of the Virgin with her Son upon
it and also smelled a fragrance so delicious … great processions … viewed
the hive … and repented greatly and wept freely, praising Holy Mary who
brings about many miracles with her son, Jesus Christ.]

Of course, the beehive not only served as a figure for the Church but
was essential to its operation, owing to the importance of candles in
Christian ritual, in addition to the value of honey. In fact, beekeepers
were often asked to provide beeswax to be used by local clergy, and
tithing was sometimes raised to pay for the expense of candle making in Spain and elsewhere. This can be seen in another miracle in
the *Cantigas*, "A Santa María muito ll' é gréu" [Holy Mary is very dis-
tressed, no. 326], which depicts a beekeeper who – unlike the sinners of
cantigas 128 and 208 – righteously donates his hives to a Marian shrine
founded by the Order of Calatrava in the Extremadura mountains of
Tudia: "de que podéss' aver a eigreja muita cera e mél" [from which the
church might have much wax and honey] (v. 10).[7] These hives, which
might have been given as an *exvoto* to thank Mary for favouring the
beekeeper, were located directly behind the church and tended by a
poor woman. This left them vulnerable to thieves, who soon after stole
the hives, described as belonging to the Blessed Mother. The property is
immediately returned, after the criminals are hunted down by a knight
of Calatrava who is devoted to the Virgin of Tudia: "non envergonn-
aron ren a ela neno que morreu na cruz" [they disrespected her and him
who died on the Cross] (vv. 32–3). Apart from the value of the *exvoto*
itself, their crime is heightened by the significance of hives, bees, and
honey making as signs of the Incarnation in earlier songs that I have
discussed. It has been shown how the "colmêa" becomes a tabernacle
to miraculously house the king bee, Jesus, born of the Virgin, who is
brought back into churches from which he was stolen, in the form of
the honeyed Eucharist.

The song that most closely associates *mater ecclesiae* with the hive,
however, is *cantiga* 211, "Apostos miragres faz todavía" [She keeps

performing perfect miracles], in which pure white bees return from gathering early summer nectar and enter through a hole in the wall of the Marian church in Elche, a large town located on the Mediterranean coast, just north of Murcia. Illuminations depict this hole in a way that recalls entrances in hives pictured in *cantiga* 128, concerning the greedy beekeeper. Making the place their home, they first repair a paschal candle for the feast of Pentecost and thereafter produce an abundance of honey for parishioners to eat:

Esto foi un día de Pentecóste, / que a sa eigreja vééron tóste / d' ómes e molléres come grand' óste / por oír a missa que s' i dizía … Mui cantada come en atal fésta … Ca viron o ciro pasqual queimado / muito dũa parte e mui menguado … Eles en aquesto assí cuidando, / viron un eixame vĩir voando / abellas mui brancas, que entrou quando / o crérig' a sagra dizer quería … E tanto que as abellas chegaron / en un furado da pared' entraron / e ben dalí o cirío lavraron / daquela cera, que en falecía … loaron a Virgen … E as abellas irss en non quiseron / mas un gran tempo ali esteueron / e mel muit e cera depois ar fezeron / que nõ quedauan a mui gran perfia. (vv. 15–48)

[This was the day of Pentecost, when a great host of men and women came to her church to hear the mass there, beautifully sung as it is on such a holy day … They say the paschal candle burned and melted down on one side … While they were worrying about this, they saw a swarm of pure white bees flying towards them, which entered when the priest began to say the secret. As soon as the bees arrived, they came in through a hole in the wall and began to mould the candle with that wax where it had melted away … they praised the Virgin … The bees did not go away but remained there a long time. They did not desist and diligently made a lot of wax and honey.]

The honeybees' physical appearance could be attributed to white pollen dust on flowers in the area that covered their bodies. In the tale, however, their colour seems to convey the purity of the Virgin, as the miraculous bees will make the cleanest wax and honey in her ecclesiastical hive, unstained by Original Sin. This emphasis is not surprising, since purity was also a constant, practical concern of medieval beekeepers, who laboriously removed dirt and dead bees from the honey as well as broken pieces of comb by filtering it, as mentioned earlier. Beeswax also needed to be carefully cleaned and rendered before candles like the one in the song could be produced.

Critics have, for the most part, limited their discussion of this song, like the story of the stolen hives, to formal considerations. In my view, the most striking aspect of the miracle is its evocation of the initial blessing and lighting of the paschal candle, which consisted of a great column of beeswax set in a candlestick of precious metal, at the start of the Easter season. The candle would be burned through the fifty days of Eastertide, until the feast of Pentecost which is being celebrated in Alfonso's *cantiga*. The blessing was performed by a clergyman wearing a white tunic, in keeping with the colour of the bees in the tale from Elche, and again representing the innocence of the Lamb of God and his virgin birth.[8] In the words of Church historian Herbert Thurston: "the paschal candle typified Jesus Christ, the true light" and its "virgin wax ... recognized the most pure flesh which Christ derived from his blessed Mother ... the five grains of incense" embedded in it "recalled the sacred wounds retained in Christ's glorified body" (1911, 516). The candle, in other words, like the honeyed production of the hive, represents the Body of Christ issued from the Virgin, sacrificed, and resurrected. A characteristic description of the symbolism of the liturgical candle being lit can be found in eleventh-century writings of Anselm of Canterbury, who understood that the wax, "the production of the virginal bee, is the flesh of our Lord supplied by the Virgin Mary" (Guéranger 1904, 534). These connotations again coincide with and build on the pattern of apian imagery that we have seen in other songs featuring incarnational beehives.

More specifically, I would contend that the reconstruction of the melted candle in this *cantiga* is reminiscent of the text of the *Exsultet* prayer sung during the blessing of the candle. It was recited as an offertory, like the secret pronounced by the priest in the Alfonsine text that summons the white bees into their churchly hive to restore the candle's wax.[9] The prayer invokes the triumphant divine and eternal king (*regis*), refers to the candle representing Christ and the Virgin as a pillar of fire (*columnae*) that purifies and removes the darkness of sin, and recalls the happy fault (*felix culpa*) that led to human redemption through the sacrifice of the Virgin Mary's son. What follows is an evocation of the bees that originally made wax for the candle: "accept this candle, a solemn offering, the work of bees (*operibus apum*) ... for it is fed by melting wax, drawn out by mother bees (*apis mater*) to build a torch (*lampadis*) so precious ... may it persevere undimmed ... receive it as a pleasing fragrance" (cited in Taylor 2013, 233). In keeping with the *Exsultet*, and other *cantigas*, the arriving bees in the tale can be seen as chaste, female imitators of Mary, being led by a Saviour who is the king of the hive. The prayer intoned during the offering is answered by the restorative power of these apian candle makers. The removal of Original Sin through Mary and the doctrine of *felix culpa* coincide with Alfonso's famous praise of the Virgin elsewhere in the *Cantigas*, as the new Eve or "Ave Eva" (no. 320).

What is more, the flaming, smoking pillar and torch of the blessing that can be seen in manuscript illuminations corresponds with one of Mary's names, taken once more from the Song of Songs: "who is she that cometh … as a pillar of smoke of aromatic spices" (3:6). St Bonaventure, among others, identified this image as a prefigurement of the Virgin, emitting the smoke of prayers and an "incense of pardon," received by sinners after being "generated" through their "contrition" – in addition to naming the Blessed Mother as the flower pollinated by the honeybee (Bonaventure 1932, 12.3). At the same time, such Paschal, Marian imagery brings to mind beekeeping practices, and in particular the use of smoking torches to protect against stings or kill bees in a dying or unproductive hive. One of the *Cantigas* manuscripts seems to allude to the danger of stingers by concluding that "E aquel eixam' estar y leixaron, / que per ren tanger sol no o ousaron, / e as abellas log' aly criaron / e fezeron mel a mui gran perfia" [they left that swarm alone, for they dared not touch it, and the bees nested there and made a lot of honey] (45–8). This sense of intangibility might also echo the gospel words from the Vulgate ("noli me tangere"), spoken by the resurrected Christ at the moment he is first recognized (John 20:17). In any case, the candle itself, having been burned throughout the season and reconstituted as virginal beeswax in the miracle, evokes the destruction of sinful impurities and the protection of a spiritual apiary for white bees who symbolize repentance and contrition, and are thus attracted to, instead of driven away by, the delicious smelling smoke of Marian prayer. The aroma of the wax anticipates the sweetness of the Eucharistic honey that the bees produce in abundance, having made the Marian church their home.

Finally, it is significant that the miracle of the candle takes place in a religious space that served as the mosque of Elche, prior to the town's recent conquest by Alfonso X around 1250. An uprising of Moors had necessitated a second military campaign in the 1260s.[10] Areas where apiculture could thrive continued to be occupied by Muslims after the thirteenth-century expansion of Castilian territories under Alfonso and his father Fernando III. These populations had long before developed apiaries in the countryside, and continued to operate them in areas near the Mediterranean coast and in parts of Andalucía that Christians would not fully repopulate for some time. In light of the apicultural history of the region, the entrance of the liturgically conjured bees appears to symbolically commemorate the recent conquest and consecration of the city's mosque as Mary's church. This can be related to the overall politics of religious conversion of Muslims and Jews in the collection, recently studied by Amy Remensnyder. She shows how Marian discourse in the *Cantigas* relies on a threat of force and triumphant conversion, as well as syncretistic – though still often antagonistic – strategies that make implicit connections between Passover and Easter, cite the name Rachel from the Torah as a type of Mary, or refer to Islamic veneration of Maryam in the Qur'an.

The centrality of honeybees in the miracles that have concerned me fit into this sort of propaganda. Scholars involved in the creation of the *Cantigas* would have been aware that the Hebrew word for the honeybee (according to St Jerome, as well as Jewish sources) was "Deborah" – that is, the name of the prophetess and Mother of Israel from the Book of Judges, who was viewed by glossators as prefiguring the motherhood of Mary (part 17).[11] It is also possible that they were aware of the famous *surat* in the Qur'an named after the bee, *An-Nahl*, in which collecting sweet nectar from many flowers to make honey exemplifies obedience to the will of Allah in nature, and Muhammad's role in bringing together all divine revelations to make the Islamic holy book (no. 16). Similarly, readers of the Christian Bible could find numerous passages that compare the making and tasting of honey with gathering and speaking God's words, as we have seen. Scholastic writers more generally used the same metaphor to discuss the memorization and edifying recollection of spiritual wisdom through the spoken word and from books, which would include the *Cantigas* itself.

It is no accident that Alfonso's collection associates honeybees with the mosque-church at Elche, and depicts a Jewish witness viewing the host-hive on the altar and a young convert from Judaism taking a communal wafer from Mary that tastes sweeter than honey. These and other Christianizing miracles draw on an apian, melliferous tradition of understanding religious truth that could resonate in other faith traditions, mixing and harmonizing the senses of taste and sound. The text offers the sweetness of honey and the sweet music of Alfonso's songs as a spiritual food and medicine, which, as we have seen, had long been equated to the Incarnation of Christ in the womb of Mary, and his presence in the taste of the Eucharist and in the souls of believers. The *Cantigas* in this way figuratively represent a communion of penitents and converts as a swarm of honeybees, following their Christian king to a unifying hive.

NOTES

1 Emily Francomano has recently studied the various allusions to sweetness in the *Libro de buen amor*. Unless otherwise noted, translations are by the author.

2 See the prologue to the *Conde Lucanor* (Manuel 1984, 50).

3 See, for example, the Introduction to David Howes and Constance Classen's recent study (2014, 11).

4 On the years Alfonso X spent in Seville during the heyday of his reign, as well as his illnesses, see the study of H. Salvador Martínez (2010, 154–9, 251–91).

5 On beekeeping and honey making during the Middle Ages, as well as other periods, see the studies of Eva Crane and Gene Kritsky.

6 See, respectively, *Georgics* (4), *Fasti* (1.363–80), *Natural History* (2.4–23), *City of God* (15.27), and *Etymologies* (2.4:3). Melissa, whose name meant "bees," was known as a nymph, and according to one version of the myth, bees were born from her dead body. Aristaeus was told to slaughter cattle in order to use their carcasses for the formation of new bee swarms.

7 The sanctuary is mentioned in several *cantigas*. It was founded by members of this military order in a mountainous region near the Badajoz. See the editions of Mettman (Alfonso X 1986–9, vol. 3, 152) and Kathleen Kulp-Hill (Alfonso X 2000, 394).

8 The implication being that the whiteness of the bees is related to the colour of the Eucharistic host, and – by extension – to the whiteness and honeyed taste of manna as described in Exodus (16:31).

9 "Regis victoria … aeterni Regis … haec igitur nox est, quae peccatorum tenebras columnae illuminatione purgavit … O felix culpa quae talem ac tantum meruit habere Redemptorem … hace cerei oblatione solemni … de operibus apum … alitur enim liquantibus ceris, quas in substantiam preti-osae huius lampadis apis mater eduxit … ad noctis huis caliginem destru-endam, indeficiens perserveret. Et in odorem suavitatis acceptus" (cited in Taylor 2013, 233).

10 The uprising and subsequent military campaign are described in Salvador Martínez's biography (2010, 164–9).

11 For a comparison of Christian and rabbinical readings of this name (for the latter, sometimes associated with the hornet), see the first chapter of Joy Schroeder's study (2014).

WORKS CITED

Alfonso X. 1986–9. *Cantigas de Santa Maria*. Edited by Walter Mettmann. 3 vols. Madrid: Castalia.

Alfonso X. 2000. *Songs of Holy Mary of Alfonso X, the Wise*. Translated by Kathleen Kulp-Hill. Tempe: Arizona Center for Medieval and Renaissance Studies.

Ambrose of Milan. 1896a. *Concerning Virginity*. Translated by H. de Romestin, E. de Romestin, and H.T.F. Duckworth. *Nicene and Post-Nicene Fathers, Second Series*. Vol. 10. Edited by Philip Schaff and Henry Wace. Buffalo: Christian Literature Publishing. www.newadvent.org/fathers/34071.htm.

Ambrose of Milan. 1896b. *On the Holy Spirit*. Translated by H. de Romestin, E. de Romestin, and H.T.F. Duckworth. *Nicene and Post-Nicene Fathers, Second*

Series. Vol. 10. Edited by Philip Schaff and Henry Wace. Buffalo: Christian Literature Publishing. www.newadvent.org/fathers/34022.htm.

Augustine of Hippo. 1999. *City of God*. Translated by Marcus Dods. New York: Random House.

Bartholomew of England. 1905. *Mediaeval Lore from Bartholomew Anglicus*. Edited and translated by Robert Steele. London: Alexander Moring.

Berceo, Gonzalo de. 1987. *Milagros de Nuestra Señora*. Edited by E. Michael Gerli. Madrid: Cátedra.

Bible. 1941. Douay-Rheims Version. New York: Benziger Brothers.

Bollo-Panadero, María Dolores. 2008. "Heretics and Infidels: The *Cantigas de Santa María* as Ideological Instrument of Cultural Codification." *Romance Quarterly* 55.3: 163–73. https://doi.org/10.3200/RQTR.55.3.163-174.

Bonaventure. 1932. *Mirror of the Blessed Virgin Mary*. Translated by Sr Mary Emmanuel. Chap. 12. St Louis: B. Herder Book Company.

Burrus, Virginia. 2000 *"Begotten, Not Made": Conceiving Manhood in Late Antiquity*. Stanford: Stanford University Press.

Carmona Ruiz, María Antonia. 2000. "La Apicultura Sevillana a Fines de la Edad Media." *Anuario de estudios medievales* 30: 387–421. https://doi.org/10.3989/aem.2000.v30.i1.501.

Crane, Eva. 1999. *The World History of Beekeeping and Honey Hunting*. New York: Routledge.

Ciruelo, Pedro. 1978 *Reprovación de las supersticiones y hechizerías*. Edited by Alva V. Ebersole. Valencia: Albatros Hispanófila.

Fife, Austin E. 1964. "Christian Swarm Charms from the Ninth to the Nineteenth Centuries." *Journal of American Folklore* 77.304: 154–9. https://doi.org/10.2307/537564.

Francomano, Emily. 2013. "'Este manjar es dulçe': Sweet Synaesthesia in the *Libro de buen amor*." *eHumanista* 25: 127–44.

Gambero, Luigi. 2005. *Mary in the Middle Ages*. San Francisco: Ignatius Press.

Gitlitz, David, and Linda Kay Davidson. 1999 *A Drizzle of Honey: The Lives and Recipes of Spain's Secret Jews*. New York: St Martin's Press.

Guéranger, Prosper. 1904. *The Liturgical Year*. Translated by Laurence Shepherd. Vol. 2. 3rd ed. London: Burns and Oats.

Howes, David, and Constance Classen. 2014. *Ways of Sensing: Understanding the Senses in Society*. New York: Routledge.

Isidore of Seville. 2007. *Etymologies*. Edited and translated by Stephen A. Barney et al. Cambridge: Cambridge University Press.

Jerome. "Letter 54." 1893. Translated by W.H. Fremantle, G. Lewis, and W.G. Martley. In *Nicene and Post-Nicene Fathers, Second Series*, vol. 6, edited by Philip Schaff and Henry Wace. Buffalo: Christian Literature. www.newadvent.org/fathers/3001054.htm.

Kritsky, Gene. 2010. *The Quest for the Perfect Hive: A History of Innovation in Bee Culture*. Oxford: Oxford University Press.

Kulp-Hill, Kathleen. 1980. "Figurative Language in the *Cantigas de Santa Maria*." *Kentucky Romance Quarterly* 27.1: 3-9. https://doi.org/10.1080/03648664.1980.9931013.

Manuel, Juan. 1984. *El Conde Lucanor*. Edited by Ian Michael. Madrid: Castalia.

Montoya Martínez, Jesús. 2007. "El culto a la Eucaristía y sus derivaciones mágicas en el siglo XIII." *La corónica* 36.1: 189–96. https://doi.org/10.1353/cor.2007.0032.

Nadeau, Carolyn. 2012. "Contributions of Medieval Food Manuals to Spain's Culinary Heritage." *Cincinnati Romance Review* 33: 59–77.

Neal, J.M., ed. and trans. 1856. *Medieval Preachers and Medieval Preaching*. London: J.C. Mozley.

Ovid. 2011. *Fasti*. Translated by Anne and Peter Wiseman. Oxford: Oxford University Press.

Pliny the Elder. 1856. *The Natural History*. Translated by John Bostock and H.T. Riley. Vol. 4. London: H.G. Bohn.

Prado-Vilar, Francisco. 2011. "*Iudeus sacer*: Life, Law and Identity in the 'State of Exception' Called 'Marian Miracle.'" In *Judaism and Christian Art: Aesthetic Anxieties from the Catacombs to Colonialism*, edited by Herbert L. Kessler and David Nirenberg, 115–42. Philadelphia: University of Pennsylvania Press.

Qur'an. 2004. Translated by M.A.S. Abdel Haleem. Oxford: Oxford University Press.

Remensnyder, Amy. 2014. *La Conquistadora: The Virgin Mary at War and Peace in the Old and New Worlds*. Oxford: Oxford University Press.

Ruiz, Juan. 1988. *Libro de buen amor*. Edited by G.B. Gybbon-Monypenny. Clásicos Castalia 161. Madrid: Castalia.

Salvador Martínez, H. 2010. *Alfonso X, the Learned*. Translated by Odile Cisneros. Leiden: Brill.

Schroeder, Joy A. 2014. *Deborah's Daughters: Gender Politics and Biblical Interpretation*. Oxford: Oxford University Press.

Sommerfeldt, John R. 2004. *Bernard of Clairvaux on the Life of the Mind*. Mahwah, NJ: Paulist.

Taylor, Anna Lisa. 2013. *Epic Lives and Monasticism in the Middle Ages, 800–1050*. Cambridge: Cambridge University Press.

Thurston, Herbert. 1911. "Paschal Candle." In *The Catholic Encyclopedia*, vol. 11. New York: Robert Appleton Company. www.newadvent.org/cathen/11515b.htm. Accessed 2 June 2014.

Virgil. 2005. *Georgics*. Translated by Janet Lembke. New Haven: Yale University Press.

Vogelzang, Robin M., trans. 2008. *The Book of Sent Sovrí: Medieval Recipes from Catalonia (Llibre de Sent Sovrí)*. Woodbridge: Tamesis.

2 European Perspectives on the *Olla podrida* and Other Early Modern Spanish Fare

CAROLYN NADEAU

To understand Spanish gastronomy of the sixteenth and seventeenth centuries, scholars have turned to historical texts that include legal documents, political essays, travelogues, and especially cooking manuals. Together with fictional narratives, plays, and poems, these primary documents provide cultural contexts for the time period that include foodstuffs, modes of production and consumption, and insight into the politics, economics, and social forces that both define food and are defined by it. Recent scholarship has focused on internal perspectives on Spanish fare to explore elements of Jewish and Arab heritage (Castro Martínez; Aguilera Pleguezuelo; Arbelos; García), class (Alvar-Ezquerra), New World influences (Garrido Aranda; Hernández Bermejo; Pérez Samper 1996; Terrón), and a general historic overview (Nadeau; Campbell; Valles Rojo; Sánchez Meco), to name the most salient perspectives. Scholars have also produced impressive editions of cookbooks written for the court (Cruz Cruz), the university (Pérez Samper 1998), and the privileged household (Martínez Crespo). This essay contributes to this rich ongoing dialogue on Spain's early modern gastronomy by first contextualizing the two most important court cookbooks of the early modern period, Ruperto de Nola's *Llibre de coch* [Book of cookery] (1520) (which was translated five years later into the Castilian *Libro de cocina*) and Francisco Martínez Montiño's *Arte de cocina, pastelería, vizcochería y conservería* [The art of cooking, pie making, pastry making, and preserving] (1611). It then examines images of Spanish cuisine from beyond Spain's borders. Using cookbooks, service manuals, and journals from other parts of Europe, this essay seeks to understand how different European cooks and gastronomes identify and describe Spanish cuisine. My objective, then, is to enhance our understanding of the evolution of Spanish cuisine between the sixteenth and seventeenth centuries with a comparative view both from inside Spain and from without.

Across Europe, one of the clear distinctions between the early modern period and the Middle Ages is the development of national cuisines. Cookbooks both at court and within aristocratic circles proliferate, palace cooks are no longer anonymous figures but well known by their reputations, and, in their writings, these culinary artists begin to emphasize both regional and national dishes. Cooks such as Ruperto de Nola and Francisco Martínez Montiño lay the foundation for the court cooking of the Iberian peninsula. From these manuals we get a clear view of the early foundations of Spanish food consumed by the elite, but rarely are recipes defined as "a la española" [Spanish-style] or "a la catalana" [Catalan-style] in these works. Rather, we must turn to cooking manuals from beyond Spain's borders – for example, by Bartolomeo Scappi, Gervese Markham, and Pierre de Lune – for evidence of how Europeans understood and helped to define "Spanish" cuisine.

Historians often refer to the year 1800 as the "great divide" that marks a radical shift in how time, society, and nation are understood. Critics such as Benedict Anderson, Ernest Gellner, Eric Hobsbawm, and others argue that "national consciousness was essentially a nineteenth-century phenomenon" (Burke 2013, 21).[1] For these critics, and particularly Gellner, the aristocratic elite belonged to a larger community than nation and spoke other national languages, while the peasantry belonged to a smaller one, the region or even the village, and communicated in a local dialect. Universal education that fostered national consciousness and other industrialized indicators – railroads, newspapers, and urbanization, for example – also fostered this shift. But, according to Burke, this "great divide" does not take into account distinctions between social and political nationalism and a broader sentiment of national pride. Burke also argues that critical reactions point to a standardization of languages that began much earlier. In the case of Spain, this is certainly true, as attention to a national language is apparent with the publication of Antonio de Nebrija's 1492 *Gramática de la lengua castellana* [Grammar of the Castilian language], the first book dedicated to the grammar of a modern European language, and later in the early seventeenth century with Sebastián de Covarrubias's 1611 *Tesoro de la lengua castellana o española* [Treasure of Castilian or Spanish language], the first vernacular monolingual dictionary in Europe. In terms of language, national consciousness was very much on the mind of those seeking to codify Spanish grammar and lexicon.

I would argue that in the realm of the gastronomic arts something similar is occurring as national identities are tied to the names of specific recipes found in the earliest printed cookbooks. Noted author Alberto Capatti calls dishes that are anchored to a specific place *gastrotoponyms* (cited in Krohn 2015, 10). Recipes whose titles indicate a specific geographic source provide evidence that an author (or compiler) was not only aware of "foreign" tastes and gastronomic customs but also privileged them by including them in a particular work. These recipes indicate both a sense of national consciousness and an openness to external tastes. Their appearance in cookbooks shows a willingness to acknowledge and embrace external modes of preparation and provide for readers, both cooks and those for whom the recipes are created, an understanding of another "foreign" cuisine. At first, gastrotoponymic recipes quite simply identified a different approach to the dish without any clear indication of what foodstuffs or cooking methods linked it to a particular place. We find examples of this approach in the early part of the fifteenth century and throughout the early modern period. But beginning in the late sixteenth century, specific dishes are attached to a national cuisine with more intentionality as they often include a brief comment related to the recipe's place of origin. In the case of Spain, the *olla podrida* [hodgepodge stew] serves as an excellent example of how dishes come to represent the external vision of what another "national" cuisine is.

I. Nola and Other Sixteenth-Century Perspectives

At the dawn of the sixteenth century, our understanding of taste and food habits primarily concerns nobility and aristocracy. From professional cooks who served the elite prior to the early modern period, some one hundred manuscripts have been identified. One of the earliest available today is the Catalan *Sent Sovi* (1324). In this work of 72 recipes there are no references to a national or regional designation. But a century later, of the 66 recipes that make up the French manuscript *Vivendier*, three reference nations: "To make a German Meat broth of rabbit, of chicken or of some other meat" (Scully 1997, 49), "To make a subtle English broth" (50), and "Hungarian broth" (76). And, in the more extensive anonymous *Neapolitan Recipe Collection* (second half of fifteenth century), many more national and regional references, some 10 per cent of the 220 recipes, form part of the recipe titles.[2] The author includes 16 references to Italy and states located within the Italian peninsula. The second most frequent designation is of four "Catalan-style" recipes, as well as one Aragonese, and the first reference ever to a *Spanish* mode of preparation: "Spanish squid sauce" (*Neapolitan Recipe Collection* 206).[3] We can see, then, that even during the latter half of the fifteenth century, an awareness of food preparation based on geographic distinction increasingly informed different cooking manuals, although none of these recipes mark a definitive style of cooking attached to the region.

Turning to Spanish cuisine as represented in the cookbooks of Ruperto de Nola and Francisco Martínez Montiño, we can trace how it evolves over an almost hundred-year trajectory and how these authors privileged specific dishes. To be clear, Nola himself had little, if anything, to do with the Castilian court; rather, he developed his culinary talents in the courts of Aragon and/or Naples. But, his cookbook, *Llibre de coch*, was quickly translated into Castilian, edited several times in both Catalan and Castilian, and laid the groundwork for Christian court cuisine of the Iberian peninsula. Not much is known about Ruperto de Nola's life, but most critics agree that he was either Catalan or born of Catalan parents relocated to Naples. Nola served under don Ferrante, illegitimate son of Alfonso I (previously Alfonso V of Aragón), who ruled Naples from 1458 to his death in 1494.[4]

In Nola's *Llibre de coch* he writes with pride about the three most important dishes in his collection: "y debéis saber que de cuantos manjares hay en el mundo son la flor estas tres y más principales, y son estas: Salsa de pavo, Mirrauste y Manjar blanco" [and you should know that of all the foods in all the world the best are these three main ones and they are: peacock sauce, *mirrauste*, and blancmange] (1997, 263).[5] All three of these recipes are poultry dishes, whether it be peacock, capon, or hen in the first case; squab in the second case; or hen in the third case. All three also use ground almonds and either bread (the first and third) or rice flour (the second) and include cinnamon and sugar (the first two) or just sugar (the third). It comes as no surprise that his most prized recipes are made with poultry because it was the privileged meat among the aristocracy, or that they include nuts, flour, and spices, as these items are among the most popular of early modern Spanish and other European cuisines.

In Platina's *On Right Pleasure and Good Health*, the recipe "Catalan mirrauste" begins with words of praise for the Catalan people and their level of cooking expertise: "The Catalan race, which is indeed distinguished and considered not much different in talent and physical form from the Italian level of skill, prepared a dish which they call *mirrauste* in this way ... I remember having eaten nothing more pleasant" (1998, 275). Platina also includes Catalan blancmange (293, 295) and a Catalan dish for partridge (287, 289), and again praises this cuisine. In both the Catalan cookbook and the Italian ones that reference Catalan cooking, there are no indicators that define a particular style of cooking or specific ingredients. Instead, those that carry a "Catalan" or "Spanish" denomination seem to simply acknowledge their existence and pay homage to the way different nations prepare a dish.

In addition to his top three, Nola's collection is filled with dozens of sauce recipes; a handful of *mirrauste* and blancmange recipes; many soups, stews, and one-pot meals; fish, meat, and vegetable dishes; pies both savoury and sweet; desserts and sweet fruit recipes; dishes for abstinence or partial abstinence days; and dishes for the ill. Nola's cookbook serves as a model for future writers and signals the direction that cookbooks will take. *Llibre de coch* sheds the exclusive late medieval features of former cooking manuscripts and reveals a Renaissance character. Like Miguel de Cervantes with his publication of *Don Quixote* over a century later, the work contains a "modern" sensibility. In his introduction Nola highlights the valued position of the cook and that cooking is a culinary *art*. Among his many stew recipes, we find the "Potaje *moderno*" [*modern* stew] (1997, 299, emphasis mine) and "Otro potaje *moderno*" [another *modern* stew] (299, emphasis mine) that reveal Nola's awareness of changes to cooking styles and ingredients.

Similar to the Italian *nuova cucina* movement reflected in the *Neapolitan Recipe Collection*, Nola's work emphasizes regional and international cooking and, in doing so, aids in developing a distinct national style. The work contains regional Aragonese, Genoese, and Venetian recipes like "toronjas de Xativa que son almojávanas" [Xativa *toronjas* which are cheese fritters] (323),[6] "rosquilla de fruta que llaman casquetas en Valencia y en Barcelona" [fruit ring called *casquetas* in Valencia and Barcelona] (323–4), "torta a la genovesa" [Genoese cake] (320), or "xinxanella a la veneciana" [Venetian jujube] (320–1). The recipe for Venetian jujubes is actually a broth with pasta. The pasta is made with cheese, fine bread crumbs, eggs, saffron, and other herbs, and pressed through a large grater that forms the dough into gnocchi-sized shapes that are then served in a broth. *Xinxanella* is a variant of *guinja*, synonym of *azufaifa* or *jujube*, the red, teardrop-shaped fruit of the jujube tree. Thus, the title of the dish, like the previous cheese fritter recipe in the shape of *toronja* or so many others in the text, reflects its form, a visual image, rather than its content.

Like its Italian counterparts, *Llibre de coch* also contains two recipes that signal specifically *Catalan* dishes. "Fruta llamada robioles a la catalana" [Fruit called *robioles* Catalan-style] (327) is a sweet fried dough recipe made with rose water batter, mixed with a hazelnut and pine nut egg yolk mixture, and seasoned with cinnamon, sugar, ginger, and more rose water. After they are fried, they are sprinkled with rose water, honey, cinnamon, and sugar. This recipe has evolved today into *rubiols*, a Holy Week turnover famous in Mallorca. The second "Catalan" dish is "Frutas llamadas garbias a la catalana" [Fruit called *garbias* Catalan-style] (328). Here, borage and Swiss chard are cooked, drained, and chopped up with a soft cheese (like ricotta).[7] Egg yolk is added as well as more soft cheese. This mixture is then used as a filling for turnovers, which are deep-fried and sprinkled with rose water, honey, cinnamon, and sugar. In these "Catalan" recipes as well as those designated "Catalan" in the *Neapolitan Recipe Collection* the authors recognize the idea of a Catalan cuisine even though specific definitive features have not yet taken shape.

Nola also underscores the contributions of other cultures, specifically Moorish and Jewish, in the development of Spanish gastronomy. He references several food items and dishes that are inspired by Arab and Jewish culinary traditions found throughout Spain and that form such an essential part of the country's heritage: the already cited *mirrauste* (266), "potaje dicho morteruelo" [hot paté stew] (275), three recipes for "potaje de culantro llamado primo" [coriander soup called the first] (275–6),[8] "salsa Granada" [Granada sauce] (313), "berenjenas a la morisca" [Morisco-style eggplant] (285–6), and "calabazas a la morisca" [Morisco-style squash] (287). The "salsa Granada" recipe is for a chicken liver purée thickened with egg yolk and flavoured with orange juice and spices. It had previously appeared in the Catalan manuscript *Sent Soví*, but in his *Libre de coch*, Nola omits all references to *tocino* [fat back], of which no fewer than four appear in the *Sent soví* version. Comparing the two *a la morisca* recipes, it is possible that the label refers to a finishing style of adding finely grated cheese, ground spices that may include coriander, cumin and/or caraway, and whipped egg batter. Even the "toronjas de Xátiva" mentioned earlier show the Muslim influence in the recipe's second name, *almojávanas*, which comes from the Hispanic Arabic *almuğábbana*, meaning *made with cheese*, which comes from the classical Arabic *ğubn*, or *cheese*.

Before the 1611 publication of Martínez Montiño's *Arte de cocina, pastelería, vizcochería y conservería*, the premier Italian cookbook, *Opera dell' arte del cucinare* [Book on the art of cooking], written by Bartolomeo Scappi, was published in 1570, around the time of the author's death. This opus is nothing short of a masterpiece of the early modern kitchen and takes an innovative approach in treating "Spanish" food. Scappi's six-volume work contains over 1000 recipes and 28 illustrations divided into sections on meat, fowl, fish, pasta, diets for the infirm and convalescent, and recipes for Lent. Scappi cooked for five different popes and was the private cook of Pope Pius V. For over two months in late 1549–early 1550 he prepared meals for the conclave that chose Pope Julius III as successor to Paul III (Dal Col and Gutiérrez Granda 2004, 13–14). He was also responsible for the coronation feast of Charles V as Holy Roman Emperor in Bologna in 1536 for which 780 dishes were prepared.

Scappi's love of his art form is apparent from the opening pages as he passionately describes food and commits to the smallest details. Before entering into a formal discussion of creating a dish, Scappi highlights seasonal ingredients and how to recognize good quality. He incorporates vivid descriptions of cooking techniques and is very particular about how to present food. His tone is consistently positive. As a closing for many recipes, he offers variations to accommodate changing seasons and different tastes. Like the earlier cooking manuals, Scappi includes references to regional dishes – Venetian, Roman, Milanese, Lombardian, Neapolitan, Genovese, Sardinian, Salernitan, and Sienese – and recipes with titles that include nationality: "to stew an ox loin in the German fashion" (2008, 140), "to cook trout in the German fashion" (321), and "to cook pike in a pottage in the French fashion" (330). But, as with the earlier cooking manuals, these recipes give no indication of a cooking method specific to the named country.

However, his treatment of other "national" food is groundbreaking in that he cites specific ingredients from specific countries – salted salmon from Flanders, salted head cabbage from Germany, fowl tongue from Cyprus, wine from Greece, and francolins and honey from Spain. The act of citing an ingredient from a specific region or nation (he also cites Milanese almonds, Roman cherries, and Neapolitan *mostaccioli*) implies an excellence in the quality of that product and reflects a modern sensibility of discriminating taste. In the case of Spain, Scappi singles out francolin that are brought to Italy. In "To spit-roast and otherwise cook rock partridge, old common grey partridge and francolin," he clarifies the size of birds worthy of import: "francolins brought from Sicily and Spain to Rome are the same size as rock partridges and have a greyish plumage" (205). In "To prepare jelly from wether's feet," he again highlights Spanish offerings when he specifically calls for two and a half ounces of *Spanish* honey to be combined with vinegar, verjuice, white wine, egg whites, cinnamon, pepper, cloves, ginger, and nutmeg (261).[9]

Scappi again shows his pioneering spirit when he includes recipes unique to two specific countries: "to prepare a thick milk soup popularly called Hungarian Soup" (226) and "to prepare a dish of various ingredients called, in Spanish, *olla podrida*" (215). What Calderón would later dub "la princesa de los guisados" [the princess of stews], the *olla podrida* was a fashionable dish during the Hapsburg monarchy. In fact, Gómez Laguna speculates that Scappi became aware of this stew when he prepared the banquet for Carlos V's coronation feast (1993, 10). In seventeenth-century Spain, the *olla podrida* represented the culinary taste of nobles both for its ostentation and its opulence. Yet everyone from kings to canons, from rectors to peasants, enjoyed it. Although its beginning as a simpler stew with humbler ingredients is generally agreed upon, no one really knows its point of origin. Some postulate that it is originally Gallic or perhaps Visigoth; others theorize that the *olla podrida* comes from the Jewish *adafina*, a stew prepared on Fridays to avoid cooking on the Sabbath.[10] The Spanish recipe also bears a striking resemblance to the recipe "On Cooking a Dish Called *Ṣinhājī'*" found in Ibn Razîn al Tujibî *Fiḍālat al-Khiwān fī Ṭayyibāt al-Ṭáām wa-l-Alwān* (Best of delectable foods and dishes).[11] At each table, ingredients for the stew would invariably change depending on the area, season, and economic level of those cooking. But in the sixteenth century, *olla podrida* becomes the fashion among the aristocracy and for three centuries is served from the richest tables to the poorest. Recipes would vary from one cook to the next, but all agreed that the ingredients must be many and varied.

Scappi, who is the first to ever publish a recipe for *olla podrida*, opens by explaining the very name of the dish: "This preparation, *oglia potrida*, is named thus by Spaniards because it is made mostly in earthenware stewpots called *oglias*, and *potride* [*sic*] means a variety of well cooked ingredients" (215–16). He then goes on to enumerate the quantities of pork, beef, fowl, legumes, vegetables, grains, and spices that are combined to make this stew. In total there are seven different pork products; five beef, goat, and domestic fowl; six different wild birds (including twenty thrush and twenty quail); twelve vegetables and legumes; and three different types of seasoning. His detail in presentation is also exceptional as he explains how to present the meal in a series of layers over different platters, allowing time for each layer to rest and a final addition of spices before serving:

> Then set out great platters and put part of the mixture on them without the broth: get all the large fowl, quartered, and the large meats, and the salami sliced, leaving the small birds whole; divvy those up onto the platters over that mixture. On top of that put some of the other mixture with the saveloy cut into pieces. Make three layers like that. Get a spoonful of the fattest broth and splash it over top. (216–17)[12]

Another *olla podrida* recipe appears in the sixteenth-century Hungarian cookbook *The Science of Cooking*. While much shorter than Scappi's, this recipe also includes pork, beef, and a wide variety of poultry:

> Boil the pig's leg, then some beef, sausage and liver, and ten kinds of bird meat if you can have it, cook them all in one pot, begin it with the older animals, then the younger ones, add some salt, red cabbage, carrot, wild carrot, mix them together with meat, then pour boiled beef broth onto it, add some salt and black pepper, saffron and ginger, serve it once cooked. (*The Prince of Transylvania's Court Cookbook* 117)

One notes here the insistence on cooking the older animals first, a clear reminder of the time needed to make the meat more tender. The author finishes his recipe for *olla podrida* with the following statement: "This dish is cooked twice or thrice a year for the Holy Roman Emperor" (117). Again, we find connections between this dish and royalty.

Almost thirty years later, Diego Granado copies Scappi's recipe for *olla podrida* and many others of his to publish in Spain *Libro del arte de cozina* [Book on the art of cooking] (1599), and, as a result, the first published recipe of *olla podrida* in its native country.[13] Granado naturally eliminates the explanation of the name that opens Scappi's version and also edits out the seasonal suggestions offered at the end of the entry, but essentially all else remains identical. While Granado's cookbook brings to Spain the creative cooking found among the pages of Scappi's work, the 1611 publication of Francisco Martínez Montiño's cookbook overshadowed Granado's, which left little mark on Spain's culinary development and was not published again until late into the twentieth century.

II. Martínez Montiño and Other Seventeenth-Century Perspectives

As with so many cooks of the early modern period, little is known about Francisco Martínez Montiño's life. He was possibly Galician and worked his entire life in kitchens, beginning as a humble kitchen boy (*galopín*) and making his way up to master cook for Philip III and Philip IV. In the opening pages of his cookbook, Martínez Montiño alludes to having served in the kitchens of Philip II's sister, doña Juana, in Portugal. Pérez Samper notes that he then moved to the royal kitchens in Madrid and began serving Philip III in 1585. He later worked for Philip IV until his retirement or death in 1629 (1998, 29–30). Martínez Montiño's work is recognized as the most published Spanish cookbook before the twentieth century, with at least twenty-eight editions known to scholars today.[14] It is separated into two chapters. The first deals with cleanliness of the kitchen and staff, how to serve banquets, and suggested banquet menus; the second, which contains 506 recipes, is organized, much as the title suggests, into various sections on cooking, pies, pastries, and preserves.

Martínez Montiño shares many recipes with Granado, including regional and international dishes. Both authors include ingredients and recipes that reflect Spain's Hispanic-Muslim past.[15] Internationally, Granado includes more recipes with Italian influences, and Martínez Montiño, French and Portuguese. They also share a similar sense of herbs and seasoning, a consciousness of varying cooking temperatures, a wide range of cooking verbs, and a more sombre tone than is found in either Scappi's or Nola's cookbook.

By the time Martínez Montiño publishes his cookbook, the *olla podrida* is already firmly established in the culinary culture of Spain, as evidenced by its appearance in the works of numerous fiction writers.[16] Martínez Montiño puts his own signature on this classic recipe when he includes "Una olla podrida en pastel" [A hodgepodge stew in a pie] as part of his collected recipes. Like Scappi and Granado, Martínez Montiño includes a wide variety of pork, beef, fowl, legumes, and vegetables. He cooks them separately and produces an excellent broth in which he stews vegetables.

Has de cocer la vianda de la olla podrida, cociendo la gallina, o vaca, o carnero, y un pedazo de tocino magro, y toda la demás volatería, como son palomas, perdices, zorzales, y solomo de puerco, longanizas, salchichas, liebre, y morcillas: esto todo ha de ser asado, primero que se echen a cocer. En otra vasilla has de cocer cecina, lenguas de vaca, y de puerco, pies de puerco, orejas, y salchichones; del caldo de entrambas ollas echarás en una vasija, y cocerás allí las verduras, berzas, y nabos, perejil, y hierbabuena y los ajos, y las cebollas han de ser asadas primero. (100v)

[Cook the ingredients for a hodgepodge stew including hen, beef, mutton, a piece of lean lard, all other fowl like pigeons, partridges, and thrushes, pork loin, hare, cooked sausage, cured sausage, and blood sausage. All of this should first be roasted then put on to boil. In another pot, cook cured beef, beef and pork tongue, pig's feet, ears, and sausage. Fill another pot with stock from the first two and in that cook vegetables like collard greens, turnips, parsley, spearmint, garlic, and onions, which should first be roasted.]

His unique approach is that he then uses these many and varied ingredients as a filling for a pie. Once the ingredients are cooked he explains how to assemble and bake the pie:

Sacarás toda esta vianda en piezas, que esté dividida una cosa de otra, y las verduras en otra pieza, de manera que no esté nada deshecho, déjalo enfriar, y harás un vaso muy grande, bien gordo de masa negra de harina de centeno, o de [a]cemite, y lo asentarás sobre una hoja de horno, e irás asentando de toda la vianda que tienes cocida dentro del pastel, e irás sazonando con todas especias, y alcaravea, y echarás de las verduras, ni mas ni menos. Y cuando estuviere lleno el pastelón, ciérralo, y métalo en el horno de pan, porque no habrá horno de cobre tan grande, que se pueda cocer dentro; y pondrás sobre una hoja de horno de cobre, y no lo quites

de la hoja donde está, hasta que se cueza: y cuando la masa del pastel estuviere más de medio cocida, agujerá el capirote de la cubierta, y hínchelo
de caldo, y cueza en el horno por espacio de una hora. (100v–101r)

[Put all the ingredients in bowls, each one separate from the other, and
the vegetables in another bowl, and don't let anything fall apart. Let them
cool. Make a big, thick crust with rye or whole wheat dough. Place it on a
baking sheet and fill the pie with all the cooked ingredients. Season with
all spices and caraway.[17] Add in all the vegetables, no more, no less. When
the pie is full, seal it and place it in the bread oven because no copper
oven would be able to hold it. Place it on a copper baking sheet and don't
remove it from the sheet until it's done baking. When the crust is half
baked, stick a needle in the top and fill with stock and let it continue baking in the oven for an hour.]

Like Scappi's recipe, Martínez Montiño's is opulent and crafted for the
most wealthy.

Within Spain, other versions of the dish appear in more modest cookbooks, like *Libro del arte de cocina* [Book on the art of cooking] (1607) by
Domingo Hernández de Maceras, who was cook in a residence hall at the
University of Salamanca. He presents a significantly more modest version of the dish, although it too contains all types of animal products, garbanzos, garlic, turnips, and seasoning (1998, 217). This dish that is key to
Spain's culinary history continues to appear over two hundred years later
in *La cocina de los jesuitas. Común modo de guisar, que observaban en las casas
de los regulares de la Compañía de Jesús* [Jesuit cuisine. The common way of
cooking that was followed in the houses of clerks regular of the Society of
Jesus] (1818). In this much-reduced version, the author explains that it is a
meal to be consumed on regular (non-abstinence) days: "Esta lleva de dos
carnes, aves, conejos, carnero, jamon, vaca, etc. Hervirá á fuego manso, y
en estando tierna se echa la especia fina, y si quieren echarle vitualla que
sea poca, y el caldo tasado, y con poco grasa: al principio se pone como
la ordinaria" [This has two meats, poultry, rabbit, mutton, ham, beef, etc.
Simmer it all and when it is tender, add fine herbs, and if you want to add
vegetables then just a few, and the broth portioned and with little fat. It is
generally served as a regular meal] (1994, 9).

Outside of Spain, the *olla podrida* rapidly becomes one of Spain's rich
gastronomic contributions to Europe. Between the times that Diego
Granado and Martínez Montiño publish their respective cookbooks
in Spain, versions begin to appear across Europe. For example, in the
1604 cookbook *Ouverture de cuisine* [Opening the kitchen], Lancelot de
Casteau titles his version "Pour faire un pot pourry dict en Espaignolle

Oylla podrida" [To make a potpourri called *olla podrida* in Spanish]. De Casteau's recipe, even more extravagant than Scappi's, begins with beef, chicken, mutton, and duck, to which he adds numerous other meats, poultry, and vegetables, including raviolis filled with almonds and candied quince. The platters are finished with "a dozen feet of sheep well washed to put all around the plate" that are then decorated with cooked dates placed between the feet (de Casteau 1604).

Only a few years later, in the 1612 Dutch cookbook *Koocboec oft Familieren Kevkenboec, bequaem voor alle jouffrouwen, die hun van keuckenhandel oft backen van toertkens ende taertkens willen verstaen* [Cookery book or familiar kitchen book suited to all young women who want to understand the workings of the kitchen or how to bake pies and tarts], writer Antonius Magirus includes a lengthy version of the recipe, "Hoe dat men een goede menghelinghe oft Spaenschen huspot maecken sal, int Spaens gheheeten: oglia potrida" [How to made a good mixture or Spanish 'hutspot,' that in Spanish is called olla podrida].[18] Schildermans and Sels have pointed out that Magirus substitutes ingredients that were available to the Dutch (2003, 61). As noted by the book's subtitle, the shift from royalty to familiar kitchens is clear. Additionally, historian Deborah Krohn notes that this cookbook project appeals "to bourgeois women who could presumably learn both general things – the workings of the kitchen – and more specific instruction regarding the creation of particular dishes" (2015, 45). Similar to Martínez Montiño, who writes recipes for men and women cooking both in the royal kitchen and in private homes, it is clear that this Spanish recipe has appeal to a wide audience.

Attempting to adapt recipes from abroad to conform to the availability and tastes of a specific locale is again present in Gervase Markham's 1615 English version of the recipe which appears in *The English Housewife*. He adds personal commentary on the exceptional quality of this dish as he opens his recipe: "To make an excellent *olla podrida*, which is the only principal dish of boiled meat which is esteemed in all Spain ..." (1986, 77). While elements of the Spanish recipe are recognizable in Markham's version – for example, the many meat, poultry, and vegetable selections – Markham, like de Casteau and Magirus before him, includes ingredients that differ from the Spanish version: tubers like potatoes and skirret and leaf vegetables like strawberry leaves, succory, and marigold leaves. In the explanation of its presentation he includes Spanish dishware and layers of fruit seen also seen in the French version:

> dish it up upon great chargers, or long Spanish dishes made in the fashion of our English wooden trays, with good store of sippets in the bottom;[19]

then cover the meat all over with prunes, raisins, currants, and blanched almonds, boiled in a thing by themselves; then cover the fruit and the whole boiled herbs with slices of oranges and lemons, and lay the roots round about the sides of the dish, and strew good store of sugar over all, and so serve it forth. (78)

Again in 1660, Robert May opens his cookbook *The Accomplisht Cook* with the recipe "To make an Olio Podrida," showing once again the importance of this dish for the British (1685, 1–3).

Returning to Italy, the German-born Mattia Giegher (Mathias Jäger) published a 1623 treatise on serving, *Lo scalco* [The steward], in which he illustrates how to serve an *oglia podrida*. For these instructions he includes a table map with the *oglia podrida* as the centrepiece surrounded by different meat dishes (see fig. 2.1). Giegher organizes dishes to be served seasonally and places the *oglia podrida* as a third course among those served in winter. He writes: "è una vivanda alla Spangnuola, nella qual' entran diverse cose, como Quaglie, Tordi, Pippioni, Pernici, Capponi, Pollastri, Carne de Vitella, de Castrato, e di Porco salvatico, Salsiccie, Salsiccioni, Prosciutto, Lingue, Peducci, e Grugni di Porco, Cavoli, Rape, Finocchi, Fave, Specierie, ed altri ingredienti" [(It) is a Spanish-style dish, in which various things are included, such as quail, thrush, squab, partridge, capon, chicken, veal, ox, and boar, regular sausages, big sausages, ham, tongue, pig's feet and face, cabbage, turnips, fennel, broad beans, spices, and other ingredients] (Giegher 1639, 49).

Moving beyond the early modern period, the nineteenth-century culinary giants Marie-Antonin Carême, in his work *L'art de la cuisine française au dix-neuvième siècle* [The art of French cooking in the nineteenth century] (1994, 129), and Auguste Escoffier, in *Le guide culinaire* [The culinary guide] (1921, 115), both include the *olla podrida* as a Spanish national dish, albeit more simplified versions compared to those of the early modern period.

In addition to cookbook citations of the *olla podrida* as an excellent Spanish dish, European travellers to Spain repeatedly note its unique and excellent quality. In 1669 Samuel Pepys writes in his journal of an "olio," his term for *olla podrida*, that was prepared by a cook who had spent time in Spain: "Sheres is to treat us with a Spanish *Oleo* by a cook of his acquaintance that is there, that was with my Lord in Spain. And without any other company, he did do it, and mighty nobly; and the *Oleo* was indeed a noble dish, such as I never saw better, or any more of" (Latham and Matthews 1976, 509). And in James Howell's letter to Lady Cornwallis he calls the dish "The reverend matron" and compares it to a living being with mutton, beef, and bacon as her soul,

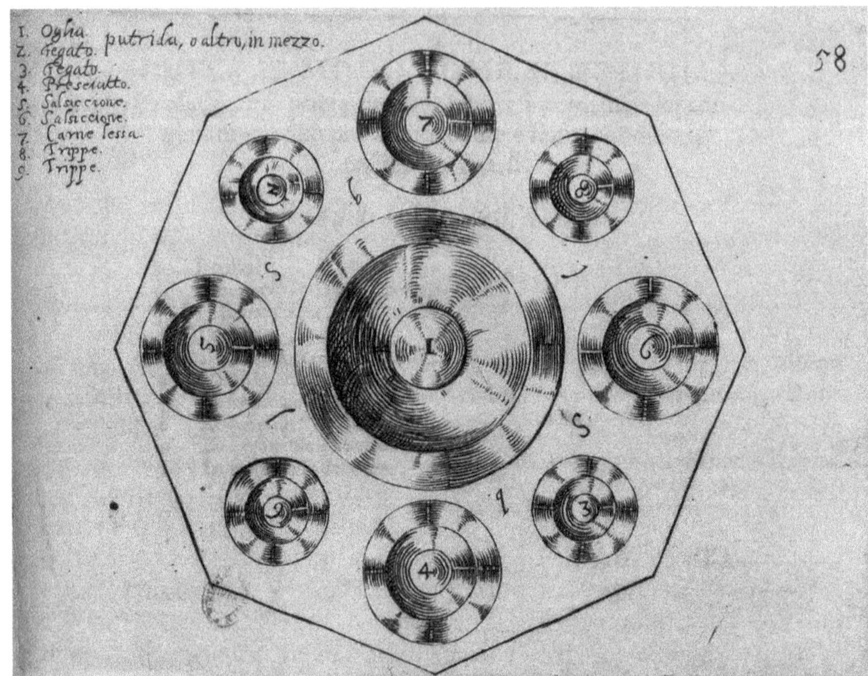

Figure 2.1. Illustration from Mattia Giegher, *Le Tre trattati de Messer Mattia Giegher*... P. Frambotto, 1639. Bibliothèque nationale de France, département Réserve des livres rares, V-11149. http://catalogue.bnf.fr/ark:/12148 /cb30504819t.

cabbage, turnips, artichokes, potatoes, and dates as her five senses, and pepper as her common sense (1907, 156–7). We can see that not only in cookbooks but also in personal narratives, writers admire what they describe as an extravagant Spanish dish.

By examining cookbooks throughout Europe, we can trace the rise of this Spanish national dish from its first recorded beginnings in the sixteenth century to its honoured place on the Spanish table in the seventeenth century. We also begin to get a sense of how famous cooks, historians, and gastronomes recognized the *olla podrida* as the definitive Spanish contribution within European gastronomy. Today, the *olla podrida* has evolved into *cocido*. Its rich regional variances give unique qualities to what is still a meat, bean, and vegetable one-pot delight. This dish is typically eaten in three courses: meat-based broth with noodles, garbanzos and cabbage, and a variety of meats (pork, beef, and fowl). The *cocido madrileño, puchero andaluz, escudella catalana, cocido de Murcia, cocido montañés,* and *cocido maragato de Asturias* are some of the regional varieties that come from this early modern tradition.[20]

The interest in Spanish court cuisine culminates in a French cookbook authored by Pierre de Lune, published in 1662 in Paris, that contains almost two hundred recipes: *Le nouveau et parfait maistre d'hostal royal enseignant la maniere de couuvrir les Tables dans les Ordinaires & Festins, tant en Viande qu'en Poisson, suiuant les quatre Saisons de l'Année. Le tout representé par un grand nombre de Figures. Ensemble un nouveau Cuisinier à l'Espagnole, contenant vne nouuelle façon d'apprester toutes sortes de Mets, tant en Chair qu'en Poisson, d'vne methode fort agreable* [The new and perfect chief royal butler teaching the way to set tables, on ordinary days and holidays, as much for meat as for fish, following the four seasons of the year. All of this depicted by many illustrations together constitutes a new Spanish cookbook containing a new way to prepare all sorts of dishes, such as meat and fish, in a very enjoyable way].[21] Little is known of de Lune, although Spanish historians propose that he is Spanish, from either Aragon or Valencia. He was cook in the house of the Duke of Rohan before serving the English princess and Duchess of Orléans, Henrietta Anne Stuart. Prior to *Le nouveau et parfait maître d'hostal royal,* de Lune published another cooking manual, *Le cuisinier* [The cook] (1656), recognized as the first cookbook published in France that treats in detail how to serve courses. But it is his second publication that holds particular relevance for understanding European perspectives on Spanish cuisine. In *Le nouveau et parfait maître d'hostal royal,* de Lune describes in detail the oversight of food preparation and its service throughout the seasons and in addition provides an entire treatise on Spanish cooking. This part of the cookbook is divided into five sections: fatty and lean soups (sixty-four recipes), meat entrées (thirty-three), roasts (thirty-nine), pastries (twenty-one), and fish (thirty-six).

In his prologue he communicates his passion for the culinary arts and specifically for the contributions of Spanish gastronomy:

> Vous verrez aussi un Nouveau Cuisinier à l'Espagnole, dans le quel il se voit une maniere d'apprester toute sorte de Mets tant viande que poisson, & autres délicatesses de bouche, d'une methode toute nouvelle non encore veuë dans d'autres Livres; ce que, sans doute, sera fort agreable à toutes sortes de personnes.

> [You will also see a new Spanish cookbook in which appears a way of preparing all sorts of dishes, as much meat as fish, and other delectables, using an all new method not yet seen in other publications; which will, undoubtedly, be most pleasing to all sorts of people.]

The presence of Spanish influences is transmitted on several levels. The first and most obvious are the almost three dozen recipes that include *Spanish* in the title: "Potage d'escargots à l'Espagnole" [Spanish snail soup] (1662, 271), "Fricassée de poulets à l'Espagnole" [Spanish chicken fricassee] (285), "Ragoust de canarts à l'Espagnole" [Spanish duck stew] (287), etc. Some of these include ingredients found only in France. For example, the recipe "Potage de chapons à l'Espagnole" [Spanish capon soup] calls for *prunes de brignolle* [Brignolle prunes] (255). Other recipes include specific Spanish ingredients. In "Autre potade de chapons" [Another capon soup], de Lune begins: "Faites cuire des cardons d'Espagne …" [cook Spanish cardoons …] (255). Still other recipes provide commentaries for cooks unfamiliar with Spanish cuisine. In the first recipe of the collection, "Potage de santé" [Healthy soup], de Lune begins his explanation with the following: "Pour le bien faire, empotez un chapon avec un ris de veau, *qu'il sout assez rare en ce païs-là*, & le faites cuire avec eau" [In order to make it well, put a capon in a pot with a veal sweetbread, *even though it is rare in this country*, and cook it with water] (253, emphasis mine). Here de Lune reassures his readers of the unfamiliar procedure. In "Potage de pois, ou purée" [Pea soup or purée], again de Lune's recipe accommodates differences of cultural norms between those who wrote the recipe and those who will prepare it: "Elle se fait de mesme qu'à la Françoise, sinon que vous y pouvez mettre raisins de corinthe, pignons, huile, capres, & safran" [This is made the same way as the French, except you can add currents, pine nuts, oils, capers, and saffron] (273). Finally, de Lune also includes recipes with other geographical designations but that are favoured by Spaniards. In "Potage de paste de Genes qu'on appelle vermiguelly en lengue Genoise" [Genovese pasta soup, called *vermiguelly* in the Genovese language], de Lune explains its inclusion: "Ce potage est fort estimé des Espagnols, comme aussi toutes les autres pastes de Genes" [This soup is highly esteemed by the Spanish, as are all of the other pastas from Genoa] (262). As is made clear with these examples, de Lune's project not only shares Spanish recipes with his French audience but also explains what foods and flavours Spaniards value.

Curiously, de Lune does not include the famed *olla podrida* among his selections, but his rich collection of Spanish soups and stews, poultry, beef, pork, and seafood dishes, pâtés, sausages, and pies, written for cooks working in the French court and among its aristocracy, is a powerful testament to how Spanish cuisine was valued beyond the borders of its own country. As the seventeenth century drew to a close, cultural shifts followed political trends, and Spanish influences across Europe waned as French cultural hegemony began to take shape. In the world of gastronomic arts, the creative forces of the French chef La Varenne, who was a contemporary of de Lune's, and later Carême and Escoffier, would gain the attention of both Spain and the rest of Europe. But, before that shift in European gastronomy took hold, the works of Nola and Martínez Montiño provide us with evidence of which dishes from Spain were valued among the early modern aristocracy and which dishes endured the test of time. Voices beyond the borders of Spain – Scappi, de Casteau, Magirus, Markham, Giegher, de Lune, and others – provide evidence of how early modern Spanish cuisine was perceived and valued throughout Europe and what role the *olla podrida* played in shaping Spanish cuisine.

Appendix 1. "Mirrauste," Ruperto de Nola, *Libro de guisados* (1525)

La salsa de mirrauste se hace de esta manera. Tomar una libra de almendras y cuatro onzas solamente para cinco escudillas y después tostarás las almendras; y majarlas y después tomar un migajón de pan que sea remojado con buen caldo; y después majarlo has con las almendras; y pasarlo has, que sea bien espeso; y después vaya al fuego con una onza de canela, mas la canela se ha de poner cuando pasarás las almendras; y después tomarás los palominos y asarlo has; y desque sea cuasi medio asados, quitarlos has del fuego; y córtalas a pedazos; y después harás cocer la salsa con media libra de azúcar dentro de la salsa; empero traerlo has, siempre con un palo de madera o cucharón de palo; y desque sea cocida pornás en esta salsa los palominos con las otras aves o pollas o gallinas; sea hecho todo de esta manera; y después toma de la gordura de la olla;[22] y pornásla dentro de la salsa con los palominos, y después puedes hacer escudillas; y de las tajadas de las aves puedes poner cuatro en cada escudilla; y encima poner azúcar y canela de buena manera; y así se hace el mirrauste perfecto. (1997, 266)

[*Mirrauste* sauce is made in this way. Take exactly one pound and four ounces of almonds for five bowls and then toast the almonds and grind them. Then take the insides of bread that have soaked in good stock and then grind them with the almonds. Strain them; it should be fairly thick. Then put it on the flame with one ounce of cinnamon but the cinnamon should go in when straining the almonds. Then take the wild squab and roast them. Once they are half roasted, remove them from the flame and cut them into pieces. After, bring the sauce to a boil with a half pound of sugar in the sauce, but always stir it with a wooden spatula or wooden spoon. Once it has boiled add the wild squab with the other birds, either young or mature hens, and let it be done this way. After, skim some of the fat from the pot and add it to the sauce with the wild squab. Then you can arrange the bowls. With the pieces of poultry, you can put four into each bowl and on top sprinkle a good amount of cinnamon and sugar. In this way the perfect *mirrauste* is made.]

Appendix 2. "To prepare a dish of various ingredients called, in Spanish, *olla podrida*," Bartolomeo Scappi, *L'arte et prudenza d'un maestro cuoco* [The art and craft of a master cook], (1570)

This preparation, *oglia potrida*, is named thus by Spaniards because it is made mostly in earthenware stewpots called *oglias*, and *potride* [*sic*] means a variety of well cooked ingredients. To make that preparation, get two pounds of salted, marbled pork jowl, four pounds of desalted sowbelly, two pig's snouts, two ears, four feet split in half and semi-salted for a day, four pounds of wild-boar meat with its brisket fresh, and two pounds of good *salsicciono*. When everything is cleaned, cook it in unsalted water. In salted water in another copper or earthenware pot also cook six pounds of wether rib, six pounds of salted veal kidney-fat, six pounds of fat beef, two capons or hens, and four fat domestic doves; remove from the broth whatever of all those ingredients is cooked first without disintegrating; set it aside in a vessel. In another earthenware or copper pot, in the broth from the above meats, cook two hindquarters of a hare, cut up into pieces, three partridges, two pheasants or two wild ducks, large and fresh, twenty thrush, twenty quail and three rock partridge. When the above things are cooked, strain and mix the broths together, minding that they are not too salty. Then get peas, brownish-red chickpeas and white chickpeas that have soaked to soften them, cleaned garlic bulbs, chopped old onions, hulled rice, shelled chestnuts and parboiled haricot beans. Cook all of that together in the broth. When the vegetables are almost done, put in kohlrabi, Savoy cabbage, yellow rape, and saveloy or sausage. When it is all cooked and rather more thickened than broth-like, stir it up so that everything blends together, testing it from time to time for its saltiness. Into that add pepper and cinnamon. Then set out great platters and put part of the mixture on them without the broth: get all the large fowl, quartered, and the large meats, and the salami sliced, leaving the small birds whole; divvy those up onto the platters over that mixture. On top of that put some of the other mixture with the saveloy cut into pieces. Make three layers like that. Get a spoon-ful of the fattest broth and splash it over top. Cover everything over with another platter and let it sit in a warm place for half an hour. Serve it hot with mild spices over top. That preparation is more common in win-ter than at any other time. The partridge, pheasants, thrush, ducks and quail can be not only boiled but also roasted on a spit, then right after-wards cut up. Instead of the capons and hens you can boil fat domestic geese and ducks, and of those ducks or geese take only the rump and breast. If you want to make that dish in the summer, get the meat that is available. Instead of hare, get a kid's hindquarters roasted on a spit and cut into pieces. That dish can be made with a variety of more or fewer ingredients, entirely at your discretion. (2008, 215–17)

NOTES

1 For an excellent monograph on culinary nationalization in nineteenth-century Spain, see Lara Anderson (2013).

2 The *Neapolitan Recipe Collection* forms part of one of four culinary manu-script styles that emerged in late medieval Italy. Terence Scully calls this style the Martino tradition (cited in *Neapolitan* 2000, 11), named after Mar-tino da Como, who authored *Libro de Arte Coquinaria* [The art of cooking] (c. 1465) and is best described in 1474 by Platina as "the prince of cooks of our age, from whom I have learned the art of cooking food" (1998, 119).

3 Other recipes from the *Neapolitan Recipe Collection* include "Twelve serv-ings of a Catalan-style White Dish" (176), "Rice in the Italian Style" (177), "Sicilian macaroni" (178), "Roman macaroni" (178), "Cabbage in the Ro-man style" (179), "Catalan-style gourds" (180), "Catalan-style Mirausto" (181), "Florentine-style goat kid in a baking dish" (182), "Florentine-style meat in a baking dish" (183), "Catalan-style partridge" (185), "French-style *Tremolette* on partridge" (185), "Aragonese sops" (191), "Lombard sauce" (193), "French-style sauce for partridge, chicken or other" (194), "French mustard" (195), "Italian mustard" (195), "Slavic cooking sauce or serv-ing sauce: Garlic sauce" (195), "Bolognese Torte" (195), "A Sienese-style *tartara*" (196), "Florentine-style *Fasanitico* Millet Pudding" (197), "Ger-man-style scrambled eggs" (198), "Florentine-style deep-fried eggs" (199), and "[Florentine-style] stuffed deep-fried eggs" (200).

4 For more on the flourishing culture of Naples at this time period, see Hersey (1969).

5 The recipe for *mirrauste* is for roasted poultry with toasted almond sauce. For the complete recipe, see Appendix 1. All translations of Spanish texts are my own.

6 Although today the *toronja* translates as *grapefruit*, this translation is inade-
quate, as the grapefruit is a cross between two different fruits that occurred
in the Caribbean in the eighteenth century. Thus, I have decided to leave the
word in its original to note that it is not grapefruit but rather its own unique
citrus fruit. Covarrubias explains that it is a type of citron (1987, 969).

7 Borage is a versatile green-leaf vegetable whose flower, leaves, and stem
are all used in different ways. Here the recipe is most likely using the
leaves in a way similar to chard. Today in Aragón, Rioja, and Navarra, the
stems are boiled and then sautéed in olive oil. They are often served with
scrambled eggs or combined with boiled potatoes.

8 *Culantro* and *cilantro* are often used interchangeably even though they are
two different plants.

9 A wether is a castrated goat. The jelly is released from the bones upon boil-
ing, left to set, mixed with the other ingredients, boiled again, filtered, and
mixed with pine nuts, almonds, and quince cooked in wine.

10 On the origins and history of the *olla podrida*, see Gómez Laguna (1993, 13)
and Rodríguez Marín (1947, 424–9).

11 My thanks to Nawal Nasrallah for pointing out this connection. For more
information, see *al-Tujībī*.

12 For Scappi's complete recipe, see Appendix 2.

13 Of the 755 recipes that make up Granado's *Libro del arte de cozina*, 556 are
from Scappi (almost 75 per cent).

14 *Arte de cocina, pastelería, vizcochería y conservería* was published ten times
in the seventeenth century (1611, 1617, 1620, 1623, 1628, 1637, 1653, 1662,
1674, 1676), thirteen times in the eighteenth century (1705, between
1705–28, 1725, 1728, 1732, 1754, 1756, 1760, 1763 [twice], 1778, 1790, 1797),
and five times in the early part of the nineteenth century (1800, 1807,
1809, 1822, and 1823). The cookbook was published again in 1982 when
Tusquets printed a facsimile version, and again in Valencia, 1994 and 1997.
Additional facsimiles also appeared in Valladolid, 2006; Seville, 2008; and
Madrid, 2009. The first three facsimiles are based on the 1763 edition and
the latter two on the 1778 edition.

15 Inés Eléxpuru writes about the Arab influences seen in both Granado and
Martínez Montiño. She has found that Martínez Montiño includes more
Hispanic-Muslim cooking in his work than Granado does (1994, 132).
This comes as no surprise, given that Granado reworked Scappi's Italian
recipes that do not share the same cultural heritage with those of Martínez
Montiño.

16 For more on the appearance of the *olla podrida* in literature, see Suárez
Granda (2006, 205–7) and Chamorro (2002, 125).

17 "Todas especias" [all spices] refers to a proportioned mix of ginger,
nutmeg, pepper, cloves, and saffron.

18 My thanks to Sebastiaan Faber for his help in translating this title. He also notes that *hutspot* is still today a traditional Dutch dish which consists of mashed potatoes, chopped carrots, and onions cooked with bacon and typically served with smoked sausage.

19 *Sippets* are pieces of bread used to sop up the juices of a dish.

20 For more on regional varieties of *cocido,* see Calera (1982).

21 My thanks to Laura Edwards for her translation of de Lune's cookbook. All translations are hers.

22 The author is referring to another pot, for example a stock pot, from which he can draw the fat that would be floating on top.

WORKS CITED

Aguilera Pleguezuelo, José. 2002. *Las cocinas árabe y judía y la cocina española.* Málaga: Arguval.

al-Tujībī, Ibn Razīn. *Best of Delectable Foods and Dishes from al-Andalus and the Maghreb: A Cookbook by Thirteenth-Century Andalusi Scholar Ibn Razīn al-Tujībī.* Edited and translated by Nawal Nasrallah. Brill: 2021.

Alvar-Ezquerra, Alfredo. 2009. "Comer y 'ser' en la Corte del Rey Católico. Mecanismos de diferenciación social en el cambio de siglo." In *Materia crítica. Formas de ocio y de consumo en la cultura áurea,* edited by Enrique García Santo-Tomás, 295–320. Madrid: Iberoamericana.

Anderson, Benedict. 1991. *Imagined Communities: Reflections on the Origin and Spread of Nationalism.* London: Verso.

Anderson, Lara. 2013. *Cooking Up the Nation: Spanish Culinary Texts and Culinary Nationalization in the Late Nineteenth and Early Twentieth Century.* Woodbridge: Tamesis.

Arbelos, Carlos. 2004. *Gastronomía de las tres culturas: recetas y relatos de los siglos XIII y XVI.* Granada: Caja de Granada.

Burke, Peter. 2013. "Nationalisms and Vernaculars 1500–1800." In *The Oxford Handbook of the History of Nationalism,* edited by John Breuilly, 21–35. Oxford: Oxford University Press.

Calera, Ana María. 1982. *La cocina regional española.* Barcelona: Mundo Actual de Ediciones.

Campbell, Jodi. 2017. *At the First Table: Food and Social Identity in Early Modern Spain.* Lincoln: University of Nebraska Press.

Carême, Antonin. 1994. *L'art de la cuisine française au dix-neuvième siècle. Traité élémentaire et pratique.* Paris: Editions Payor & Riuages.

Castro Martínez, Teresa de. "Iberian Peninsula: Moorish Heritage in the Cuisines of Spain and Portugal." 21 October 2011. http://www.teresadecastro.com /papers/IberianPeninsula.htm.

Chamorro, María Inés. 2002. *Gastronomía del Siglo de Oro español.* Madrid: Herder.

La cocina de los jesuitas. Común modo de guisar, que observaban en las casas de los regulares de la Compañía de Jesús. 1994. Seville: Portada Editorial.

Covarrubias, Sebastián. 1987. *Tesoro de la lengua castellana o Española* (1611). Edited by Martín de Riquer. Barcelona: Editorial Alta Fulla.

Cruz Cruz, Juan. 1997. *La cocina mediterránea en el inicio del Renacimiento.* Huesca: La Val de Onsera.

Dal Col, Raffaello, and Juan Luis Gutiérrez Granda, ed. and trans. 2004. *Del arte de cocinar. Obra del maestro Bartolomeo Scappi, cocinero privado del papa Pío V*. By Bartolomeo Scappi. Gijón: Ediciones Trea.

de Casteau, Lancelot. 1604. *Ouverture de cuisine.* Liège: Leonard Streel. Medieval Cookery. http://www.medievalcookery.com/notes/ouverture .html. Accessed 9 April 2019.

de Lune, Pierre. 1662. *Le nouveau et parfait maistre d'hostal royal enseignant la maniere de couuvrir les Tables dans les Ordinaires & Festins, tant en Viande qu'en Poisson, suiuant les quatre Saisons de l'Année. Le tout representê par un grand nombre de Figures. Ensemble un nouveau Cuisinier à l'Espagnole, contenant vne nouuelle façon d'apprester toutes sortes de Mets, tant en Chair qu'en Poisson, d'vne methode fort agreable.* Paris: Estienne Loyson.

Eléxpuru, Inés. 1994. *La cocina de al-Andalus.* Madrid: Alianza Editorial.

Escoffier, Auguste. 1921. *Le guide culinaire.* Translated by H.L. Cracknell and R.J. Kaufmann. New York: Mayflower.

García, L. Jacinto. 2007. *Un banquete por Sefarad. Cocina y costumbres de los judíos españoles.* Gijón: Ediciones Trea.

Garrido Aranda, Antonio, et al. 1999. "La revolución alimentaria del siglo XVI en América y Europa." In *Los sabores de España y América*, edited by Antonio Garrida Aranda, 197–212. Huesca: La Val de Onsera.

Giegher, Mattia. 1639. *Li Tre trattati di Messer Mattia Giegher, bavaro di Mosburg, … nel primo si mostra … il modo di piegare ogni sorte di panni lini … nel secondo … s'insegna … la maniera di mettere in tavola le vivande … nel terzo … s'insegna il modo di trinciare ogni sorte di vivande …* P. Frambotto. Bibliothèque nationale de France. https://gallica.bnf.fr/ark:/12148/bpt6k3101729/f85. item. Accessed 9 October 2020.

Gellner, Ernest. 1983. *Nations and Nationalism.* Ithaca: Cornell University Press.

Gómez Laguna, Santiago. 1993. "Aclaraciones sobre la olla podrida." *Cuadernos de Gastronomía* 3 (June): 9–14.

Granado, Diego. 1991. *Libro del arte de cozina.* Edited by Xavier Benet I Pinós. Lleida: Pagès.

Hernández Bermejo, J. Esteban, and J. León. 1994. *Neglected Crops: 1492 from a Different Perspective. Published in Collaboration with the Botanical Garden of Córdoba (Spain) as Part of the Etnobotánica 92 Programme (Andalusia, 1992).* Rome: Food and Agriculture Organization of the United Nations.

Hernández de Maceras, Domingo. 1998. *Libro del arte de cocina*. In *La alimentación en la España del Siglo de Oro*, edited by María de los Ángeles Pérez Samper. Huesca: La Val de Onsera.

Hersey, George L. 1969. *Alfonso II and the Artistic Renewal of Naples 1485–1495*. New Haven: Yale University Press.

Hobsbawn, Eric. 1992. *Nations and Nationalism since 1780: Programme, Myth and Reality*. Cambridge: Cambridge University Press.

Howell, James. 1907. *Epistolæ Ho-Elianæ. The Familiar Letters of James Howell*. Introduced by Agnes Repplier. Boston: Haughton Mifflin.

Krohn, Deborah. 2015. *Food and Knowledge in Renaissance Italy: Bartolomeo Scappi's Paper Kitchens*. Farnham: Ashgate.

Latham, Robert, and William Matthews. 1976. *The Diary of Samuel Pepys*. Vol. 9. Berkeley: University of California Press.

Magirus, Antonius. 1612. *Koocboec oft familieren kevkenboec, bequaem voor alle jouffrouwen, die hun van keucken-handel oft backen van toertkens ende taertkens willen verstaen*. Leuven: Johannes Christoph.

Markham, Gervase. 1986. *The English Housewife*. Edited by Michael R. Best. Kingston and Montreal: McGill-Queen's University Press.

Martínez Crespo, Alicia, ed. 1995. *Manual de mugeres en el qual se contienen muchas y diversas reçeutas muy buenas*. Salamanca: Ediciones Universidad Salamanca.

Martínez Montiño, Francisco. 1611. *Arte de cocina, pastelería, vizcochería y conservería*. Madrid: Luis Sánchez. http://books.google.com. Accessed 9 October 2020.

May, Robert. 1685. *The Accomplisht Cook or the Art and Mystery of Cookery*. 1660. London. https://www.gutenberg.org/files/22790/22790-h/cook1.html. Accessed 9 April 2019.

Nadeau, Carolyn. 2016. *Food Matters: Alonso Quijano's Diet and the Discourse of Food in Early Modern Spain*. Toronto: University of Toronto Press.

The Neapolitan Recipe Collection. Cuoco Napoletano. 2000. Edited and translated by Terence Scully. Ann Arbor: University of Michigan Press.

Nola, Ruperto de. 1997. *Libro de guisados*. In *La cocina mediterránea en el inicio del Renacimiento*, edited by Juan Cruz Cruz. Huesca: La Val de Onsera.

Pérez Samper, María de los Ángeles. 1996. "España y América: el encuentro de dos sistemas alimentarios." In *Las raíces de la memoria. América Latina, ayer y hoy, quinto encuentro debate*, coordinated by Pilar García Jordán, 171–88. Barcelona: Universitat de Barcelona.

Pérez Samper, María de los Ángeles. 1998. *La alimentación en la España del Siglo de Oro. Domingo Hernández de Maceras. "Libro del arte de Cocina."* Huesca: La Val de Onsera.

Platina. 1998. *On Right Pleasure and Good Health*. Edited and translated by Mary Ella Milham. Tempe, AZ: Medieval and Renaissance Texts and Studies.

The Prince of Transylvania's Court Cookbook from the 16th century. The Science of Cooking. Edited by Glen F. Gorsuch. Translated by Bence Kovacs. Medieval Cookery. http://www.medievalcookery.com/etexts/transylvania-v2.pdf. Accessed 23 February 2018.

Rodríguez Marín, Francisco. 1947. "El yantar de Alonso Quijano el Bueno." In *Estudios cervantistas*, 421–39. Madrid: Ediciones Atlas.

Sánchez Meco, Gregorio. 1998. *El arte de la cocina en tiempos de Felipe II*. El Escorial: Consejalía de Cultura.

Scappi, Bartolomeo. 2008. *The Opera of Bartolomeo Scappi (1570): l'arte et prudenza d'un maestro cuoco*. Translated by Terence Scully. Toronto and Buffalo: University of Toronto Press.

Schildermans, Jozeph, and Hilde Sels. 2003. "A Dutch Translation of Bartolomeo Scappi's Opera." *Petits Propos Culinaires* 74 (December): 59–70.

Scully, Terence, ed. 1997. *The Vivendier: A Fifteenth-Century French Cookery Manuscript*. Translated by Terence Scully. Totnes: Prospect Books.

Suárez Granda, Juan Luis. 2006. *El cielo de la boca. Antología del paladar español*. Gijón: Ediciones Trea.

Terrón, Eloy. 1992. *España, encrucijada de culturas alimentarias. Su papel en la difusión de los cultivos americanos*. Madrid: Ministerio de Agricultura, Pesca y Alimentación.

Valles Rojo, Julio. 2007. *Cocina y alimentación en los siglos XVI y XVII*. Valladolid: Junta de Castilla y León.

3 The Politics of the Origins of Maize

JOHN SLATER

An undetected fungus from America once made its way into a Bavarian brewer's wort. Thanks to that fungus – a cold-resistant or cryotolerant yeast – early modern brewers could brew at lower temperatures, using less energy. New efficiencies inspired new techniques, ultimately resulting in the production of lager beer. In this way, a microbial traveller from the New World, floating in motes and scattered bits of dust, altered the cuisine of Bavaria.[1] Perhaps as early as the sixteenth century, American life forms became so prevalent that Europeans who had never given a thought to emigrating were breathing in America all the same, filling their lungs with exotic microbes and pushing them out again as they spoke familiar words.

Other American life forms depended on human beings for their dispersal. Maize was one these. Maize (*Zea mays* L.), unlike wheat, will not grow on its own in the wild; it needs human intervention to propagate. Despite this, it may have spread across Europe even more quickly than our brewer's New World yeast.[2] The case of maize was very different from that of microbes; its arrival in Europe did not prompt new techniques for exploiting its nutritional possibilities. Europeans were quick to integrate maize into their diets, but they did not employ Indigenous American techniques for processing corn (nixtamalization), nor did they invent new ways of preparing it (Katz 1989, 127). The fact that maize was generally treated "just like Old World cereals," rather than as something new, indicates that maize frequently spread without much cultural information at all (Warman 2003, 145). It picked up and lost a string of names and supposed origins (it was called all sorts of things – Turkish, Asian, Egyptian, Indian, Italian); and without its American identity it travelled unaccompanied by knowledge of the old methods used to make it into a healthy food. Marcy Norton explains that American plant products are cultural artifacts "that would not exist without knowledge and techniques developed over millennia in the western hemisphere" (2008, 4). This is true, but it does not mean that those techniques or that knowledge necessarily circulated along with the plants. In sixteenth-century Europe, maize was frequently an undocumented traveller whose lack of fixed cultural status or identity allowed centuries of historians to read in kernels and cobs their own ideas about belonging and difference.

We have told stories about the origins of maize for a very, very long time, and new ways of telling these stories – some relying on genetic testing – are still being drafted. The variety and persistence of some old stories, however, has shaped the diet, the landscape, even the life expectancy of people around the world. The stories told in Europe, Mexico, and the United States after 1492 offer vastly different accounts of the origin and the dissemination of maize. Frequently, the most unlikely stories are the most influential. Even what appear to be rigorously scientific accounts of the origins of maize can be political allegories that dress racial and national ideologies in the trappings of phytogeography. But, of course, allegory says one thing and means another.

In practice, stories about the origins of corn are often a way of constructing an identity, telling a story of racial difference, or resisting a dominant narrative. There are nationalist and anti-imperialist stories about where corn is from (which are, Arturo Warman notes, the same thing) (2003, xi). For a few very peculiar reasons, when we talk about maize, natural history is often indistinguishable from national history: its "theme is *man* rather than *maize*" (Weatherwax 1923, vii). When we change the narrative context for the consumption of maize – if we say, for example, that maize is Asian rather than American – we characterize particular forms of cultivating, preparing, and consuming it as more or less appropriate or authentic. This has dietary and health effects because some maize-rich diets make you sick while others do not. Examining differing points of view at three moments in the history of maize's narrative development – Spain in the seventeenth century, France in the nineteenth, and the United States in the twentieth – illustrates how stories of the origin and dissemination of maize have been deployed in political mythologies.

I. The Origins of Confusion

By the 1620s, maize was a familiar plant in Madrid. The naturalist Bernardo de Cienfuegos (c. 1580–c. 1640) tells that maize was cultivated from Galicia, in the far northwest of the Iberian Peninsula, to Valencia, in the east (Cienfuegos c. 1630, I:36–158). Cienfuegos was the author of the monumental *Historia de las plantas*, a seven-volume manuscript in the vernacular of some five thousand pages.[3] A careful observer of plants and people, Cienfuegos tells a number of marvellous stories about maize. He explains, for example, how Moriscos – forcibly converted Muslims cast out of Spain in 1615 – made tortillas.[4] Cienfuegos describes in detail who was growing maize, how and where they were doing it, and, most importantly, the different cultural strata within which maize was disseminated.

He identifies three networks for the exchange of maize and information about the plant. They are the poor who eat maize, the rich who grow it as an ornamental, and naturalists who write about it. Each of these groups is interested in corn for different reasons, each has different values, and each – in Cienfuegos's *Historia* – possesses different information.[5] Sharing within groups is common, but what we would today call "trading zones" for exchange between groups do not always develop (Galison 1997, 52). Additionally, information about plants, the plants themselves, and techniques for cultivating or processing harvests are all disseminated at different rates even within the same cultural stratum. None of this is exceptional when it comes to exotic flora in the sixteenth century; as Antonio Regueiro y González Barros points out, information about plants and the plants themselves often followed "caminos muy diversos" [very different paths] (1983, 208).[6] What is exceptional is to have these networks as clearly delineated as we find them in the *Historia de las plantas*.

The first of the three groups that Cienfuegos names is the rich landowners who grow maize as an ornamental: "en las tierras fértiles de España en algunas huertas y jardines se siembra más por ostentación y galantería que porque se aprovechen del para pan" [in the fertile lands of Spain, in some fields and gardens, maize is grown for its showiness and elegance rather than being grown in order to make bread] (c. 1630, I:144). Growing maize as an ornament was quite common at the time (Warman 2003, 100). In fact, the first representation of maize of any kind in Europe (textual, visual, or otherwise) may have been the festoons painted by Giovanni Martini da Udine about 1515–17 in the Villa Farnesina (Janick and Caneva 2005, 79). What is uncommon is the other claim that Cienfuegos makes about wealthy enthusiasts. He says that those who have "en Indias haciendas" [lands in the colonies] are often more knowledgeable than famous naturalists, specifically more knowledgeable than Conrad Gesner, Valerius Cordus, and Jacob Dietrich (Tabernaemontanus), among others (Cienfuegos c. 1630, I:36).[7]

While Spanish landholders were "wary about corn as human food," poor subsistence farmers, the second group that Cienfuegos mentions, were not (Weatherwax and Randolph 1955, 2).[8] The rich grew maize in fertile soil, but the poor tended to grow it in "tierras faltas y miserables" [poor and miserable lands], especially in Galicia and the mountains of Burgos (c. 1630, I:144). Unlike wealthy landowners, the poor did not seem to possess much natural or cultural information about maize. Cienfuegos is clear about this; the poor grow different varieties "sin distinción" [without regard to the best cultivars], and "se cría de todos colores" [varieties of every colour are grown]. So there are two clear differences between the cultures of maize that Cienfuegos identifies among the rich and the poor in Spain: landowners grow maize as an ornamental (they do not eat it) and they are more knowledgeable than many naturalists. The poor eat corn – "que remedia la necesidad" – but they do not distinguish among different varieties or seem to possess much cultural or natural information about maize.[9] Poor farmers, as David Rindos noted, unconsciously select for "immediate benefit": squeezing more calories per acre out of their labours (1984, 4). For the rich, maize cultivation was part of a ritualized possession of New World cultural practices and a New World aesthetic.

Spanish farmers did not call maize "maíz" (a word borrowed from Arawak) and they did not associate maize with Amerindian practices for preparing it. When farmers substituted maize for what they used to grow – millet or sorghum, for example – they kept the old names. So in the north of Spain, "borono" had referred to millet and was applied to maize; in Valencia "dacsa" (or "adacça") ended up referring both to sorghum and maize (López Gómez 1974, 148–9).[10] As a substitute for familiar crops, maize was not only called what the old crops had been called but also prepared as the old crops had been, generally ground dry and made into bread or porridge. However, throughout the Americas maize was soaked in an alkali bath and ground wet, a process called nixtamalization. Without this treatment, the niacin in maize is not bioavailable and cannot be properly digested by humans. As Daphne Roe explains, "the alkali or lime treatment frees the bound niacin, and there is evidence from studies of experimental pigs that the amount of niacin so freed can be just sufficient to prevent pellagra" (1973, 15). Pellagra is a serious disease that causes a characteristic rash on the face, diarrhoea, dementia, and death. Niacin deficiency and the pellagra it caused would, for centuries, afflict Europe and especially the United States, where, until the advent of the obesity epidemic, pellagra was the most fatal disease caused by malnutrition.

Pellagra was a danger wherever maize spread for a number of reasons, as Solomon Katz (1989) explains: nixtamalization was never successfully introduced to a European or African culture during the early modern period; alkali processing was never reinvented independently outside the Americas; and no similarly effective technique for processing maize was ever developed outside the Americas. What was clear neither to wealthy landowners nor to struggling farmers were the costs associated with disseminating corn *without* knowledge of Amerindian customs.

Cienfuegos – who did not visit the Indies himself – was perfectly aware of nixtamalization; he describes soaking corn in "agua de cal" [lime slaked with water] to prepare it (c. 1630, I:146). Although Cienfuegos follows Acosta's *Historia natural y moral de las Indias* (1590) closely in his discussion of corn, he takes the description of nixtamalization from Felipe de Pamanes's *Notables del Perú*, a manuscript now lost.[11] The use of lime in the alkali processing of corn would have been familiar to readers of Francisco Hernández's natural history of New Spain, completed before 1582; Hernández's work was consulted in manuscript at the Escorial near Madrid and circulated widely in manuscript copy and various published forms throughout the seventeenth century.[12] In addition to Hernández and Pamanes, other sixteenth-century authors – such as Diego de Landa and Diego Durán – wrote about nixtamalization.[13] Early modern histories of New Spain even mention lime being necessary ["menester"] for the preparation of corn in lists of provisions: "un almud de maíz para cada semana, y una libra de carne para cada día, *y la cal que hubiesen menester para cocer el maíz*" [a portion of maize for each week and a pound of meat for each day, and *however much lime might be necessary for preparing the maize*] (Cepeda and Alfonso Carrillo 1637, 15, emphasis mine). So Spanish chroniclers in the New World and Spanish naturalists in the Old had a good understanding of how Indigenous communities prepared maize.

The authors who described American flora – particularly Acosta, Pamanes, Nicolás Monardes, Pedro Cieza de León, and Francisco López de Gómara – were considered one half of the third group that Cienfuegos describes. Even more than subsistence farmers or landowners, naturalists attract Cienfuegos's scrutiny. There are essentially two groups of naturalists in the *Historia de las plantas*: careful Spanish observers of nature, on the one hand, and obtuse northern chauvinists, on the other.[14] Cienfuegos understands sixteenth-century German naturalism much as Julius von Sachs would centuries later: for the "northerners," naturalism or proto-botany was Protestant and national (Sachs 1906).[15] For Sachs, this was logical and even good; for Cienfuegos, it is pathetic and wrong. Cienfuegos insists that the works of Leonhart Fuchs, Hieronymus Bock (Tragus), Rembert Dodoens, Matthias de l'Obel (Lobelius), and even the much-lauded Charles de l'Écluse (Carolus Clusius) are *intentionally* flawed.[16]

Specifically, Cienfuegos says that the "alemanes" [Germans] do not have the right information, they lard their accounts with fictions, and they treat the truth cavalierly because their values are corrupt. They also copy one another "outright," giving their works an overall sense of ideological and aesthetic uniformity (Weatherwax and Randolph 1955, 2).[17] Authors had an obligation to get the story right before going to print, thought Cienfuegos, because printed books were copied, reedited, and plagiarized for centuries afterward. He singles out the repeated use of woodcuts of maize from Dietrich's 1588 *Neuw Kreuterbuch* (which would be reused in subsequent works for almost a century) (Finan 1950, 179).[18] He also believed that printed works of natural history, taken together, constituted an echo chamber in which friends congratulated one another for their seriousness – a rhetorical manoeuvre designed to obfuscate the fact that they were copying one another's errors uncritically – and in which a veil of idealism hid political motivations.

One of the things that most enrages Cienfuegos is that the "alemanes" act as if they do not know where corn is from: "los alemanes a cualquiera cosa que no conocen y es nueva en su país o peregrina venida del nuevo mundo le llaman 'de Italia' como cosa comunicada de aquella Provincia" [the Germans call anything they have not seen before and that is new to their country or exotic and from the New World "from Italy" as if it were something imported from that province] (c. 1630, I:149). Indeed, early herbals printed in northern Europe did tend to attribute the origins of maize to Anatolia or Turkey, Egypt, Italy, or generally to North Africa or Asia, making "el verdadero origen del maíz algo desconocido" [the true origin of maize somewhat unknown] (Pardo-Tomás and López-Terrada 1993, 146). Bock, for example, called the plant *Frumentum Asiaticum* in 1539, and in 1542 Leonhart Fuchs used the term *Turcicum Frumentum*. Different origin stories necessarily implied different routes of introduction and transmission, whether maize moved north from Africa, or west from Asia Minor.

This speculation drives Cienfuegos crazy (despite the fact that Oviedo may have encouraged these mistakes) (Bonavia 2008, 15–16). Calling out Bock (known as Tragus or Trago) for particular derision, Cienfuegos writes: "Los autores Alemanes y Flamencos pintaron y describieron el maíz con nombre de Trigo Turquesco. Jerónimo Trago que escribió en tiempo del Emperador Carlos V (de gloriosa memoria) y imprimió sus obras el año 1552 *cuando ya había muy copiosas relaciones del descubrimiento de Indias y sus frutos*, no supo el nombre de maíz ni el de trigo de las Indias" [German and Flemish authors depict and describe maize with the name Turkish wheat. Tragus, who wrote during the reign of Charles V, of glorious memory, and published his works in 1552 *when there were already extensive accounts of the discovery of the Indies and of its fruits, did not know the name of maize*] (c. 1630, I:149, emphasis mine). The thrust of the critique is that if by 1552 Bock did not know the origin of maize, his ignorance was wilful.[19] A few pages later, Cienfuegos makes a more sweeping statement about the "obstinada pertinacia desta nación" [obstinate pertinacity of that nation], claiming that the Germans distort natural history just as they distort religion. He says, "aunque conoce la verdad [esta nación] no quiere confesarla claramente, buscando falsos sentidos como lo hacen no solo en materia de hierbas y historia sino en la verdad evangélica; que aunque la conocen (a lo menos los doctos) no quieren confesarla de puro obstinados y ciegos" [although they know the truth, this nation does not want to state it plainly and they search for false interpretations, just as they do not only with regard to plants and history but also with respect to the truth of the Bible; although they know the truth (or at least the learned Germans do) they do not say so, because they are altogether obstinate and blind] (c. 1630, I:152). These northern naturalists may seem to know as little as poor farmers, but Cienfuegos feels as if the errors in printed books are a kind of strategic disinformation, materiel in a propaganda war. Bock, Fuchs, and other "Germans" called the maize of New Spain either "Saracen wheat" or "Turkish corn" at precisely the same time that northern Europeans started calling Spaniards Saracens and Turks in the early salvos of the Black Legend (Fuchs 2007, 94). This may have been coincidence in the 1550s, but by the 1620s it looked like chicanery.

In Cienfuegos's discussion of the three European maize cultures – the distinct cultures of farmers, wealthy gardeners, and naturalists – a few things come into sharp focus. Knowledge about nixtamalization does not make it to the people who eat maize, nor does it appear in printed herbals, despite the fact that it circulates widely in Spanish-language texts. Seeds spread faster than information and thus maize's appearance in printed herbals cannot be used as a way to track the diffusion of maize.[20] The American origins of maize are well known to Cienfuegos and his correspondents, although early herbals printed in the north located maize's origins in Asia or Africa. (To be fair, this was quickly corrected – most herbals written after 1580 do not contain the mistake – but Cienfuegos is unforgiving.) Last, and just as important, Cienfuegos believes that national allegiances influence "northern" accounts of the origins of corn. There is no uncoupling national identity and science for Cienfuegos, and accounts of the origin of maize are where this is clearest.

The fact that a few naturalists during a few decades got one aspect of the natural history of maize wrong would not be significant if Cienfuegos's fears had not proven spectacularly prescient. Well into the twentieth century, historians would wonder if there weren't some truth to Bock's and Fuchs's surmises about an Asian origin of maize. Daniela Bleichmar (2012, 151) has shown how scientific writing and illustration involve a complicated tension between what is made visible and what is rendered invisible. Cienfuegos complained that the "fathers of German botany" were involved in a calculated attempt to render the Hapsburg monarchy invisible: their silence about Spain denied the empire credit for what would be called "uno de los más insignes servicios prestados a Europa por los españoles" [one of the greatest services rended to Europe by the Spanish] (Álvarez López 1945, 234).[21] Cienfuegos may have been right and Bock wrong about where maize was from, but ultimately that would not matter when political interests dominated science. Over the coming centuries, the desire to believe alternative histories of the origin and diffusion of corn would be particularly common among historians who wanted to write Spain out of the history of science.

II. Race and the Origins of Maize

As we have seen, accounts of the origin of maize revealed what Cienfuegos believed to be vast religious and political differences between himself and the "Germans." But he did not write of those differences in specifically racial terms. By 1836, when Matthieu Bonafous published his *Histoire naturelle, agricole et économique du maïs*, race would become a much more important part of the debate. Bonafous was a wealthy member of the French industrial class; his family business was silk, and family members shuttled betweeen Lyon and the Piedmont (Zanier 2012). Rather taken with his own scepticism, Bonafous decided to treat the origin of maize as an unsettled question, a mystery to solve.

Bonafous conjectured that terms like "Turkish" or "Saracen wheat" were clues, not mistakes. In his methodology, the oldest written stories were the most important because the earliest nomenclature might help recover a lost story of maize's travels. This philological approach only worked, however, when terminology was understood in light of national cultures. If one follows this method and assumes that the key is to go back to the first printed mentions of maize to reconstruct its genesis, then two things happen. First, Bock – who in 1539 called maize *Frumentum Asiaticum* – and Leonhart Fuchs – who called maize *Turcicum Frumentum* in 1542 – become the most reliable authorities on the origins of maize (which is now clearly Asian). Second, claims that maize is *not* Asiatic and was introduced by Spain start to sound propagandistic.

Bonafous proposes that Spain will get credit for the introduction of maize, if the Spanish can prove that it did *not* arrive in Europe before 1492 (1836, 15).

The most famous part of Bonafous's argument about the origins of maize has to do with the probable date of first cultivation in China. He is a firm believer that words track seeds closely and that written mentions of maize cultivation, interpreted in light of national culture, will enable him to estimate the time of introduction. In the case of China, national culture is crucial because it is incontrovertibly true (in this worldview) that the Chinese hate change. Bonafous believed that the first written mention of maize dated from the 1570s; this meant, he thought, that it started to be grown widely about then. But the idea that maize was grown in the 1570s in China was actually an argument for *pre-Columbian* diffusion, given "la lenteur de ce peuple à adopter les cultures étrangères" [the slowness with which this people adopts foreign cultures] (1836, 15).[22] Given the Chinese character, Bonafous explains, it necessarily would have taken more than a century for maize to become widely grown there, and since it was grown widely in the 1570s, it follows that maize must have been present in China before 1492. Ergo, Spain could not have disseminated maize. When added to the fact that Bock calls maize Asian, the question is put to rest.

Bonafous makes racial stereotypes an essential factor in reconstructing rates of dissemination: some cultures adopt maize quickly, others, like the Chinese, less so. As William Eamon (2009, 13) and Víctor Navarro and Eamon (2007, 27) have powerfully shown, eighteenth- and nineteenth-century attitudes in France towards Spanish cultural achievements – especially in the areas of science and agronomy – were "racist." Bonafous's innovation was disguising racism as a coefficient of diffusion: a way to calculate the spread of a good or technology through a society with known racial or cultural qualities. Whether maize is assumed to spread slowly or quickly turns out to be a crucial building block of subsequent historical phytogeography. For more than a century afterward, authors would make tacit calculations about how quickly maize *ought to have travelled* through particular human communities. As in the case of Bonafous and the Chinese, these calculations are a pseudo-scientific way of measuring cultural belatedness and merely reveal the authors' preconceptions about attitudes towards those communities.[23]

In addition to Bonafous's ideas about probable rates of diffusion, his work would go on to be influential in two very different ways. First and most basic, his version of the introduction of maize into China – complete with woodcut – would be reproduced repeatedly, even by sceptics.[24] (Collins [1909, 24], for example, reproduces all of the elements of Bonafous's argument.) Second, Charles Darwin would praise the *Histoire naturelle* in his *Variation of Animals and Plants under Domestication*. Darwin drew on Bonafous's "great work" to argue that American corn cultivated in Europe undergoes an almost immediate transformation: "In the second generation the plants were from nine to ten feet in height and had ripened their seed better ... the original beautiful white color had become duskier ... In the third generation nearly all resemblance to the original and very distinct American parent-form was lost. In the sixth generation this maize perfectly resembled a European variety" (1998, 1:340). What clearly seem today like Darwin's racial preoccupations – his fascination with whiteness and duskiness, and so on – have received critical attention from scholars such as Catherine Innes (2002, 77), so it is not surprising that plant acclimation is rendered in what we recognize today as the language of cultural and racial assimilation. For both Bonafous and Darwin, the domestication of plants tells a racial history – maize is still divided into "races" or "landraces" – and in Bonafous's racial schema, positive contributions of Spaniards and Indigenous Americans are simply too unlikely to be considered.[25]

In 1883, Alphonse de Candolle dealt the Asian-origin hypothesis a serious blow. In a classic of phytogeography, *Origin of Cultivated Plants* [*Origine des plantes cultivées*], Candolle makes two succinct claims: first, maize is American, and second, it was introduced to Europe "since the discovery" of the New World (1959, 387). "I consider these two assertions as positive," Candolle went on, "in spite of the contrary opinion of some authors, and the doubts of the celebrated agriculturalist Bonafous" (1959, 387). Rather than put an end to their doubts, Candolle's formulation would split Bonafous's twentieth-century followers into two camps: those that continued to argue for an Asian origin, and those that insisted that maize was American but introduced to Asia and perhaps to Europe long before 1492 (a group generally known as "diffusionists"). Both of these groups would continue to cite Bock and Fuchs as evidence, just as Bonafous had. A third group argued for American origins, drawing on Candolle, but maintained the political fervour that had infected debates for centuries. In other words, the situation in the 1920s looked much as it had in the 1620s: with some scholars staking reputations on an Asian origin (against increasingly long odds), and others understanding maize's American origins only in light of a national mythos.

How maize moved through human societies – when, who gets the credit, what it says about our views regarding Indigenous communities, what it says about us – became such a polarizing and encompassing question during the twentieth century that its sensationalist phase seems inevitable in hindsight. This was the maize debate's *Kon-Tiki* moment. Scholars looking back at Bock and Fuchs, and *Frumentum Asiaticum* and *Turcicum Frumentum*, and the old debates about if not Asian origin at least an Asian introduction, wondered if there were not some likelihood of transpacific, pre-Columbian diffusion. Thor Heyerdahl sailed across the Pacific on a balsa-wood raft in 1947 – a craft he named the *Kon-Tiki* – to demonstrate that oceanic travel via very basic means was possible. For good and ill, Heyerdahl became a figurehead for anthropological diffusionists (some of whom argued that maize could have been spread from the Americas to Asia centuries before Columbus).[26]

Appealing convictions motivated the search for an Asian introduction. Historians, anthropologists, linguists, and others were justifiably trying to come to terms with the consequences of colonialism and imperial domination. Crediting Spain with the dissemination of a crop that contributed to increased world population might be seen as saying that Spain had despoiled the Americas for the good of humankind.[27] Historiographic efforts to focus on Indigenous communities and to recognize their cultural achievements led to further attempts to eliminate Spain from the story of maize's transmission to Europe (e.g., Stonor and Anderson 1949). The work of Carl Sauer is significant in this respect.

Sauer, a seminal figure in the history of agriculture, repeated the most important elements of Bonafous's argument in 1962. There was something, Sauer felt, in the Asiatic names Bock and Fuchs had used; after all, "the German herbalists were competent describers and did know what they were talking about" (Sauer 2009, 215). What is more, "There is strangely little evidence in support of the theory that maize [was] disseminated eastward through the Old World from Spain" (216).[28] Bonafous's overt racism was gone, but the "mild form of racism" that makes it perfectly acceptable to imagine human history without Iberian influence is still present in Sauer's analysis (Mignolo 2007, 317). Sauer actually believed that maize was introduced to Europe from India (2009, 192),[29] and one of his students, Carl Johannessen, made this argument even more forcefully (1988; Johannessen and Parker 1989).[30]

By the time Sauer was writing in the 1960s, the idea that maize had an American origin but reached Europe via Asia was not widely accepted, but it was a more or less plausible theory with reasonable adherents and instances of intriguing evidence.[31] Unfortunately, for much of the twentieth century, Sauer and others who accepted an American origin could be confused with those who still argued for an Asian origin (or at least wanted to teach the controversy).[32] More recently, the intersection of postcolonial theory and diffusionism has occasionally reached a thrillingly vehement if rhetorically unproductive pitch. For example, Alice B. Kehoe contends that "the notion of America cut off from the world until 1492 fits Anglo-American political rhetoric legitimating conquest," and she blames Manifest Destiny, fascist WASPs, the Monroe Doctrine, and "Scottish bourgeois culture" for the refusal to "investigate transoceanic contacts" (2003 and 2010, 202–4). Taking a step back, the most striking thing is that what so annoyed Cienfuegos – fanciful accounts of the origins of maize – would continue in our own time to play a role in the way that historians and anthropologists imagine the interactions of early modern cultures. (And of course in Bonafous's pseudo-science and Sauer's postulating, the true subject is not maize at all, but men.)[33]

One of the consequences of assuming that Bock and Fuchs knew something that Cienfuegos did not is that it makes nixtamalization a moot question. In other words, if the most authoritative sources do not mention alkali processing, histories based on those sources do not mention it either. But many of the twentieth-century accounts that did accept an American origin overlooked nixtamalization, too. This is where the stakes start to get higher.

The United States as Corn Country

The grand narrative of the United States' corn culture often rests on linguistic slippage and what it properly means to be American. When Edward Enfield wrote in 1866 that "America is clearly and beyond question the native *country* of Indian corn," he conflated "America" the nation state and "America" the hemisphere (Enfield 1866, 36, emphasis mine).[34] The same confusion is apparent in Weatherwax's description of maize's place in a cosmic, racial plan (where the Aryan and the Semite break bread together); when he explains that maize "grows best and is still most appreciated in its native land," the primordial origin of the plant (its "native land") is the United States (Weatherwax 1923, 2).[35] Maize, proclaimed Walden (1966, 18) in a similar vein, was "the kernel of a civilization." The ubiquity of this bombast led Fussell (1999, 56) to say that "corn," an "all-American grain," itself became "the language of a new nationalism."[36]

The history of European colonization was retold in the language of this new nationalism; colonization became a grand drama in three acts in which maize is the protagonist, beckoning Europeans to the New World, revealing secrets of prosperity, and ordering the state. In the first act, Squanto teaches new arrivals escaping religious persecution to sow

Indian corn: "the Puritan planted a crop whose ways he little knew, and, with only a savage for his teacher, he learned his lesson in agriculture" (Weatherwax 1923, 217–18). This was the passing of an agricultural mantle from a primitive culture to a more deserving one, because not even "enlightened Incas, Aztecs, or Mayas" were "sufficiently curious about the corn kernel to have taken it apart and experimented with its components" (Walden 1966, xv–xvi). "Indians" are merely custodians of a resource that will come to fullness under new masters; this logic makes the twentieth-century development of "corn products" in the US a "native accomplishment" (Walden 1966, xx). Europeans seamlessly added their number to a timeless tradition, modifying that tradition only for universal betterment.[37] (Maize's European sojourn, and the fact that some farmers coming to the Americas had already grown maize, plays no part in this tale.)

In the second act, maize spurs the settling of the continent. Maize acts as the "bridge over which English civilization crept, tremblingly and uncertainly at first, then boldly and surely to a foothold and a permanent occupation of America" (Parker 1910, 15). Once here, maize became "the bridge by which the pioneers crossed America to the Missouri" (Wallace and Brown 1988, 10). In fact, maize becomes the mechanism that makes possible the conquest of the Americas by Europeans. From the Pequot War in 1636 to 1779, "every march of invasion was rendered possible by the corn found in the Indian granaries" (Sturtevant 1894, 339). Not only military losses but also Indigenous demographic collapse was due to lack of access to corn (rather than to smallpox, for example) (Esteva 2003, 19). The providential transfer of maize was the motor of westward expansion; as Wallace and Brown, almost comprehensibly, explain: "This great corn country had first to be made solidly American, before the United States could extend to the Pacific" (1988, 10).

In the third act, maize – which the Indigenous people bestowed upon Europeans in order to make colonization possible – structures the life of the new Americans. It is more than a food, it is a defence against enemies,[38] the source the American people's "exceptional energy" (Wallace and Brown 1988, 10), optimism (Crosby 1994, 167), and prosperity (Emerson 1878, "Preface"); it is the basis of American philosophy[39] and identity.[40] More than a bridge, proclaims Giles (1940, 6), it is a way and a creed: "Corn is life. Its life is the life of men. Sown in weakness, it is raised in power. It dies, yet it lives. It is eaten; and lo! of it there springs a greater life." This is John 11:25 – "I am the resurrection and the life" – with maize playing the Son of Man.[41]

If maize was eaten and of it sprang a greater life, it is also the case that, when Giles wrote those words (in the 1930s), corn was causing a public health crisis. This crisis was a pellagra epidemic that killed three hundred thousand Americans during the first half of the twentieth century. Pellagra is a systemic disease caused by niacin deficiency in people who eat a maize-rich diet without nixtamalizing the maize or enriching cornmeal with extra B vitamins.[42] Even what seems like a relatively varied diet of "biscuits, gravy, cornbread, grits, rice, syrup, collard greens, and yams" is so poor in available niacin that it quickly made (unfortunate) test subjects very ill (Bollet 1992, 217).

The paeans that credited maize with creating and ordering US society could not accommodate the notion that it might make people sick. As we have seen, US maize cultivation was supposed to be part of an authentically American culture stretching back to time immemorial, and colonists had a right to maize because ignorant Native Americans lacked the technical proficiency to unlock the plant's potential. The unfortunate reality of the situation in the US during the first half of the twentieth century, however, mirrored almost exactly what Cienfuegos observed in Spain three hundred years before: the mostly poor people who ate a great deal of maize used it as a "wheat substitute" to make cornbread (and did not use Indigenous American techniques), while books adjusted natural history to suit nationalist ends (Fussell 1999, 51).[43] This made what Roe calls "the disadvantages of a maize culture" almost inconceivable (1973, 8).

So, the two bases of maize mythology – that US agriculture was authentically American, and that colonists' ingenuity had flawlessly improved primitive techniques – were wrong. The origins of US agricultural practices were European cereal cultures, not Amerindian maize cultures. And it was the lack of nixtamalization (or any other technique to improve the bioavailability of niacin) that made people sick in the US.[44] The relationship between maize and pellagra had been guessed at since the early eighteenth century when it was first diagnosed in Spain.[45] But the Americans who understood "Spain as America's antithesis" could never draw lessons from Spanish history (Kagan 1996, 430). In the US, any connection between corn and malnutrition was narrative impossibility and a political non-starter. Both Bollet (1992) and Lanska (1996) compare pellagra to AIDS because political inertia impeded medical research; physicians and politicians refused to allow clinical trials, while other officials refused to report cases or to recognize that there was even a problem. "Politicians and the general public," explains Bollet, "felt that it was more acceptable for pellagra to be infectious than for it to be a form of malnutrition" (1992, 211).[46] Politics and motivated reasoning condemned many to die. This is not unique – ideas about cuisine, like ideas about landscape, grow out of the "fertile intercourse" of reality and preconception – but the consequences were exceptional (Turner 1979, 116).

The ultimate misfortune was that at the very moment that fascination with maize was rendering the US incapable of solving one public health crisis related to corn, the government was inadvertently creating another. In 1933 hybrid corn was first cultivated in the United States; this would allow for mechanization, more acreage brought under cultivation, and enormous yields. The year 1933 was also when farm subsidies were introduced, the subsidies that many have blamed for the proliferation of inexpensive processed foods that led to the current obesity epidemic (Hawkes 2007). Narrative failures – the refusal to understand where the US maize culture came from, how the adaptation of corn cultivation to European agriculture (rather than borrowing from Indigenous peoples) shaped the diet of the nation, and so on – at a pivotal moment in the history of agricultural policy played a role in the development of US cuisine.[47]

Conclusion

Maize's story is one of careful cultivation, close scrutiny, and unintended consequences. No one could have predicted the lasting effects of Bock's simple mistake, any more than they could have guessed the paths invisible microbes would travel. Recently, however, genetic studies have confirmed some of what Cienfuegos believed – that maize originated in Mexico and was introduced to Europe after 1492 – as well as what many have suspected for a long time: that there were multiple introductions from both North and South America to Europe.[48] The exciting thing about this research is that scientists are finding new ways to tell the story of maize *and* men.

As we saw in the cases of Bonafous and Sauer, there were a number of political reasons that authors might write maize's history without Spain. The diffusion and natural history of maize made an ideal discourse within which to encode these polemics because as an undocumented traveller maize could be made to suit vastly different accounts. This ultimately is the marvel of maize: it has as many narrative utilities as it does culinary or industrial uses. It can be a lens through which to view the present and the past. And it can just as easily be an allegory of national history. As Giles (1940, 7) would have it, "To us, in America, it is the strength of our past, the power of our present, the security of our future. For corn is the symbol of American democracy. And the story of corn is the story of the American people."[49] However, allegory, as many have complained, is unnatural. This is where the problem arises.

Confusing the high artifice of allegory with natural history is the text-book definition of ideology: "the confusion of linguistic with natural reality" (de Man 1986, 11).

Whatever the ideological impetus that obscured the American origins of corn – and the ways in which the excision of Spain from world history contributed to the creation of ersatz national cuisines that masqueraded as aboriginal – it would be an overstatement to say that the Black Legend is responsible for the obesity epidemic in the United States. We hunger for sweet and fat, markets shape our habits in ways that we do not always perceive, and innumerable other factors contribute to the way that we eat. At the same time, the centuries spent neglecting a simple fact that was evident to Cienfuegos, Landa, Pamanes, Durán, and Hernández and missing in the ostensibly more authoritative accounts of Bock, Fuchs, and others – that people in Europe generally did something very different with corn from people in Mexico – had consequences. A general distrust of Spanish natural history enabled historians such as Finan to consider Spanish accounts "inexact" and northern accounts "precise," and permitted Bonafous, Sauer, and many others to believe that Bock was probably right. Leaving Spain out of twentieth-century maize narratives made it possible to believe that the United States had inherited a maize culture that was passed directly from Natives to Pilgrims: this culture was authentically American and made even more so by the ingenuity of crop scientists and government subsidies. So the story went. Leaving out nixtamalization and the knowledge of Indigenous Americans, leaving out Columbus and Spain, all of this simplified the narrative that made the United States' corn-based cuisine seem providential. The motivations of anti-imperial and patriotic storytellers alike were usually noble; but we sometimes pay for these stories in human lives.

NOTES

1 Libkind et al. explain that "lagers require slow, low-temperature fermentations that are carried out by cryotolerant *Saccharomyces pastorianus*" and that this yeast was domesticated through a "fusion of *Saccharomyces eubayanus*, found in Southern beech forests of Patagonia, and other yeasts" (2011, 14539). This possibility is intriguing, because lager beer brewing was pioneered in the fifteenth century, suggesting, perhaps, a very early arrival of American microbes in Europe. However, in a personal communication, one of the article's authors, Mark Johnston, conjectured that another

cryotolerant yeast must have been used in lager beer brewing prior to the arrival of *S. eubayanus*. Thus, it is unclear precisely when American yeasts arrived in Bavaria.Unless otherwise noted, translations are by the author.

2 Some historians maintain that Europeans arrived in the Americas much as New World microbes ended up in Bavarian beer, driven by biological vagaries and not by conscious choices. For example, Arnold (1996) criticizes Alfred W. Crosby's *Ecological Imperialism* and *The Columbian Exchange* for attributing "too much to biology and too little to conscious human agency" (89). Maize provides a helpful contrast to yeasts, in this sense, precisely because maize must be passed from hand to hand intentionally. Even a corncob buried in fertile ground will not thrive. Kernels must be removed from the cob and spaced, or they will choke one another.

3 For a description of the contents, see Blanco Castro, Morales Valverde, and Sánchez Moreno (1994); Arévalo (1935).

4 "Los moriscos del Reino de Valencia le cultivaban [maíz] con cuidado y después de molido y hecho harina le amasaban y hacían unas tortillas muy delgadas que se cocían en los hornos" (Cienfuegos c. 1630, I:144). Cienfuegos devotes an entire section to the "diversidad de Puches de los Moriscos" (c. 1630, I:229).

5 Such "círculos culturales" [cultural circles] are often unaware of one another, as Álvarez López has noted (1945, 227).

6 On the differential rate of diffusion of plants and technologies associated with plants (the cultural "tool kits" for such things as grinding and preparing), see Staller (2010, 1–2).

7 On Dietrich and American flora, see López Piñero and López-Terrada (1997, 109–11).

8 On the early association of maize and poverty, see Brandes (1996, 259).

9 Cienfuegos makes a notable exception in the case of Moriscos, a community of farmers that he admires. In volume II of the *Historia de las plantas*, the expulsion of the Moriscos was a *medical* disaster, because skilful healers – "mujercillas y muchos moriscos o africanos" – were "expelidos destos Reinos" (c. 1630, II:i).

10 Some of the confusion surrounding early nomenclature is present in Paz Sánchez (2013).

11 Cienfuegos cites many manuscripts that have been lost. See Arévalo (1935, 325).

12 For Hernández's description of the use of lime to prepare corn, see Hernández (2000, 112). López Piñero and Pardo-Tomás (1994 and 1996) painstakingly trace the diffusion of Hernández's work. For a further idea of the influence of Hernández's pioneering work, see Chabrán (2009).

13 On sixteenth-century accounts of nixtamalization, see Staller (2010, 28–33) and Méndez Martínez (2011, 286–90). Roe takes it for granted that the

"Indian's age-old process of corn preparation was known to the Spanish conquerors" (1973, 14).

14 This perfectly inverts traditional accounts of the history of botany; Finan, for example, maintains that in "the literature of exploration, the descriptions of maize are mostly fragmentary and inexact; in the herbals they are generally precise and well illustrated" (1950, 180).

15 The differences between the two scientific communities that developed during the reign of Charles V are vast. One, the group Cienfuegos calls "Germans," tended to represent plants in text and illustration by abstracting natural originals from human communities; these naturalists tended to print their work. Another, working closer to the imperial metropolis, focused much more on what José de Acosta called "natural and moral history," a way of studying the life histories of plants within human communities; a significant number of naturalists in this group disseminated their work in manuscript. Arévalo (1935, 333) examines some of the reasons Cienfuegos did not want to publish.

16 On Cienfuegos's criticisms of Clusius, see López Pinero and López-Terrada (1997, 88). Paul Weatherwax (1954, 34–7) contains a classic account of "How the Old World Received Corn."

17 See also Finan (1950, 179).

18 López Piñero and López-Terrada (1994, 28) point out that Fuchs's illustrations would be reused in new editions until 1774.

19 Cienfuegos is complaining that Bock's work, originally published in 1539, still has not been corrected in 1552. This may seem a bit unfair, but Álvarez López (1945, 232) would still be accusing Bock of "exagerada pasión nacionalizadora." For Cienfuegos's further criticisms of Bock, see Rey Bueno (2004, 253). It is true that Spain zealously "guarded the secrets of its American natural resources"; at the same time, it is important to keep in mind Cienfuegos's belief that foreigners simply aren't paying attention (Schiebinger and Swan 2005, 1).

20 On some of the problems associated with using mentions in printed herbals to document the dissemination of maize, see Warman (2003, 99).

21 This silence would still sting, centuries later; Álvarez López accuses northern naturalists of "emulación, acaso teñida con secreta envidia" (1945, 232).

22 As Walter Mignolo (2007, 317) discusses, this is much the same way that Kant spoke about the hidebound Spanish character.

23 For arguments based on the probable rate of diffusion of corn (i.e., how fast maize ought to have spread among different peoples), see Enfield (1866, 34); Emerson (1878, 23); Bowman (1915, 1); Álvarez López (1945, 265–6); and Mangelsdorf and Oliver (1951, 275).

24 For subsequent reproductions of Bonafous's account and image, see for example Hance and Mayers (1870, 523); Weatherwax (1923, 2), and Weatherwax (1954, 132–8).

25 As Warman (2003, 102) discusses, the supposed inferiority of American
   nature was long an argument against an American origin of maize. "Lan-
   drace" is not directly related to sociological racism, although Kumar notes
   that such terminology reveals "unconscious feelings and hidden social
   relationships" (1995, 191).

26 Mangelsdorf and Oliver begin their rather arch rejection of the diffusion-
   ist position, "Whence Came Maize to Asia?," with a sporting reference to
   Heyerdahl (1951, 263–4). Johannessen and Parker (1989, 164) would mention Heyerdahl positively.

27 Crosby believes that wheat allowed the urbanization of medieval Europe,
   but that maize allowed for subsequent population growth (2004, 18).

28 A decade after Sauer, the philological argument would turn up again in
   Jeffreys (1973). For Jeffreys, the fact that Fuchs, Bock, Dodoens, and Ruel
   were "convinced of the Asiatic origin of maize" is evidence in favour of
   early introduction (1973, 399), and evidence of Spanish belatedness, because maize moved "from Asia Minor into Europe and into Spain" (400).

29 Sauer (2009, 192). Characterizing Columbus as insignificant and uncurious
   was a minor piece of his important critique of colonialism.

30 See also Johannessen and Parker (1989). For earlier conjectures about early
   maize in Asia, see Marszewski (1962), Jeffreys (1973), and Singh (1977, 6).

31 See, for example, Sorenson and Raish (1990).

32 See Hance and Mayers (1870), Collins (1909), and Stonor and Anderson
   (1949).

33 For an idea of the extraordinary intensity of the debates about the origins
   of maize in the 1960s and 1970s, see Wilkes (2004).

34 On the implications of these contrary uses of "country," see Williams
   (1973, 1–12).

35 Weatherwax was a sensible historian, but helped popularize the sublime
   school of maize histories: "It was deep in the mists of the past, long before
   the advent of the human race, that Nature ... devised for oriental lands
   their rice and their millets, for Africa and parts of Asia the sorghum family,
   and for the Semite in his desert garden and the Aryan on his westward mi-
   grations, the small grains of Europe and Asia. For the vast wilderness of the
   Western Hemisphere, however, she had only a single corn plant" (1923, 2).

36 There is a Mexican nationalist discourse that similarly confuses nation
   states and places of origin, apparent when Kato Yamakake et al. (2009, 10)
   explain in the "executive summary" of *Origen y diversificación del maíz* that
   maize's "origin, domestication and diversification all took place in *our
   country.*"

37 Roe examines the ways in which nineteenth-century writers "attributed
   to the pre-Columbian inhabitants of the American continents the same
   motives for maize cultivation" that they held (1973, 9–10). US authors were

not alone in thinking that they formed part of an ancient tradition; Mangelsdorf and Oliver dryly point out that on every continent where maize is grown, people believe that they have grown maize "from time immemorial" (1951, 280–1).

38 In the chapter "Too Long a Secret Weapon," Walden explains that maize's "indispensability when the chips are down lies not only in food but in the products of industries which make the machines, firepower, and habiliments of war" (1966, 165).

39 Giles (1940, 83) argues that the thinking of Ralph Waldo Emerson and the "Concord philosophers" was "the direct fruitage of cornfields." The "corn belt," according to Weatherwax, is "the land of rationalism" (1923, 2).

40 Fussell, in an impassioned passage, writes, "my search for the hidden roots of corn was a search for a homeplace, a search ultimately for myself" (1992, 282).

41 There are even un-American, urban unbelievers – located at the "schools of the eastern cities," according to Wallace and Brown – who "all too often have neglected to teach their pupils to understand and appreciate corn as the sustenance of our civilization" (1988, 10).

42 On the social and economic factors that contributed to pellagra epidemics in Europe and the United States, see Katz (1989, 127–37), Bollet (2004, 169–70), Warman (2003, 148–72), and Roe (1973, 170).

43 See also Staller (2010, 3). Weatherwax and Randolph (1955, 3) explain that English colonists in particular used the methods they already knew and did not tend to adopt Indigenous practices. Nixtamalization was not unknown in the US; hominy is essentially nixtamalized corn. However, many people relied on cornmeal that was not nixtamalized and increasingly had the healthy germ of the kernel removed to improve shelf life (Bollet 2004, 170).

44 Pellagra was not a problem in cultures where nixtamalization is prevalent; see Brenton (2004, 37).

45 See López Piñero (2006) and García Guerra and Álvarez Antuña (1993).

46 See also Roe (1973, 81–3), and Etheridge (1972).

47 Warman (2003, 172) explicitly connects the end of pellagra to the beginning of epidemic obesity.

48 Weatherwax (1923, 12) assumed, as did others, that maize introductions to Europe were fairly constant. Genetic studies confirm this, and confirm that maize was introduced to Europe from the Americas, post-1492. See Rebourg et al. (2003), Dubreuil et al. (2006), and Tenaillon and Charcosset (2011).

49 In *Sin maíz no hay país* (2003, 10), Galicia García reaches for the same purple heights as Giles's "the strength of our past, the power of our present": "El maíz como testigo fiel del pasado y del presente mexicanos, como protagonista central del futuro que nos acerca acompañado simultáneamente de esperanza e incertidumbre ..."

WORKS CITED

Álvarez López, Enrique. 1945. "Las plantas de América en la botánica europea del siglo XVI." *Revista de Indias* 6: 221–88.

Arévalo, Celso. 1935. "Bernardo de Cienfuegos y la Botánica de su época." In *Estudios sobre la ciencia española del siglo XVII*, edited by the Asociación Nacional de Historiadores de la Ciencia Española, 324–35. Madrid: Gráfica Universal.

Arnold, David. 1996. *The Problem of Nature: Environment, Culture and European Expansion.* Oxford: Blackwell.

Blanco Castro, Emilio, Ramón Morales Valverde, and Pedro M. Sánchez Moreno. 1994. "Bernardo Cienfuegos y su aportación a la botánica en el siglo XVII." *Asclepio* 46.1: 37–123. https://doi.org/10.3989/asclepio.1994.v46.1.476.

Bleichmar, Daniela. 2012. *Visible Empire: Botanical Expeditions and Visual Culture in the Hispanic Enlightenment.* Chicago: University of Chicago Press.

Bollet, Alfred Jay. 1992. "Politics and Pellagra: The Epidemic of Pellagra in the U.S. in the Early Twentieth Century." *Yale Journal of Biology and Medicine* 65: 211–21.

Bollet, Alfred Jay. 2004. *Plagues and Poxes: The Impact of Human History on Epidemic Disease.* New York: Demos.

Bonafous, Matthieu. 1836. *Histoire naturelle, agricole et économique du maïs.* Paris: Madame Huzard.

Bonavia, Duccio. 2008. *El maíz: Su origen, su domesticación y el rol que ha cumplido en el desarrollo de la cultura.* Lima: Universidad de San Martín de Porres.

Bowman, M.L. 1915. *Corn: Growing, Judging, Breeding, Feeding, Marketing.* Waterloo, IA: Waterloo Publishing.

Brandes, Stanley. 1996. "El misterio del maíz." In *Conquista y comida: Consecuencas del encuentro de dos mundos*, edited by Janet Long, 255–63. Mexico City: UNAM.

Brenton, Barrett P. 2004. "Piki, Polenta, and Pellagra: Maize, Nutrition and Nurturing the Natural." In *Nurture: Proceedings of the Oxford Symposium on Food and Cookery 2003*, edited by Richard Hosking, 36–50. Bristol: Footwork.

Candolle, Alphonse de. 1959. *Origin of Cultivated Plants.* New York: Hafner.

Cepeda, Fernando de, and Fernando Alfonso Carrillo. 1637. *Relacion universal legitima y verdadera del sitio en que esta fundada la muy noble, insigne y muy leal Ciudad de Mexico ...* Mexico City: Imprenta de Francisco Salbago, ministro del Santo Oficio.

Chabrán, Rafael. 2009. "Dr. Francisco Hernández and Denmark: The Presence of the Mexican Treasury in the Work of Ole Worm. An Introduction." *Colorado Review of Hispanic Studies* 7: 169–83.

Cienfuegos, Bernardo de. c. 1630. *Historia de las plantas*. Biblioteca Nacional de España. Mss 3357–Mss 3363.

Collins, G.N. 1909. *A New Type of Indian Corn from China*. Washington, DC: Government Printing Office.

Crosby, Alfred W. 1994. *Germs, Seeds, and Animals: Studies in Ecological History*. Armonk, NY: M.E. Sharpe.

Crosby, Alfred W. 2003. *The Columbian Exchange: Biological and Cultural Consequences of 1492*. Westport, CT: Praeger.

Crosby, Alfred W. 2004. *Ecological Imperialism: The Biological Expansion of Europe, 900–1900*. Cambridge: Cambridge University Press.

Darwin, Charles. 1998. *The Variation of Animals and Plants under Domestication*. Edited by Harriet Ritvo. 2 vols. Baltimore: Johns Hopkins University Press.

de Man, Paul. 1986. *The Resistance to Theory*. Minneapolis: University of Minnesota Press.

Dubreuil, P., et al. 2006. "The Origin of Maize (*Zea mays* L.) in Europe As Evidenced by Microsatellite Diversity." *Maydica* 51: 281–91.

Eamon, William. 2009. "'Nuestros males no son constitucionales, sino circunstanciales': The Black Legend and the History of Early Modern Spanish Science." *Colorado Review of Hispanic Studies* 7: 13–30.

Emerson, William D. 1878. *Indian Corn and Its Culture*. Cincinnati: Wrightson & Co.

Enfield, Edward. 1866. *Indian Corn: Value, Culture, and Uses*. New York: Appleton.

Ensminger, Audrey, et al. 1994. *Foods and Nutrition Encyclopedia*. 2 vols. Boca Raton: CRC Press.

Esteva, Gustavo. 2003. "Los árboles de las culturas mexicanas." In *Sin maíz no hay país*, edited by Gustavo Esteva and Catherine Marielle, 15–28. Mexico City: Consejo Nacional para la Cultura y las Artes.

Etheridge, Elizabeth W. 1972. *The Butterfly Caste: A Social History of Pellagra in the South*. Westport, CT: Greenwood Publishing Company.

Finan, John J. 1950. *Maize in the Great Herbals*. Waltham, MA: Chronica Botanica.

Fuchs, Barbara. 2007. "The Spanish Race." In *Rereading the Black Legend: The Discourses of Religious and Racial Difference in the Renaissance Empires*, edited by Margaret R. Greer, Walter D. Mignolo, and Maureen Quilligan, 88–98. Chicago: University of Chicago Press.

Fussell, Betty. 1992. *The Story of Corn*. Albuquerque: University of New Mexico Press.

Fussell, Betty. 1999. "Translating Maize into Corn: The Transformation of America's Native Grain." *Social Research* 66.1: 41–65.

Galicia García, Griselda. 2003. Presentación. In *Sin maís no hay país*, edited by Gustavo Esteva and Catherine Marielle, 9–10. Mexico City: Consejo Nacional para la Cultura y las Artes.

Galison, Peter. 1997. *Image and Logic: A Material Culture of Microphysics.* Chicago: University of Chicago Press.

García Guerra, Delfín, and Víctor Álvarez Antuña. 1993. *Lepra asturiensis: La contribución asturiana en la historia de la pelagra (siglos XVII y XIX).* Madrid: CSIC.

Giles, Dorothy. 1940. *Singing Valleys: The Story of Corn.* New York: Random House.

Hance, H.F., and W.F. Mayers. 1870. "Introduction of Maize into China." *Pharmaceutical Journal* 3.1: 522–5.

Hawkes, Corinna. 2007. "Farm Subsidies, Duties, Quotas, and Tariffs." In *The Oxford Companion to American Food and Drink*, edited by Andrew F. Smith, 214. Oxford: Oxford University Press.

Hernández, Francisco. 2000. *The Mexican Treasury: The Writings of Francisco Hernández.* Stanford: Stanford University Press.

Innes, Catherine Lynette. 2002. *A History of Black and Asian Writing in England, 1700–2000.* Cambridge: Cambridge University Press.

Janick, J., and G. Caneva. 2005. "The First Images of Maize in Europe." *Maydica* 50: 71–80.

Jeffreys, M.D.W. 1973. "Pre-Columbian Maize in Asia." In *Man across the Sea: Problems of Pre-Columbian Contacts*, edited by Carroll L. Riley et al., 376–400. Austin: University of Texas Press.

Johannessen, Carl L. 1988. "Indian Maize in the Twelfth Century BC." *Nature* 332: 587. https://doi.org/10.1038/332587a0.

Johannessen, Carl L., and Anne Z. Parker. 1989. "Maize Ears Sculptured in 12th and 13th Century A.D. India as Indicators of Pre-Columbian Diffusion." *Economic Botany* 43.2: 164–80. https://doi.org/10.1007/BF02859857.

Kagan, Richard L. 1996. "Prescott's Paradigm: American Historical Scholarship and the Decline of Spain." *American Historical Review* 101.2: 423–46. https://doi.org/10.2307/2170397.

Kato Yamakake, Takeo Ángel, et al. 2009. *Origen y diversificación del maíz. Una revisión analítica.* Mexico City: UNAM.

Katz, Solomon H. 1989. "Biocultural Evolution of Cuisine: The Hopi Indian Blue Corn Tradition." In *Handbook of Psychophysiology of Human Eating*, edited by Richard Shepherd, 115–40. Chichester: Wiley.

Kehoe, Alice B. 2003. "The Fringe of American Archaeology: Transoceanic and Transcontinental Contacts in Prehistoric America." *Journal of Scientific Exploration* 17.1: 19–36.

Kehoe, Alice B. 2010. "Consensus and the Fringe in American Archaeology." *Archaeologies: Journal of the World Archaeological Congress* 6.2: 197–214. https://doi.org/10.1007/s11759-010-9132-x.

Kumar, Pushpam. 1995. "Intellectual Property Rights and Biodiversity: Emergence of Biobattles." In *Intellectual Property Rights*, edited by Krg Nair and Ashok Kumar, 186–95. New Delhi: Allied Publishers.

Lanska, Douglas J. 1996. "Stages in the Recognition of Epidemic Pellagra in the United States: 1865–1960." *Neurology* 47: 829–34. https://doi.org /10.1212/WNL.47.3.829.

Libkind, Diego, et al. 2011. "Microbe Domestication and the Identification of the Wild Genetic Stock of Lager-Brewing Yeast." *PNAS* 35.108: 14539–44. https://doi.org/10.1073/pnas.1105430108.

López Gómez, Antonio. 1974. "La introducción del maíz en Valencia y la sustitución de otros cereales." *Estudios geográficos* 35: 147–56.

López Piñero, José María. 2006. "Gaspar Casal: Descripción ecológica de la pelagra, primera enfermedad carencial." *Revista Española de Salud Pública* 80: 411–15. https://doi.org/10.1590/S1135-57272006000400010.

López Piñero, José María, and Maríaluz López-Terrada. 1994. *La traducción por Juan de Jarava de Leonhart Fuchs y la terminología botánica castellana del siglo XVI.* Valencia: Universitat de València, CSIC.

López Piñero, José María, and Maríaluz López-Terrada. 1997. *La influencia española en la introducción en Europa de las plantas americanas (1493–1623).* Valencia: CSIC, Universitat de València.

López Piñero, José María, and José Pardo-Tomás. 1994. *Nuevos materiales y noticias sobre la* Historia de las Plantas de Nueva España *de Francisco Hernández.* Valencia: Universitat de València/CSIC.

López Piñero, José María, and José Pardo-Tomás. 1996. *La influencia de Francisco Hernández (1515–1587) en la constitución de la botánica y la materia médica modernas.* Valencia: Universitat de València/CSIC.

Mangelsdorf, Paul C., and Douglas L. Oliver. 1951. "Whence Came Maize to Asia?" *Botanical Museum Leaflets, Harvard University* 14.10: 263–91.

Marszewski, T. 1962. "The Age of Maize Cultivation in Asia." *Folia Orient.* 4: 240–95.

Méndez Martínez, Jorge Luis. 2011. *Caos-Nixtamal: Materia y energía de una técnica alimentaria mesoamericana.* Mexico City: Centro de Investigaciones y Estudios Superiores en Antropología Social.

Mignolo, Walter. 2007. "What Does the Black Legend Have to Do with Race?" In *Rereading the Black Legend: The Discourses of Religious and Racial Difference in the Renaissance Empires,* edited by Margaret R. Greer, Walter D. Mignolo, and Maureen Quilligan, 312–24. Chicago: University of Chicago Press.

Navarro Brotóns, Víctor, and William Eamon. 2007. "Spain and the Scientific Revolution: Historiographical Questions and Conjectures." In *Más allá de la Leyenda Negra: Beyond the Black Legend,* edited by Víctor Navarro Brotóns and William Eamon, 27–38. Valencia: Universitat de València, CSIC.

Norton, Marcy. 2008. *Sacred Gifts, Profane Pleasures: A History of Tobacco and Chocolate in the Atlantic World.* Ithaca: Cornell University Press.

Pardo-Tomás, José, and Maríaluz López-Terrada. 1993. *Las primeras noticias sobre plantas americanas en las relaciones de viajes y crónicas de Indias (1493–1553).* Valencia: Universitat de València, CSIC.

Parker, Arthur C. 1910. *Iroquois Uses of Maize and Other Food Plants*. Albany: University of the State of New York.

Paz Sánchez, Manuel de. 2013 "El trigo de los pobres. La recepción del maíz en el Viejo Mundo." *Revista Batey*. 21.11: 1–106.

Rebourg, C., et al. 2003. "Maize Introduction into Europe: The History Reviewed in the Light of Molecular Data." *Theoretical and Applied Genetics* 106: 895–903. https://doi.org/10.1007/s00122-002-1140-9.

Regueiro y González Barros, Antonio M. 1983. "La flora americana en la España del siglo XVI." In *America y la España del siglo XVI: Homenaje a Gonzalo Fernández de Oviedo*, edited by Francisco de Solano and Fermín del Pino, vol. 1, 205–17. 2 vols. Madrid: CSIC.

Rey Bueno, Mar. 2004. "Juntas de herbolarios y tertulias espagíricas: el círculo cortesano de Diego de Cortavila (1597–1657)." *Dynamis* 24: 243–67.

Rindos, David. 1984. *The Origins of Agriculture: An Evolutionary Perspective*. Orlando: Academic Press.

Roe, Daphne A. 1973. *A Plague of Corn: The Social History of Pellagra*. Ithaca: Cornell University Press.

Sachs, Julius von. *History of Botany (1530–1860)*. 1906. Translated by Henry E.F. Garnsey. Oxford: Clarendon.

Sauer, Carl. 2009. *Carl Sauer on Culture and Landscape: Readings and Commentaries*. Edited by William M. Denevan and Kent Mathewson. Baton Rouge: Louisiana State University Press.

Schiebinger, Londa, and Claudia Swan. 2005. Introduction. In *Colonial Botany: Science, Commerce, and Politics in the Early Modern World*, edited by Londa Schiebinger and Claudia Swan, 1–16. Philadelphia: University of Pennsylvania Press.

Singh, Bhag. 1977. *Races of Maize in India*. New Delhi: Indian Council of Agricultural Research.

Sorenson, John L., and Martin H. Raish. 1990. *Pre-Columbian Contact with the Americas across the Oceans: An Annotated Bibliography*. Provo, UT: Research Press.

Staller, John E. 2010. *Maize Cobs and Cultures: History of Zea mays L*. Berlin: Springer.

Stonor, C.R., and Edgar Anderson. 1949. "Maize among the Hill Peoples of Assam." *Annals of the Missouri Botanical Garden* 36: 355–404. https://doi.org/10.2307/2394398.

Sturtevant, E. Lewis. 1894. "Notes on Maize." *Bulletin of the Torrey Botanical Club* 21.8: 319–43. https://doi.org/10.2307/2477991.

Tenaillon, Maud Irène, and Alain Charcosset. 2011. "A European Perspective on Maize History." *Comptes Rendus Biologies* 334: 221–8. https://doi.org/10.1016/j.crvi.2010.12.015.

Turner, James. 1979. *The Politics of Landscape: Rural Scenery and Society in English Poetry 1630–1660*. Oxford: Blackwell.

Walden, Howard T. 1966. *Native Inheritance: The Story of Corn in America*. New York: Harper and Row.

Wallace, Henry A., and William L. Brown. 1988. *Corn and Its Early Fathers*. Ames: Iowa State University Press.

Warman, Arturo. 2003. *Corn and Capitalism: How a Botanical Bastard Grew to Global Dominance*. Translated by Nancy L. Westrate. Chapel Hill: University of North Carolina Press.

Weatherwax, Paul. 1923. *The Story of the Maize Plant*. Chicago: University of Chicago Press.

Weatherwax, Paul. 1954. *Indian Corn in Old America*. New York: Macmillan.

Weatherwax, Paul, and L.F. Randolph. 1955. "History and Origin of Corn." In *Corn and Corn Improvement*, edited by George F. Sprague, 1–16. New York: Academic Press.

Wilkes, Garrison. 2004. "Corn, Strange and Marvelous: But Is a Definitive Origin Known?" In *Corn: Origin, History, Technology, and Production*, edited by C. Wayne Smith, Javier Betrán, and E.C.A. Runge, 3–63. Hoboken: Wiley, 2004.

Williams, Raymond. 1973. *The Country and the City*. New York: Oxford University Press.

Zanier, Claudio. 2012. "Overcoming the Barrier of the Alps. Silk and the Intellectual Legacy of Mathieu Bonafous between Lyon and Turin." *Cromohs* 17: 1–14. http://www.cromohs.unifi.it/17_2012/zanier_bonafous.html.

SECOND COURSE

What to Eat and How

4 Dietetic Prescriptions for the Ruling Elite of the Kingdom of Navarra during the First Half of the Sixteenth Century: The Cases of Juan Rena and Juan de Alarcón[1]

FERNANDO SERRANO LARRÁYOZ

The currency of the *regimina sanitatis* during the Renaissance is evident in medical Hispanic literature in the quantity of treatises published throughout the sixteenth century in Latin as well as in Romance languages (Castilian or Catalan) and in the proliferation of re-editions of ancient medieval texts.[2] This is a type of literature whose predecessors must be sought in the medieval Galenic tradition, which put special emphasis on what were called the *sex res non naturales* – factors which, unlike the *res naturales*, did not constitute the individual nature of each person and yet still contributed to the better maintenance of health. The spread of these ideas through vernacular languages reflects in good measure certain attitudes of contemporary social elites in which Galenism continued to be relevant into the seventeenth century.[3]

In this work we present four dietetic prescriptions from the first half of the sixteenth century that have been preserved in the Archivo General de Navarra (AGN). The project deals with documents that are valuable because of the scarcity of known examples of these types of sources for the field of the Spanish Renaissance; these documents show doctors' and patients' interest in dietetics, which they understood as a general regimen for an individual's life in order to maintain or restore good health. The individualized medicine practised in medieval times and in the early Renaissance required the analysis of the particular constitution of the organ being treated, which implied the existence of "muchas saludes diferentes" [many different types of health] in the same individual. Thus, the distinct constitution of each person justified the existence of different health regimens, "reglas de vida individuales hechas a la medida del sujeto que las utiliza, con el fin de mantenerle sano" [individual sets of rules made according to the subject using them, with the intent of keeping him healthy] (Gil-Sotres 1996, 478).[4]

For instance, the documents included in this text practised this type of personalized medicine, adapted to the necessities of each patient.

It is difficult to frame the four Navarrese texts in conventional categories, especially during a period of transformation such as the sixteenth century. The diversity in the formal expression of the individualized treatments makes it difficult to label them as part of the *regimina sanitatis*,[5] since the *regimina* are broad-prescriptive texts that plot a complete and organized course through the "six non-natural things." The documents presented here, in contrast, constitute a series of dietetic recommendations thought to treat an individual's specific illness. For this reason, they must be considered more like the *consilia* than the *regimina sanitatis*. This relationship is evident in three of the cases studied, even though the structure does not entirely correspond to what are considered the classic characteristics of this genre: short texts, generally written in an epistolary mode and usually divided into three parts. In the first section, these texts would set forth the *casus*, followed by a diet consisting of health recommendations – generally with a well-developed section dedicated to nutrients – and finally, a cure based on a specific pharmacopoeia (Nicoud 2010, 18).[6] If the *consilia* form a consistent, structured academic genre, the prescriptions presented here do not correspond in form to this pattern, but they do share with the *consilia* the objective of offering a collection of medical recommendations adapted specifically to a patient's characteristics. In fact, it has been shown how, together with the printed circulation of traditional medical genres for maintaining health, health regimens proliferated in this period, along with formularies and other similar writings adapted and individualized by the users themselves.[7] In that sense, it is important to highlight that one of the four documents transcribed was written by the patient himself, Juan Rena, who was able to base his work on a "health regimen" and select only what interested him in order to alleviate his own illness.

The four dietetic prescriptions are kept in the Archivo General of Navarra and, except for one, lack any dating. Nonetheless, looking at the content, the links with other texts, and the characters associated with those texts, an approximate chronology can be suggested. The two oldest ones are those intended for Juan Rena, dated in 1524 and around 1528; the two other texts were prescribed to Juan de Alarcón, his servant.

I. Dietetic Prescriptions for Juan Rena (c. 1480–1539)

One characteristic to point out in the dietetic prescriptions for Juan Rena is that the oldest one, which is also the only one with a date – May of 1524 – corresponds to notes that he himself wrote, at least in part. The patient lays out chronologically the steps to take in everything related to ingesting food, taking medicine, and the baths and the massages that had to be used. It would not be surprising if, besides the advice of a doctor, his preparation involved a *regimen sanitatis* that was inventoried in his home in Pamplona in 1525.[8] The second diet, developed around 1528, was doubtless written by a doctor. Its structure is different from the previous one, putting special emphasis on the food that Rena should and should not consume and then proceeding to prescribe certain medical compounds. Where the first text ends with the prescription of an unguent that Rena should use, the second one collects a series of simple medicines that he has to take. Nonetheless, it is important to point out that the prescription for the unguent and the list of simple medicines are written in different hands from the general aspects of each diet, which would suggest the involvement of diverse people in their production.

Venetian by origin, Juan Rena was born around the year 1480, and we know nothing about his family or where he acquired the solid training that allowed him to take on responsibilities in the Spanish administration in the early part of the sixteenth century. What is clear is that his political-administrative journey and his religious status allowed him to occupy the bishopric of Pamplona towards the end of his life. Named *capellán* of Queen Juana I of Castile in 1508, he was the right hand of Ferdinand II of Aragon (Fernando el Católico) after the conquest of Navarra in the administrative restructuring, and he served as, among other activities, financial overseer for the extraordinary public works and expenses of Navarra from 1512 until his death. As *capellán* of Carlos V, he served on numerous commissions to the Spanish crown, also until his death. The ecclesiastical prebends of which he was a beneficiary and that he desired so much became constant starting in 1523; he served as treasurer of the cathedral of Pamplona between 1530 and 1538. The greatly desired episcopal mitre of the diocese of Pamplona arrived in the spring of 1538.[9]

Regarding his dietetic prescriptions, it is necessary to note the weight accorded by the Arab and Latin medieval traditions of Galenism to bathing and massages. In spite of the consideration given to bathing as part of preventative medicine in the health treatises of the period, in 1524 the Venetian expected a purely curative benefit. His plan is clear, and the proposal is to make use of baths before ingesting food, first thing in the morning as well as in the afternoon before dinner, leaving a prudent amount of time after the noon meal. The use of bathing was seen as a substitute for exercise or as a way of completing its action

(Gil-Sotres 1996, 629). Luis Lobera de Ávila, doctor of Emperor Carlos V, in his *Banquete de nobles caballeros* [Banquet of noble gentlemen] (1530), collected some of the benefits of bathing centuries before they were recommended by Rhazes.[10]

Rena used both full-body bathing and specific bathings of the affected body parts, although in the morning, before entering the bath, he proposed "vntar el hígado con vngüento sandalino e rosado, e cada mañana antes de vntar el hígado haré con un lienço linpiar lo que de la vnçión del día antes quedado oviere" [anointing the liver with rose and sandalwood unguent, and every morning before anointing the liver I will clean away with a piece of linen what has remained of the anointing from the day before] (Appendix 1, 3). Problems in his legs – probably gout – and stomach seem to have been his main sources of pain. The long baths, between a half-hour and an hour, must have alleviated his pain, and the treatment was completed with compresses of hot urine (whose source is not specified) and a hot unguent. In the afternoon, after the unguent was applied, his legs had to be wrapped in lukewarm linen, and he had to lie down for an hour before dinner. In the mornings, on the other hand, it does not seem that his legs were covered before resting. These practices, which were performed from 12 May until "no hiziese eçessivo calor" [it was no longer excessively hot], formed part of a perfectly regulated treatment in which pills and unguents were included (Appendix 1, 7).[11]

On more than one occasion, hot weather was not considered agreeable. For this reason, Rena affirms that if "hiziere de muncho calor haré poner sobre la vnçión del hígado vn lençezico delgado mojado en agoa rosada e vnas gotas de vinagre templado" [the weather is very hot, I will place a thin piece of linen, dampened with rose water and a few drops of lukewarm vinegar, over the anointing of the liver] (Appendix 1, 3). The importance given to hot medicinal treatments and to the humidity contributed by baths in the prescriptions intended for Juan Rena should not be surprising, especially when we take into consideration that in 1524, the date of the earlier "regimen," Rena might have been forty-four years old. For the medicine of the time, a person reached old age between forty-five and fifty-five years of age, as a function of the degree to which by that point the two principal characteristics of a person's constitution, which were also the fundamental principles of life, had diminished: natural heat and root moisture (Gil-Sotres 1996, 845–6). These arrangements would be in force again four years later, when Rena was attended by the physicians Juan de Elizondo, doctor of Pamplona and of the dethroned kings of Navarra, and Martín de Santacara, first *protomédico* of Navarra.[12]

The close relationship between Juan Rena and Juan Vallés, named protonotary and treasurer of Navarra in 1524 and 1528 respectively, is reflected not only in their epistolary relationship, preserved from the time in which Vallés was present at court in the service of Carlos V between 1519 and 1528,[13] but also in a series of prescriptions that Vallés provided to treat Rena's problems with his leg. Vallés's inclinations towards medicine are well known.[14] It would not be surprising if in one of his medical works that is now missing, *Flores de medicina y cirugía* [Collection on medicine and surgery], he included some of the prescriptions that he offered Rena for his leg:

Tómese una cabeça de carnero y pélese y quebrántese y quítensele los sesos, y tanbién se tomen los pies y las manos y se pelen. Ítem se tomen rayzes de maluauisco dos libras, mancanilla, corona de rey y heneldo, de cada uno dos manojos, simiente de alholuas y de lino, entera la simiente, de cada uno media libra. Todas estas cosas cuezan en la quantidad de agua que fuere sufficiente y cuezan hasta que la carne de la cabeça y de las manos se aparte de los huesos. Y con este baño quanto más callente se pueda suffrir se laue un ratico, y después de bañado y enxugado con un paño callente luego de presto se ponga el emplastro que está hecho y tenga siempre la pierna leuantada, digo tendida sobre alguna caxa. Este cozimiento se guarde para que en estos cinco o seys días se bañe con él cada día una vez o dos callentándolo siempre muy bien. Y los huessos se echen a mal por que se pueda lauar con las mesmas cosas que entran en el cozimiento.[15]

[Take the head of a ram and let it be skinned and cracked and its brains taken out, and also take the feet and the hands and let them be skinned. Then take two pounds of marshmallow roots, chamomile, encrusted saxifrage (*saxifruga longifolia*), and dill, two bunches of each, fenugreek seed and flaxseed, the whole seed, a half-pound of each. Cook these things in whatever amount of water is sufficient and cook them until the flesh of the head and of the hands pulls away from the bones. And with this bath – as hot as can be borne – wash yourself for a little while, and after bathing and drying with a hot cloth, then quickly apply the plaster that has been made and keep the leg raised, or rather stretched out upon a chest. The mixture that has been cooked should be kept so that for the next five or six days you bathe with it every day once or twice, always heating it very well. The bones may be tossed because you may wash with the very things that are in the mixture that has been cooked.]

The use of pharmacological elements like pills, syrups, tablets, and unguents is complemented by the food and drink that the Venetian had to consume according to his social status and his pain; this is evident in the 1524 text as well as in the one he was prescribed in 1528. The number of meals to be prepared depended on factors like age, constitution, strength, the time of the year, and whether or not there was a *cuadro morboso* [clinical case] present. The most appropriate thing for those who had a dry constitution, which was accompanied by a strong innate heat, and who were used to eating exquisite meals was to prepare two meals per day (Gil-Sotres 1996, 653–6). The two prescriptions considered lunch and dinner obligatory. The first established the time for lunch at ten in the morning and dinner between eight and nine at night, consistent with what had been established by Arnau de Vilanova two centuries before (Gil-Sotres 1996, 656–7).

Regarding meals, the prescription of 1528 that the bread "sea hun día cozido" [be cooked the day before] (Appendix 2, 5) coincides with the proposal of some medieval regimens not to eat warm bread or bread prepared more than two days ago (Gil-Sotres 1996, 677). Nor does it mention legumes except for "garbanzos tostados" [toasted chickpeas] (Appendix 2, 4), although some regimens allow the consumption of fava beans, peas, green beans, and lentils, especially those that are cooked, with the recommendation not to waste the broth because of its diuretic and unblocking qualities for the body's veins (Gil-Sotres 1996, 680–1). Onions and garlic, cooked and roasted, along with aromatic herbs to which were attributed certain medical properties, like *hierba santa* [*piper auritum*], hyssop, and parsley, formed part of the roots considered appropriate to combat pains (Appendix 2, 4), although the dietetic treatises recommended not eating them raw (Gil Sotres 1996, 684). In terms of other vegetable products, the prescription of 1524 did not reject the ingestion of raisins and almonds. Raisins could be eaten "sin granos" [without seeds] before the main meal ("antepasto"), while toasted almonds could be consumed in the "sobremesa"[16] of the meal. During dinner, raisins and almonds could be consumed with the yolks of fresh eggs (Appendix 1, 3). In the second dietetic prescription, among the fresh and dried fruits and nuts allowed were included pine nuts, dates, figs (dried?), raisins, almonds, hazelnuts, and "nuezes moscadas en que sirua toda confitura, con que no sea calabacate o limones, y quando quisiere carne de membrillo sea con speçias" [nutmeg in preserves, as long as it is not squash or lemon, and when you desire quince meat, let it be with spices] (Appendix 2, 4). These arrangements accord with medieval and Renaissance doctors' negative views of fruits and vegetables as nutrients, and their valuation as medication, similar what occurred with sweets – with a sugar or honey base – and with spices (Gil-Sotres 1996, 687–8).

Juan Rena proposes a broth either of roasted chicken, of boiled chicken, or of lamb to eat on 14 May 1524. Two days before he had planned to eat "yantar cozido" [a cooked or boiled lunch], and the next day a broth and "comeré como suelo" [I will eat as I am accustomed], while at night he forced himself to eat his "diet" (Appendix 1, 1, 2, 3). The text of 1528 is more explicit. Broths are abandoned, although the prescription follows similar parameters to 1524 regarding the varieties of meat: chicken "y su linaje" [and its kind], partridge chicks, turtle doves, young pigeons, "y toda manera de aues del canpo o criadas, eçepto las de agoa y su natura, y sobre todo posarides gruesos y carnero … la mayor parte asado o en pasteles" [and every manner of birds of the field or domesticated birds, except those of the water and their kind, and above all fat *posarides* (haunches?) and mutton … the greater part roasted or in pies] (Appendix 2, 1). In fact meat constituted one of the principal elements of medieval and Renaissance nutrition, and medicinal virtues were attributed to it, especially to fowls, which were considered suitable for the elite in their ideal nutrition. Nevertheless, health regimens reject all types of aquatic birds, just as proposed in the text of 1528 (Gil-Sotres 1996, 693).

Regarding fish, the diversity of opinions about their advisability – or not – is a regular theme of the medieval health regimens as a whole. The case of the author of the 1528 diet for Juan Rena offers evidence of this: "De pescados ningunos son buenos y quando hubiere de ser sea pescado fresco de vna cola o cangregos de río o cancros de la mar, o truchuelas muy frescas o yomejuelas, y desto pocas vezes" [Of fish none of them are good, and when it is necessary, let it be fresh fish from the tail or crayfish from the river or crabs from the sea, or very fresh trout or yomejuelas (not identified), and of these very rarely] (Appendix 2, 2).[17] So scarce is the appreciation for this type of food that Rena does not even mention it in 1524. Something similar occurs with milk and dairy products. The diet of 1528 clearly establishes which foods must be got rid of: "todas cosas agres y verdes y de todo pescado, ecepto lo dicho, y de todas cosas saladas y carnes peliagudas y todas cosas de leche" [all things bitter and green and all fish, except those named, and all things salted and the meats of long-haired animals and all things of milk] (Appendix 2, 7). The complete opposite happens with eggs. The most valued part is the yolk, and this is shown in the document of 1524, when for 12 May Rena proposes eating "yemas blandas" [soft-cooked yolks] for dinner, and two days later "yemas frescas e passas e almendras" [fresh yolks and raisins and almonds]. In 1528, fresh yolks had to be prepared "asadas con azúcar y canela o echas en agoa de azar con açúcar y canela" [roasted with sugar and cinnamon or tossed in orange blossom water with sugar and cinnamon] (Appendix 1, 1, 3; Appendix 2, 3).[18] Cinnamon is the only spice highlighted, even though any type is allowed, including sugar – which was then considered a spice – and honey. These are meant to be used not only in solid items like egg yolks or toasted bread soaked in wine, to which are added a variety of other things ("dust"), but also in sweet watered-down wines "con agoa cozida con canela" [with water boiled with cinnamon] (Appendix 2, 3, 5, 6). The medicinal virtues of the spices are reflected in the medical texts, and their use depended on the type of patient, given the high price of the majority of them (Cruz Cruz, 1997, 176–7).

The only drink which is alluded to is wine, a fundamental element of the diet of the time along with bread. Wine comes out at the top of the recommended nutrients, followed by the juice of meat and eggs *sorbidos* [slurped]. The properties that health regimens attributed to wine were the capacity to transport nutrients to the body's organs, its nutritious quality, the possibility of restoring the natural heat of the spirits, facilitating the digestion, improving bowel movements, and a whole series of actions beneficial to the central nervous system (Gil-Sotres 1996, 717). The wine suggested in 1528 is white, "maduro olorioso y dulçe" [mature, fragrant, and sweet], diluted by water boiled with cinnamon, of the same kind as Juan Rena proposed four years earlier to make a decoction with other ingredients (Appendix 2, 5; Appendix 1, 7). One wine – white – was considered weak, which satisfied thirst. The characteristics attributed are positive, since wines with strong smells are capable of nourishing the body and of "multiplicar los espíritus sutiles" [multiplying the subtle spirits]. On the other hand, sweet wines are considered ideal for their "extraordinario alimento, aunque suelen provocar mucha sed" [extraordinary nutrition, even though they tend to provoke thirst]. Regarding the necessity of watering down the wines, opinions differed according to the physician (Gil-Sotres 1996, 721, 723–4).[19]

Sleep and the emotions, included respectively in the non-natural things as numbers four and six, also are reflected in these prescriptions. Their therapeutic character is discerned in the text of 1524. Juan Rena recognizes that after dinner and a few massages of the kidneys, performed with rose unguents, it is necessary to sleep. One senses that the objective was to recover from physical weariness.[20] Regarding emotions, the prescription of 1528 urges Rena to "procurad muchos juegos y plazeres, y sea dos o tres oras después de aver çenado o comido, y el día que esto se hubiere de azer el comer sea mediado y no muy repleto" [seek out many games and pleasures, and let it be two or three hours after eating, and on the day in which this is to be done, let the food be moderate and not over-full] (Appendix 2, 12). Happiness was the "accidente del alma" [accident of the soul] – somatic alterations unleashed to the rhythm of the emotions and which occur at the level of the heart – most valued by physicians so long as it was moderate. Games and pleasure could lead to this happiness, with various advice to promote it, while seeking to avoid worries (Gil-Sotres 1996, 815–19).

II. Dietetic Prescriptions for Juan de Alarcón († 1551)

If it is problematic to date one of the dietetic prescriptions intended for Juan Rena, it is even more difficult to do so in the case of those addressed to Juan de Alarcón, since his texts do not contain any dating. One of them is signed by a physician named Medrano, who served in Pamplona between 1541 and 1543,[21] even though it is quite possible that his activity began years earlier. We know that in 1537, between the last days of August and the beginning of October, Alarcón purchased various medicines at the price of thirty Navarrese pounds, three *sueldos*, and eight *dineros*.[22] Medrano's prescription, which I have dated to around 1538, is explicit about the hepatic and stomach issues in his patient (Appendix 3, 1).

Of Castilian origin, Juan de Alarcón appears for the first time in Navarra linked to the figure of Juan Rena, his master, in the 1520s. He then becomes one of Rena's right-hand men. He lived in Pamplona, in the same house as Rena, who taught him how to manage accounts. On his way to court in 1529, Juan Rena names him "apoderado" [attorney], entrusted in Rena's absence with the responsibilities of the "pagador real" [payer] for public works and expenses. Until Rena's death in 1539, Juan de Alarcón was also in charge of managing his master's house and estate. When Rena passed away, Alarcon took his place as *pagador* until his death in 1551.

Apparently, Alarcón's pains were prolonged because he was advised to "[hacer] exercicio en aiunas yugando a la pelota un rato ata que comience a sudar y otro tanto antes que cene y hacer exercicio moderado antes de comer y de cena, y no sobre comer ni cena hata que passen tres horas" [exercise while fasting, playing ball for a while until he begins to sweat and the same again right before eating dinner and to exercise moderately before eating lunch and dinner, and let the food not be excessive and not to eat lunch or dinner until three hours have passed]. According to Avicenna, increasing body heat would allow the thick materials in the body's interior to dissolve and, as the pores dilated, it would facilitate the exit of fluids from the body. Bernardo de Gordon highlighted the importance of exercise in increasing natural heat and its action on the heart, which would activate the cardiovascular system and the body's senses (imagination and memory). In this light, we can better understand a prescription for a poultice for the heart from 1537. The strengthening of the limbs is also one of the functions of exercise, an activity that, according to medieval authorities and as the Navarrese physicians suggest, had to be moderate. The ball game was one of the most recommended (Appendix 4, 5; Appendix 3, 4).[23] Here we might wonder if these "games" that were prescribed to Juan Rena had to do with implementing physical exercise, mainly due to the problems in his leg. Another important factor in bringing about Alarcón's recovery was the recommendation that he reach emotional stability, separating himself from "de toda tristeza y enojo" [all sadness and anger], as was also suggested to Rena. To achieve this stability, it is recommended that he separate himself from "exercicio de las mugeres" [exercise of women] and avoid conversations with them, "porque a él le pesará" [because it will weigh him down] (Appendix 4, 5; Appendix 3, 4). The medieval medical tradition considered sexual activity necessary to avoid illnesses because of its evacuating function, although it rejected this practice for those who were sick (Gil-Sotres 1996, 764, 767). The damages posed by coitus, in the opinion of contemporaries, were also set forth by the previously mentioned Luis Lobera de Ávila (Lobera de Ávila 1996, 57).

Juan de Alarcón's stomach issues are confirmed by the last prescription. In it, he is ordered to take *cassia fistula* (the golden rain tree, used as a purgative) and the sap of fir trees (with the properties of both a balm and a diuretic [Appendix 4, 1]). One prescription written by the same person recommends that he take the sap with certain pills and to follow the treatment:

> Tomará su mercet de quinze en quinze días dos píldoras de esas, vn poquito antes de cena *et sunt sine custodia* más que si no las tomasse. Y después al tercero día tome su trementina como ha acostumbrado, y en todo lo demás guarde su regimiento lo mejor que pudiere.[24]

> [His grace will take for fifteen days two of these pills a little before dinner and he will be with less care than if he did not take them. And on the third day let him take the sap as he is accustomed and in everything else let him keep his regimen as best he can.]

On the other hand, Doctor Medrano's treatment included taking a tablet in the morning "de las que se ordenaron" [from the ones prescribed], accompanied by white wine with two leaves of bitter wormwood, and before eating mixed spices ("polvora," or dust) or a few cinnamon and anise pills. The rose unguent for the kidneys that was prescribed for Juan Rena is also prescribed to Alarcón, to be applied in the afternoons, even if it had to be covered by a cloth dampened with rosewater (Appendix 3, 3; Appendix 4, 2).

The consideration of both beneficial and harmful nutrients for Juan Rena's "servant" follows the parameters seen in the regimens intended for Rena himself, even if the variety of quadrupeds prescribed for Alarcón is somewhat more explicit. No milk, cheese, "ni carnes de pelagudo sino fuesse cabrito o de algún gazapo o ternera, haunque de la liebre puede comer el caldo" [no meat from long-haired animals except a kid, a young rabbit, or a calf, although a broth of hare's meat may be eaten] and mutton. Doctor Medrano allowed him to eat fowl (without specifying) and also lamb boiled in the morning to eat, all of it seasoned with *hierba santa* (*piper auritum*) and parsley, and he recommended foods that were roasted in the afternoons (Appendix 4, 3; Appendix 3, 4). Because of how well these meats were digested, medieval health treatises recommended the meat of kids, lambs, and rabbits, although this last one was not recommended roasted (Gil-Sotres 1996, 691–2). The variety of fowl allowed in the first prescription is vast, but, speaking in general terms, there are no substantial differences in the principles mentioned in the proposals for Juan Rena: chickens "o su linage" [or their kind], partridges, quail, and "todo linage de aues saluo ánades y ánsares" [every kind of birds except ducks and geese].[25] Nor is it surprising that Medrano recommends that his client "buscar un poco de hígado de lobo y yo le diré que a de hazer para su salud" [seek out a little wolf liver and I will tell him what he has to do for his health] (Appendix 4, 4), because even in the educated medicine of the time, some symbolic considerations proper to sympathetic magic had not been completely dismissed (Appendix 3, 5).

Salty and bitter foods, greens, radishes, and legumes, except for chickpea broth, "el qual deue mucho usar" [which should be used often], are not advised in the dietetic prescriptions (Appendix 3, 4; Appendix 4, 3).[26] While the diet intended for Juan Rena in 1528 allowed him to consume roasted onions and garlic, in the more recent document intended for Alarcón a cooked mixture of radish leaves, chard, borage, and nettles "con su perrexil" [with parsley] (Appendix 4, 4)[27] was considered somewhat useful. These different things, in general, were used to treat intestinal complaints (Gil-Sotres 1996, 683). Once more the physician's mistrust of vegetables is evident. Similarly, fresh fruit was proscribed in both diets; the second diet emphasized the disagreeable quality of grapes, even though they were one of the most commonly used laxatives. Among dried fruits and nuts, chestnuts were rejected, but raisins and almonds were accepted – with which one could make *almendrada* – and pine nuts (Appendix 3, 4; Appendix 4, 3, 4).

As in the dietetic prescriptions for Juan Rena, fish received little praise, with the exception of trout or headstander [*megaleporinus obtusidens*] (Appendix 3, 4; Appendix 4, 4).[28] In the same way, eggs – fresh and "blandos" [soft] – enjoyed high regard. The 1538 text approves the intake of "alguna manteca fresca" [some fresh butter] (Appendix 3, 4; Appendix 4, 4), in spite of the general rule that milk and dairy products, with few exceptions, were not considered adequate nutrients. The same text recommends not drinking "agua cruda" [raw or unprocessed water] (Appendix 3, 4) because of the ease with which the water of wells, lakes, and ponds was contaminated. To make it drinkable, according to physicians, it was necessary to boil it, add vinegar, and aerate it multiple times by pouring it from container to container.[29] Regarding wine, while in the prescriptions for Rena he was advised to drink "maduro" [mature] white wine mixed with water that had been boiled with cinnamon, Doctor Medrano suggests that Alarcón drink "vino blanco muy bueno serenado de por noche con dos o tres oijas de acensones amargas machacadas puestas dentro" [a very good white wine chilled overnight with two or three crushed leaves of bitter wormwood (*artemisia absinthium*) placed within], which would be of great benefit in spite of its bitter taste, and white or red wine "claro maduro, amesado medianamente" [clear, aged, moderately mixed]. In the more recent diet, it is suggested that he drink white wine that has been watered down. Both documents suggest moderation in drinking during meals and, implicitly, not eating or drinking between meals. Hence the advice of Doctor Medrano to Juan de Alarcón not to "haga collaciones" [eat anything] (Appendix 3, 2, 4; Appendix 4, 5)[30] in order not to harm his delicate stomach.

Moderation in drink was to be accompanied by the habit of not sleeping during the day, "y menos sobre comer y ni cena" [especially after lunch and not even after dinner] – that is to say, after the most important meals (Appendix 4, 5). It was necessary to wait for the food, which was to change into the organism's substance, to reach a place agreeable to its transformation. These recommendations were intended to discourage naps or sleep during the early afternoon.[31]

The massages of the kidney with rose unguent that had to be performed by Juan Rena in 1524, and the advice to Juan de Alarcón in the last of these prescriptions not to wear "demasiada ropa sobre los riñones" [too many clothes over the kidneys], have their origin in the idea that "superficialidades de la segunda digestión se eliminan a través de los riñones, que actúan a modo de filtro, separando de los líquidos lo inútil, lo que no puede ser aprovechado por el organismo" [the super-ficialities of the second digestion are eliminated through the kidneys, which act as a filter, separating what is of no use from the liquids, what cannot be used by the body] (Gil-Sotres 1996, 756). Both arrangements were meant to facilitate the proper functioning of his organs. Similarly, the instruction to Alarcón that he not hold "mucho la orina" [often his urine] aims at the same end, since after sleeping, and once the second and third digestion were finished, a full bladder had to be emptied, and the same applied to the rest of the day, as many times as necessary.

III. Final Considerations

In addition to reflecting a textual genre not well known for the Spain of the sixteenth century, the documents that we have presented here are significant for a better understanding of the actual practice of the theoretical postulates of university medicine and Galenism in concrete individuals. These texts are difficult to classify in categories that are, in-evitably, artificial, but they show the efforts of physicians and patients to adapt and individualize the knowledge found in specialized manu-als for maintaining good health. In this way, they offer a fully person-alized vision of illness and its treatment that serves as counterpoint to the homogenization and the generalizations of health regimens dissem-inated through printed materials during the Renaissance. In spite of the differences that can be seen in the recommendations for Juan Rena and Juan de Alarcón, coincidences of a practical nature exist. The sim-ilar kinds of meats recommended, the mistrust of vegetables, legumes, tubers, and fresh fruit, along with the little regard given to fish, with few exceptions, as with milk and dairy products, or the pursuit of the pleasures of life and of happiness, with the exception of sexual activity, are just some examples.

It is important to highlight the value that these texts must have had for their owners. One of them, the oldest, was written by the patient himself, Juan Rena, which shows how involved he was. It is also signifi-cant that the language of these prescriptions is Spanish instead of Latin, a point that should not be disregarded, since these prescriptions were written by educated physicians for people who knew Latin well. This highlights the importance that the vernacular had acquired in transmit-ting medical knowledge even among the elite.

Finally, regarding the medical tradition represented in the original documents studied here, a perfect transposition may be seen of what is recommended in prescriptive medical treatises to the world of practice. Medieval approaches continued to be in force. In this way, the appeal to allopathic principles to fight off illnesses and the feeding of the sick with diets contrary to the constitutional qualities typical of the *cuadro morboso* [clinical case] are reflected in the individual examples of Juan Rena and Juan de Alarcón.

APPENDIX

1 *Prescripciones dietéticas de [Juan Rena] para seguir a partir del 12 de mayo de 1524*

Archivo General de Navarra, Archivos Particulares-Rena, caj. 105, no. 17–7.

[1r] [1] El jueues en la noche tomeré antes de çenar dos píldolas de 12 granos cada una; abré comido al yantar cozido y ceneré entre las 8 y 9 vna (sic) yemas blandas. [2] El viernes tomeré 1 caldo y comeré como suelo. A la noche çeneré de dieta. [3] El sábado tomeré 1 bano (sic) a las 6 y staré en él vna ora; salido dél me lauaré los pies con vrinas calientes y me yré a la cama en la qual staré dos oras. Comeré a las 10 [çumo] de vn pollo assado e de polla cozida o vn poco de çumo de carnero. Por antepasto passas sin granos. Sobremesa almendras tostas. A las siete de la tarde tornaré al baño por media hora e después lavaré los pies con las vrinas e después de linpios de la humedad me haré vntar con la vnçión caliente e enboluerán los pies en vnos lienços tenplados, e estaré vna hora sin çenar en la cama. Haré la çena de vnas yemas frescas e passas e almendras y vna hora después me vntarán los reñones con vngüento rosado e después dormiré. A la mañana antes de entrar en el bano me haré vntar el hígado con vngüento sandalino e rosado, e cada mañana antes de vntar el hígado haré con un lienço linpiar lo que de la vnçión del día antes quedado oviere. Si días hiziere de muncho calor haré poner sobre la vnçión del hígado vn lençezico delgado mojado en agua rosada e vnas gotas de vinagre templado. [1v] Abiendo vsado el baño quatro días desta manera al quinto tomaré vna píldora de la massa que queda, la quoal pese quinze granos; digo que la tomaré martes en la noche e el miércoles no haré baño fasta la noche ante de çena. [4] Jueues e los tres días siguientes me haré bañar como antes, e domingo en la noche tomaré otra píldora e lunes no me bañaré fasta la noche. [5] El martes siguiente haré tomar vna onça del vngüento e añedirle peso de ocho granos de poluo de euforbio, e salido del baño de esa mañana e linpio de la humedad de las vrinas me haré vntar los pies con esta vnçión caliente e la tendré por dos horas, e después me haré linpiar della los pies para me levantar, e a la noche dexarela toda la noche. [6] El viernes añediré a lo

que del vngüento quedare a vna onça doze granos de euforbio e con este vngüento me vntaré los días que restare de baño. [7] Después que me dexaré de bañar me haré cada mañana por quatro días poner vn paño de agua ardiente que sea buena en cada pie por vna hora, el qual paño se tienple entre las manos. De quatro en quatro días vsaré vna píldora ante çena mientra no hiziese eçessivo calor. [2r] Pondrán para cada decoçión vn cántaro de vino blanco e otro de agua de ferreros e vn açumbre de vinagre, e de las yerbas la quantidad que señale de cada vna \vn puno (sic)/, e de rosas e granos de arraihán de cada vno dos puños. Lo que pondrán para cozer es los granos de arraihán e cozerá ochavo de hora e luego las hojas de laurel, e como vn buen fervor ayan passado echen todas las otras yerbas eçepto la mançanilla e melliloto, que se pondrán al vltimo fervor, e las rosas que se han de poner quitando la caldera del fuego basta que mengue este cozimiento el vn terçio e queden los dos terçios.En lugar de saluia pondrán ruda con lombrizes \vna dozena/. Haziendo tienpo tenplado durará cada decoçión para quatro dias, y si muncho calor hiziere se renovará pasados tres días.

Recepta del ungüento
Olei antiqui, olei yrini, ana uncias v.
Opoponaci, galbani, bdeli, storacis, ana uncias semis.
Resolutis gumarum in vino con cera alba.
Fiat unguentum.
Evforbium, sicut supra dictum est.
[2v] A XI de mayo 1524
16875 Martes 26 de abril empecé a tomar los banos.

2 *Prescripciones dietéticas destinadas a Juan Rena* [1528]

Archivo General de Navarra, Archivos Particulares-Rena, caj. 105, no. 17–5

[1r] El regimiento que el señor micer Joan a de tener es lo seguiente:

[1] Primeramente quanto a las carnes comerá galina y su linage, perdigón, tórtolas, palominos caseros y toda manera de aues del canpo o criadas, eçepto las de agoa y su natura, y sobre todo posarides gruesos y carnero, y esto sea de la manera que su merçé mandare, pero la mayor parte asado o en pasteles. [2] De pescados ningunos son buenos y quando hubiere de ser sea pescado fresco de vna cola o cangregos de río o cancros de la mar, o truchuelas muy frescas o yomejuelas, y desto pocas vezes. [3] Yemas de huebos frescas, asadas con açúcar y canela o echas en agoa de azar con acúcar y canela. [4] De las frutas

piñones y dátiles, higos y pasas, garbanços tostados, almendras y abelanas, nuezes moscadas en que sirua toda confitura, con que no sea calabacate o limones, y quando quisiere carne de membrillo sea con speçias. Puede comer cebolas cozidas y asadas y ajos cozidos o asados e hierbasanta, ysopo y perexil. [5] Todas espeçias coma y miel, el pan sea de hun día cozido, el bino sea blanco maduro olorioso y dulçe, agoado tenpradamente con agoa cozida con canela.

[1v] [6] Tomareys por sobre comer y çenar vna tostada muy delgada mojada en vino que bebeys puro, y sacado del binno cargarle a de ambas partes de la póluora y comerlaeys, y después de comida no bebaes nenguna cosa. [7] Guoardaos de todas cosas agres y verdes y de todo pescado, ecepto lo dicho, y de todas cosas saladas y carnes peliagudas y todas cosas de leche, y de agoa cruda. Andad muy aropado y mucho secando a los pies y a la cabeça. Procúrese en todo caso mucho plazer e euítese de todos enojos. [8] Las cosas señor que abeys de azer de medeçinas son las siguientes: en el quarto postrero desta luna, ocho días antes tomad tres maynanas y tres noches los xarabes que quedan ordenados y la tablila primero d'eyllos. Después, al quarto día, tomad las siete pilloras que quedan ordenadas y ese día se se xiga como las que se purguan. [9] Después de purgado nuebe días aseo, tomad la tablila que queda ordenada y beber sobre ello hun trago de vino primero o agoa de asençios. [10] Después desto echo cumplido cada noche vos huntad las caderas y el petineon con esta huntura, la mano bien caliente y después denbebido el vnguinte ponga hun paño caliente, y esto se aga dentro en la cama bien caliente y abrigado. [11] Tome agora cada maynana vna ochaua de metridato desecho en vino blanco tibio en amaneçiendo.

[2r] [12] Quoando quisieredes antes, procurad muchos juegos y plazeres, y sea dos o tres oras después de aver çenado o comido, y el día que esto se hubiere de azer el comer sea mediado y no muy repleto.

[2v] [en blanco]

[3r] Jesuchristo

[Col. A] Clabos de girofre, nuezes mozcadas, ginginbre blanquo, zedoari, graringal, pebre longo, pebre redondo, granos de genebro, scorçio de citrón, scorcio de toronjas, flor de salbia, basili, flor de romero, ençens masclo, aloe, exatic, menta redonda, grana de laurel.

[Col. B] Poleo, regal, genciana, calamenti, flor de sabico, rosas blanquas, ameos, spicanardi, cunbebas doméstiquas, cardamoni, magna, calami aromatiçi, camapiteos, semiente de nigela, maçis, flor d'abet, semiente de artamisa. De todo lo susodicho sendas dragmas con sus escriptos cada uno en su paperico. Anbre gris, roybarbo, romero, ruda, salbia, tomillo, poleo y picon sendas dragmas otras cada uno por sí con su scripto, y si todo lo susodicho es doblado ya es muy mejor.

3 *Prescripciones dietéticas destinadas a Juan de Alarcón* [1538]

Archivo General de Navarra, Archivos Particulares-Rena, caj. 82, no. 9–1

[1] El señor Alarcón tiene vna complexión muy regalada y delicada porque tiene el hígado algo flaco en virtud y el sthómago húmedo y el vaço muy ventoso y la digestión primera y segunda débiles y tardías, y para esto a my me paresce que será bien que continúe para el reparo de su sthómago a traer sobre él el talengoncito que le ordoné bien faxado. [2] Ítem que tome cada mañana mientras durare una tableta de las que se ordenaron con vn trago o dos de vino blanco muy bueno serenado de por de noche con dos o tres oijas de acensones amargos machucadas puestas drentro, porque aunque al tomar del dicho vino le paresca amargo serle a muy probechoso. [3] Ítem tomará sobre comer o de la pólbora que tiene o de vna poca de dragea de canela y de anís hechan. [4] Ítem hará exercicio en aiunas yugando a la pelota un rato ata que comience a sudar y otro tanto antes que cene. Coma de su ave y carnero cozido en las mañanas con ierbasancta y perexil y assado en las tardes. Beba buen vino blanco o tinto claro maduro, amesado medianamente. No beba agua cruda, no coma fruta cruda ny coma cosa agre ny salada ny pelaguda, ny legumina ny pescado sino fuese de alguna truncha. Coma algunos huebos frescos y de alguna manteca fresca. No duerma entre día ni haga collaciones, beba poco a sus comeres, quítese de enojos y tome quanto plazer pudiere excepto que no conversse con mugeres porque a él le pesará. [5] Haga buscar un poco de hígado de lobo y yo le diré lo que a de hazer para su salud, y con tanto Dios le tenga de su mano y quedo a su seruicio.

Doctor Medrano (*rubricado*).

4 *Prescripciones dietéticas destinadas a Juan de Alarcón* [1539/1540–51]

Archivo General de Navarra, Archivos Particulares-Rena, caj. 82, no. 9–2

Jesucristo, María

[1] Lo que al señor Alarcón conuiene es que esté vn mes continuo cada semana vna vez de tomar de mañana a las vi horas vna onca de cañafístula en caña li[...] y chupando la pulpa de dentro, y desque la aya tomado tome detrás cuarto vna almendra de trementina de abet

que sea muy buena y después no duerma, y passada vna hora o dos se podrá llebantar, y no coma \después de tomado esto/ hasta las xi horas ni salga de casa hasta después de comer, y así lo continuará esto como está dicho:

[2] Ítem se haga traer dos oncas de vnguiento rosado y con él le vntarán cada tarde vna vez todos los riñones detrás y encima le pernan vn paño mojado en agua rosada, y de mañana no se vnte. [3] Et haziendo esto \y después/ es menester que se guarde de comer leche ni queso ni carnes de pelagudo si no fuesse cabrito o de algún gaçapo o ternera, haunque de la liebre puede comer el caldo, ni coma cosas saladas ni agres, ni vercas ni castañas ni ráuano, sino las hojas, y legumina si no fuesse caldo de garbancos, el qual deue mucho usar, ni coma pescado de mar \ni enguilas/, ni fruta y menos ubas, no coma roz.[4]Deue comer gallina o su linage, carnero o perdiz o codornizes y todo linage de aues saluo ánades y ansares. Puede comer guebos frescos y blandos y de alguna trucha o madrilla, de algún caldo de garbancos y alguna almendrada o de algunas acelgas y borraynas y ortigas cozidas con su perrexil. Puede comer pasas y almendras y piñones. [5] No beua sino al comer, y entonces su buen vino blanco bien aguado, no duerma entre día y menos sobre comer ni cena. Procure de hacer exercicio moderado antes de comer y de cena, y no sobre comer ni cena hata que passen tres horas, e sobre todo guarde el exercicio de las mugeres, especialmente sobre comer. Aparte de si de toda tristeza y enojo y no trayga demasiada ropa sobre los riñones ni retenga mucho la orina.

NOTES

1 This work was carried out as part of the research group Sciència.cat (www.sciencia.cat), currently funded as a project of MICIU-AEI/FEDER PGC2018–095417-B-C64. I would like to thank Montserrat Cabré i Pairet, Jon Arrizabalaga Valbuena, Lluís Cifuentes i Comamala, Juan Jesús Virto Ibáñez, Carmen Sánchez Téllez, Félix Segura Urra, Itzíar Zabalza Aldave, and the two anonymous readers for their comments and clarifications to the original text, an earlier version of which was published in *Dynamis* 34.1 (2014): 169–92. Unless otherwise noted, translations are by Gregory Baum.

2 On the importance of vernacular languages in this kind of work, see Gutiérrez Rodilla (2009, 39). Regarding their spread in Catalan, see Cifuentes i Comamala (2006, 96–105). *Il Perché* o *Liber de homine* [Book about man] (1474), a health regimen and a treatise on physiognomy by the Bolognese physician Girolamo Manfredi, was translated into Catalan

(1499) and Spanish (1567). Its first part, dedicated to preserving health, corresponds to a health regimen divided into seven parts. On this last matter, see Carré and Cifuentes (2006, 171–2). Printed texts could also become open collections, as may be seen in a copy of a health regimen from Salerno that was published by Jacobum Myt expensis Bartholomei Trot in Lyon in 1516 – *Regimen sanitatis Salerni: accurate castigatum adiecta tabula in calce libri hactenus non impressa* [The Salerno health regimen, carefully corrected in the attached and hitherto unpublished table at the bottom of the book] – and which is kept in the Biblioteca Navarra: "At the end of the text, annotated by a hand from the same period, follows a list of more than forty prescriptions written by two anonymous hands in Latin, Spanish, and Catalan, a collection that completes the domestic advice offered by the health regimen for maintaining health and preventing illness" (Cabré 2008, 180).

3 A complete overview on the vernacularization and continuity of the medieval scientific tradition during the Renaissance may be found in Cifuentes i Comamala (2008, 123–48), and a brief approach, with regard to some of the Renaissance works in Spanish connected to the *regimina santitatis*, in López Piñero (2006, 449–50). The influence of this literature reached the seventeenth century, as the Spanish version of the *Regimen sanitatis ad regem Aragonum* [Health regimen to the king of Aragon] of Arnau de Vilanova (composed around 1305) was published in Barcelona (1606) by Jerónimo de Mondragón, whose title is *Maravilloso regimiento i orden de vivir, para tener salud, i alargar la vida; que compuso, el doctisimo Medico Arnaldo de Vilanova, para el serenisimo Rei de Aragon, don Jaime el Segundo: sacado de vn libro latino de mano mui antiguo, traslado del mesmo original del Autor; i puesto en esta lengua, por el Licenciado Hieronymo de Mondragón: porque de tan singular Obra, pueda gozar todo el mundo* [Marvellous regimen and order of living to have health and extend life; composed by Arnaldo de Vilanova, learned doctor, for the most serene king of Aragon don Jaime the Second: taken from a Latin book of a very old hand, translated by the author himself and translated into this language by Hieronymo de Mondragón: so that everyone can enjoy such singular work] (1609) (Cruz Cruz 1997, 295–6).

4 On the proliferation of texts for individual use in the sixteenth century, see also Solomon (2010). For the Italian world, see Cavallo (2011, 196–200).

5 One of the documents is alluded to as a "regimiento" (Appendix 2). During the medieval period and the Renaissance, dietetics forms part of the teaching of practical medicine, together with pharmacopeia and surgery for the treatment of illnesses. The Latin term used most frequently to define it was *diaeta*, a term with a double meaning. In its strict sense, it referred to food and drink, although in a broader sense it referred to what

was mentioned at the beginning of this work: the "not natural things."
Unlike pharmacopeia or surgery, diet was used not only as a cure but also
as a way of preventing disease and preserving health (Nicoud 2010, 16).

6 On the evolution of the medical *consilia*, see Nicoud (2007, 314–36). From
the final years of the Middle Ages, in the Spanish world, I am familiar
with the medical *consilium* of one *licenciado* Antonio, physician to the
Duke of Brittany, who moved to Vitoria to treat García Álvarez de Toledo, first Duke of Alba († 1488) (García Ballester 2001, 357–8), and with a
magnificent example, of Catalan origin and very similar to the Navarrese
documents, whose intended recipient is unknown and the physician/
author of which can be inferred, without total certainty, from surrounding
papers: "Primo, vos guordau de pa alís e mal cuyt e calent; de vi agre, ni
fort ni agut; de tota carn vella, ni grossa ni en ast (la demés, en olla, jove
e grassa); de formatge, nous, castanyes, codonys, nesples; de totes coses
estíptiques e caldes; de allada, de pebrada, de peix, especialment salat o
bestinal. De les coses demunt vedades podeu menjar poch e a tart. – Los
remeys. – Beureu alguns matins aquestes coses següents: licor d'ordi ab let
d'amenles e sucre; let de amenles ab gra de carabasses, melons, cogombres
e semblant; dragagant, let de somera, let de cabra, e sobretot lo serigot,
que val més; aygua de indívia o de licsons, stil·lades, de seba blancha,
tota hora ab sucre, adés una, adés altre. – Les viandes. – Tota carn grassa e
carabasses, letugues, spinachs, bledes, borratges, ortigues ortolanes, fonoll
marí e semblants. Ítem, si voleu fer axarob, recipe rel de fonoll, de juyvert,
de gram, *pentafilon* (que és peucrist), ciurons negres (quatre o sinch), figues
blanques, pances, tot bollit ab ayga de font; e beureu d'aquella aygua de
matí un gotet, e de vespre, ab sucre. E si·n voleu fer axarob, com l'aygua
sia colada e samada, meteu-hi sucre e feu-ne exerob. A part de fora, ajau
draps prims banyats ab aygaròs o de plantatge o de morella vera" [First,
beware of unleavened bread, poorly cooked and hot; of sour, strong, or
spicy wine; of all kinds of old, tough, or roasted meat (the rest, in a pot,
young and with fat); of cheese, walnuts, chestnuts, quinces, medlars; of all
kinds of hot and styptic things; of sauces like those made of bread mixed
with water, salt, and crushed garlic, or made of peppers, garlic, parsley,
and vinegar; of fish, especially those that are salty or without scales. You
can eat a little of these forbidden things from time to time. – The remedies. –
Some mornings you will drink the following things: barley liqueur with
almond milk and sugar; almond milk with pumpkin seeds, melons, cu-
cumbers, and the like; tragacanth, donkey's milk, goat's milk, particularly
the whey, which is more worthwhile; endive and lettuce water, distilled,
and white onion, always with sugar, now one, now the other. – Meats. –
All kinds of fatty meat and squash, lettuce, spinach, chard, borage, garden nettles, rosemary, and the like. Also, if you wish to make syrup, take

fennel root, parsley, grass root, *pentafilon* (which is creeping cinquefoil [*potentilla reptans*]), black beans (four or five), white figs, and raisins, all boiled with spring water; and you will drink of that water, in the morning, a glass, and in the evening, with sugar. And if you want to make syrup with it, when the water is strained and has been reduced, add sugar and make the syrup. For your skin, take thin fabrics bathed with rose water, plantain, or black nightshade] (Arxiu Històric de la Ciutat de Barcelona, Fons notarial, IX.2, carp. 5, manid 110 (http://www.sciencia.cat/db /scienciacat-db.htm).

7 On several of these questions, see Cabré (2011).

8 Together with the *Regimine sanitatis*, another notable work is a book of *cozina* [cookery] (Archivo General de Navarra [AGN], Archivos Particulares-Rena, caj. 105, no. 14–1). It is interesting that both these copies stand out among almost half a hundred, the majority of which have religious content, that are collected in that year (1520). Another hand adds the annotation *antidotariu[m]* [antidote] to the book *Postillas de Nicolás de Lira*, an error perhaps from confusing this with the *Antidotarium Nicolai* (a book from Salerno), when in reality it is a theological work.

9 See Goñi Gaztambide (1985). For an updated study on the biographies of Juan Rena and Juan de Alarcón, see Chocarro Huesa and Segura Urra (2013, 37–68 and 70–4).

10 See Lobera de Ávila (1996, 59).

11 The two essential organs that participate in the digestive function are the stomach and the liver (Gil-Sotres 1996, 738).

12 See Appendix 2, 10. On the activities of the physicians mentioned, both of whom were connected to the Navarrese elite, see Sánchez Álvarez (2010, 40–4 and 129–39). Though it is not possible to clarify Juan Rena's general state of health throughout his life, what is certain is that, aside from his time in Navarra, several lists of medicines that he acquired are preserved. In June of 1528 there is notice of his purchase of "exaropes, agoas cordiales, vna mededina laxatiba" [syrups, cordial waters, a laxative medicine] by order of Master Juan de Elizondo, "echa con decotión cordial y pectoral" [made with heart and pectoral decotion]; on 10 September, "xaropes y agoas y vna medecina laxatiba para pugar a su merced … Ata XXVIII del dicho mes llebaron para su merced vnos julepes y vnas tabletas" [syrups and water and a laxative medicine to purge your Grace … until the 28th of said month they brought him some juleps and tablets]; between 20 and 24 October he purchased different syrups; on the 28th, "vna presa de píldoras por hordinació del doctor Sanctacara" [pills by Doctor Sactacara's orders]; the 30th, "vn vngüento magistral" [a magistral unguent] together with other medicines; on 1 November, "hun lectuario confortatibo hordenado por el Doctor Sanctacara echo con polbos cordiales y

otras diversas cosas" [a comforting medicine made with cordial powder and other things], taken to Antonio Caparroso. Further purchases were postponed until 18 March of the following year (AGN, Archivos Particulares-Rena, caj. 105, no. 15–3, fol. 1r–2v). Such purchases implied a "crisis" of a certain importance in Juan Rena's health, which very well might have had something to do with the second dietetic prescription.

13 See, for example, AGN, Archivos Particulares-Rena, no. 7–1 and 7–2, caj. 87.

14 On the biography of Juan Vallés and his literary activity, see Serrano Larráyoz (2008).

15 AGN, Archivos Particulares-Rena, caj. 105, no. 17–2. Other cures supplied by Juan Vallés for the same pain may be found in the same document. A "recebta del señor don Juan de Viamont" [recipe delivered by Juan de Viamont] is also preserved, on the back of which is annotated: "para la hijada" [for the flank] (AGN, Archivos Particulares-Rena, caj. 105, no. 17–4).

16 *Sobremesa* refers to "after-meal conversation, digestion, and relaxation."

17 On fish and how it was regarded in medieval health regimens, see Gil-Sotres (1996, 695–9).

18 On the medical consideration of eggs, see Gil-Sotres (1996, 699–701).

19 Included in the treatment to follow in 1528 was the instruction to drink every morning "en amaneciendo" lukewarm white wine, to which he would add an eighth part of mithridate; see Appendix 2, 11.

20 On sleep hygiene, see Gil-Sotres (1996, 736–40).

21 In 1542, Doctor Medrano was "quarenta y dos anos poco más o menos" [more or less forty-two years old] (AGN, Tribunales Reales. Procesos, 130784).

22 On 5 August, he buys "vn xarope conpuesto, echo con III onzas de reubarbaro y otras diversas cosas con su decotión muy copiosa en quantidat de IIII libras por hordinación del Doctor Leggasa" [a syrup made with three ounces of rhubarb and other things with a copious three-pound decoction, by orders of Doctor Leggasa] (AGN, Archivos Particulares-Rena, caj. 105, no. 15–5).

23 On exercise in medieval medical authorities, see Gil-Sotres (1996, 601–25).

24 AGN, Archivos Particulares-Rena, caj. 82, no. 9–3.

25 As in the case of Juan Rena, physicians absolutely reject migratory aquatic birds, as occurs in the medieval period; medieval health regimens consider birds less nutritious than quadrupeds, but they were also more digestible, for which reason physicians gave preferences to eating them (Gil-Sotres 1996, 693–4).

26 Doctor Medrano considers eating any kind of vegetable unsuitable. Even rice, an item of some luxury at the end of the Middle Ages and the beginning of the Renaissance, is not considered ideal for curing Juan de Alarcón.

27 According to Arnau de Vilanova, a vegetable broth opens and cleans the capillary veins of the liver and the urinary tracts, being a good remedy for stones, especially if parsley is added to the broth (Gil-Sotres 1996, 681).
28 Trout also appears in the 1528 diet intended for Juan Rena.
29 See Bau and Fernanda Canavese (2006, 136).
30 The medieval medical tradition advised against drinking while fasting (Gil-Sotres 1996, 726).
31 On these issues, see Gil-Sotres (1996, 740–3).

WORKS CITED

Bau, Andrea María and Gabriela Fernanda Canavese. 2006. "'Agua que cura, agua que alimenta'. La dietética para sanos y el uso del agua en la sociedad española bajomedieval y moderna." *Cuadernos de Historia de España* 80: 127–46.

Cabré, Montserrat. 2008. "Los consejos para hermosear ('libros' I–III) en el *Regalo de la vida humana* de Juan Vallés." In *Regalo de la vida humana [Juan Vallés]*, coordinated by Fernando Serrano Larráyoz, vol. 2, 171–202. Pamplona and Vienna. Gobierno de Navarra and Österreichische Nationalbibliothek.

Cabré, Montserrat. 2011. "Keeping Beauty Secrets in Early Modern Iberia." In *Secrets and Knowledge in Medicine and Science, 1500–1800*, edited by Elaine Leong and Alisha Rankin, 169–73. Farnham and Burlington: Ashgate.

Carré, Antònia, and Lluís Cifuentes. 2006. "Éxito y difusión de la literatura de Problemas en la Castilla del siglo XVI: la traducción castellana de *Il Perché* de Girolamo Manfredi (Zaragoza, 1567)." *Asclepio* 58.1: 149–96. https://doi.org/10.3989/asclepio.2006.v58.i1.5.

Cavallo, Sandra. 2011. "Secrets to Healthy Living: The Revival of the Preventive Paradigm in Late Renaissance Italy." In *Secrets and Knowledge in Medicine and Science, 1500–1800*, edited by Elaine Leong and Alisha Rankin, 191–212. Farnham and Burlington: Ashgate.

Chocarro Huesa, Mercedes, and Félix Segura Urra. 2013. *Inventario de la documentación de Rena. Archivo Real y General de Navarra*. Pamplona: Gobierno de Navarra.

Cifuentes i Comamala, Lluís. 2006. *La ciencia en català a l'Edat Mitjana i el Renaixement*. 2nd ed. Barcelona and Palma de Mallorca: Universitat de Barcelona and Universitat de les Illes Balears.

Cifuentes i Comamala, Lluís. 2008. "La ciencia en vulgar y las élites laicas, de la Edad Media al Renacimiento." In *Regalo de la vida humana [Juan Vallés]*, coordinated by Fernando Serrano Larráyoz, vol. 2, 123–48. Pamplona and Vienna. Gobierno de Navarra and Österreichische Nationalbibliothek.

Cruz Cruz, Juan. 1997. *Dietética medieval. Apéndice con la versión castellana del "Régimen de salud" de Arnaldo de Vilanova*. Huesca: La Val de Onsera.

García Ballester, Luis García. 2001. *La búsqueda de la salud. Sanadores y enfermos en la España medieval*. Barcelona: Península.

Gil-Sotres, Pedro. 1996. "Introducción." In *Opera Medica Omnia [Arnaldi de Villanova]*, edited by Luis García Ballester, Luis McVaugh, et al., vol. 10.1, 471–885. Barcelona: Universitat de Barcelona and Fundació Noguera.

Goñi Gaztambide, José. 1985. *Historia de los obispos de Pamplona, siglo XVI*. Vol. 3, 254–82. Pamplona: Ediciones Universidad de Navarra and Gobierno de Navarra.

Gutiérrez Rodilla, Bertha. 2009. "La adecuación lingüística al destinatario en los textos médicos instructivos y de divulgación del Renacimiento castellano." *Res Diachronicae* 7: 37–46.

Lobera de Ávila, Luis. 1996. *Banquete de nobles caballeros*. Donostia/San Sebastián: R&B Ediciones.

López Piñero, José María. 2006. "Los orígenes de los estudios sobre la salud pública en la España renacentista." *Revista Española Salud Pública* 80.5: 445–56. https://doi.org/10.1590/S1135-57272006000500003.

Nicoud, Marilyn. 2007. *Les régimes de santé au Moyen Âge: naissance et diffusión d'une écriture médicale (XIIIe–XVe siècle)*. Vol. 1. Rome: École Française de Rome.

Nicoud, Marilyn. 2010. "La dietética medievale: testi e lettori." *Minerva* 23: 15–34.

Sánchez Álvarez, Julio. 2010. *El Protomedicato navarro y las Cofradías sanitarias de San Cosme y San Damián. El control social de las profesiones sanitarias en Navarra (1496–1829)*. Pamplona: Gobierno de Navarra

Serrano Larráyoz, Fernando. 2008. "Juan Vallés (c. 1496–1563): vida y obra de un humanista navarro de la primera mitad del siglo XVI." In *Regalo de la vida humana*, coordinated by Fernando Serrano Larráyoz, vol. 2, 17–75. Pamplona and Vienna: Gobierno de Navarra and Österreichische Nationalbibliothek.

Solomon, Michael. 2010. *Fictions of Well-Being: Sickly Readers and Vernacular Medical Writing in Late Medieval and Early Modern Spain*. Philadelphia and Oxford: University of Pennsylvania Press.

5 Etiquette on the Stage: Spanish Renaissance Theatre and the History of Manners (Juan del Enzina and Lucas Fernández)

JULIO VÉLEZ-SAINZ

The thirteenth-century *Quisquis es in mensa* [For those at the table] warns the nobleman that "a morsel which has been tasted should not be returned to the dish"; the English *Book of Nurture* asserts "A man who blows his nose in the table cloth is ill-bred"; Erasmus of Rotterdam's *De civilitate* [On civility] reprimands the passers-by who greet someone "qui urinam reddit aut alvum exonerat" [urinating or defecating]. These acts, now openly considered "disgusting," were common enough that a major European author such as Erasmus dedicated time to the matter. This evolution in social customs points to the formation of a conscience on manners. Albeit most of the treatises of good manners were designed for noblemen, once printed they arguably established a set of social customs that were passed on to the paying masses. These customs were first attained by the nobility and then trickled down on to the rest of society in a slow but inexorable process.[1] The immense number of treatises on good manners, which flourished from fourteenth- through eighteenth-century Europe, dwell on the most insignificant aspects of life (eating, drinking, proper bed and table manners), and are mostly directed to courtiers, and showcase their progression. These treatises are a largely understudied part of a bigger discussion on the fashioning of a philosophical ideal of manhood – treatises on the nature of man, scholarly *tractati* on notions of nobility and citizenship, medical treatises on proper eating and exercise, and, significantly, courtly treatises defending female nature from the scorn of medieval misogyny (defences of women, *querelles des femmes*).[2] With the help of the printing press, many of these treatises, mostly intended to educate noblemen, were broadcast to a greater public, which found in them a set of behaviours that endowed them with the prestige and mystique of the nobility.[3] These notions were part of the discourse of a number of scholarly academies, and artistic performances served to underscore these modes of behaviour. At the same time, the appearance of public entertaining and *otium* on the stage served as a means to publicize modes of behaviour that were present in the medieval *mirrors of princes*. This combination served to foster a set of arts of eating and drinking (*artes edendi* and *bibendi*): behaving, conversation, courtliness, virtuosity, and a set of social manners that created what was considered acceptable, educated, and "civilized." The present article studies the creation, consolidation, and dissemination of a set of behaviours in the social life of early modern Europeans, and its reverberations within Spanish Renaissance drama, a much-neglected field of study, even among Hispanists. In order to do that, I will examine some influential plays against the backdrop of what Norbert Elias has aptly termed *The History of Manners*. Under this lens, the work of Spanish Renaissance playwrights Juan del Enzina and Lucas Fernández offers new insights into how the early modern European self was constructed.

The majority of scholarship devoted to the art of living has centred on very particular aspects of the history of manners through the optics of sociohistorical research. Elias's groundbreaking *Über den Prozeß der Zivilisation* [*The Civilizing Process*] vividly depicts the process by which western society has repressed the natural instincts and bodily functions that we find distasteful nowadays.[4] The western subject internalized moral standards and feelings of disgust and contempt that, far from being natural or rational, represented another stage in the individual psyche dealing with society. The latter controls the psychological and social completion of the individual, who is now seen as a child. Elias utilizes Freudian theoretical underpinnings that were widespread at the time his book was written but are now largely contested. For Elias, we repress taboo subjects such as defecation, the naked body, or violence through the standards of good manners at the table, proper use of utensils, adequate speech, or, simply, rational or hygienic ways of treating our bodily waste. From this perspective, the fork and the napkin become ways of sheltering the self from other people as a reaction to the fear of contamination from them. The present article attempts to describe and analyse the means by which the "civilizing process" grew out of the restricted circles for which it was intended, and how it went from being a courtly ideal to widespread notions of good social behaviour, manners, and civility. The printing press and the emergence of a literary field and theatre for the masses played a significant role in this process.

The anonymous *Diálogos en que se muestra cuánto convengan a su majestad las reformaciones que se han propuesto* [Dialogues that show his majesty the usefulness of the reforms that have been proposed], from around 1590 and edited by Fernando Bouza, is proof of theatre's role. Within the context of the well-known concept of the world as theatre, one of the interlocutors asks a lady about the criteria for judging plays:

De que las ha oído alabar?
Al que compuso la comedia, si hizo hablar a cada personaje conforme al *decoro* de la persona que introduce. Y el maestro y representantes se alaban, se representan las comedias conforme a los tiempos, si los vestidos son conforme a las personas que representan, si los ademanes y posturas y aseo del vestido es tal cual conviene a la persona que representa.
Dice v. M. que esa es la obligación de los representantes, de modo que parecería mal el que representase el personaje de una dama si sólo entrase mal aseada en el tablado, un galán si entrase cayéndosele la capa, si no fuese que las palabras o la ocasión del galán que representa lo requiriese. (Bouza 2001, 17)

[What have you heard about their worth?
I have heard the praise of the author of the comedy, if he made each character speak according to the decorum of the person introduced. Comedies are represented according to the times and the director and actors are praised, if the dresses are according to the people represented, if the gestures, postures, and cleanliness of the dress suit the person represented.
Your Grace says this is the obligation of the actors, so it would be wrong to represent a lady if she came on stage in an untidy manner, or a gallant if he came on with a drooping cape, unless the words or the occasion required it.]

The two speakers make it clear that the stylistic notion of *decorum* is related to the actors' clothing, gestures, stage positions, and hygiene [*aseo*] being in accordance with the characters being represented. A *galán*, as a representative of the nobility, must behave according to his social stature. His cloak must be perfectly placed on his shoulders; subsequently, the lady must enter the stage with suitable manners. The anonymous author of the *Diálogos* develops the notion of decorum as seen in Horace's *Ars* (158–60) and Aristotle's *Rhetorics* (3,7). In a work well known in the late fifteenth and early sixteenth centuries, *Praenotamenta Terentii*, Badius Ascensius devotes four chapters to the notion of decorum. In one of them, he highlights the Horatian example of the difference in speech between Davo, the slave, and a hero (1053–4). *Decorum*, as a point of judgment for the quality of the play, is intricately related to the adequacy of the characters' condition, state, and representation. The world as a stage motif serves to provide, among other things, a representation of the ideals that inform the society that produces these works. In my view, and very much like seventeenth-century didactic French drama,[5] sixteenth-century Spanish plays performed a set of behaviours and manners derived from the medieval court that could be framed within courtly ideals and the notion of ennobling love in the autumn of the Middle Ages.

At the time of Lucas Fernández and Juan del Enzina, arts of eating and drinking (*artes edendi* and *bibendi*) sanctioned ways of eating and nourishing. For instance, Luis Lobera de Ávila´s 1530 *Banquete de nobles caballeros* [Banquet of noble gentlemen] collects previous medical knowledge and recommends "en el comer no ha de ser mucha la quantidad, de manera que ni quede repleto ni tampoco ambriento sino que medianamente contento, antes quede con algún apetito que con repleción" [in eating you should not ingest a great amount, so as not to feel replenished or hungry but adequately content. You had better feel a bit hungry instead of fed up] (1952, 24v). Lobera asserts that the nobleman should follow the medieval ideal of *mesura* so as to be considered acceptable and "civilized." Opposed to this aristocratic notion of eating, we find instances in which characters gorge on food as an example *ex contrario*. In Lucas Fernández´s *Farsa del Nacimiento de Nuestro Señor* [Farce of the birth of Our Lord], the shepherd Pascual celebrates the advent of Christ by overeating:

Digo que de aquí adelante
quiero andar más perpujante,
comer, beber de contino
tasajo, soma y buen vino. (vv. 24–7)

[From here on now / I want to walk stronger / by constantly eating and drinking / cold cuts, bread, and good wine]

A number of rustic foods are mentioned: cottage cheese ("buenos requesones"), crumbs ("miga cocha"), milk ("remamar la cabra mocha"), piglets ("lechones"), castrated goats ("castrones"), ducks ("ansarones"), unborn lambs ("abortones"), lambs ("corderitos"), twin cows ("mielgos"), younger and older goats ("chibos y cabritos"), etc. Pascual includes an almost infinite list of meals completely unfit for the Renaissance nobleman. The contraposition between noble and rustic behaviour is repeated in Fernández's *Égloga o farsa del Nascimiento* when Macario and Gil reprimand ill-bred shepherds ("pastorcicos malcriados") for not knowing how to eat ("gallofear") (vv. 281–7). Accordingly Gil in his *Comedia de Bras Gil y Berenguella* feels that he cannot eat properly due to his inordinate lovesickness:

El comer, ño ay quien lo coma,
el dormir, ño se me apega,
como modorra borrega
estoy lleno de carcoma (vv. 33–6)

[I cannot eat, / I cannot sleep, / I feel like a sick lamb / full of malady]

These examples show that a tremendous stage performativity of the self is at play in Lucas Fernández's depiction of the shepherds, even more acute since Fernández pits his shepherds against already courtly characters such as the soldier, a particularly odd combination of *miles gloriosus* and Renaissance courtier who is able to provide definitions and species of love. Fernández's *Farsas y églogas* (1514) have traditionally been seen as merely the first continuations of Enzina's model of pastoral plays. The book, however, is important for other matters: first and foremost, it is the first autonomous collection of dramatic pieces given to the printing press in Europe.[6] Secondly, it quickly changes between the secular and religious, as the collection includes seven plays, four of which are devoted to worldly matters while the rest delve into spirituality. Another one of Lucas Fernández's main achievements is the introduction (unique in purely theatrical performances) of a soldier as a stock character. The eclogue in which this character has a most significant role will serve to show the development of the history of manners in Fernández's play. I am here referring to the *Farsa o cuasicomedia en la cual se introducen cuatro personas, conviene a saber: dos pastores e un soldado e una pastora* [Farce or quasicomedy in which four characters are introduced, that is, two shepherds, and a soldier and a shepherdess].

The play opens with the mournful laments of Prabos, the shepherd, for Antona, his beloved. The soldier will immediately show up and express his surprise at how these marginal, slightly beastly characters have even heard of love. During his speech on the forms of love, lovesickness is described as a real illness with consequences for the body and the physical appearance of the shepherd. Specially interconnected with his lonesomeness are mentions of his capillary extensions, thickness, and proportion. Prabos claims:

La greña se me'spelunca,
tómame pasmo y terito;
afrácaseme este'sprito.
El redemio espero nunca.
Siempre me estó esperezando
y bocezando.

Traygo caýdos los braços,
contino me vo arrojando
y rellanando,
Qu'el cuerpo se me'az pedaços. (vv. 21–30)

[My hair bristles, cold and trembling take over me, my spirit dies. I hope for
no remedy. I am always stretching out and shouting. My arms are dangling.
I am constantly falling and losing control, my body is falling to pieces,
dismembered.]

Prabos's immediate characterization as a loving shepherd is properly
described in terms of his hair. His love is represented by the "maddening" of his hair, which is followed by the rest of his body. The shepherd
makes, in this regard, abundant use of rusticized Latinisms, which emphasize the ludic and performative nature of the sketch. The shepherd's
hair ("greña") is described as "espeluncado," a term probably derived
from the Latin *spelunca-ae*, which means cavern, concavity. *Espeluncar*
becomes the vulgarized concept of "despeluzar" or to loosen one's hair,
which, according to José Lamano y Beneite's *Dialecto vulgar salmantino*,
is of common usage around Ledesma (Salamanca, Spain) and is related
to *espelufar/despelufar* and *espelujar/despelujar* (to rob, to steal). As we
can see, an intricate web of burlesque meanings is associated with the
"maddening" of hair. Beyond the hair, the next step towards his process of falling in love involves his body ("tómame pasmo y terito") as
cold and chills take over his limbs. *Terito* is a vulgar derivative from
"teritar" or "tiritar" [to tremble] and is related to cold. *Teritona*, then,
means "temblor," trembling. For instance, Juan del Enzina's Bras Gil
claims: "Pues en prados y en verdura / tománme cint mili teritos"
[In prairies and meadows, I feel a hundred thousand tremors]. Also
Gonzalo Correas commented in his *Vocabulario*, "Más vale sudar, que
toser y teritar. – De frío y resfrío" [It is better to sweat than to cough
and tremble – of cold and flu] (1906, 452). The shepherd's spirit follows
immediately thereafter: "afrácaseme este'sprito." Correas's *Vocabulario*
of rustic terms makes clear that "Esprito dice el aldeano por espíritu"
[Villagers say *espirito* instead of *espíritu*] (137). The recklessness of the
shepherd's soul is reflected in the disintegration of his body: his limbs
stretch (*esperezando*, a common term in the famous wine region of the
Ribera del Duero) to the point of complete dismemberment as his body
is pulled apart into tiny pieces ("qu'el cuerpo se me'az pedaços"). Here
we find again a theatrical representation of a process of disintegration,
in this case a psychological process. Instead of tearing apart his clothes,
the protagonist compares himself to a dog with rabies ("A rauia doy

tal dolencia") that forces him to go forlorn through hills ("cerros") and groves ("carrascales"), half dead and afflicted with deadly incursions ("terrerías mortales") (v. 40). Quite interesting are the many insults to which the soldier subjects the shepherd. The soldier calls him a villain ("auillanado"), a bastard ("bastardado"), a brute ("bruto"), and rude ("tosco"), but the climax falls on yet another reference to his bushy hair ("melenudo") (v. 308).

Having long and thick hair was undoubtedly related to poor manners at the time. Paul Lacroix's classic *A History of Manners, Customs and Dress during the Middle Ages and the Renaissance* (1874) mentions that it was customary for the noble and the plebeian to swear by their hair, and it was considered the height of politeness to pull out a hair and present it to someone (2012, 540). Specific minority groups, such as gypsies, whose custom involved having long hair, were looked down upon. An account of a meeting between a courtier and gypsies stresses the former's fascination with how the men were very swarthy with curly hair (2012, 565). In Lucas Fernández's eclogue, the soldier invokes natural effects to compare with the shepherd's laments by referencing cyclic pastoral notions: the moon, the seasons. Accordingly, he relates the shepherds' bushy beards to their lack of courtliness: "Barbudos, por espantar, / Mostráys los gestos sañudos; / vuestro oficio es renegar" [Bushy bearded men, frowning and attempting to frighten, all you do is complain] (vv. 490–2). He also expresses his great surprise that people with such big eyebrows could even recognize love. Their big thick eyebrows give them away:

> Estas rizones me nota:
> los ahuncos y descrucios,
> sobrecejos, respelluzios
> qu'es amorío remota. (vv. 670–4)

[I can see [that] these big locks, the grooves and stretches, the frowning eyebrows, and the bristling hair, give away that it is love.]

Fernández enumerates a number of physiognomic and psychological terms conflating both fields of meaning. *Auncar* literally means "to fill the soul with grief" (Castro y Rossi 1852, 127.2), while *descruciar* is related to a liberating effort (Coll Sansalvador 2007). These psychological terms are followed, through some sort of logical association, by physiognomic expressions such as *sobrecejos* [frowning] and *respelluzios* [hair bristling]. As Andreu Coll Sansalvador states: "La disposition sur deux vers semble tracer une dernière frontière fragile entre contenu et expression" [The distinction in these two verses traces a fragile frontier between content and expression] (2007, 118). At the same time, it is a clear indication of the performative nature of self-fashioning on stage. Love prompts both psychological and physical reactions. Disdainful love triggers a number of physical and mental reactions that are capable of disintegrating the shepherd's body.

A similar example, albeit a much more tragic scene, can be found in Juan del Enzina's *Égloga de Fileno, Zambardo y Cardonio* [Eclogue of Fileno, Zambardo and Cardonio].[7] Set as a pastoral eclogue, it presents three shepherds: Fileno, who is smitten with Zéfira, and his two friends, Zambardo – deeply in love with his beloved Oriana – and Cardonio, who is just interested in tending to his flock. Enzina crafts a very tenuous plot where Fileno laments and his friends prescribe remedies for his unrequited love. Although the two women do not appear on stage, they are constantly referenced. Fileno suffers from frenzy, as can be seen in his diatribe with Cardonio (vv. 257 et passim). Zéfira quite paradoxically references the zephyr wind, the wind from the west that silences heaven's madness with its gentle breezes. Enzina adds topoi concerning misogyny, the defence of women, and the medical knowledge of the time (Vélez-Sainz 2019).

Subjected to an unrequited love, Fileno will eventually show his incapacity to control himself. His friend Zambardo emphasizes his ill-mannered status: "En tus vestiduras no nada compuesto / te veo, y solías andar muy polido" [I see in your dress bad composure / when you used to be so refined]. Fileno's lack of poise, balance, and grace identifies him as a disdained lover while at the same time pointing out his uncourtliness. Fileno has mislaid the most visible elements of his courtly configuration, his dress and gestures, as he recognizes himself to be undergoing "passions" that "muestran de fuera señales muy cierto / del corto camino lieva la muerte" [show very true signals / of the short path towards death] (vv. 35–6).

Fileno openly acts moved by wrath: "la ravia, Cardonio, que mi pecho encierra / de ver olvidados mis muchos servicios / hace salir la lengua de quicios" [the wrath enclosed in my chest / of seeing my many services forgotten / makes my tongue speak ill] (vv. 265–7). The key word here is "quicios," which is related to adequateness and constraint; his tongue is loose and out of control. Cardonio indicates the cause of the suffering: "¡O pobre de seso! Más que de plazer, / de sola pintura te dejas vencer" [¡Oh light-headed! You are vanquished by a painting, not even by pleasure] (vv. 374–5). Fileno is, in fact, in love with a representation of beauty, not beauty itself. He embraces his lack of courtliness and, accordingly, strips himself of each of the elements that configure him as a courtly shepherd. This is an example of courtly performativity common to the theatrical models of the time. He first says goodbye to his lute:

> E tú, mi rabé, pues nunca podiste
> un punto ni ver aquella enemiga,
> ni menos jamás tan dulce tañiste
> que el alma aliviasses de alguna fatiga. (vv. 553–6)

> [And you, my lute, were never able to see that foe, nor played sweet melodies that alleviated the burden of my soul.]

The musical instrument of the literary shepherd is arguably the most codified feature of the eclogues. The Virgilian model endowed the shepherd with either a string or a wind instrument, which served as a metonymy of the character. Fileno's instrument, however, has not functioned well as either seducer of the lady or relief for the disappointments of love. After the lute, he looks for other pastoral tools inside his bag:

> ¿Qué es lo que queda en aqueste çurrón?
> No me ha de quedar salvo el cuchillo,
> pedernal terrena, yesca, eslavón,
> que vos en dos partes iréis, caramillo.
> ¿Queda otra cosa, si bien la cuchar?
> Çaticos de pan ten tú, venturado,
> pues el çurrón no me ha de quedar,
> ni vos en mal ora tanpoco, cayado. (vv. 561–8)

> [What is left inside my bag? Only this knife, flint, earth, swivel, and tinder. You will be split in half, my flageolet. What other thing is left but my spoon? Have some bread crumbs, you fortunate, for nothing will remain of my bag, and neither will you, damned staff.]

Inside the bag ("çurrón"), he finds a knife, some flint, earth, swivel, tinder, a flageolet, a spoon, bread crumbs ("Çaticos de pan"), and, finally, the staff ("cayado"). We know that the shepherd Mingo metamorphoses into a courtier in *Eclogues VII* and *VIII* by requesting visual signals. He starts by demanding a "galardón" [gift] from the female shepherd (*VII*, 62, vv. 21–32); then, he changes his dress, already that of a courtier (*VIII*, 84–5, vv. 411–21), and his gestures and manners (*VIII*, 85, vv. 438–40), in a process of social transformation (García-Bermejo Giner 2011; Vázquez Melio 2012). In the case of Fileno, his loss of self-control guides him to the path of despair and to lose the traits that conform to his courtliness. The fact that Fileno is stripped of pastoral features can be seen in the light of what Stephen Greenblatt defines as *self-fashioning* – though the latter does not pay attention to the education of the masses or utilize Elias's works – which describes the building of public personalities among the Renaissance elite. In this piece, we are confronted with a further step. Fileno exemplifies how the concept of nobility was transformed from lineage to a set of societal behaviours. These were present in the public representations of the elite in forms of portraits, memories, and theatre. In dramatic terms, it is also to be noted that the brevity of the scene foregrounds the kinesics of the characters and the representability of stage-space through a few iconic elements.

How did these works broadcast their message? Criticism shows abundant proof that both Enzina and Fernández worked at the court of the Albas between 1496 and 1498. Enzina's *Égloga representada en reqüesta de unos amores* [Eclogue staged at the request of certain loves] makes it clear that it was staged "en la sala donde el Duque y la Duquesa estaban" [in the room where the Duke and the Duchess were] (Enzina 2001, 61); and his *Representación por Juan del Encina ante el muy esclarescido y muy illustre príncipe don Juan* [Staging by Juan del Enzina before the enlightened and illustrious prince don Juan] was prepared in 1497 for the prince's arrival in Salamanca (del Río in Enzina 2001, 101nA). In fact, Enzina's *Égloga de las grandes lluvias* [Eclogue of the great deluge] alludes to his rivalry with Fernández for the favour of the Duke of Alba. Explaining this piece in his critical edition, Alberto del Río states: "seguramente el poco interés mostrado por sus amos en que la vacante del puesto de cantor de la catedral fuese a parar a Encina sería el detonante para que este decidiera a cambiar de suerte y abandonar tierras salmantinas" [the little interest that the dukes showed in helping Enzina attain the position of main singer at the cathedral would probably trigger his leaving Salamanca] (Enzina 2001, 95n110). Fernández's piece was also very likely performed for the greater public in the Corpus festivities of 1503. The representation was included among various other festivities. Framiñán states that he was paid 1,200 *maravedís*:

> 204 maravedíes del adorno del templo; 942 maravedíes del cortejo musical y el porte de hachones encendidos; 306 maravedíes del paso animado de san Sebastián; 2,040 maravedíes por una danza de serranas y "los personajes con su dama"; 2,000 maravedíes de un *Auto de los estordiones*; y 1,200 maravedíes de un *Auto de los pastores*, a cargo de Lucas Fernández. (Framiñán 2016, 74)

[204 *maravedis* for the adornment of the church; 942 *maravedis* for the musical entourage and lit torches; 306 *maravedis* for the animated statue of Saint Sebastián; 2,040 *maravedis* for a *serrana* dance with damsel characters; 2,000 *maravedis* for the *Auto de los estordiones*; and 1,200 *maravedis* for the *Auto de los pastores*, by Lucas Fernández.]

It is important to note that Lucas Fernández's name is the only one singled out. The already familiar figure of the soldier ("çoyço" or "infante") will become prevalent in subsequent Salamanca Corpus festivals. In 1508 we find three momos and a dance with three characters, a lady, ten haughty women with bell arches, seventeen "zoizos," three dancing black male characters and one black female character, four dancing Portuguese with rattles, and three ploughmen playing with three drummers. For all these characters the stage practitioners Rueda and Cristóbal were paid 5,400 *maravedis*, to which we must add another 2,000 *maravedis* for the *Auto de Fortuna y el rey y la reina y el ermitaño con el pastor* [The farce of fortune and the king and queen, and the hermit with the shepherd] (Framiñán 2016, 294). Sometimes the performers were paid in food. Framiñán notices that the payment for a "danza de espadas," a noble dance, was an invitation to overeat: "Iten se hizo una danza de espadas y con lo que les di y se gastó en comer, según convine con ellos, cuatrocientos y setenta y cinco maravedís" [and a sword dance was performed and the payments and the invitation to eat, as negotiated, was 475 *maravedís*] (registro 96; Framiñán 2016, 68). Another time, Lucas is given three *reales* to pay for chickens for the singers. Framiñán believes that they were paid in food because they were considered servants of the cathedral (Framiñán 2016, 52).

To sum up, these works, which were designed to be performed at court, were shortly thereafter put on display for the public to see, and then they reached an even broader audience through the printing press. Thus, a message that was initially intended for the nobility was spread to other social strata. We find a democratization of etiquette and manners in which Fileno and the unnamed shepherd in Lucas Fernández's quasi-comedy are pitted against a set of social customs to provide examples *ex contrario* on how to behave.

The great divide between rustic and courtly figures is more than likely intended to provoke both laughter and a certain sense of disdain towards the semi-savage rustics. The plays present lowly pastoral characters as laughingstocks for the courtly audience, whose customs and behaviour are codified in courtly treatises, and whose overeating is but a sign of savagery. Juan del Enzina and Lucas Fernández aptly showcase how the civilizing process became a way for educating the diverse social orders in a culture of law and civility. Stephen Jaeger, in *The Origins of Courtliness*, probably the most significant revision of Elias's work, believes that the urge to civilize responds to very concrete political ideologies in an attempt to control the warrior by teaching him to restrain his natural urges within the confines of the court.

If theatre in the Middle Ages was mostly entertainment for clerics and courtiers, what made these pieces attractive for publication to the greater public? One answer might lie in the process of "courtlyfication" that the public underwent. We can view it as a movement aimed at raising this class from an archaic and primitive stage of social and civil life to a higher stage, thus imbuing it with ideals of modesty, humanity, elegance, restraint, moderation, affability, and respectfulness. What was once meant to educate the elite became a public mode of behaviour. A *habitus* (to utilize the Bourdieuan term) was created which was later to be identified with the European Man.[8]

NOTES

1 This piece attempts to complement previous research on the formation of courtly ideals in the later medieval Castilian court of Juan II (2013). European treatises on good manners that were printed and therefore were read by an audience other than their intended one include, among others, *Ein spruch der ze tische kêrt* [A word to those at the table]; Bonvicino da Riva's *Courtesien* [The courtesan] and *De le zinquenta cortexie da tavola* [On the fifty table manners], *Quisquis es in mensa, S'ensuivent les countenances de la table* [To those at the table. Followed by table manners]; Erasmus's *De civilitate morum puerilium* [On the good manners of children]; Giovanni della Casa's *Galateo, Il cortegiano* [Galateo, the courtesan]; Calviac's *Civilité* [Civility], Antoine de Courtin's *Nouveau traité de civilité* [New treaty on civility]; Pedro de Gracia Dei's *Crianza e virtuosa doctrina* [Education and virtuous doctrine]; and Andrés de Li's *Summa de Paciencia*. For a summary, see Elias (1994). For a more extensive bibliography, see Montandon (1995) vol. 1 for treaties in France, the United Kingdom, and Germany, and vol. 2 for Italy, Spain, Portugal, Rumania, Norway, the Czech Republic, Slovakia, and Poland. Unless otherwise noted, translations are by Gregory Baum.

2 Major attention should be given to medical treatises on hygiene; among others, the *Arte cisoria, Arte complida de cirugía (Cirugía menor)* [Art of surgery]; *Primera y Segvnda y Tercera Partes de la Historia Medicinal: de las cosas que se traen de nuestras Indias Occidentales, que siruen en Medicina* [First, second and third parts of medical history: Of the things brought from the

Indies, which serve as medicine]; *Discvrso breve, sobre la cvra y preservacion de la pestilencia* (all in *ADMYTE*) [Brief discourse about the cure and preservation of pests]; and *artes edendi* such as *Banquete de nobles caballeros* [Banquet of noble gentlemen]. In a sense, defences of women and treatises on female education should also be included in the list of treatises on good manners. These are, among others, courtly defences of women such as John Gower's *Confessio amantis, Dives et pauper* [Confession of a rich and poor lover]; Christine de Pizan's *Livre de la cité des dames* [Book of the city of ladies] and *Le livre des Trois Vertus* [Book of the three virtues]; Chaucer's *Legend of Good Women*; Boccaccio's *De claris mulieribus* [On famous women]; Álvaro de Luna's *Libro de las virtuosas e claras mugeres* [Book of virtuous women]; Juan Rodríguez del Padrón's *Triunfo de las donas* [The triumph of women]; and Diego de Valera's *Defensa de virtuosas mugeres* [Defence of virtuous women]. Treatises on female education include *Castigos y doctrinas que un sabio daba a sus hijas* [Punishments and doctrines that a wise man gave to his daughters]; Martín de Córdoba's *El jardín de las nobles doncellas* [Garden of noble maidens]; Juan Luis Vives's *Introductio ad sapientiam* [Introduction to knowledge] and *De ratione studii puerilis* [On the education of children]; and Fray Luis de León's *La perfecta casada* [The perfect wife], among many others. I have dedicated a monograph to these treatises (in press).

3 Treatises on nobility include Bartolo de Saxoferrato's *Bartoli Commentaria in tres libros* [Commentary in three books]; Juan Rodríguez del Padrón's *Cadira de onor* [Chair of honour]; and Diego de Valera's *Espejo de verdadera nobleza; Ceremonial de príncipes y caballeros*; and *Doctrinal de príncipes* [Mirror of true nobility; Ceremonial of princes and gentlemen; and Doctrine of princes].

4 Sociohistorical research following Elias has been launched to a great extent by the Norbert Elias Foundation in the Netherlands (http://www .norberteliasfoundation.nl/).

5 With the significant exception of French seventeenth-century theatre, whose didacticism has been underscored by critics of old with clear examples in Molière's comedies of manners satirizing the hypocrisy and pretension of the *ancièn regime* such as *L'École des femmes* [School of women] or *Tartuffe* (Howarth 1978), European national theatrical traditions have not been seen as representing social role models. The major critics on the rest of the national dramatic traditions have not devoted enough attention to the interrelationship of the civilizing process and theatre. Among others, we can include Ferdinando Taviani's (1969) or Roberto Tessari's (2013) work on Italian authors from *Commedia dell'arte* companies such as the *Intronati* or the *Gelosi*; and Laura Giannetti and Guido Ruggiero's work on Italian Renaissance authors such as Bernardo Dovizi de Bibbiena, Niccolò Machiavelli, and Pietro Aretino (2003). Even Stephen Orgel's (1975) or Stephen Greenblatt's (1980) groundbreaking work on the English national theatre

from Sackville and Thomas Kyd to Shakespeare does not utilize Elias's work, although the latter does wonderfully describe the ways Renaissance authors fashioned self. Some articles have specifically made this point, such as Jean Howard's wonderful depiction in her article on "The New Historicism in Renaissance Studies" (1986). A dissertation by Ann E. Garner on "Shakespeare and the Theatrical Code of Conduct" alone speaks to this tradition (2012).

6   Other authors such as Juan del Enzina and Bartolomé de Torres Naharro also give their works to presses, with greater success than Fernández in most cases, but they combine drama and poetry. The generic status of the fifteenth-century dialogue *Celestina*, which for some might be the first example of published theatre in Spain, is under scrutiny. Encina's *Égloga de Plácida y Victoriano* [Eclogue of Plácida and Victoriano] made it to the section for books in the Romance languages within the 1559 *Index inquisitorum prohibitorum* [Index prohibited by the Inquisition] (Bujanda 1984, 465), along with many theatrical plays of the time, including Torres Naharro's *Jacinta*, *Aquilana*, and *Propalladia* (his complete works); the anonymous *Orfea*; Jaime de Huete's *Thesorin*; the Portuguese Gil Vicente's *Amadis*; and the Italian Giambatista Gelli's *Circe*.

7   Considered the "patriarch of the Spanish stage," Juan del Enzina (1468–1529) was a poet, translator, and playwright with ties to the Dukes of Alba. His theatre is usually divided into two categories: the early "Castilian" phase, which divides the plays by cycles (Nativity, Easter) following medieval practice; and the later "Italian" one, which presents a clear evolution towards the dramatic practices of the Italian Renaissance such as the use of mythological characters and pastoral themes. For a general overview, see Surtz (1979).

8   Tentatively titled *The Making of the European Civilization*, the book project of which this piece is part attempts to dissect the means by which literature (mostly theatre but also poetry and prose) has been utilized as a venue to form notions of civility, citizenship, hygiene, education, and manners in early modern Europe. By showing how theatre became a privileged mode of educating the masses, I hope to challenge José Antonio Maravall's very influential book *La cultura del barroco*, which states that theatre was a means to promote not a set of customs but the social ideology of the nobility with an interest in preserving the *status quo*. While there is some contestation by Melveena McKendrick, Fernando Rodríguez de la Flor, and Frederick A. de Armas, among others, there is no major redefinition of the *telos* of the gigantic body of literature (unequalled in numbers by any other contemporary European dramatic tradition). By placing the books of manners and theatre together, I hope to describe properly the process by which the courtly ideals of social behaviour were funnelled to the paying masses.

WORKS CITED

ADMYTE. 1992–8. *Archivo digital de manuscritos y textos españoles*. Edited by Francisco Marcos Marín, Gerardo Meiro, Charles B. Faulhaber, Ángel Gómez Moreno, Aurora Martín de Santa Olalla, Julián Martín Abad, and John Nitti. Madrid: Micronet. 5 CD-ROMS 0–4.

Ascensius, Badius. 2013. *Praenotamenta Terentii [Anotaciones previas a Terencio]*. Edited by José Manuel Ruiz Vila. Madrid: Cátedra.

Barthes, Roland. 1977. *Fragments d'un discours amoureux*. Paris: Éditions du Seuil.

Bartolo de Saxoferrato. 1549. *Bartoli Commentaria in tres libros*. Petrus Parisius, Lugduni, 64 Bl;2-o. Online ed. 2011. http://digital.ub.uni-duesseldorf.de/urn/urn:nbn:de:hbz:061:1-76060. Accessed 4 April 2015.

Boccaccio, Giovanni. 2001. *Famous Women*. Edited by Virginia Brown. Cambridge, MA: Harvard University Press.

Bouza, Fernando. 2001. *Palabra e imagen en la corte. Cultura oral y visual de la nobleza en el Siglo de Oro*. Madrid: Abada Ediciones.

Bujanda, J.M. 1984. *Index des livres interdits: Index de l'Inquisition Espagnole. 1551, 1554, 1559*. Sherbrooke: Centre d'Études de la Renaissance.

Cano Ballesta, Juan. 1992. "*Los Castigos y dotrinas que un sabio daua a sus hijas*, un texto del siglo XV sobre educación femenina." In *Actas de la Asociación Internacional de Hispanistas X*, edited by Antonio Vilanova, 139–50. Barcelona: PPU.

Castro y Rossi, Adolfo de. 1852. *Biblioteca Universal. Gran Diccionario de la Lengua Española*. Madrid: Oficinas y establecimiento tipográfico del *Semanario* Pintoresco y de La Ilustración.

Cátedra, Pedro. 1989. *Amor y pedagogía en la edad media: estudios de doctrina amorosa y práctica literaria*. Salamanca: Universidad de Salamanca.

Coll Sansalvador, Andreu. 2007. *La théâtralité dans l'ouvre de Lucas Fernández*. Unpublished dissertation. Toulouse: Université de Toulouse le Mirail.

Córdoba, Martín de. 1974. *Jardín de nobles doncellas*. Edited by Harriet Goldberg. Chapel Hill: University of North Carolina Press.

Correas, Gonzalo. 1906. *Vocabulario de refranes y frases proverbiales y otras fórmulas comunes de la lengua castellana*. Madrid: J. Ratés.

de Armas, Frederick. 2011. "Claves políticas en las comedias de Calderón: el caso de *El mayor encanto, amor*." *Anuario Calderoniano* 4: 117–44. https://doi.org/10.31819/9783954879915-007.

de León, Fray Luis. 1985. *La perfecta casada*. Edited by Joaquín Antonio Peñalosa. Mexico City: Porrúa.

de Pizan, Christine. 2000. *Le livre de la cité des dames*. Edited by Thérese Moreau and Eric Hicks. Paris: Stock.

Elias, Norbert. 1994. *The Civilizing Process: The History of Manners and State Formation and Civilization*. Translated by Edmund Jephcott. Oxford: Blackwell.

Enzina, Juan del. 2001. *Teatro*. Edited by Alberto del Río. Barcelona: Crítica.

Fernández, Lucas. 1974. *Farsas y églogas*. Edited by Mª Josefa Canellada. Madrid: Castalia.

Framiñán de Miguel, María Jesús. 2016. *El espectáculo dramático-festivo del Corpus en la Salamanca del Renacimiento*. Madrid: Iberoamericana.

García-Bermejo Giner, Miguel M. 2011. "Disfraz, máscara e identidad en el primer teatro prelopesco (De Enzina a Torres Naharro)." In *Máscaras y juegos de identidad en el teatro español del siglo de oro*, edited by María Luisa Lobato López, 75–90. Burgos: Visor.

Garner, Ann E. 2012. "How Should I Act?: Shakespeare and the Theatrical Code of Conduct." *Dissertations*. Paper 551. http://scholarworks.umass.edu/open_access_dissertations/551.

Giannetti, Laura, and Guido Ruggiero. 2003. *Five Comedies from the Italian Renaissance*. Baltimore: Johns Hopkins University Press.

Gower, John. 1899–1902. *The Complete Works of John Gower*. Oxford: Clarendon Press.

Greenblatt, Stephen. 1980. *Renaissance Self-Fashioning from More to Shakespeare*. Chicago: University of Chicago Press.

Greene, Roland. 1999. *Unrequited Conquests: Love and Empire in the Colonial Americas*. Chicago: University of Chicago Press.

Howard, J.E. 1986. "The New Historicism in Renaissance Studies." *English Literary Renaissance* 16: 13–43. https://doi.org/10.1111/j.1475-6757.1986.tb00896.x.

Howarth, William Driver. 1978. *Molière: A Playwright and His Audience*. Cambridge: Cambridge University Press.

Jaeger, C. Stephen. 1985. *The Origins of Courtliness: Civilizing Trends and the Formation of Courtly Ideals 939–1210*. Philadelphia: University of Pennsylvania Press.

Kristeva, Julia. 1980. *Pouvoirs de l'horreur: essai sur l'abjection*. Paris: Éditions du Seuil.

Lacroix, Paul. 2012. *A History of Manners, Customs and Dress during the Middle Ages and the Renaissance*. [London, 1874]. London: Emereo Pty Ltd.

Lamano y Beneite, José. 1915. *El dialecto vulgar salmantino*. Salamanca: Tipografía Popular.

Lobera de Ávila, Luis. 1952. *Banquete de nobles caballeros*. [Augsburg, 1530]. Madrid: Castilla.

López de Villalobos, Francisco. 1999. *Sumario de la medicina*. [Salamanca: Impresor de la Gramática de Nebrija, 1498]. *Electronic Texts and Concordances of the Madison Corpus of Early Spanish Manuscripts and Printings*. Edited by John O'Neill. CD ed. Madison and New York: Hispanic Seminary of Medieval Studies.

Luna, Álvaro de. 2009. *Libro de las virtuosas e claras mugeres*. Edited by Julio Vélez-Sainz. Madrid: Cátedra.

Maravall, José Antonio. 1975. *La cultura del Barroco. Análisis de una estructura histórica*. Madrid: Ariel.

McKendrick, Melveena. 2000. *Playing the King: Lope de Vega and the Limits of Conformity*. London: Tamesis.

Miller, William Ian. 1997. *The Anatomy of Disgust*. Cambridge, MA: Harvard University Press.

Montandon. Alain. 1995. *Bibliographie des traités de savoir-vivre en Europe, du Moyen Âge à nos jours*. 2 vols. Clermont-Ferrand: Association des Publications de la Faculté des Lettres et Sciences humaines de Clermont-Ferrand.

Orgel, Stephen. 1975. *The Illusion of Power*. Berkeley: University of California Press.

Pfander, H.G. 1933. "Dives et pauper." *The Library*, s4-XIV. 3: 299–312. https://doi.org/10.1093/library/s4-XIV.3.299.

Rodríguez de la Flor, Fernando. 2002. *Barroco: Representación e ideología en el mundo hispánico (1580–1680)*. Madrid: Cátedra.

Rodríguez de Montalvo, Garci. 1988. *Amadís de Gaula*. 2 vols. Edited by Juan Manuel Cacho Blecua. Madrid: Cátedra.

Rodríguez del Padrón, Juan. 1982. *Obras completas*. Edited by César Hernández Alonso. Madrid: Editora Nacional.

Rojas, Fernando de, and ancient author. 2000. *La Celestina*. Edited by F.J. Lobera et al. Barcelona: Crítica.

San Pedro, Diego de. 1995. *Cárcel de amor, Arnalte y Lucenda, Sermón*. Edited by José Francisco Ruiz Casanova. Madrid: Cátedra.

Schloss, Dietmar, ed. 2009. *Civilizing America: Manners and Civility in American Literature and Culture*. Heidelberg: Universitätsverlag Winter.

Serés, Guillermo. 1996. *La transformación de los amantes. Imágenes del amor de la Antigüedad al Siglo de Oro*. Barcelona: Crítica.

Solomon, Michael. 1979. *The Literature of Misogyny in Medieval Spain: The "Arcipreste de Talavera" and the "Spill"*. Cambridge: Cambridge University Press and Madrid: Castalia.

Surtz, Roland E. 1979 *The Birth of a Theater: Dramatic Convention in the Spanish Theater from Juan del Encina to Lope de Vega*. Madrid: Castalia.

Taviani, Ferdinando. 1969. *La Commedia dell'Arte e la società barocca. La fascinazione del teatro*. Roma: Bulzoni.

Tessari, Roberto. 2013. *Commedia dell'arte: la maschera e l'ombra*. Gius: Laterza.

Valera, Diego de. 2009. *Defensa de virtuosas mugeres*. Edited by Federica Accorsi. Pisa: Edizioni ETS.

Vázquez Melio, María. 2012. "La configuración del personaje masculino en el teatro de Juan del Enzina." *Dicenda. Cuadernos de Filología Hispánica* 30: 207–19. https://doi.org/10.5209/rev_DICE.2012.v30.41372.

Vélez-Sainz, Julio. 2013. *"De amor, de honor e de donas": Mujer e ideales corteses en la Castilla de Juan II (1406–1454)*. Madrid: Editorial Complutense.

Vélez-Sainz, Julio. 2015. *La defensa de la mujer en la literatura hispánica. SS. XV–XVII*. Madrid: Cátedra.

Vélez-Sainz, Julio. 2019. "Curing the Malady of Lovesickness: Medicine and Physicians in Early Spanish Theatre." In *Science on Stage in Early Modern Spain*, edited by Enrique García Santo-Tomás, 103–22. Toronto: University of Toronto Press.

Vives, Juan Luis. 1995. *Instrucción de la mujer cristiana*. Translated by Juan Justiniano. Edited by Elizabeth Teresa Howe. Madrid: Universidad Pontificia de Salamanca.

6 Celestial and Transgressive Banquets in the Theatre of the Spanish Golden Age

FREDERICK A. DE ARMAS

Banquets are highly theatrical affairs and fit seamlessly as scenes within Golden Age plays which often exhibit their own theatricality. These metatheatrical moments are not mere adornments; they are also instances that reflect or reflect upon the work as a whole while at the same time deepening the sense of life as theatre. Michel Jeanneret, who has studied banquets from the classical through early modern periods, affirms that they are particularly significant instances: "The combination of words and food in a convivial scene gives rise to a special moment when thought and the senses enhance rather than tolerate each other" (1991, 1). But I would argue that in the *comedia*, words in banquet scenes are often in competition with the senses. In some cases, words will lash out against them, while in others they will highlight the sensuous and luxurious banquet. The banquet can also trigger vivid descriptions that seek to vie with the lushness of this practice; or it can call for simple stage machinery that can bring down a "celestial" banquet from the heavens. This essay is a first attempt to classify different key repasts in the *comedia*; it also seeks to foreground the many dramatic possibilities and the many registers and symbolic significance of these scenes.[1] Twelve plays have been selected by five of the major playwrights and by two lesser-known figures of the period: Calderón de la Barca, Claramonte, Lope de Vega, Moreto, Ruiz de Alarcón, Tirso de Molina, and Valdivielso. The plays will be divided into five general categories in terms of the types of "banquets" they depict: celestial suppers, unholy banquets, rustic repasts, banquets of sense, and demonic feasts. Each has its own relationship to the senses. Only five types are featured in what could become a much more extensive list – one particularly gruesome form that deserves further attention is the banquet of human flesh.[2] I would like to stress that these categories are not mutually exclusive, since a dramatic scene can fit more than one type. For example,

Lope's *La niñez de San Isidro* [The childhood of Saint Isidro] depicts a rustic repast, but it is also a celestial supper. Although terms such as *colación, fiesta,* or *merienda* are often used in the texts that are to be studied here, most often the meal staged is called a *cena*, the most important meal of the day. We have chosen to include a number of types of repasts under the rubric "banquet" because the suppers or lighter meals that are featured in the scenes to be studied are not everyday occurrences, but events that are highly theatricalized and are designed for a special occasion or purpose. Their theatrical nature, the blend of words and appetites, make them stand out. The term "banquet" is also significant because it underlines the use of the term by critics such as James F. Burke, Michel Jeanneret, and Frank J. Kermode. It brings up numerous associations such as the Banquet of the Gods as depicted by Juan Luis Vives, where humans and deities commingle (Jeanneret 1991, 14); the Platonic symposium (often translated as banquet), where intellectual nourishment is more important than any food or drink; the "banquet of sense," which, for Kermode, stands for the quasi-bestial man; the Christian Last Supper and the Eucharist, often depicted as a banquet. This study will often exhibit scenes where the *comedias* contrast the sumptuous banquets with the simple yet fulfilling "celestial" meal.

The term "banquet" seems to have been invented by the Renaissance. Starting in fourteenth-century Italy, it passed on to France in the fifteenth century and to Spain in the sixteenth. It was meant to signify a particularly extravagant feast and meal where many dishes were set at a long table or *banco*, thus the term banquet.[3] While, in the Middle Ages, feasts were set on particular religious occasions and also for weddings and other key events, no periodicity was needed for the Renaissance banquet. It just had to be an extravagant meal foregrounding conspicuous consumption. Wines would be there for drinking and exotic foods would serve to be admired and astonish the invited guests. While in humbler homes the main meal was taken after work, at Court there were so many different meals and types of meals at so many different times that physicians often complained that this was detrimental to health. During the Renaissance and Golden Age, banquets were most often evening affairs, although in the seventeenth century some claimed that they should be held in the late morning or at noon (Albala 2007, xi). In seventeenth-century Spain, Sebastián de Covarrubias does not set a time but defines the banquet by the abundance of foods and sumptuousness of presentation: "Vale tanto como un festín, combite y comida espléndida, abundante de manjares y rica en aparato" [It is the same as a feast, invited dinner, with splendid food, abundant delicacies and with much splendour] (1987, 191).

The banquet became such a coveted event that it was often depicted in Renaissance art. Taking as a point of departure the interpolated tale of "Cupid and Psyche" in Apuleius's *Golden Ass*, Raphael and Giulio Romano depicted the "lavish wedding feast" (Apuleius 1990, 115; Hartt 1950, 164) ordered by Jove, a banquet that included all the senses, according to Apuleius: there was music, dance, cups of nectar, golden plates for delicious morsels, and even a little theatrical representation that was sung by "a Satyr and a little Pan" (1990, 115). While the Seasons displayed colourful flowers, the Graces "sprinkled perfumes" (115). Apuleius's description is not far from the Renaissance Banquet, which included many wines or nectars and was often supplemented by theatre, dance, or music. Raphael's many frescoes dealing with the story of Cupid and Psyche can be found in the entrance loggia of the Villa Farnesina in Rome. Even the tale that surrounds the execution of the paintings mirrors the importance of the senses. Since Raphael was not progressing substantially on his commission, Agostini Chigi, the merchant who wished to enjoy the new decorations at the Villa Farnesina, "worked things out in such a way that he finally managed to bring this woman of Raphael's to come and stay with him on a constant basis in the section of the house where Raphael was working, and that was the reason why the work came to be finished" (Vasari 1991, 328). The sensuality of the scenes to be painted called for actual sensual gratification, while the celestial banquet in the ceiling tempered desire as Psyche now abided with the gods (see fig. 6.1).

Giulio Romano's commission was equally impelled by the passions and the senses. In Mantua, Giulio worked for Federigo Gonzaga, who asked him to construct and decorate the Palazzo del Te. This "island paradise" just outside the city was built for the sensual enjoyment of Federigo and his mistress Isabella Boschetti, an affair that was rebuked and opposed by Federigo's mother, Isabella d'Este (Hartt 1958, 1:92).[4] In order to emphasize the passions of the god of love and his beloved, Giulio set out a very ambitious program. The story of Cupid and Psyche is told through twenty-three scenes divided into lunettes, octagons, larger wall frescoes, other paintings (even some unrelated to the tale), and, of course, the central scenes of the banquet, where luxury and the play of the senses have more than some hints of debauchery (Hartt 1958, 1.130; de Armas 2006, 194–204). The decorations made a point that although Federigo would never marry Isabella, his palace would stand as a symbol of his unwavering and unrestrained passion for her. It would also stand as a bulwark against forced marriage and the many roles he was expected to play as ruler. At the Palazzo del Te, his guests at banquets and other feasts would

Figure 6.1. Raphael, *The Wedding Banquet of Cupid and Psyche*, 1517. Heritage Image Partnership Ltd / Alamy Stock Photo.

admire his ability to contest such rules and were invited to succumb to most pleasurable enjoyments. Thus, the art works and the events that transpire at the island-palace are very much in tune: "In the centre of the ceiling the marriage ceremony is celebrated in the celestial theatre, amongst gods standing on clouds, seen sharply from below, and on the walls of the room the marriage feast is being prepared" (Hartt 1950, 166). There seems to be a major difference between Raphael's banquet and Giulio's frescoes on the walls. While the first depicts a more decorous feast in heaven, the second shows the preparations for the feast on earth, with all manner of sensuous detail, including the nude couple lying next to each other, frolicking cupids and satyrs, and even exotic animals mingling with humans and gods (Malaguzzi 2008, 34) (see fig. 6.2).

Banquets and other meals can then range from the celestial to the transgressive and even demonic. In Raphael's *The Wedding Banquet of Cupid and Psyche* a celestial feast is enjoyed by the deities, and some would interpret it in an allegorical manner, as the triumph of true love

Figure 6.2. Giulio Romano, *Banquet of Amor and Psyche*, c. 1530. Palazzo del Te. ImageBROKER / Alamy Stock Photo.

over the snares of the world; it could be seen to celebrate the soul's joining with the god of love. On the other hand, Giulio Romano's *Hall of Psyche* at the Palazzo del Te, although partaking of the allegorical, points to the sensual. The range, meaning, and possible dramatic appeal of banquets and other meals made them an ideal scene to be staged. After all, the meal itself invites the banqueters to become actors and follow a script, as Ken Albala contends: "Any meal, past or present, thus contains a script. It might be said that every participant in the eating event is equally an actor. Sometimes the rules are rigidly set ... but the parts can also be improvised and negotiated in the course of a meal. In this respect, a meal is a form of theatre. In the case of the banquets ... this is literally the case replete with an audience, stage sets, props and interludes" (2007, 4).

I. Celestial Suppers

Valdivielso, *Psiques y Cupido* [Psyche and Cupid] (1622)
Calderón, *Psiquis y Cupido* [Psyche and Cupid] (1640)
Calderón, *Ni amor se libra de amor* [Not even love is exempt from love] (1662)
Calderón, *La dama duende* [The phantom lady] (1629)

This first section will examine two examples of celestial banquets in the sacramental plays of the Spanish Golden Age. This type of banquet often contrasts with the banquet of senses and is limited to very few ingredients. Its numinous qualities almost negate the luxurious and abundant nature of the Renaissance banquet as depicted by Raphael and Giulio Romano. In addition to the two sacramental plays, we will also view in this section a banquet from a mythological court play and one from a comedy. Here, the banquets will be more fulsome. All four works will be based on the myth of Cupid and Psyche, this being a way to contrast the paintings just discussed with representations of "celestial" banquets on the Spanish stage. With the translation of Apuleius's *Golden Ass* by Diego López de Cartagena in 1513, the tale became an important model for literary works. It could be turned into long mythological poems as in the case of Juan de Mal Lara, Gutierre de Cetina, and Fernando de Herrera.[5] More importantly, its allegorical meanings were ideal material for sacramental plays. Already in classical times, Fulgentius had given the myth an allegorical meaning, and mythographers of the Italian Renaissance and Spanish Golden Age continued this practice. In these works, Psyche is often identified with the human soul; her fall is attributed to curiosity and sensuality, defects/sins that are then purged, leading to the contemplation of the divine.[6] In 1622 Joseph de Valdivielso published *Doze autos sacramentales y dos comedias divinas* [Twelve sacramental plays and two plays rendered in a sacred manner], which includes *Psiques y Cupido* [Psyche and Cupid], a sacramental play where Psyche has three suitors, *Mundo*, *Deleite*, and *Lucifer* [World, Enjoyment, and Lucifer], three "princes" that have come to ask for her hand in marriage. But she wishes to marry Amor, who appears "de morado con velo de plata delante del rostro" [wearing purple with a silver veil over his face] (1622, 59v).[7] The numinous, then, is removed from the world, only partially glimpsed. This does not prevent Psyche from seeking her vision. At the wedding banquet with her mysterious Cupid, he urges her to eat the bread and drink the wine: "ella es mi cuerpo, Razón / y ella mi sangre" [she is my body, Reason / and she is my blood] (1622, 63r). But Psyche does not seem so interested in the mystery of the Eucharistic meal; she seeks to solve a different mystery, wishing to see Cupid's face, to uncover what hides behind the veil. Unhappy with her wishes, her beloved causes the banquet to disappear as he departs. Her sisters, her three suitors, all worldly and demonic forces are intent on preventing a hierophany, where the sacred, manifesting itself, brings new insight and meaning to an individual or group of individuals. As Mircea Eliade explains: "the sacred manifests itself in space, the real unveils itself" (1959, 63). The test of the veil serves to bring about a true hierophany. After her transgression and after she laments her loss, the god of love forgives her: "y para perdonarte / basta que tú lo quieras" [and to forgive you / it is enough that you desire it] (1622, 68r). He then brings about a celestial union. At this point, Psyche's black and mended garments are transformed into a luminous white: "queda de blanco y sin parches" [white and patchless] (1622, 68v). She is offered a crown by *Cielo* as a Chorus lauds the union in a celestial feast of sound and colour, in a theatrical theophany that approaches apotheosis. Although Raphael can paint a celestial banquet, Valdivielso, following a more rigorous decorum, prefers to view the heavens as light and harmony, devoid of terrestrial delights. The banquet in this sacramental play had been staged earlier, where Psyche was shown the mystery of the Eucharist. After all, these sacramental plays were performed during the feast of Corpus Christi.[8] There, Amor had wanted Psyche to have faith in his mysteries. For Eliade, "the Christian incarnation is the supreme hierophany or theophany" (Allen 2002, 115). The Eucharist celebrates through transubstantiation the coming together of the divine and the human. Here, the Eucharist and the marriage of Cupid and Psyche are moments of harmony and union, a doubling of the celestial banquet, one of bread and wine and a second of light and harmony. These two banquets contrast with Raphael's painting and even more with Giulio Romano. They are spiritual and symbolic feasts that shun the senses, although the spiritual feasts are theatricalized in such a way as to please sight and hearing.

More than a decade after Valdivielso's publication, Calderón de la Barca wrote a sacramental play on the myth of Cupid and Psyche for Toledo (1640).[9] Enrique Rull, in his edition of the *auto*, has shown how Calderón blends the story of Cupid and Psyche with the sacramental play by Valdivielso, vastly improving the dramatic elements with a better understanding of the myth.[10] Sebastian Neumeister speaks of Calderón's daring in drastically transforming the story into sacred history (2000, 141); and this is indeed the case according to Rull. While Valdivielso had dealt with a narrower theme, the salvation of the soul, Calderón deals with a broader historical landscape, including as characters Paganism and Judaism, which are echoed in Idolatry and Synagogue (Psyche's sisters) (Calderón 2012, 50–6). In the Toledo play, Psyche (the soul in Valdivielso) becomes Faith (*La Fe*). She is, according to Vincent Martin, human faith and not the more specific Christian faith (2002, 94); while Valdivielso's *Cielo*, her father, is now the World (*Mundo*). Cupid remains as Christ here as in Valdivielso, and he is also "invisible," wearing a white veil (Calderón 2012, 268). Once again, this is the veil that hides divinity from the world, a hierophany in the making, since he is as yet to unveil himself. He challenges others to believe in him as deity: "Sin verlo, lo has de creer / con oírlo" [without seeing, you must believe / by hearing] (2012, vv. 259–60). Although many try, none can remove the veil from his countenance. The father seeks revenge through his daughter: "en ella nos venguemos / el deshonor que es de todos" [let us take revenge on her / for the honour that belongs to all of us] (2012, vv. 442–3). Cupid views the sea voyage and exile of his beloved from above, as the vessel takes the shape of the emblematic ship of the world, tossed about by storms. Faith (Psyche) is then abandoned on a deserted island. Here a rugged mountain opens to reveal a palace and its lush gardens. We are back to the moment in the myth where Psyche is sacrificed to Venus but finds herself in an enchanted palace. Mysterious voices greet her and songs praise her. Turning to the chivalric tradition, Calderón has the figure of *Albedrío* (Free Will), who accompanies Faith, worry: "Que es un palacio encantado, / y que algún mágico intenta / encantarnos en él" [It is an enchanted palace, / and some magician tries / to enchant us in it] (2012, vv. 755–7). As Cupid enters, he extinguishes the light: "como para Fe te quiero / ciega has de ser para Fe" [because I want you for Faith / you shall be blind for Faith] (2012, vv. 827–8). Psyche/Faith falls for his arguments, but asks that her family be brought to witness her joy. At first all are amazed at the richness of her dress and the beauties of the palace. But soon they conspire to have her use her senses to know her beloved.[11] There is no banquet here, as there would be in Apuleius and in the chivalric version of the myth, *El Conde Partinuplés*. Calderón eschews the banquet to deny the importance of the senses, since he wishes to foreground Faith. Still, falling to temptation, and the advice of her envious sisters, Faith/Psyche seeks to view Cupid with a light brought by *Albedrío*, but she cannot.[12] Given her trespass, Cupid vanishes and the palace reverts to savage nature. But the latent theophany is soon to become a glorious appearance of the god. Once Psyche/Faith confesses her wrongdoing, she is forgiven. The denouement exhibits a celestial banquet in her honour: high above, Cupid appears with a table, a chalice, and the host (2012, 249). Thus, the double banquet in Valdivielso has been compressed into one final feast. The only script here is that of the deity who exhibits and explains the mysteries of the Christian faith as its enemies flee in fright or express disdain, and as Cupid announces that Toledo will become a central site for faith: "donde más la Fe se ensalza" [where Faith is more extolled] (2012, v. 1537). Just as one age moves to the next, so paganism must give way Judaism and then to Christianity, and the pagan banquet of the senses must be replaced by the Eucharist. This is the point of Calderón's use of the myth. The pagan has been transformed in the Christian age into an allegory of sacred history, salvation, and the power of the Eucharist: "De Psiquis y Cupido / la alegoría aquí acaba" [Of Psyche and Cupid / here the allegory ends] (2012, vv. 1538–9).[13]

Calderón also used the myth of Cupid and Psyche in one of his mythological court plays, *Ni amor se libra de amor*, performed with music at the Retiro in 1662.[14] It precedes the second version of the sacramental play *Psiquis y Cupido* (1665), written for Madrid, and is a most lyrical and enticing *comedia* where Calderón brings the myth closer to our world, adorning it with a series of palace intrigues. What Louise Stein has called a "court play with music" (1993, 270) follows Apuleius from the start. Venus becomes envious of Psyche as people think her more beautiful than the goddess and thus profane her rituals. Furious, Venus seeks vengeance: "Infelice tu hermosura, / Siquis será, pues tu dueño / un monstruo ha de ser" [Wretched your beauty will be, / Psyche, for your owner / a monster shall be] (Calderón 1969, 1948). She is ordered to be sacrificed at a ruined temple in Mount Oeta (1969, 1955). As opposed to the sacramental plays, Cupid is not at first disposed to love Psyche. Upon seeing her striking beauty, he debates between vengeance and love. In a slumber she calls out, "Monstruo, detente" [stop, Monster] (1969, 1957). He drops his arrow, and it is picked up by Psyche, who, waking up, wounds him, and in so doing, unwittingly makes the god of love fall in love. In this play, violence is never far away and always has unforeseen consequences. If it were not for Venus's desire for vengeance, Cupid would never have met Psyche; and were it not for Psyche's violent outburst, the god might not have fully embraced the love for her.

In the second act Psyche laments her fate: "ni imaginada tragedia / como que desamparada / de un padre ... / en tan remota isla, bárbara y desierta" [unimagined tragedy / as abandoned / by a father... / in such a remote, barbarous, and deserted island] (1969, 1962). Very much as in the 1640 *auto*, there is a sudden transformation. A nymph comes to guide her to a sumptuous palace and tells her she has been saved. When Cupid appears, he attempts to woo her, but must remain invisible; a behaviour that does not allay her suspicions. All that is of value in this world is placed at her feet by Cupid: precious stones such as diamonds, rubies, and emeralds; metals such as gold and silver (1969, 1969). Music and song surround her, and she is bidden to enjoy in her meals all possible delicacies: "registrará tu mesa / cuanto hay que el mar circunde, cuanto hay que el monte corre / cuanto hay que el aire cruce" [your table will have / everything that circles the sea, everything that roams the mountain / everything that crosses the air] (1969, 1967). Thus she will partake of foods that derive from three of the four elements: earth, water, and air. Calderón subtly transforms the banquet of the senses into one that foregrounds the elements, showing how Cupid's love for Psyche is all-encompassing. Although staged on earth, this banquet can be considered as celestial since it is orchestrated by a god, it is made of the elements necessary for the creation of the cosmos, and the servers are beings from another realm. In the midst of all these bountiful gifts, Psyche will not follow the expected script, she will not fall for her invisible lover. This is her banquet, but one she disdains, as she is suspicious of Cupid. The fire of love (the fourth and missing element) has not as yet enraptured her. Fire brings about her doom and deliverance in the third act as she takes a candle to see her monstrous beloved and finds him to be the god of love. Thomas A. O'Connor has recognized the importance of the offence-vengeance cycle in the play. At this point "it resumes its deadly trajectory" (1988, 235), with Psyche wanting revenge on all for her loss. But it is the gods' forgiveness that brings about a happy conclusion. Even the courtly intrigues (not at all part of Apuleius's tale) are resolved as the characters Astrea and Selenisa marry the suitors they once disdained, Arsidas and Lidoro. Even though Cupid has to act as *deus ex machina* in these two worldly marriages, the love between him and Psyche has been earned through numerous trials and stands as unique. There is no final banquet, but one is not needed since the earlier banquet had encompassed all earthly and cosmic delights. This is instead a moment of apotheosis where even Venus has forgiven her human counterpart and accepts her as part of the family of the gods. Spectators would be enabled to imagine a version of Raphael's celestial banquet.

At the beginning of the third act, the servant Friso contends that his master and lady, Psyche and Cupid, deserve to be named: "ella es la dama duende / y él es el galán fantasma" [she is the phantom lady / and he the handsome ghost] (1969, 1968). Clearly, Calderón is quoting here the titles of two of his most popular comedies. Of the two, the first one is based on a gender reversal of the tale of Cupid and Psyche. Indeed, Calderón was not the first to fashion the "Invisible Mistress" plot. Italian *novelle* had already used the topic, and by the time he would write

La dama duende in 1629, Lope de Vega and Tirso de Molina had written plays on the subject.[15] In all of these works, it is the woman, not the god of love, who is veiled, masked, or in darkness. And the suitor is the one who expresses confusion and curiosity. Following the myth, in *La dama duende* the gallant is taken to doña Ángela's abode (Cupid's mysterious palace in the myth), where she offers the man a light meal (*colación*) to make him at ease and underline notions of desire. Again, it is this early meal that is the centrepiece, which is much more earthly and modest than the one in *Ni amor se libra de amor*. In this and other plays featuring the Invisible Mistress, what we have is an attenuated banquet of the senses. While in Lope de Vega's *La viuda valenciana* the meeting and the meal take place early on, in Calderón's *La dama duende* they do not occur until the third act.[16] Don Manuel is taken in darkness to the lady's rooms where he is greeted by her, her attendants, and her friend doña Beatriz. The curious gallant is surprised at the luxurious surroundings:

> ¡Qué casa tan alhajada!
> ¡Qué mujeres tan lucidas!
> ¡Qué damas tan bien prendidas!
> ¡Qué beldad tan estremada! (1999, vv. 2278–82)

> [What a beautiful house!
> What brilliant women!
> What adorned ladies!
> What admirable beauty!]

The stage directions stress the elegance of the moment and the availability of food and drink: "Salen todas las mujeres con toallas y conservas y agua, y haciendo reverencia todas" [All the women come out carrying cloths and preserves and water, making all kinds of curtsies] (1999, 103). Soon, he is being served water and sweets to set him at ease and to further the appearance of comfort and luxury. The offering of water rather than wine may be a nod to decorum, since don Manuel is in the lady's own apartments, a situation that could reflect on her honour. The meeting and "banquet" follow Ángela's script: she is the author of this theatrical moment, much as Cupid had overseen the banquet in Calderón's mythological play. Don Manuel seems to embrace his role, praising the lady and her surroundings, but he is still troubled because he does not know her identity. Although he had tried to see his invisible lady before by bringing in a light, that event had not affected their relation; it did not cause banishment as in the case of Psyche. In Calderón, it is at the moment of heightened anticipation during the banquet that the situation unravels. Doña Ángela's brother, don Luis, knocks at the door. After scenes of concealment, confusion, confrontation, and imminent danger, the comedy ends in marriage.[17] The Invisible Mistress, through her ruses, has been able to turn the rooms where she is confined in her brothers' house into a place of fantasy. She has lured don Manuel into her imaginative spaces and thus gained his love. The banquet, then, is not fully a banquet of sense, but one of the imagination, where the lady wishes to obtain the love of a man who rescued her while she was veiled at the beginning of the work. She is both Cupid, who fosters love, and a phantom hidden in her home. Thus she becomes a true *duende*, a trickster and a quasi-supernatural being who is able to go beyond her brothers' watchful eyes and conquer the man she loves.[18]

In this first section, then, we have seen how the myth of Cupid and Psyche blends in very well with the sacramental plays of Golden Age Spain, bringing together the celestial banquet found in the myth and the celebration of the Eucharist, a main trait of the *autos*. When Calderón transfers the story to a play dealing with mythology, he prefers to emphasize the banquets in Psyche's mysterious palace, which are ordered by the god of love. These banquets partake of the celestial since they seek to convince Psyche that she is loved and cared for, and that the bounties he provides are cosmic in nature, partaking of the four elements. When Calderón converts the myth into a comedy, he again focuses on the palace banquet, but this time it seems to slide in the direction of the banquet of sense, although it is more of exaltation of the imagination and of woman's power to envision a better future. All four banquets, then, are ways to dramatize hope and future fulfilment.

II. Unholy Banquets

Calderón, *La cena del rey Baltasar* [King Baltasar's feast] (c. 1635)[19]
Claramonte, *El secreto en la mujer* [Woman's secret] (c. 1617)
Moreto, *La cena del rey Baltasar* [King Baltasar's feast] (1642–8)

Banquets in the sacramental plays can also have the very opposite meaning of a sacred supper or a heavenly feast. This section will turn to a sacramental play and two secular *comedias* to view unholy banquets that challenge the divine. The biblical tale of Baltasar's banquet followed by the divine letters of doom was used as subject by Cristóbal Suárez in a work that is now lost but was performed in Seville in 1613 (Sánchez Arjona 1887, 283; Parker 1986, 160). It may be that Calderón knew this early work and used it for his *La cena del rey Baltasar*. For Alexander Parker, the pay deals with "a conflict between a vain, idolatrous King and the Prophet of God's chosen people whom he has enslaved" (1986, 194). This critic also points out that most characters are aspects of Baltasar's mind. At the *auto*'s inception, Baltasar, already married to *Vanidad*, announces that he will take a second wife, *Idolatría*. At the same time, the prophet Daniel tries to have him see reason through the figure of *Pensamiento*. Once married, the two wives promote the deceit of the senses. As Antonio Sánchez Jiménez and Adrián J. Sáez, the editors of the play, point out, God seeks Baltasar's conversion through a meditation on power and through warnings of mortality (2013, 27–36). After all, as Daniel asserts:

> Baltasar quiere decir
> "tesoro escondido," y yo
> sé que en los hombres las almas
> tesoro escondido son (2013, vv. 754–6)

> [Baltasar means
> "hidden treasure," and I
> know that souls are hidden treasures
> in men]

While Daniel seeks to bring out this hidden treasure, Baltasar continues to be comforted by the deceits of his wives. Not even a striking ekphrastic dream featuring an equestrian portrait and a tower is able to shake Baltasar's course. Thus we move to the banquet or *cena* of doom, which is amplified from its biblical source, becoming a sumptuous feast. Idolatry announces to the king:

> Una opulenta cena
> de las delicias y regalos llena
> que la gula ha ignorado
> te tiene prevenida mi cuidado,
> adonde los sentidos
> todos hallan sus platos prevenidos (2013, vv. 1236–42)

> [An opulent dinner
> abundant in delicacies and gifts
> that gluttony has ignored,
> where all the senses find their dishes]

In this lavish banquet, the sideboards showcase plates and utensils of silver and gold that delight the eyes. Aromas of flowers and delicious dishes play to the sense of smell; music pleases the ears; the elaborate tablecloth satisfies the touch; and the costly drinks highlight taste (2013, vv. 1236–68). All his senses, Idolatry claims, should be satisfied: "olfato, ojos y oídos, gusto y tacto" (2013, v. 1284). As Ignacio Arellano has noted, the vivid description even includes "ingeniosos trueques de atribuciones que mencionan el hambre del olfato y la sed del oído" [ingenious exchanges of attributions that mention hunger for smell and thirst of hearing] (2001, 74). The sumptuousness of the meal is not Calderón's invention (fig. 6.3). It is hinted at in the source and led Rembrandt to paint the scene with the king wearing a golden cloak, shining in the chiaroscuro of the work. But his golden robe pales in brightness next to letters written on the wall by the divine hand. In the play, it is up to Baltasar to decide on the final script, on how he will play his part. Will he remain tied to earthly power, riches, and sensual gratification, or will he seek to transcend them? Indeed, this last Chaldean king of Babylon utilizes at the feast the cups that Nebuchadnezzar had stolen from the temple in Jerusalem to toast the leading god of Assyria: "Moloc, dios de los asirios" (2013, v. 1375). In the Old Testament, this god is associated with the sacrifice of children. Given Baltasar's double sacrilege (using the stolen cups and invoking a pagan deity), the figure of Death now explains to him how opposites may inhabit the same object. In the cup of life Baltasar can discover nectar or hemlock, antidote or poison. Accepting the script of Idolatry, and savouring the unholy banquet, he is condemned as Daniel reveals the meaning of the mysterious letters that have appeared on the wall: the end of Baltasar's empire. The unholy banquet thus ends in doom. In Calderón's play the banquet of sense is opposed to the banquet which Daniel wishes for the king: a celestial banquet that points to the Eucharist and is tied to the salvation of humanity through Christ's sacrifice.[20] Once Baltasar has been punished, Daniel prophesies a new banquet for humankind which is then shown to the audience: "Descúbrese con música una mesa con pie de altar y en medio un cáliz y una hostia, y dos velas a los lados" [With music, a table is uncovered, with an altar and in the middle a chalice and a host, and two candles on the sides] (2013, 241). *La cena del rey Baltasar* features two banquets: the terrestrial (replete with the sensual) and the celestial, in what is perhaps one of the clearest and most effective contrasts between the two extremes in the theatre of the Golden Age.

Very much like the myth of Cupid and Psyche, the biblical story of Baltasar's feast became part of secular theatre. Andrés de Claramonte's *El secreto en la mujer* (c. 1617), for example, makes use of the story for extended allusion. When the suitor, Lelio, receives a letter from his beloved Clavela, his reaction is one of great joy as he describes the writing as burning letters. This reminds his servant of those letters "que

Figure 6.3. Rembrandt van Rijn, *Belshazzar's Feast* (detail), 1635, National Gallery, London. FineArt / Alamy Stock Photo.

vió escritas Baltasar / en el templo" [that Baltasar saw written / in the temple] (1991, vv. 313–14). This is followed by an attempt at interpretation from both the servant and his master. The latter, as is the case with Daniel in the biblical text, turns to the Hebrew. Being a lover, he interprets the letters in a positive manner. However, the letter, given to him by Clavela, recalls the second term that God used in his judgment of Baltasar as found in Calderón's *auto. Tecel* is judgment itself: "y que en el peso / no cabe una culpa más" [and in the balance / not a single additional guilt fits] (2013, vv. 1458–9). Instead of a banquet, Lelio, at the end of the play, wishes to cook for his beloved a meal and, given his poverty, he offers her a falcon. But this turns out to be a banquet of doom since it goes against two of three precepts that his father had ordered him to follow: not to act against his patron and not to confess his secret to a woman. Clavela turns him in to the duke, who had ordered that whoever is found guilty of stealing his falcon would be condemned to death. Once again, we have a character who prefers to follow the senses instead of the dictates of the "father." The cooking of the falcon is his banquet of doom. Although Claramonte saves Lelio at the very end with a surprising peripety, there is little question that the work follows closely the biblical tale, and may even have borrowed from the lost *auto* by Cristóbal Suárez. If such is the case, it may even be possible to reconstruct some of the *auto*'s basic elements from Claramonte's play and thus come up with some of the elements Calderón could have utilized from Suárez. Indeed, even the opposition antidote/ poison, found in Calderón, is clearly present in Claramonte.[21]

Agustín Moreto writes a full play on the subject: *La cena del rey Baltasar* (before 1648). Very much like Calderón's *Ni amor se libra de amor*, where a mythical tale is brought down to earth with a series of courtly intrigues, Moreto's *comedia* takes a biblical tale and removes many of its sacred elements, turning it into a play of palace intrigue. The first two acts have very little to do with the biblical tale, centring on courtly scheming and in particular the amorous rivalries between two ladies (Fénix and Diana) and two suitors (Ciro and Baltasar) (Lobato 2012, 604). Only in the last act does Moreto borrow from both the biblical tale and Calderón's sacramental play.[22] Here, instead of toasting the pagan gods as in Calderón, Baltasar toasts the beauty of Fénix as the music plays: "Haga la música salva / la hermosura sin igual / de Fénix divina viva" [Let music protect / the unequalled beauty / of the living divine Phoenix] (Moreto 1798, 29). For Fénix, the toast carries poison, since she loves another. But for Baltasar, this is a banquet of the senses as he delights in food, drink, and his beloved's beauty, which he describes in terms of "sol, nieve, rosa y coral" [sun, snow, rose, and coral] (1798, 30). As they toss away the glasses, thunder strikes, the banquet table disappears, and fateful words appear on the wall, which Daniel interprets. This is a strikingly theatrical moment where an earthly banquet is upstaged by the divine, who denies Baltasar's power and even the reality of the banquet as the table disappears. However, this scene is diminished by the conclusion. Fenix's beloved, Ciro, has conquered the city and enters to claim his bride and kill Baltasar. The king, unable to draw his sword, has to defend himself with the plates from the banquet and is finally brought down by many soldiers and swords. Moreto's play, then, conjoins the biblical and the theatrical to forge a denouement that may be pleasing to the audience but that fails to coalesce. The disappearance of the banquet would have made for a striking denouement. Instead, Moreto delivers a violent and melodramatic ending.

This second section has underlined that sacramental plays can include unholy banquets, where the main figure rebels against God's script of salvation, turning instead to the senses. The cup of salvation is turned into poison. Baltasar's biblical disobedience is reformulated in Claramonte as a man's disregard for his father's precepts. Once again, by rejecting the script and embracing inordinate passion, the character suffers. Moreto reworks the sacramental play to create a work of love and intrigue at court, but one that preserves the biblical story, albeit adorned and deprived of some of its power. Here, the banquet is once again unholy. By this I mean that it rejects the divine script and foregrounds rebellion that delights in earthly power, the senses, and the unrepentant will. The term holy derives from *hagios*, which means "different" – in other words, different from the world. In these plays, the characters seek difference in the world, which only makes them more subject to its allurements and to deceit and mortality. In the sumptuous banquet, the unruly king is ruled by his will and ego; he thinks himself different but is actually rejecting difference, distancing himself from the divine and embracing the unholy.

III. Rustic Repasts: Nature and Symbol

Lope de Vega, *La niñez de San Isidro* [The childhood of Saint Isidro] (1622)
Lope de Vega, *Peribáñez y el comendador de Ocaña* [Peribáñez and the commander from Ocaña] (c. 1610)

From the celestial and unholy, we now turn to rustic banquets where nature and symbol go hand in hand. There are many variations on this type of repast, from those showing the excesses of the senses to symbolic banquets and to works where the rustic banquet becomes the food for the true Christian. Before I discuss in greater detail the two plays by Lope that are the focus of this section, I will briefly point to Valdivielso. His sacramental play *El villano en su rincón* shows how Juan Labrador, a wealthy farmer, enjoys the delights of *Apetito* and *Gusto*, living without knowledge of his king. *Apetito* describes an opulent banquet which even includes quail, but the many symbolic dishes hide their subjection to the pagan, such as "una holla / que a las de Egypto parece" [a stew that resembles those of Egypt] and "del rey Nabuco una lengua" [a tongue of king Nabuco] (1622, 6v). The play shows how the farmer comes to know the king and learns from him how to act properly: "que el apetito y el gusto / solo ha de hazer lo que es justo / que es servir a la razón" [that appetite and taste / only do what is fair / that is, to serve reason] (1622, 11v). In a reversal of the opposition court/sensuality versus country/simplicity, the sensual banquet is to be found in the countryside, while the celestial meal is at court. Lope's *La quinta de Florencia* [The Florentine villa] also shows the opposition between court and country, but here it is the farmer who teaches the duke how to behave. The work exhibits a fully symbolic meal in which the Duke of Florence is shown the meaning of rustic honour.

Hagiographical plays often seek to depict a celestial banquet, and these can occur in a rustic setting. Lope de Vega wrote a number of works dealing with the patron saint of Madrid, San Isidro. He began with a lengthy poem written in 1599, which gave impetus to Isidro's future beatification in 1619 and canonization three years later.[23] It was followed by *San Isidro Labrador*, which recounts the life of the saint. In 1622, for the feast of canonization, Lope composed two more plays.[24] The first of these two is of interest here in relation to food and banquets. *La niñez de San Isidro* is a devotional work written to celebrate the patron saint of Madrid, composed in two acts and with a *Loa*. The relation between a coming Age of Gold and the birth of this future saint is a key motif. In the *Loa*, the new rule of Philip IV is praised as "el tiempo feliz en que reina Astrea" [the happy times when Astrea rules] (1965, 327). Although the new ruler may be seen as the figure who is to bring the new age, it is a saintly child, San Isidro, who will be canonized shortly after his coronation and who will foreground a new Christian Golden Age. The first act centres on his birth: the mother, Inés, prays to have a saintly child, while the father, Pedro, has a dream vision that confirms that this child will be a saint. Inés equates the child with the grains of wheat from the crops, and offers them to God: "que cada grano de espiga / precioso diamante fuera" [that every grain of wheat / be a precious diamond] (1965, 329). As Françoise Cazal reminds us, Isidro's mother offers to heaven not just her child but also the crops of the fields: "En su discurso, Inés ofrece conjuntamente a Cristo el fruto de sus entrañas y los granos de trigo de la próxima cosecha de su esposo Pedro, estableciéndose de este modo una equivalencia entre los dos ofrecimientos" [In her speech, Inés offers to Christ both the fruit of her womb and the grains of wheat of her husband Pedro's next harvest, establishing an equivalence between the two offerings] (2005, n.p.). This action points to the offering of the host in Christian churches. The Eucharist's bread (made of wheat) turns into the body of Christ. Thus, Inés's offering echoes Christ's sacrifice. The act ends with Isidro's birth and baptism. The goodness of the child, his charity and devotion, are foregrounded in the second act, as well as his first miracles. The act concludes when Jesus descends from the heavens disguised as a shepherd.

He asks Isidro for a *merienda*, but after a pious conversation, Christ offers one to him: "Baje una mesa y una silla entre dos ángeles, con unas flores y un panal" [Bring down a table and a chair between two angels, with flowers and a honeycomb] (1965, 358). With the use of rudimentary stage machinery, the spectators can view how a celestial banquet is brought down from heaven. The honeycomb, as Ryan Giles explains in an essay in this volume, is often equated with the sweet word of God.[25] This is truly a celestial meal where the sweetness of honey and the smell of the flowers (used by the bees for their honey) elevate the senses to the divine. Isidro, realizing the nature of his guest, kneels as Jesus blesses the table. The play ends as the labourers offer their crop of wheat to the Virgin of Atocha in Madrid, while the child Isidro offers a cross to the Virgin's child. The repetition of the wheat image reinforces the relation between the sacred and political action of the play. Astraea, goddess of the new Golden Age under Philip, is often represented with a sheaf of wheat. Thus, the play is a celebration of a new political and religious age with a new monarch and a new saint.

Turning to a secular work by Lope, we find the same symbolic equivalency between wheat and the fruits of the marriage, as well as the relation of wheat and the Eucharist. Lope de Vega's peasant honour play *Peribáñez y el comendador de Ocaña* begins with the bliss of the newly married Peribáñez and his wife Casilda. What we have at the inception is a feast of words in which each compares the other to elements from nature. Peribáñez views Casilda in terms of an olive grove, a field, an apple, oil, wine, and wheat harvested in August (1986, 1.41–66), while she envisions him as a brave bull in the fields (1986, 1.111–12). Around them, others sing and dance, also praising the fertility of the fields and the couple's union. This rustic wedding feast is interrupted by the Comendador, who immediately falls for the bride and spoils the feast with his untimely appearance.[26] Although Peribáñez is immediately suspicious, the wedded harmony is not shattered. Later, Casilda affirms her love for her new husband as she recounts the rustic banquet she prepares for Peribáñez when he returns from the fields. Here all the senses are invoked. She claims to know in her very soul the moment he returns from his labours and seeks to enter the home. She goes to open the door, embracing him "y yo me arrojo en sus brazos" [and throwing myself into his arms] (1986, 1.175). The couple gladly hears the sound of cooking and the smell the garlic and onion from the kitchen. Sitting for the meal, they are gratified by the sight of the "limpios manteles" [clean tablecloths] (1986, 1.748); and while there is no silver, the plates are of high quality: "no en plata, aunque yo quisiera / platos son de Talavera" [they are not silver, though I would want them to be / they are from

Talavera] (1986, 1.749). Silver was the mark of aristocratic tableware, while pottery from Talavera was highly praised, but signified lower ranks in society. Here, as with the finer porcelain, Lope compares the plates to carnations.[27] They are then beautiful to the eye, and represent conformity with one's station and the bounty and magnificence that is hidden in the countryside. The rustic banquet in Lope's play points to the praise of the country. It contrasts with the excessive opulence of the court, which often hides danger, poisonous cups, and numerous faults and vices. The Comendador is a good example of such perils as he attempts to bring disharmony to rustic marital bliss. There is indeed a banquet of sense here, but one that is attenuated through simplicity and equated with goodness and innocence.

Rustic banquets display or at least connote a dislike for the sumptuous meals at court. These simple feasts derive from products of the earth that surround the banqueters. Even more so when it comes from the heavens, the ingredients are pure, wholesome. The script here is that the labourers have an innocence and a relation to nature that is absent in the artificiality of the court.

IV. The Banquet of Sense

Ruiz de Alarcón, *La verdad sospechosa* [Suspect truth] (1618–21)
Lope de Vega, *El anzuelo de Fenisa* [Fenisa's hook] (1604–6)

What has been called the Banquet of Sense derives from both the biblical and the classical tradition. The first is based on the passage on the Eucharist in Corinthians 10 where Paul admonishes: "Ye cannot drink of the cup of the Lord and the cup of devils, ye cannot be partakers of the Lord's table and of the table of devils" (Kermode 1961, 69). The classical version is echoed by Marsilio Ficino's commentary on Plato's *Symposium*, as he discusses the three Venuses (celestial, terrestrial, and bestial) (1985, 53–4).[28] Frank Kermode asserts: "Ficino draws ... strong contrasts between the extremes of bestial and heavenly love with reference to the banquet – the banquet of heavenly love which the man who abandons himself to voluptuousness is giving up" (1961, 78). The bestial man replaces the heavenly banquet (symbolized by the Eucharist in Christianity and foreshadowed by Plato's banquet) with the biblical table of devils, which becomes a banquet of the senses. Kermode explains: "The danger is that the gratification of the senses becomes an end in itself, so that a sensual *Voluptas* is taken for the highest good" (1961, 72). As noted by Ficino, and continued in the tradition, there is a hierarchy of the senses with sight at the top, which can lead to the celestial, and touch at the bottom, which is associated with the venereal and infernal.

Throughout this essay we have noted how plays during the early modern period stage either celestial or unholy banquets often connoting the opposition between the pure, simple, and divine versus the courtly, sensual, and devilish. Only in Cupid's enchanted or supernatural palace is the sumptuous banquet considered positive, since its script and ingredients are derived from the god of love. In other cases, the courtly, as evinced by Baltasar, points to deceit and rebellion as it revels in the senses. There is perhaps no better example of this banquet of sense in Golden Age theatre than Juan Ruiz de Alarcón's *La verdad sospechosa*. In this complex and dazzling play, don García comes up with at least ten lies or inventions in order to amaze those around him at court. Learning of his fault, his father is intent on marrying him as soon as possible, while the gallant comes to love at first sight one of two ladies he sees emerging from a coach, the one he considers "la más bella" (1982, v. 558) When his servant Tristán asks the coachman for the name of the most beautiful of the women, he is told that she is Lucrecia de Luna. Don García cannot even conceive that the *cochero* is naming the other lady. He thus believes he has fallen for Lucrecia while in reality his beloved's name is Jacinta.[29] The plot revolves around this confusion and García's many lies and inventions. Of all the inventions, there is one that stands out and brings us to the banquet. García runs into two former friends, don Juan and don Félix, who are in the midst of discussing a mysterious banquet that took place by the river, where a gallant wooed a lady. García immediately sets out to improvise, claiming that he was the suitor. His invention is surprisingly detailed. García explains that at his banquet, the set-up was quite elaborate. Six tents were erected, each containing a different part of the meal: appetizers, desserts, meats, etc. In addition, there were four sideboards with dinner services and utensils of gold, silver, crystal, and pottery (1982, vv. 677–80). The mixture of precious metals and pottery can signify the blending of a courtly banquet with a rustic feast – it is held outside, by the river. In their midst was a "limpia y olorosa mesa" [clean and fragrant table] (1982, v. 670) with an elaborate tablecloth and napkins. Again, the clean table contrasts with the coverings to suggest a blending of spaces. It is as if García is imagining the best of the country and the best of the court and offering it to his beloved. Actually, he is offering it as an act of rhetorical perfection and bravado to his stunned listeners.

And yet, this is but the prelude to García's invention. As the listeners come to terms with the fact that all of this had to be somehow transported to the banks of the river, García describes the arrival of the lady and the full feast. James F. Burke, who has studied the subsequent fabrication in detail, argues that it derives from the Banquet of Sense: "It showed how man, through an ever increasing involvement with sensual experience, could descend through the senses until his only concern was the gratification of the lower soul. Through such a fall he would in effect become a beast or an adherent to bestial love" (1986, 52). At the same time this critic believes that this invention shows, first of all, García's love for Jacinta; and secondly, his detachment from the scene, since it is an invention. Thus, it cannot portray García as a fallen being, enslaved by the senses.[30]

However, I would argue the opposite on both points: that since the invention presents the senses from highest to lowest, it may intimate and/or foreshadow García's slow descent towards the devilish; and that it does not really signify Garcia's love for his lady, but his desire to be heard, to amaze others with his feats, albeit fictitious. In addition, the presentation of the senses is rather ambiguous, evincing a penchant for the devilish. He first regales the lady with fireworks, thus turning to the sense of sight. This may appear as a celestial image for the banquet, but already here there are premonitions of a fall, since fireworks mimic stars but really do not belong in the heavens. One of the verses clearly calls them "sulfúreas luces" [sulphuric lights] (1982, v. 702), and the smell of sulphur is associated with the devil and the infernal regions. Twenty-four torches light the scene while music plays in the background. Thirty-two dishes are brought out, not counting appetizers or desserts. We thus move from celestial sight and hearing to an amount of food that points to gluttony. The many aromas saturate the air, thus pleasing the sense of smell. Touch comes last as García presents his lady with a jewel in the form of a man pierced by the golden arrows of love. All this is followed by singing, so that the god Apollo, envious of a human feast, has to send in the dawn to end it. The envy of the gods, of course, is yet another reminder that this banquet challenges the divine. Let us recall that García imagined that there were twenty-four torches lighting the banquet. These torches may represent the hours in a full day and night, expressing the desire to be with the lady at all hours. As master of day and night, García challenges Apollo and approaches the rebellions of Baltasar.

Particularly telling is don Juan's comment on the banquet: "Que fue el festín / más célebre que pudiera / hacer Alejandro Magno" [the feast was more noted than any Alexander the Great could have given] (1982, vv. 761–3). Alexander was renowned for banquets that featured excess. In the Renaissance and early modern period, his banquets are featured in art and music, from Domenico del Barbiere's *Banquet of Alexander the Great* to Dryden's *Alexander's Feast or the Power of Music* (1697). In this latter piece, we see how music (and rhetoric) can transform Alexander, puffing him up with pride, driving him to drink or to burn with passion for his mistress Thais. Indeed, this is part of one of the best-known anecdotes concerning Alexander. On winning Persepolis, he gave a grand banquet to celebrate the victory and, according to Diodorus (as recorded by Plutarch), one of the famed courtesans, Thais, said in jest that they should burn all the temples of the city. Intoxicated by drink, Alexander ordered this done. He led a parade with torches, in honour of Dionysus, god of ecstasy. He was followed by Thais and then by the rest of his drunken revellers, who all had a hand in torching Persepolis (Wood 1997, 114). In many ways, don Juan's comments are directed at García. Like Alexander, he is too passionate, too proud of his "conquests." And like Alexander's, his banquet is surrounded by torches, recalling the torching of Persepolis. Indeed, later in the play we discover that García is in love with fame most of all (de Armas 1996). He indicates that he would torch the temple of Diana at Ephesus if this is what was needed: "Ser famosos es gran cosa / el medio cual fuere sea … / pues uno por ganar nombre / abrasó el templo de Efesia" [To be famous is a great thing / no matter the means … / for to be renowned someone burned the temple at Ephesus] (1982, vv. 861–2, 865–6). It seems, then, that don Juan is correct. García craves fame and would do anything for it, including the fashioning of a verbal banquet of sense that would rival the legendary banquets of Alexander the Great and the torching of temples.

If García can throw a verbal banquet for his beloved, a figure that compares to the courtesan Thais can also be the hostess for a banquet of sense. Lope de Vega's *El anzuelo de Fenisa* has been singled out for its "spirit of freedom" (Stoll 1991, 256), questioning strict social mores of the period.[31] Anita Stoll has summarized the main action of the work thus: "Fenisa is a beautiful woman who, by her own testimony, was once deceived by a man. Now she devotes her beauty and her wiles to deceiving men for pleasure and money … Her victim in the play is Lucindo, a Spanish merchant who has just arrived with goods to sell" (1991, 245). On seeing him arrive at the port of Palermo in Sicily, Fenisa, as an experienced courtesan who understands that he is a rich merchant, immediately sets out to seduce him.[32] Even though he holds as his motto that women can be worse than pirates (2009, vv. 299–301), she does not hesitate, wishing to seize all his possessions and abandon him love-lorn: "El cuerpo en cueros dejalle / y el alma con mataduras" [Leave his body naked / and his soul full of sores] (Lope de Vega 2009, vv. 445–6). She invites Lucindo to her home, where she shows him an

162   Frederick A. de Armas

astonishing art collection, featuring many mythological subjects. Indeed, she may see herself in some of the art, as a new Helen of Troy or a new Cleopatra.

After they engage in intimate conversation, servants bring out a *colación* or light meal, made up mainly of sweets. Lucindo's servant warns him of treachery and Lucindo even turns down wine in favour of water, but Fenisa begins to make inroads. Even though the banquet itself is minimal, it certainly involves seeing the beautiful artworks and the beautiful courtesan, hearing her many blandishments and praises, and tasting, even if the drink he chooses is only water. Her gifts to him call on the missing senses: incense relates to smell and amber gloves relate to both smell and touch. Touch is of course the lowest of the five senses, and the one that Lucindo most wants to experience with Fenisa. The banquet is but a prelude to sexual satisfaction, a promise which is subtly dangled before the befuddled merchant. It is all too much for him as he succumbs and lists all the precious objects he will bring for her. The banquet of sense has had its effect; Fenisa's script has worked to such an extent that Lucindo, in the end, falls for her, albeit not without qualms.[33] Although Lucindo will return from Spain in the third act to dupe Fenisa in a counter-trick, what is of importance here is that the banquet of sense has become the tool of a courtesan to dupe and steal from her client. She uses all five senses to accomplish this. The banquet of sense has reached a low point. While with García it had a somewhat higher purpose, the acquisition of fame no matter the cost, with Fenisa it seems to descend to gratification of the senses and particularly of touch.[34] Although never as transgressive as the unholy banquet, the banquet of sense points to a rebellious figure that wills to win at all costs, be it through lies or through the senses.

V. A Demonic Banquet

Tirso de Molina, *El burlador de Sevilla* [The trickster of Seville]
   (1617–29)

As we reach the conclusion of this essay, let us briefly view how Tirso de Molina's *El burlador de Sevilla* moves beyond the unholy banquet to the realm of the demonic. While Baltasar's banquets in Calderón and Moreto exhibited sumptuous earthly delights which would lead to doom and damnation, no such foodstuff is found in Tirso's play.[35] After his many conquests and transgressions, don Juan, who insults the stone statue of don Gonzalo de Ulloa, a man he has killed, asks him to dinner. In a doubling of the invitation, the statue appears at the inn at dinner time and then invites don Juan to dine with him. The following night, an ill-fated Tuesday, the very night he is to wed, don Juan goes to the church, where he is greeted by the dead man. While his servant declines the meal since he has "merendado esta tarde" [eaten this afternoon] (1991, v. 2800), don Juan and the walking statue face each other in front of don Gonzalo's tomb and sit in two chairs brought by servants in black. The banquet consists of creatures associated with the nether regions such as the scorpion and the viper. When the *gracioso*, Catalinón, is asked to drink the wine, he exclaims that it tastes like gall, and that it has turned to vinegar. This transformation of wine into vinegar underscores the metamorphosis of don Juan's pleasurable life into its opposite. In many ways this moment echoes the biblical description of the crucifixion of Christ, as he refuses to drink cheap Roman vinegar wine (Matthew 27:34). In the play, a buffoonish servant is made to drink it, while the living statue of the Commander explains that such wine is brewed in the infernal regions. Don Juan claims he will eat or drink anything. And indeed "hiel" [gall], a bitter humour, is said to make men impetuous. This impetuosity is but one of many faults in don Juan, who partakes of a demonic banquet, an earthly example of his coming sufferings in the nether regions. The Commander's first-hand knowledge of hellish beverages may point to the fact that he is one of the condemned, although it is difficult to determine if he comes from above or from below to bring retribution.[36]

Whatever the answer, once the meal is ended, the statue asks for don Juan's hand in an allusive gesture that recalls the many deceptions by don Juan where he has asked for a woman's hand in marriage. Giving it, don Juan begins to experience the torments of hell. Fire and ice, the two opposite sensations he experiences, are also Petrarchan images of love. Once again, there is a careful symmetry and a *contrapassio*.[37] Don Juan is soon taken to the nether regions as the sepulchre caves in. This has been a banquet of sense in reverse. Instead of leading to pleasure, the senses serve to terrorize and torment. The sight of a walking statue inspires awe; hearing a fateful song at dinner that calls for punishment foreshadows the coming doom. Although smell is not mentioned, the reader or spectator would imagine the rancid smell of the drink or the mustiness of the tomb. The taste of infernal foods anticipates upcoming torments; and touch (the hand) leads to pain. It recalls the hand of God at Baltasar's banquet. The sweet touch of sexual satisfaction has turned into the infernal fires of hell. For James Mandrell, don Juan is a new Cupid, a demonic figure of passion, that brings harmony in spite of himself.[38]

We have gone full circle, once again encountering the multifaceted god of love: we began this study with the figure of Cupid in the celestial suppers based on Apuleius's myth, and have ended it with a demonic Cupid. In works featuring celestial banquets, the human being is reminded of his divine origins through repeated hierophanies, including supernatural suppers at a mysterious palace on earth. Although Psyche rejects the demands of her divinity, acting against his commands, she eventually repents. Psyche is wedded to Love as she is taken to the heavens and enjoys the celestial banquet which on earth is tied to the Christian Eucharist, as seen in the sacramental plays by Calderón and Valdivielso. Even when the myth is transformed into a secular palace performance, some of the main features remain; and even as it is displaced into a comedy, there is a vague hint of the celestial. Turning to unholy banquets, we have witnessed the allure of the senses and how the celestial script is foiled once and again, leading to Baltasar's doom in Calderón, Claramonte, and Moreto. As for rustic repasts, they seem much closer to the celestial, often opposing courtly pomp to the innocence of the countryside. Christ can even descend to dine with one of his saintly labourers. The banquet of sense is often tied to the feast of devils, as the sensual overwhelms the human being in Ruiz de Alarcón and Lope de Vega. This excess of desire leads to the demonic banquet where a figure no longer redeemable is made to feel the terrors of hell through the senses. The banquet, then, is an essential component of the theatre of the Golden Age, with its many dramatic elements, its malleable script, and its metatheatrical and performative nature. Five types of banquets have been exhibited in relation to the five senses. From the sight of the celestial to demonic touch, these feasts provide insights into the purpose, uses, and meanings of these culinary events during the times of Lope de Vega and Calderón.

NOTES

1 As Jeanneret has pointed out, detailed classification of meals already existed in the Renaissance. Stuckius of Zurich (1582), for example, elaborated a catalogue of "symposiac science" from antiquity and early Christian times, divided into three books: "the first on different kinds of meals ordered according to menu, time of day, occasion, types of guests, whether it is public or private, religious or profane; the second on décor, equipment and service; the third on the items on the menu" (Jeanneret 1991, 71). Unless otherwise noted, translations are by the author.

2 In Tirso's *La venganza de Tamar* [Tamar's vengeance], Amon's body is displayed at the banquet table; and in Guillén de Castro's *Progne y Filomena* [Procne and Philomela], Progne serves her child to her husband as

revenge (Castañeda 2006, 104–6). There are also several other types of banquets which I am not able to cover here; for example, the inverted banquet (where the meal is served backwards) as in Tirso's *El pretendiente al revés* [The counterfeit suitor]; and the treacherous banquet (which hides a deceitful purpose) as in Lope's *Las mujeres sin hombres* [Women without men] and Tirso's *La prudencia en la mujer* [Prudence in woman].

3 "Tomó nombre de las bancas, o mesas sobre que se ponen las viandas" [The name derives from the benches or tables where food is placed] (Covarrubias 1987, 191).

4 "We see the construction of the villa on the Isola del Te in connection with Federigo's love affair with Isabella Boschetti ... Long before Federigo became marquis of Mantua, Isabella Boschetti exerted the most crucial influence on him" (Verheyen 1977, 19–20).

5 Escobar Borrego discusses these poets' use of the myth in detail: Juan de Mal Lara (2002, 77–154), Gutierre de Cetina (2002, 154–62), and Fernando de Herrera (2002, 162–6). The first has an allegorical scheme akin to Fulgentius, while the second may have borrowed from engravings by Benedetto Verino and Agostino Veneziano.

6 For a detailed account of the ancient and Renaissance mythographers and their allegories of this myth, see Enrique Rull's edition of Calderón's *Psiquis y Cupido* (2012, 19–28).

7 For a detailed account of this sacramental play, see Rull (1966, 133–93). He divides the *auto* into six sections: dispute among the suitors; the arrival of Amor and his declaration of love; the plot by Psyche's sisters to gain revenge; the wedding of Amor and Psyche, his doubts, and her fall; the labours of Psyche, her discovery of Amor's secret, and her repentance; and the reconciliation of the lovers through the Virgin and Amor's forgiveness.

8 John Cull asserts: "The Corpus plays are sermons represented" (1997, 107), while Daniel L. Heiple notes how they "have often been appreciated for the subtle way in which they encode and allegorize Catholic theology" (1997, 154).

9 A second *auto* for Madrid in 1665 is beyond our discussion.

10 "El mito de Psique, en su doble vertiente de fábula clásica y alegoría cristiana, bascula peligrosamente en Valdivielso hacia este último lado ... pierde efecto desde el lado literario-teatral en el que se inscribe" [The myth of Psyche, in its double meaning of classical fable and Christian allegory, dangerously tilts Valadivesio towards the latter ... losing its effect in the literary-theatrical side where it is inscribed] (Calderón de la Barca 2012, 54).

11 Rull explains the significance of the allegorized myth: "Por eso Cupido puede ser a la vez malo y bueno para Psique: propiciando primero, como deseo carnal, su destrucción, y luego, como transfiguración espiritual, su

salvación" [This is why Cupid can be both bad and good for Psyche: first, enabling carnal desire, he brings about her destruction, and then, as a spiritual transfiguration, her salvation] (2000, 821).

12 Vincent Martin asserts: "Calderón también convierte la curiosidad de la Psique latina en un acto de desobediencia de la Fe (Psiquis)" [Calderón turns the curiosity of the Latin Psyche into an act of disobedience of Faith] (2002, 93).

13 The significance of the banquet in sacramental plays is, of course, not only limited to reworkings of Apuleius's tale. As Ignacio Arellano asserts, it often appears at the end of the *autos*, modelled after the Last Supper, thus increasing the link between the Eucharist and the banquet scene. Arellano discusses the banquet in *El nuevo hospicio de pobres* [The new hospice for the poor], *Llamados y escogidos* [Called and chosen], and *La protestación de la Fe* [The declaration of Faith] (2001, 44–5).

14 Another important palace performance in this period was Antonio de Solís y Rivadeneyra, *Triunfos de Amor y Fortuna* [Triumphs of Love and Fortune] (1658), where each of these figures takes a mortal under their wing to see who is most successful. Amor picks Psiquis and Fortuna chooses Endimión. In the end, Jupiter judges that both are successful. See Lobato (2002) for this and other works performed in honour of Felipe Próspero. Some have claimed that since Psyche is important to this work, Calderón could not have written his play on the subject in 1662. For a conclusive analysis of 1662 as the date of composition, see Rull's edition of Calderón's *Psiquis y Cupido* (2012, 39–47). He shows, among other things, the bearing of a reference in *Ni amor se libra de amor* to *La dama capitán* [The lady captain], a play attributed to Calderón and performed at the Royal Palace in 1661.

15 On the utilization of the Invisible Mistress plot in Lope de Vega's *La viuda valenciana* [The widow from Valencia] and Calderón's *La dama duende*, see de Armas (1976, 47–91; 123–59). Antonucci, in her edition of *La dama duende*, prefers to find a model in Tirso's *Por el sótano y el torno* [Through the cellar and the turnstile] (1623/4) (Calderón 1999, xxxiiii–xxxix). Arellano finds these two plays so different that he does not see a connection, neglecting to note that both are derived from Apuleius: "La comedia de Lope ... responde a un modelo de comedia urbana conectado todavía con las formas de la baja comicidad y el tono obsceno de la comedia antigua; la de Calderón corresponde a la primera etapa de plenitud de las comedias de capa y espada aurisecular, con un decoro más estricto, siempre dentro del marco cómico" [Lope's play follows the model of an urban comedy which is still connected to low style comedy and the obscene in classical comedy; Calderón's play falls within the first stage of the triumph of the cloak and sword comedies from the Golden Age, with a more

strict notion of decorum, but always within the comic structure] (2006, 188–9).

16 Lope de Vega makes the reader/spectator aware that he is utilizing the myth of Cupid and Psyche. As Camilo seeks to catch a forbidden glimpse of Leonarda, he worries that his fate will parallel that of Psyche: "Que si Psiques vio el amor / A quien ascuras gozaba, / Perdió la gloria en que estaba, / Y negoció su dolor" [If Psyche saw love / Whom in the dark she enjoyed, / She lost the glory in which she was, / And negotiated her own pain] (2001, vv. 1829–32).

17 For some, the imminent danger and other aspects of the play point to tragic elements (Mujica 1969; ter Horst 1972), while others contend that this and other elements are part of the comic genre (Hildner 1979; Arellano 2006).

18 One of the more enticing assessments of Ángela's agency can be found in Bradley J. Nelson (2007).

19 The editors of the play, Antonio Sánchez Jiménez and Adrián J. Sáez, conclude that the sacramental play was written in 1635 or shortly thereafter. Providing a wider window of time, they add: "debe de proceder de los primeros años de la década de 1630" [it must come from the first years of the 1630s] (Calderón 2013, 14).

20 "Y es que el asunto de la celebración eucarística está siempre ligado al tema de la redención humana, al de la salvación" [the Eucharistic celebration is always linked to the theme of human redemption, to salvation] (Sánchez Jiménez y Sáez in Calderón 2013, 18). The editors also note that in *La cena del rey Baltasar* "el asunto redentor-eucarístico se aprecia a lo largo del argumento" [the redemptive-eucharistic theme is present throughout the plot] (2013, 19).

21 For a more detailed analysis of Claramonte's play, see de Armas (1994).

22 For a more detailed analysis of Moreto's borrowings, see Gavela García (2013).

23 See Antonio Sánchez Jiménez's impeccable and erudite edition of the poem in ten cantos. Here, the meal is as important as in the plays. In one of his early miracles Isidro feeds white doves with grains of wheat that belong to his master, but they begin to multiply (Lope de Vega, *Isidro* 2010, 5.636–725). This meal of love is compared to Christ's passion, to the sacrificed lamb.

24 *San Isidro Labrador* is dated 1617. On the three plays on San Isidro, see Gallego Roca (1989, 113–30).

25 The honeycomb image derives, in part, from the scene where Samson finds it in the mouth of a lion (Judges 13:8). It is often used as a eucharistic figure and it is mentioned in Calderón's *La cena del rey Baltasar* (2013, v. 1552).

26 The fact that the Comendador is overwhelmed by a young bull foreshad-
    ows what is about to happen: "It stands surely for sexual desire, and in
    particular for the guilty passion that overwhelms don Fadrique" (Dixon
    1966, 11).

27 Portús Pérez points to Lope's *Del mal lo menos* [Of evil, the less], where the
    carnation is used in a metaphor for a princess (1993, 272).

28 "The first Venus, which is the Mind, is said to have been born of Uranus
    without a mother, because mother, the physicist, is matter ... the other is
    the power of procreation attributed to the World Soul" (Ficino 1985, 53–4).

29 Examining the astrological imagery of the play, Carolyn Nadeau explains:
    "García, the symbolic sun god, searches for his complement and twin,
    Diana, the moon goddess, who appears, not as one might think as his be-
    loved Jacinta, but rather as Lucrecia de Luna whose surname reveals her
    astrological identity" (1998, 65).

30 "It is difficult to believe that Alarcón is not implying something about
    García other than that he would be absolutely firm in his love. One has to
    recall that the entire scene is the product of his imagination" (Burke 1986,
    55).

31 Gómez Canseco echoes Anita Stoll's assessment: "Italia es, pues, un es-
    pacio propicio para romper las ataduras sociales y para vivir con libertad
    moral" [Italy is a favourable space to break social ties and to live with
    moral freedom] (Lope de Vega 2009, 171). D'Antuono claims that Lucindo
    refers to Camila Lucinda, Lope's lover, and the language of the play con-
    tains "a justification by Lope for that illicit passion" (1983, 113).

32 "Among prostitutes a subgroup, to which Fenisa clearly belongs, is the
    buscona (con artist) who does not charge directly for sex but who uses her
    sexuality and her wits to separate her client-victim from his possessions"
    (Gitlitz 1988, xvii–xviii).

33 As David Gitlitz asserts: "From the very start Lope has imbued Lucindo
    with a realistic ambivalence toward Fenisa, a vacillating attitude that re-
    mains until Lucindo finds himself fleeced toward the end of the second
    act" (1988, xv).

34 To be fair to Fenisa, she has become a new Circe because in her youth she
    was betrayed and abandoned by the man she loved. Thus, as courtesan,
    she seeks revenge over and over again.

35 There is an ongoing dispute as to authorship, and new editions simply
    state that the work is attributed to Tirso. For Alfredo Rodríguez López-
    Vázquez (2011), the work was written by Andrés de Claramonte.

36 For Daniel Rogers, the figure of don Gonzalo is merely a divine messen-
    ger: "there is no indication that Don Gonzalo, having delivered his charge
    into hell, will himself be obliged to stay there" (1964, 144). Judith Arias
    contends that don Gonzalo is sent from God, but at the same time she also

argues that he is condemned: "the text means precisely what it says: the Commander suffers the same punishment as Don Juan; he burns in hell" (1990, 370).

37 Archimede Marni explains: "Counterpassion may be defined as the principle whereby justice demands that a sin receive retribution first and foremost in kind" (1952, 129). As mentioned, the statue asks for don Juan's hand just as don Juan has asked for women's hands in marriage in order to trick them.

38 "... he engenders the conditions by which desire is directed toward matrimony in socially productive ways ... Don Juan's failed promises are contradicted by the potential good of the four mutual promises made at the end of the drama" (Mandrell 1992, 82).

WORKS CITED

Albala, Ken. 2007. *The Banquet: Dining in the Great Courts of Renaissance Europe.* Urbana-Champaign: University of Illinois Press.

Allen, Douglas. 2002. *Myth and Religion in Mircea Eliade.* New York: Routledge.

Apuleius. 1990. *Cupid and Psyche.* Edited by E.J. Kenney. Cambridge: Cambridge University Press.

Arellano, Ignacio. 2001. *Estructuras dramáticas y alegóricas en los autos de Calderón.* Kassel and Pamplona: Reichenberger and Universidad de Navarra.

Arellano, Ignacio. 2006. "La dama duende y sus notables casos." In *El escenario cósmico. Estudios sobre la comedia de Calderón*, 187–202. Madrid: Iberoamericana.

Arias, Judith H. 1990. "Doubles in Hell: *El burlador de Sevilla y convidado de piedra.*" *Hispanic Review* 58: 361–77. https://doi.org/10.2307/473812.

Burke, James F. 1986. "The 'Banquet of Sense' in *La verdad sospechosa.*" In *Hispanic Studies in Honor of Alan Deyermond: A North American Tribute*, edited by John S. Miletich, 51–6. Madison: University of Wisconsin Press.

Calderón de la Barca, Pedro. 1969. "Ni amor se libra de amor." In *Obras completas*, vol. 1, edited by Ángel Vabuena Briones, 1941–81. Madrid: Aguilar.

Calderón de la Barca, Pedro. 1999. *La dama duende.* Edited by Fausta Antonucci. Barcelona: Crítica.

Calderón de la Barca, Pedro. 2012. *Psiquis y Cupido (Toledo).* Edited by Enrique Rull. Kassel and Pamplona: Reichenberger and Universidad de Navarra.

Calderón de la Barca, Pedro. 2013. *La cena del rey Baltasar.* Edited by Antonio Sánchez Jiménez and Adrián J. Sáez. Kassel and Pamplona: Reichenberger and Universidad de Navarra.

Castañeda, James. 2006. "The Classical Legend of Progne and Philomela in Spanish Golden Age Theater." In *Critical Essays on Golden Age Spanish*

Literature in Honor of James A. Parr, edited by Barbara Simerka and Amy R. Williamsen, 102–9. Lewisburg: Bucknell University Press.

Cazal, Françoise. 2005. "El santo, el trabajo y el amo, en tres obras de Lope sobre San Isidro." *Les Cahiers de Framespa* 1. http://framespa.revues.org/410.

Claramonte, Andrés de. 1991. *El secreto en la mujer*. Edited by Alfredo Rodríguez López-Vázquez. London: Tamesis Books.

Covarrubias, Sebastián. 1987. *Tesoro de la lengua castellana o Española* (1611). Edited by Martín de Riquer. Barcelona: Editorial Alta Fulla.

Cull, John T. 1997. "Emblematic Representation in the autos sacramentales of Calderón." In *The Calderonian State: Body and Soul*, edited by Manuel Delgado Morales, 107–32. Lewisburg: Bucknell University Press.

D'Antuono, Nancy. 1983. *Boccaccio's "Novelle" in the Theater of Lope de Vega*. Madrid: José Porrúa Ruanzas.

de Armas, Frederick A. 1976. *The Invisible Mistress: Aspects of Feminism and Fantasy in the Golden Age*. Charlottesville: Biblioteca Siglo de Oro.

de Armas, Frederick A. 1994. "Balthasar's Doom: Letters that Heal/Kill in Claramonte's *El secreto en la mujer*." In *The Golden Age Comedia: Text, Theory and Performance*, edited by Charles Ganelin and Howard Mancing, 58–75. West Lafayette, IN: Purdue University Press.

de Armas, Frederick A. 1996. "The Burning at Ephesus: Cervantes and Ruiz de Alarcón's *La verdad sospechosa*." In *Studies in Honor of Gilbert Paolini*, edited by Mercedes Vidal Tibbits, 41–56. Newark, DE: Juan de la Cuesta.

de Armas, Frederick A. 2006. *Quixotic Frescoes: Cervantes and Italian Renaissance Art*. Toronto: University of Toronto Press.

Dixon, Victor. 1966. "The Symbolism of Peribáñez." *Bulletin of Hispanic Studies* 43: 11–24. https://doi.org/10.3828/bhs.43.1.11.

Eliade, Mircea. 1959. *The Sacred and the Profane: The Nature of Religion*. New York: Harcourt and Brace.

Escobar Borrego, Javier. 2002. *El mito de Psique y Cupido en la poesía española del siglo XVI*. Seville: Universidad de Sevilla.

Ficino, Marsilio. 1985. *Commentary on Plato's Symposium of Love*. Translated and edited by Sears Jayne. Dallas: Spring Publications.

Gallego Roca, Miguel. 1989. "Efectos escénicos en las comedias de Lope de Vega sobre San Isidro: tramoya y poesía." *Criticón* 45: 113–30.

Gavela García, Delia. 2013. "La historia reciente, la material bíblica y la ficción en la reescritura de Agustín Moreto." RILCE: *Revista de Filología Hispánica* 292: 319–36.

Gitlitz, David M. 1988. Introduction to Lope de Vega's *El anzuelo de Fenisa/Fenisa's Hook or Fenisa the Hooker*. San Antonio: Trinity University Press.

Hartt, Frederick. 1950. "Gonzaga Symbols in the Palazzo del Te." *Journal of the Warburg and Courtauld Institutes* 13.3–4: 151–88. https://doi.org/10.2307/750211.

Hartt, Frederick. 1958. *Giulio Romano.* 2 vols. New Haven: Yale University Press.

Heiple, Daniel L. 1997. "Staging Theology in a Calderón Loa." In *The Calderonian State: Body and Soul*, edited by Manuel Delgado Morales, 154–62. Lewisburg: Bucknell University Press.

Hildner, David. 1979. "Sobre la interpretación tragedizante de *La dama duende.*" In *Perspectivas de la comedia II*, edited by Alva Ebersole, 121–5. Valencia: Albatross-Hispanofila.

Jeanneret, Michel. 1991. *A Feast of Words: Banquets and Table Talk in the Renaissance.* Translated by Jeremy Whitely and Emma Hughes. Chicago: University of Chicago Press.

Kermode, J. Frank. 1961. "The Banquet of Sense." *Bulletin of the John Rylands Library* 15: 68–99. https://doi.org/10.7227/BJRL.44.1.4.

Lobato, María Luisa. 2002. "Fiestas teatrales al Infante Felipe Próspero (1657–1661) y edición del baile *Los Juan Ranas* (XI, 1658)." *Scriptura (Estudios sobre el teatro del Siglo de Oro)* 17: 227–61

Lobato, María Luisa. 2012. "Las comedias bíblicas de Agustín Moreto (1618–1669) en el conjunto de su producción dramática." In *La Biblia en el teatro español*, edited by Francisco Domínguez Matito and Juan Antonio Martínez Berbel, 599–606. Vigo: Editorial Academia del Hispanismo.

Lope de Vega. 1965. "La niñez de San Isidro." In *Obras. Comedias de vidas de santos II*, vol. 10, 327–60. Madrid: Atlas.

Lope de Vega. 1986. *Peribáñez y el comendador de Ocaña.* Edited by Juan María Marín. Madrid: Cátedra.

Lope de Vega. 1995. *La quinta de Florencia.* Edited by Debra Collin Ames. Kassel: Edition Reichenberger.

Lope de Vega. 2001. *La viuda valenciana.* Edited by Teresa Ferrer Valls. Madrid: Castalia.

Lope de Vega. 2009. "El anzuelo de Fenisa." Edited by Luis Gómez Canseco. In *Comedias de Lope de Vega.* Parte VIII, coordinated by Rafael Ramos, vol. 1, 165–304. Lérida: Milenio-Universitat Autònoma de Barcelona, 2009.

Lope de Vega. 2010. *Isidro.* Edited by Antonio Sánchez Jiménez. Madrid: Cátedra.

Malaguzzi, Silvia. 2008. *Food and Feasting in Art.* Los Angeles: J. Paul Getty Museum.

Mandrell, James. 1992. *Don Juan and the Point of Honor: Seduction, Patriarchal Society and Literary Traditon.* University Park: Pennsylvania State University Press.

Marni, Archimede. 1952. "Did Tirso Employ Counterpassion in *El burlador de Sevilla*?" *Hispanic Review* 20: 123–33. https://doi.org/10.2307/471052.

Martin, Vincent. 2002. *El concepto de "representación" en los autos sacramentales de Calderón.* Kassel: Reichenberger.

172   Frederick A. de Armas

Moreto, Agustín. 1798. *La cena del rey Baltasar*. Madrid: Pablo Nadal.

Mujica, Barbara Kaminar. 1969. "Tragic Elements in Calderón's *La dama duende*." *Kentucky Romance Quarterly* 16.4: 303–28. https://doi.org/10.1080/03648664.1969.9926306.

Nadeau, Carolyn. 1998. "Star-Crossed Love: Spheres of Reality in Ruiz de Alarcón's *La verdad sospechosa*." In *A Star-Crossed Golden Age: Myth and the Spanish Comedia*, edited by Frederick A. de Armas, 62–73. Lewisburg: Bucknell University Press.

Nelson, Bradley J. 2002. "The Marriage of Art and Honor: Anamorphosis and Control in Calderón's *La dama duende*." *Bulletin of the Comediantes* 54: 407–41. https://doi.org/10.1353/boc.2002.0038.

Neumeister, Sebastian. 2000. *Mito clásico y ostentación: los dramas mitológicos de Calderón*. Kassel: Reichenberger.

O'Connor, Thomas Austin. 1988. *Myth and Mythology in the Theater of Calderón de la Barca*. San Antonio: Trinity University Press.

Parker, Alexander A. 1986. *The Allegorical Drama of Calderón*. Oxford: Dolphin Books.

Portús Pérez, Javier. 1993. "'Que están vertiendo claveles': Notas sobre el aprecio por la cerámica en el Siglo de Oro." *Espacio, Tiempo y Forma, Serie VII, Historia del Arte* 6: 255–74. https://doi.org/10.5944/etfvii.6.1993.2218.

Rodríguez López-Vázquez, Alfredo. 2011. "Tirso de Molina y *El burlador de Sevilla*: La hipótesis tradicionalista y el estado de la cuestión." *Castilla: Estudios de Literatura* 2: 151–65.

Rogers, Daniel. 1964. "Fearful Symmetry: The Ending of *El burlador de Sevilla*." *Bulletin of Hispanic Studies* 41.3: 141–59. https://doi.org/10.3828/bhs.41.3.141.

Ruiz de Alarcón, Juan. 1982. *La verdad sospechosa*. Edited by Alva V. Ebersole. Madrid: Cátedra.

Rull, Enrique. 1966. "Psiques y Cupido, auto sacramental de Valdivielso." *Segismundo* 2: 133–93.

Rull, Enrique. 2000. "Los límites de la comedia y el auto calderoniano." In *Calderón 2000: homenaje a Kurt Reichenberger en su 80 cumpleaños*, edited by Ignacio Arellano, vol. 2, 817–26. Kassel: Reichenberger.

Sánchez Arjona, J. 1887. *El teatro en Sevilla en los siglos XVI y XVII*. Madrid: A. Alonso.

Stein, Louise K. 1993. *Songs of Mortals, Dialogues of the Gods: Music and Theatre in Seventeenth-Century Spain*. Oxford: Clarendon Press.

Stoll, Anita K. 1991. "Lope's *El anzuelo de Fenisa*: A Woman for All Seasons." In *The Perception of Women in Spanish Theater of the Golden Age*, edited by Anita K. Stoll and Dawn L. Smith, 245–58. Lewisburg: Bucknell University Press.

ter Horst, Robert. 1972. "The Ruling Temper of Calderón's *La dama duende*." *Bulletin of the Comediantes* 27.2: 68–72. https://doi.org/10.1353/boc.1975.0026.

Tirso de Molina (attributed). 1991. *El burlador de Sevilla*. Edited by Alfredo Rodríguez López-Vázquez. Madrid: Cátedra.

Valdivielso, Josep. 1622. *Psiques y Cupido, Christo y el Alma. Doze autos sacramentales y dos comedias divinas*, 58r–69r. Toledo: Ruiz.

Valdivielso, Joseph de. 1622. *El villano en su rincón. Doze autos sacramentales y dos comedias divinas*, 1r–12r. Toledo: Ruiz.

Vasari, Giorgio. 1991. *The Lives of the Artists*. Translated by Julia Conaway Bondanella and Peter Bondanella. Oxford: Oxford University Press.

Verheyen, Egon. 1977. *The Palazzo del Te in Mantua*. Baltimore and London: Johns Hopkins University Press.

Wood, Michael. 1997. *In the Footsteps of Alexander the Great*. Berkeley and Los Angeles: University of California Press.

THIRD COURSE

Modern Appetites and Culinary Fashions

7 Extravagant Appetites, Hunger, and Identity: Food in Bourbon Spain

JAMES MANDRELL

La mejor salsa del mundo es la hambre; y como ésta no falta a los pobres, siempre comen con gusto.

[Hunger is the best sauce in the world, and because it is never lacking among the poor, they always eat with pleasure.]

Miguel de Cervantes,
Don Quijote de la Mancha 2.5

The discourse on food in eighteenth-century Spain comprises a number of distinct voices, including a variety of texts in specific genres, and competing visions as to the nature and function of food for different social and political classes at different moments. Yet, whatever the text or the voice, whatever the perspective, all were shaped by the arrival, in 1700, of the Bourbon dynasty, in the person of Philippe, Duc D'Anjou, who would become Felipe V. Felipe came to the throne at the invitation of the Spaniards because the Hapsburg dynasty, in power in Spain since 1518, ended when Carlos II died without an heir. Although Felipe V possessed close blood ties to the Spanish Hapsburgs, the question of succession was hardly a settled matter. On the one hand, his great-grandmother, Louis XIII's wife, was Ana de Austria, daughter of Felipe III and sister of Felipe IV. His grandmother, María Teresa, the daughter of Felipe IV and half-sister of Carlos II, was both wife and cousin to Louis XIV. On the other, prior to the death of Carlos II, Felipe's distant cousin José Fernando de Baviera was named Príncipe de Asturias. Then, on José Fernando's death, the Archduke Charles of Austria – later Charles VI, Holy Roman Emperor, King of Bohemia and Hungary – became the heir apparent, popularly referred to as Carlos III. Only shortly before his death did Carlos II name Philippe, Duc D'Anjou, to succeed him.[1]

Immediately upon being named King of Spain, Felipe journeyed to Madrid, where he moved to consolidate his power throughout what was left of the Spanish Empire, but always under the guidance, indeed control, of his grandfather Louis XIV, who sent with his grandson to Spain a number of French advisors. These advisors included Marie-Anne de la Trémoille, Princesse des Ursins, who served as a companion and advisor to Felipe's first queen, Maria Luisa di Savoia, and to Felipe himself. Not until well into his first reign – for Felipe V reigns twice, from 1700 to 1724, when he abdicates in favour of his son Luis,[2] who dies only eight months later, and then from 1724 until 1746 – did he begin to loosen the ties to France. First, the War of Succession increasingly compromised France in terms of its troop strength and foreign policy.[3] Second, it became clear that Spain's interests weren't necessarily those of France. Finally, following the death of his first wife, Maria Luisa di Savoia, Felipe married Elisabetta Farnese, daughter of Odoardo II Farnese, principe di Parma; at this point, especially once the new queen sent the Princesse des Ursins packing, the country's cultural compass found its North not in France, but in Italy.

This, then, is the backdrop to discussions of food in Spain in the eighteenth century. It would be tempting to claim that the connection between what is consumed and the political, social, and cultural situation in Spain reflects the degree to which all that is associated with the royal court and the French is seen as extravagant, and that things Spanish evince a kind of prudence and simplicity. Rafael Altamira, for example, explains, "Tomada en conjunto, la sociedad española de esta época aparece caracterizada en sus costumbres por la sencillez, la regularidad, la monotonía y la subordinación á principios de autoridad (el rey, la Iglesia, los padres) que recortan la iniciativa de los individuos y ordenan la conducta según ciertas normas impuestas" [Considered in its entirety, the customs of Spanish society in this period (the eighteenth century) appear to be characterized by simplicity, consistency, monotony, and subordination to principles of authority (the king, the church, parents)] (1914, 433). To be sure, things French were associated with excess and the Spanish with a degree of sobriety. Yet the reality that emerges from the texts we'll consider is somewhat more complex, demonstrating how food, one of many points of reference, functioned as a site of cultural negotiation and, as such, came to be embedded in different forms of discourse reflecting matters of appetite and hunger as well as traces of memory.

I

… mísero plato a su ambición cruel …

[… a wretched plate for its cruel ambition …]

On 17 November 1701, Liselotte, Elizabeth Charlotte of the Palatinate and Duchesse d'Orléans, writes the following in a letter to Sophia of the Palatinate, Electress of Hanover and, after the 1701 Act of Settlement, heir to the English crown:

> The *dames du palais* by whom this Queen is surrounded are wicked old things. The Queen requested to be given French food, since Spanish cooking does not agree with her, so the King ordered the Queen's food to be prepared by his French chefs. When the ladies saw that, they took the French soups and poured all the broth off; they said it might spoil their dresses and brought the Queen the soup without the broth. The same thing they did with the ragouts. They refused to touch the big platters of roasts, such as leg of mutton or loin roast, saying that their hands are too delicate to carry such platters. So they just pulled three chickens out of another platter of roast meat with their hands, put them on a plate, and served that to the Queen. It would be hard to find more wicked people than these, and on top of that they are horribly ugly. (Orléans 1984, 138–9)

The queen in question is Maria Luisa di Savoia, the first wife of Felipe V. And what Felipe's great aunt Liselotte describes in this letter are the stark differences in taste and cuisine between the kitchens of the court of Louis XIV and those in the Spanish court. We also get a good sense of the antipathy that many Spaniards in the new king's household, and, indeed, throughout Spain, will express towards the French.

The occasion of the arrival of a new dynasty, the Bourbons, and a new king, however necessary and welcome, comes to be seen in Spain as a kind of invasion by the neighbour to the north, not just politically, but also culturally, with the advent of new customs and fashions. These new customs and fashions include, as Liselotte suggests, those having to do with food, both its preparation and its consumption. To be sure, the dynastic transition from the Hapsburgs to the Bourbons that was set in motion by the death of Carlos II in 1700 was not as dramatic in principle as it was in practice. Felipe V's arrival in Spain is notable not only because of the matter of dynasty, but also because he attempted to recreate in the Spanish court, and, indeed, throughout the government and other institutions in Spain, much of what he left behind.[4] He always spoke French at court, as did those around him – one reason why he married Elisabetta Farnese after Maria Luisa di Savoia's death is because she spoke French well, as did most of the Italian aristocracy and upper classes – and he vastly preferred French styles in food and fashion, as well as in music and art.[5] Henry Kamen observes:

> The hundreds of French officials who accompanied Philip to Madrid were in agreement that they did not like the court; they shared a dislike of this way of life with which they were completely unfamiliar. The style in clothes, in decoration, in etiquette, in culture, all seemed to the fashionable Versailles courtiers to be relics of a past age. The king, accustomed to a different style of diet, refused to accept food cooked in the Castilian way. The chamberlains issued new instructions to the Spanish cooks in the royal kitchens, but they refused to obey, staged strikes, and even insisted on placing their dishes before the king. In the face of such intransigence Philip had no option but to create a completely new royal household, one in which all the key officials were French and would do things in the French manner. (2001, 8)

In fact, as María del Carmen Simón Palmer points out, the arrival of Felipe V and of the Bourbons had the effect of internationalizing Spanish cuisine, with two important consequences. First, French and Italian foods began to be included alongside "platos hechos a la española" [dishes made in the Spanish style]. Second, the inclusion of people to prepare these new dishes in the royal household, the "familia francesa" [French family], caused resentment and made the Spanish feel as if they had been "desplazados" [displaced] (1991, 12).[6]

To this brief anecdote can be added other instances reflecting on the new dynasty and the matter of food. If it appears that people in Spain initially welcomed Felipe warmly, if for no other reason than that he offered a stark contrast to Carlos II,[7] the War of Succession is proof positive that there were ongoing reservations both about Felipe and about having a foreign king, as well as a deeply ingrained sense of hostility to and ongoing suspicion of the French (Kamen 2001, 43). Iris Zavala cites as one of many expressions of distaste for the French a "Receta para fabricar franceses" [Recipe for making Frenchmen]:

> En un alambique echarás
> a Lutero y a Calvino,
> un judío, un asesino
> y todo lo mezclarás.
> La sangre de Barrabás

y de Judas inhumano:
y en el hornillo de Vulcano
destila la quintaesencia
y sacarás sin violencia
un francés, el más humano. (Zavala 1978, 267–8)

[Throw Luther and Calvin, / a Jew, an assassin, / into a still / and mix
everything up. / The blood of Barabbas / and of inhuman Judas: / and
in Vulcan's little oven / distill the quintessence / and you will effortlessly
obtain / a Frenchman, the most human.]

Even more pointed is this sonnet, which gives a sense of the threat
believed to reside in the players, composition, and workings of Felipe's
government. The players included – in addition to Felipe, the queen, and
Marie-Anne de la Trémoille, Princesse des Ursins – Jean Orry, who was
sent to Spain by Louis XIV to oversee finances, particularly as preparations for the War of Succession got underway; Melchor Rafael de
Macanaz; Pierre Robinet, Felipe's confessor; José de Grimaldo, marqués
de Grimaldo, the titular head of the government from 1714 to 1724 and
again briefly in 1726; and Michel-Jean Amelot, the French ambassador.[8]
All of the likely suspects are accounted for in the sonnet – the Princesse
des Ursins, Orry, Macanaz, Robinet, Grimaldo, Amelot – and Spain becomes like a piece of meat, something to be carved and consumed, a
"wretched dish" that mirrors the food served to Maria Luisa di Savoia.

Un anatemizado Mancanaz [*sic*],
un ateista padre confesor,
un presidente vuelto servidor,
una risible Alteza antifaz.
Un secretario en infusión de agraz,
un otro cascabel adulador,
un Orri-ble zurriago del Señor,
la hez de Francia convertida en haz.
Estos trinchan de España el cuerpo fiel
como si hubiera sido desleal:
mísero plato a su ambición cruel,
sin bastar tanto aviso celestial.
Pues inste a su justicia tanto Abel
porque llegue a su término fatal. (Egido López 1973, 211)

[An accursed Macanaz, an atheist as Father Confessor, a president become
servant, a risible Highness in a mask. A secretary in an infusion of verjuice,

> another belled as a flatterer, an "Orry-ble" whip of God, the shit of France
> changed into troop. These all carve up the faithful body of Spain as if it
> had been disloyal: a wretched dish for its cruel ambition, without even a
> celestial warning. Abel so urges justice in order to bring about the fatal end.]

Given the degree to which food is found in anecdotes about and satirical verse directed at Felipe V and the French, it comes as no surprise
that, when Felipe dies, food figures again as part of the story. Felipe's
son Fernando, now Fernando VI, is, in the words of Teófanes Egido
López, "saludado alborozadamente y en primer lugar como liberador
de esta pestilencial plaga" [greeted joyfully and in the first place as lib-
erator from the pestilent plague] of the French (2002b, 90). There was
even a rumour circulating throughout the capital suggesting that "[se]
han suprimido totalmente los empleos que ocupaban los extranjeros,
proveyéndolos de españoles; y hasta la cocina real (que eran todos
franceses e italianos) quedan despojados y ocupados por españoles,
y guarnecidos los despenseros y demás oficinas del gusto Real todos
desta misma nación española" [all foreigners have been fired and the
positions they occupied filled by Spaniards; and even in the royal
kitchen (where everyone was French or Italian) the foreigners were
cleared out and their positions taken over by Spaniards, and the position of pantryman and all the other jobs pertaining to questions of royal
taste were filled by people of the same Spanish nation] (cited in Egido
López 2002b, 91).

And yet, if the Bourbons internationalized Spanish cuisine, there
were, in fact, always foreigners in the royal kitchens. Simón Palmer
remarks on the surprising fact that "los estómagos regios, tanto de la
Casa de Austria como de la de Borbón, fueron alimentados casi siempre
por extranjeros" [the royal stomachs, those of the House of the Austria
as much as those of the Bourbons, were fed almost always by foreign-
ers]; she adds that the queen who married into the royal family almost
always included in her retinue, in addition to a doctor and a confessor,
a personal chef who would remain with her or, if he returned home,
would be replaced with a fellow countryman. Moreover, the royal
household grew under Felipe V to accommodate the larger royal family and to provide, even when the court was not in residence in Madrid,
such extravagances as water brought exclusively from Madrid's Fuente
del Berro and other delicacies (Simón Palmer 1991, 5, 7, 12–13).

Thus, from Maria Luisa di Savoia's distaste for Spanish food to
Felipe's importation of French cooks, from the "Receta para fabricar
franceses" to Spain as a "wretched dish" and "faithful body" to be
carved up, the language of food makes evident how integral it was to

the profound transformations taking place in the Iberian Peninsula. These anecdotes and verse also suggest the degree to which the discussion of food served to disclose deep cultural and class differences, even when the poor were seemingly invisible. As María de los Ángeles Pérez Samper comments, "en la Corte encontramos, idealizada y a escala reducida, la jerarquización alimentaria que se da en la sociedad. La desigualdad en la distribución de alimentos, tanto en cantidad como en calidad, abarca desde el Rey hasta el último de los criados y proporciona una interesante imagen, especial pero muy significativa, de la alimentación como hecho social" [in the court we find, idealized and on a smaller scale, the alimentary hierarchy of society at large. The inequality of the distribution of foodstuffs, as much in quantity as in quality, ranges from the king to the lowest servant and provides an interesting image, particular yet significant, of food as a social issue] (2004, 529). That is, we can read of abundance in the court of the king, but also of lack. And Pérez Samper explains just what the cuisine at court was like, again referencing what it is not:

> La cocina cortesana de la Monarquía española del siglo XVIII fue una cocina opulenta, refinada y cosmopolita, que respondía a los más elevados ideales gastronómicos y que se hallaba completamente diferenciada, por una parte de la cocina cortesana de los Austrias, y por otra parte de la cocina popular, separada por una enorme distancia. Sin embargo, como modelo que era, debido al prestigio de la Corte, sumado al de la alta gastronomía francesa de la época, el ejemplo cortesano cambió las costumbres culinarias españolas ... (2003, 155)

> [The courtly cuisine of the Spanish monarchy in the eighteenth century was sumptuous, refined, and sophisticated, responding to the most elevated gastronomical ideals and finding itself completely differentiated, on the one hand, from the cuisine of the Hapsburg court and, on the other, separated by a great distance from popular preparations. Nevertheless, as the model that it was, and due to the great prestige of the court and to the *haute cuisine* of the French at that time, the example of cuisine in the Spanish court changed Spanish culinary customs ...]

Moreover, we see in all of these examples a question of appetite, in some instances a taste for what is familiar, in others a desire for what is other, extravagant, or new, for what will enhance one's position or impress others. This appetite tends to express itself in terms of quantity as much as quality, but its effects are always in evidence. Yet there is another, more poignant dimension to Felipe's preference for things

French in general and French cuisine in particular that also haunts other considerations of food: the importance of memory as an aspect of taste. In her discussion of "doing-cooking," Luce Giard writes of food memories, remarking, "when political circumstances or the economic situation forces one into exile, what remains the longest as a reference to the culture of origin concerns food" (1998, 184). In many ways, and for all that he came to identify himself as Spanish and with the Spanish people, the notion of Felipe as a figure in exile offers a powerful means of understanding his role within Spanish culture as well as the type of ambivalence at work in cultural negotiations between Spain and France, particularly as seen in things like food and fashion. Because Felipe is a figurehead and arbiter of taste, his preferences become apparent and, in many respects, both naturalized and nationalized. But this does not mean that the process by which his taste becomes that of Spain occurs without discussion, debate, and even dissent, or that appetite necessarily corresponds to the demands of memory or runs counter to it.

II

… la lengua de oro de la caridad …

[… the golden tongue of charity …]

Two of the important eighteenth-century Spanish cookbooks implicitly engage in the discourse on food and the matter of class, as well as appetite and memory. Juan de la Mata's *Arte de reposteria* [Art of pastry and sweets] (1747) clearly represents new ways of thinking about sweets of all kinds. In the prologue, the author, who was the *repostero* [confectioner or pastry chef] in the court of Felipe V, lets his reader know that he has wide experience in the field of sweets and that he draws on different traditions,

> teniendo la experiencia en las muchas funciones en que me he hallado, y el haver sido discipulo de los mejores Maestros, que ha havido, assi Franceses, como Italianos, y de otras Naciones. Y por ser la primera impression, pido al curioso supla las muchas faltas, que en èl seràn dignas de notar: que si en esta primera impression diesse gusto, ofrezco la segunda, en que mas largamente, y con mas especialidad puedan los aficionados adquirir otras, y mas modernas noticias: y el motivo de no haver salido antes esta Obra, ha sido el haver estado quatro años fuera de Madrid. (Mata 1747, np)[9]

[having experience in the many functions in which I found myself, and having been a disciple of the best teachers there have been, French and Italian, and of other nations. And because this is the first edition, I request that the curious reader fill in the many gaps, which will be obvious. And if this first edition is successful, I will offer a second, in which more extensively and in more detail aficionados will be able to find more, and more modern, information. And the reason that this work didn't appear earlier is because I was away from Madrid for four years.]

After the prologue comes a chapter on cleanliness; thirty-eight chapters of recipes of varying complexity; two chapters on serving ware and service; and, if there were any lingering doubts as to the orientation of the volume, a concluding discussion of the tablespace, on centrepieces and table settings for ten, twenty, and up to one hundred dishes. That the recipes themselves are in the main Spanish, as well as, as Manuel M. Martínez Llopis notes, "otras de origen portugués, italiano, francés, flamenco y hasta oriental" [others of Portuguese, Italian, French, Flemish, and even Asian origin] (1989, 320), is of small matter. Mata's *Arte de repostería* is for sophisticated cooks such as himself who are responsible for entertaining large groups of people accustomed to the finest preparations.

That said, it is important to recognize that recipes are, as a genre, inherently traces of a past moment, a way to recollect and to recreate something previously experienced, whether or not as an exercise in nostalgia. Mata's explanations of how to prepare dishes from Spain – or elsewhere – become a sort of prescriptive memoir, a "doing-cooking" that fabricates the past for a present moment. When, in Mata's hands, recipes also become a means of representing not just skill but also taste, social class, or aspirations, we begin to see the potential power of food as a tool in the creation of identity, of cuisine to define a nation.

Juan Altamiras's purpose in his *Nuevo arte de cocina* (1745/58) is far different from that of Mata.[10] Perhaps because the author is a monk in the austere Franciscan order of Regular Observance (Juan Altamiras is the pseudonym of Raimundo Gómez),[11] the book is explicitly dedicated in the prologue to

gente de economía; porque siendo preciso y necesario el gasto, como la vida humana, se ha de mantener, como es justo, teniendo presente esta Cartilla, no se desperdiciará cosa alguna, pues lo calamitoso de los tiempos no permite desperdicios; a mas, de que en los Pobres de Jesucristo es más culpable cualquier gasto superfluo. (Altamiras 1994, 45)

[people of limited means; because expenses are unavoidable and necessary, like human life, one must ensure, as is right, with this little book, that nothing goes to waste, since these calamitous times do not permit for waste; moreover, for Jesus Christ's poor, any superfluous expense is worthy of blame.]

Altamiras returns to the question of waste when he remarks:

> que se haga cargo de lo que ha de guisar, y para cuantos sujetos, proporcionando las vasijas, y viandas; y advierta, que menos malo es que le falte un poco de caldo, que no el que le sobre mucho; el caldo ha de ser a proporción de lo que se pone en la olla … (1994, 47)

[one must take responsibility for what is to be cooked, and for how many subjects, supplying the serving ware and the food. And note that it is better to have too little broth than to have too much; the broth must be in proportion to the pot …]

And he concludes by clarifying his reasons for writing the *Nuevo arte de cocina*:

> no es mi intento escribir modos exquisitos de guisar, que para este fin ya hay muchos Libros, que dieron a luz Cocineros de Monarcas, pero la ejecución de su doctrina es tan costosa, como dictada por lengua de plata; en esta suena más la lengua de oro de la caridad … (1994, 48)

[it is not my intent to write of exquisite ways to cook. For this purpose there are many books brought to light by the cooks of kings. But the execution of their doctrine is so costly, as if dictated by a silvered tongue, that in this volume the golden tongue of charity resounds more …]

According to Altamiras, the new way of cooking is about economy as a form of piety in response to the troubled times in which he, and his readers, were living. Despite the meekness of his presentation, Altamiras leaves no doubt that he calls into question books like those of Mata, "brought to light by the cooks of kings," which exemplify a kind of excess that is abhorrent to the Franciscan. But we should note, too, the insistence with which Altamiras locates himself and his volume in a specific historical moment: "these calamitous times do not permit for waste," and, elsewhere, "la calamidad, y miseria de los tiempos tan apuradas" [the calamity and misery of these difficult times] (1994, 48). In so doing, Altamiras raises the spectre of hunger and deprivation as a part of that moment, which stands in stark contrast to the extravagance found in the Spanish court and among the wealthy. I think this can be pushed even further to include the general antipathy found towards the French: it's not simply the *presence* of foreigners and foreign foods at court and elsewhere, but the apparent *extravagance* associated with these foods and fashions, especially in a century in which hunger was prevalent, due to poor harvests, problems in the distribution of staples, and costs.

With respect to the matter of hunger, Vicente Palacio Atard sums up the entirety of the history of food, or nutrition, in Spain as one of "sub-alimentación crónica, motivada por la escasez de artículos alimenticios y por su deficiente conservación y distribución; motivada también por la ignorancia de una dieta racional, lo que hacía alimentarse mal incluso a las gentes hartas" [chronic malnutrition, caused by a shortage of food items and its poor storage and distribution; caused, too, by ignorance of a rational diet, which meant that even well-fed people were malnourished] (1998, 294). As for the eighteenth century, Gonzalo Anes, in his seminal study of agriculture in Spain, identifies different periods that give a good sense of the ways in which basic needs were not being met. During the early years of Felipe V's reign, the cold winter of 1708–9, which was followed by a particularly wet spring, affected the harvest and caused hunger as well as many deaths. This was followed by twenty years of relative abundance, with greater agricultural production and lower prices, yet abundance gave way to higher prices and lower wages, leading to a situation of crisis (1735–53) that deepened in the 1760s and continued well into the nineteenth century (Anes 1975, 427–38),[12] when, in Madrid, during the crisis of 1812, "la gente moría en la calle y a plena luz del día" [people died in the streets in the full light of day] (Rubí y Casals 2009, 312). In other words, when the first edition of Mata's *Arte de repostería* was published, in 1747, Spain was in a crisis of subsistence to which Altamiras's *Nuevo arte de cocina* appears to respond. Instead of the appetite for and the abundance of sweets and pastries proposed by Mata, Altamiras urges charity and economy while condemning excess. To understand the nature of this excess, we turn now to the *sainete*, a short satirical drama dealing with contemporary life.

III

... "Aquí se venden / también franceses rellenos" ...

[... "Stuffed Frenchmen are also sold here" ...]

It has long been recognized that the *sainete* provides a particularly powerful optic by which to look back at diverse aspects of the eighteenth century in Spain. To a large degree this is because these short satirical dramas are contemporary in nature and deal with current issues. Emilio Cotarelo y Mori defines the *sainete* as a dramatic work "sin argumento" [without argument], comic in nature, in which "la nota maliciosa es cualidad esencial" [the malicious tone is an essential quality] (1899, 4). But Juan F. Fernández Gómez notes that *sainetes*, in addition to being comic, are didactic, creating onstage a "gigantesco espejo que magnifica virtudes y defectos, los estiliza, y devuelve una imagen realista a los que allí se encuentran, que son los sujetos activos y pasivos de la acción" [gigantic mirror that magnifies virtues and defects, stylizes them, and projects a realistic image of those who find themselves therein, who are the active and passive subjects of the action] (1996, 363). At the same time, as Francisco Lafarga cautions, in the case of the *sainetes* of Ramón de la Cruz and those who would presume to find in them a full description of eighteenth-century life, "si los sainetes de Ramón de la Cruz pueden servir para ilustrar algunos aspectos de la vida española, en particular madrileña, difícilmente podrán ser la base de una descripción completa de la vida y costumbres de la época" [if Ramón de la Cruz's *sainetes* might serve to illustrate certain aspects of eighteenth-century Spanish life, they can serve only with difficulty as a complete description of the life and habits of the time] (1990, 25).

The glimpses of the past found in the *sainetes* may not tell the whole story in and of themselves, but they do add important details to our understanding of the discourse on food in eighteenth-century Spain. In Ramón de la Cruz's "La hostería de buen gusto" [The inn of good taste] (1773), food and where and for whom it is served are sites for cultural disputes. The Spanish wife of the French innkeeper of an establishment in Madrid, in her insistence on being a woman from Spain, from Madrid, and of the people, takes on cultural assumptions when her husband insists on serving food and drink only to his countrymen. When one of her husband's friends refers to her as "madam Grodibú," she replies indignantly, "Si usted me vuelve a llamar / Grodibú or Grodicuerno, / le he de tirar a usted cuantas / caserolas y pucheros / hay en este gabinete" [If you call me Grodibú or Grodihorn one more time, I'll throw all of the casseroles and pots in this cabinet at you] (1928, 355). She goes on to explain the reason for her indignation:

En cada tierra hay su estilo:
ya le he dicho que nombre tengo,
y me llamo Catalina

Leonarda de San Tadeo,
nacida y criada en la
misma calle de San Pedro
la baja; y por más reseñas,
hija de un real tabernero.
Y si en Francia se conocen
las mujeres por el mesmo
apellido del marido,
acá guardamos el nuestro
cada una … (1928, 355)

[Every country has its way: I've already told you my name, which is
Catalina Leonarda de San Tadeo, born and raised on the lower side of San
Pedro Street; and on further inspection, daughter of a royal innkeeper.
And if in France women are known by the very surname of their hus-
bands, here we each keep our own …]

Then Catalina subverts her husband's plans by inviting her friends to
partake of the repast, to which he eventually accedes, but not before
she asserts, "si vienen tus amigos, / mientras estén embutiendo / a la
puerta, si me enfado / se ha de poner un letrero / en que diga: 'Aquí
se venden / también franceses rellenos'" [if your friends come, while
they are stuffing themselves through the door, if I get angry, we must
put up a sign that says "Stuffed Frenchmen are also sold here"] (355).[13]
Here we see a Spaniard with extensive knowledge of and dealings with
the French who nevertheless asserts her identity while insisting, "Ni
tampoco a mis paisanos / los he de dejar yo hambrientos" [Nor am I
going to let my countrymen go hungry] (354).

A slightly different take on national identity turns up in Ramón de la
Cruz's "El cocinero" [The cook] (1769), which provides a portrait of the
kitchen of a wealthy master who, as do many who would imitate the
royal household (Simón Palmer 1991, 16), employs French cooks. The
cook of the title, Monsieur de Papillón, and his assistant, Monsieur de
Andoville, are as ridiculous as their names, as Francisco Lafarga rightly
comments (1996, 463–4). But they are also fundamentally dishonest,
which, as Patricia Mauclair observes, is typical of the representation of
the French in Spanish literary texts of the second half of the eighteenth
century (1996, 163). To be sure, all of the cooks in "El cocinero," French
and Spanish alike, seem to be ready to take advantage of their situation.
The *sainete* opens with a song performed by a male chorus in which the
advantages include "comer y beber mucho / y poco trabajar" [eating
and drinking a lot, and little work], "los mejores bocados / … / y el

amo más contento / cuanto lo paga más" [the best bites of food … and the master more content the more he pays], and the fact that "siempre en las cocinas / algo se pega" [in the kitchens something always sticks to you] (Cruz 1928, 8, 9). More detail is added somewhat later, as when one of the kitchen workers remarks, in what seems like an echo of the opening song, "hay ciertos oficios / que parece que se hicieron / para estafar y dejar / al estafado contento" [there are certain trades that seem to be made for swindling and for leaving the swindled content] (1928, 12). But it's Monsieur de Papillón who speaks most openly about his role in the kitchen when he says, "El amo tiene gran gusto / que le robe cuanto quiero" [It gives my master great pleasure when I steal from him as much as I want] (1928, 15).

Even when the cook in question is not foreign, the matter of national identity is invoked. In another *sainete* involving misappropriation on the part of servants, Sebastián Vázquez's "Paca la salada y merienda de horterillas" [Sassy Paca and supper for the poor servants] (1790),[14] Paca, who is the owner of a *fonda*, a kind of tavern, responds impertinently to all and sundry, hence her name, Paca la salada, or Sassy Paca, literally "salty Paca." After dispatching don Marcelo with one of her quips, the wealthy gentleman remarks to himself:

> ¡Habrá pícara chuzona!
> Éstas son las que han quedado
> legítimas Españolas,
> porque las de los estrados
> solo son un quiproquo
> de Francés y de Italiano. (Vázquez 1792, 4)

[What a witty wench! These are the ones [women] who are still rightfully Spanish, because those in high places are just the same as the French or the Italians.]

Don Marcelo seems to suggest that it is cooks, and people, like Paca who are truly Spanish, as opposed to those in "high places." Something has been lost, then, in the rush to appropriate the styles and tastes of the royal households.

Scenarios involving those of modest means and those in more comfortable circumstances are common in *sainetes*, allowing for people like the servants in "El cocinero" to be placed in situations where they are both less than dignified and less than honest. This is precisely what happens in "Paca la salada y merienda de horterillas," where the "horterillas," or poor servants, steal from their masters in order to be able to enjoy a fine meal in Paca's *fonda*. Similar to what we saw in "El cocinero," where Monsieur de Papillón's thievery was revealed, the servants' perfidy is discovered by their masters. In this instance, however, the servants receive a light punishment, simply the fear instilled in them by being discovered by their masters, and keep their positions in the household.

More critically, note that both the masters and their servants are possessed of hearty appetites. Just as there's not an easy opposition between French extravagance and Spanish simplicity, it's not simply a matter of excessive consumption or a fondness for extravagance on the part of the wealthy and, when it comes to the poor, scarcity and hunger. Rather, the servants, who are indeed hungry, aspire to cure their hunger by enjoying the appetites of the masters and, in so doing, they resort to all kinds of trickery before receiving their comeuppance. This is the case in many of Vázquez's *sainetes* – e.g., *El hambriento en Nochebuena* [The hungry man on Christmas Eve] (1774) and *La merienda desgraciada de plumistas y criadas* [The clerks' and the maids' unfortunate repast] (1782) – as well as those of Ramón de la Cruz and other authors. Yet, in the case of the lower classes, both appetite and aspiration are viewed as problematic, but for different reasons. Hunger is neither a vice nor criminal. Aspiration, on the other hand, especially when it involves ostentation, is viewed with alarm. In this sense, then, and references to hunger aside, there is little sympathy for the plight of the poor. As Georges Dufour remarks apropos of Ramón de la Cruz's view of the lower classes, "el obrero es responsable de su miseria" [the worker is responsible for his misery] (1996); Ramón de la Cruz effectively blames the "pauperismo que afectaba a la mayor parte de los españoles" [pauperism affecting most of the Spaniards] (335) on the poor themselves, "eximiendo de toda responsabilidad a las clases pudientes" [exempting the wealthy classes from liability] (336).

Thus, whatever the cure for hunger, it rests with the poor to find it for themselves, but always within their limited means and irrespective of their appetites, as we see, for example, in Juan Ignacio González del Castillo's "El día de toros en Cádiz" (date unknown) and Ramón de la Cruz's "El rastro por la mañana" (1770). In "El día de los toros," Clara, a woman of the upper class who has fallen on hard times, laments:

Los tiempos están perversos,
 y es preciso usar de maña
para aparentar decencia.
Yo conozco muchas damas
que llevan en las mantillas

> encajes de media vara,
> y sólo comen tres cuartos
> de pescado en una salsa
> que llaman zámpalopresto;
> y aun días sé que le mascan
> dando saltos y carreras,
> porque la mesa es la palma
> de la mano. (González del Castillo 1914, 350)

> [The times are perverse, and one must be cunning to appear to be decent. I
> know many ladies who carry in their mantillas half a yard of lace and who
> only eat three quarters of fish in a sauce they call "wolfitdownquickly";
> and I know there are even days when they chew while jumping and racing
> around because their table is the palm of their hand.]

Clara describes a literal hand-to-mouth existence, as women of her acquaintance struggle to get by while keeping up appearances. As for
how to get by, Cruz suggests an option yet to be mentioned, but one
of perhaps limited utility. When Mariana and Ignacia bump into each
other in the market, they begin to compare their situations, which
should be similar, since their husbands are coworkers, but which turn
out to be quite different. Ignacia says that, with her husband's wages
and her careful oversight, "se hace el milagro" [miracles are made], to
which Mariana replies, "¿Y a mí/ te vienes con ese ejemplo? / ¿No
sabes que tu marido / y el mío son compañeros, / y con su jornal apenas / para tres días tenemos / que comer, muy poco y malo; / y eso
que yo me ingenio / tal cual, y de aquí ó de allí / siempre alguna cosa
llevo …" [And you come to me with that example? Don't you know
that your husband and mine are coworkers, and with his daily wages
we have barely enough for three days of food, and very little of it and
very bad, as well as whatever I manage to work out, and I always pick
something up here and there …] (Cruz 1928, 134, ll. 379–88). Mariana
continues, "Pues / hacer con poco dinero / lo que otras hacen con mucho / es imposible, no siendo / de tres modos" [Well, it's impossible
to do with only a little money what others do with a lot, but for three
ways], and she explains, "hacer moneda falsa, / hurtar ó tener cortejo"
[make counterfeit money, steal, or have a beau] (Cruz 1928, 134, ll. 391–
5, 397–8). But Ignacia gets the last word, claiming, "Cuatro son, y te has
dejado / el mejor en el tintero … Buscar á Dios; / que él es tan buen
despensero / de su pan, que cada día / le da por un padrenuestro. / Él
te guarde" [There are four ways, and you've left the best in the inkwell
… Seek God, for he is so generous with his bread, that he gives it to us

each day for an "Our father." May he watch over you] (Cruz 1928, 134, ll. 399–400, 401–5).

In a world of poverty, in which work does not necessarily provide the daily bread, it may seem a bit naive or even foolish to look to God to provide what is not readily available. But because the evidence provided by the *sainetes* would appear to suggest an indifferent or even heartless approach to the problems of hunger, irrespective of the nature of the appetite being expressed, it comes as no surprise to find God listed alongside counterfeiting money, stealing, and depending on a paramour for sustenance. But we should remember that, among the *ilustrados*, or enlightened elite, there were many who attempted to address matters of both appetite and hunger in the abundant economic literature dealing with luxury and agriculture.[15] If remedies aren't forthcoming in the *sainetes* themselves, then the approach found in Leandro Fernández de Moratín's *sainete*-like *La comedia nueva* (1792) seems appealing.[16] When don Pedro realizes that Eleuterio, the author whose first play he justly disparages, writes about and from the necessity of hunger, he finds a way to give the man and his family the support they need: "Yo, amigo, ignoraba que del éxito de la obra de usted pendiera la suerte de esa pobre familia. Yo también he tenido hijos. Ya no los tengo; pero sé lo que es el corazón de un padre" [Friend, I didn't realize that the fortune of this poor family depended on the success of your play. I, too, have had children. I no longer do, but I know what a father's heart is like] (1982, 129). After paying Eleuterio's debts, don Pedro offers Eleuterio a position alongside his majordomo to learn how to run an estate while providing for his family with wages that are in proportion to his "necesidades" (131). In a play in which the lower classes must learn to keep to their proper place and women must fulfil "los oficios de esposa y madre" [the duties of wife and mother] (131), we see that the wealthy are similarly obligated by their own commitments, as don Pedro notes. When those around him exclaim over his goodness and generosity, don Pedro simply says, "Esto es ser justo. El que socorre la pobreza, evitando a un infeliz la desesperación y los delitos, cumple con su obligación; no hace más" [This is being just. He who helps the poor, saving an unfortunate man from desperation and crime, fulfils his obligations, nothing more] (32). Thus, there is a remedy beyond those proposed by Ramón de la Cruz's Mariana and Ignacia, but it appears to be more hypothetical than real.

These three vignettes demonstrate the extent to which the discourse on food in Spain in the eighteenth century is neither univocal nor possessed of a simple, straightforward history. They instead give evidence of ongoing negotiations, occasionally quite fraught, relating to appetite and hunger that will remain unresolved throughout the period. Whereas the arrival of Felipe V brought with it renewed interest in and emphasis on French customs, including French food, appetite for these plates was tempered both by what they represented and by matters of means and the availability of basic foodstuffs. Pérez Samper is undoubtedly correct when she says that the court served as model for the rest of Spain, and that "el ejemplo cortesano cambió las costumbres culinarias españolas" [the example of cuisine in the Spanish court changed Spanish culinary customs] (2003, 155). Yet, as Mata's cookbook attests, even when the means and the ingredients are available, there is an appetite for cuisines other than French, including that of Spain. And, in directing himself to those suffering from poverty and hunger, Altamiras is as if unaware of the new culinary fashions. If the same cannot be said of the masters and servants in the *sainetes* we briefly took up, hunger continues to be a vexing matter, even when appetites are so excessive.

What this suggests, then, is that the issues around food raised here, for all that they are obvious and obviously being discussed, are part of other pressing matters in Spain, including education, the economy, land distribution, and agriculture, to name only the most readily apparent. And because the problems relating to appetite and hunger prove so intractable, it isn't until much later that culinary negotiations raised here begin to resolve themselves into a surprisingly nationalized discourse on food that nevertheless admits of and assimilates the foreign while attending to the needs of the people.[17] The faithful body of Spain, lamented in the eighteenth century as a "mísero plato" [wretched dish] sacrificed to the "ambición cruel" [cruel ambition] of France (Egido López 1973, 211), finally finds its place at the table, even if what is being served is far from the traditional fare for which it hungered.

NOTES

1 Saint-Simon's account of the intrigue surrounding Carlos II's last days and the selection of the duc d'Anjou is particularly engaging and extensive. It accounts for most of his entry for 1700 (Saint-Simon 1968, vol. 1, 136–41). See also Ribot García (2004), which meticulously traces the question of lineage with respect to claims on the Spanish throne in the context of shifting aversions to – not alliances with – France and Germany.Unless otherwise noted, translations are by the author.The bibliography on Felipe V, the establishment of the Bourbon dynasty in eighteenth-century Spain, and its legacy is vast. I have found most useful the following: Baudrillart

1890–1901; Bottineau 1986 and 1993; Dubet 2008; García Cárcel 2002a, 2002b, and 2002c; Hargreaves-Mawdsley 1973 and 1979; Hernández 2002; Kamen 1969 and 2001; León Sanz 2002; Lynch 1989; Martín Gaite 1975; Saint-Simon 1968–72; San Felipe 1957; Tortella 2002; and Voltes Bou 2008. Also helpful on the eighteenth century in Spain are Haidt 1998; Martín Gaite 1987; Sarrailh 1957; and Zavala 1978.

2 On the symbolism of the name, see San Felipe (1957, 140); and Baudrillart (1890, vol. 1, 285). On Luis's ascension to the throne and short reign, see San Felipe (1957, 351–63); and Coxe (1815, vol. 3, 55–6).

3 On the War of Succession, see Kamen (1969), as well as the contemporary accounts of Saint-Simon (1968–72) and San Felipe (1957).

4 There are abundant discussions of French influence in Spain in the eighteenth century in general and in the court of Felipe V in particular. A good starting point remains Anes (1975, 347–57).

5 Sempere y Guarinos writes in his history of luxury and sumptuary laws in Spain that, thanks to Felipe's machinations, in the matter of a few years "toda la Corte se vistió a la Francesa" [the entire Court dressed in the French style] and that, "en el año de 1707, era general el vestido frances" [in 1707, French style in dress was common] (2000, 322, 323). But see, too, Descalzo Lorenzo, who writes, "Con frencuencia se viene admitiendo que con la llegada de Felipe V al trono de España llegó también la moda francesa a nuestra país. Ahora bien esto no fue así, ni llegó de lleno la moda francés, ni se adoptó inmediatamente, pues esta moda había empezado ya a introducirse en la segunda mitad del siglo XVII" [It has frequently been claimed that French fashion arrived in our country with the arrival of Felipe V to the Spanish throne. Now, this was not the case. French fashion neither arrived then nor was it immediately adopted, since this style had already begun to be seen in the second half of the seventeenth century] (2000, 197).

6 On this topic, see, too, Simón Palmer (1982 and 1997), as well as Díaz (1990, 167–8, 185–9, et passim); and Pérez Samper (2004, 2003, and 2000).

7 See San Felipe (1957, 20); the *Gaceta de Madrid* (Torrione et al. 1998, 32) and Martín Gaite's citation of an anonymous pamphlet (1975, 50).

8 On Orry, see San Felipe (1957, 43–4); Escudero (1979, 47–54); and Dubet (2008). Information on Macanaz can be found in Kamen (2001, 64); and Martín Gaite (1975). Pierre Robinet was a Jesuit priest who had a long relationship as confessor to Felipe V (Ramírez Aledón 2005). Kamen notes, "Chief among the ministers was José de Grimaldo, who was officially the head of the Council of State, but also despatched all official business with the king" (2001, 132); see also Saint-Simon (1972, vol. 3, 327). Michel-Jean Amelot, baron de Brunelles, marquis de Gournay, was a French diplomat also involved in the reorganization of the Spanish army. Teófanes Egido

López gives a good sense of the power of these people, individually and as a group (2002a, 100–1); and Saint-Simon offers perspective on the Princesse des Ursins and Orry (1968, vol. 1, 234; cf. vol. 1, 222, vol. 1, 235–42).

9 Little is known about Mata beyond what he mentions of himself in this work. Martínez Llopis (1989) mistakenly believes the 1786 edition of the *Arte de repostería* to be the first. Given that the licences in the 1747 edition are dated 1741 and that Mata says that publication was delayed because he was "quatro años fuera de Madrid" [away from Madrid for four years], this would appear to be the first edition (1747, np).

10 Although the 1758 edition is the earliest that is known, the licences indicate that the first publication took place in 1745; there are also contemporary references to this earlier edition. See Pisa Villarroya for a list of editions (1994, 22–9).

11 See Pisa Villarroya on the identity of the author (1994, 29–37), which cites in its entirety Latassa y Ortín's entry on Raimundo Gómez (1801, vol. 5, 150–1). On Regular Observance and the Franciscans, see Moorman (1968, 372–83), especially the discussion of Spain (377–80).

12 See too Kamen (2001, 68); Domínguez Ortiz (1976); and Pérez Moreda (1980, 360–74).

13 Haidt examines this *sainete* in a fine discussion of the Spanish identity of the lower classes (2011, 162).

14 The word "horterilla" is essentially untranslatable. It's possible that *horteras*, which are small bowls used by the poor and carried with them tied to a belt or sash, became so identified with the poor that the term applies to the person by extension.

15 The classic text on luxury in the eighteenth century is Sempere y Guarinos; see Haidt (1998) for a good discussion of this topic. Jovellanos (2008) gives a sense of discussions of agriculture, while Anes (1969) provides an overview.

16 Although a two-act play, *La comedia nueva* is viewed by many to be little more than extended *sainete* by Moratín's contemporaries – e.g., Mor de Fuentes (1981, 59) – as well as modern critics like Alvarez Barrientos (2000, 30) and Angulo Egea (2006, 67).

17 See Anderson (2013) for an interesting discussion of the role of food in the nationalization of Spain.

WORKS CITED

Altamira y Crevea, Rafael. 1914. *Historia de España y de la civilización española IV*. 3rd ed. Barcelona: Juan Gili.

Altamiras, Juan. 1994. *Nuevo arte de cocina*. Colección Alifara. Huesca: La Val de Onsera.

Alvarez Barrientos, Joaquín. 2000. Introducción. In *La comedia nueva o el café*, by Leandro Fernández de Moratín, 7–55. Colección ¡Arriba el telón! 12. Madrid: Biblioteca Nueva.

Anderson, Lara. 2013. *Cooking Up the Nation: Spanish Culinary Texts and Culinary Nationalization in the Late Nineteenth and Early Twentieth Century*. Colección Támesis, Serie A, Monografías 321. Woodbridge: Tamesis.

Anes, Gonzalo. 1969. *Economía e Ilustración en la España del siglo XVIII*. Esplugues de Llobregat, Barcelona: Ariel.

Anes, Gonzalo. 1975. *El antiguo régimen: los Borbones*. Edited by Miguel Artola. Historia de España Alfaguara 4. Madrid: Alianza, Alfaguara.

Angulo Egea, María. 2006. *Luciano Francisco Comella (1751–1812): otra cara del teatro de la Ilustración*. San Vicente del Raspeig: Publicaciones de la Universidad de Alicante.

Baudrillart, Alfred. 1890–1901. *Philippe V et la cour de France d'après des documents inédits tirés des archives espagnoles de Simancas et d'Alcala de Hénarès et des Archives du Ministère des affaires étrangères à Paris*. 5 vols. Paris: Firmin-Didot et Cie.

Bottineau, Yves. 1986. *El arte cortesano en la España de Felipe V (1700–1746)*. Translated by María Concepción Martín Montero. Bellas Artes 5. Madrid: Fundación Universitaria Española.

Bottineau, Yves. 1993. *Les Bourbons d'Espagne, 1700–1808*. Paris: Fayard.

Cervantes, Miguel de. 1980. *Don Quijote de la Mancha*. Edited by John Jay Allen. Letras Hispánicas 100 and 101. 2nd ed. Madrid: Cátedra.

Cotarelo y Mori, Emilio. 1899. *Don Ramón de la Cruz y sus obras: ensayo biográfico y bibliográfico*. Madrid: José Perales y Martínez.

Coxe, William. 1815. *Memoirs of the Kings of Spain of the House of Bourbon, from the Accession of Philip V to the Death of Charles III. 1700 to 1788. Drawn from the Original and Unpublished Documents*. 2nd ed. 5 vols. London: Longman, Hurst, Rees, Orme, and Brown.

Cruz, Ramón de la. 1915 and 1928. *Sainetes de Don Ramón de la Cruz en su mayoría inéditos*. Edited by Emilio Cotarelo y Mori. Nueva Biblioteca de Autores Españoles 23 and 26. 2 vols. Madrid: Casa Editorial Bailly Bailliere.

Descalzo Lorenzo, Amalia. 2000. "El arte de vestir en el ceremonial cortesano. Felipe V." In *España Festejante: El Siglo XVIII*, edited by Margarita Torrione, 197–204. Málaga: Servicio de Publicaciones, Centro de Ediciones de la Diputación de Málaga.

Díaz, Lorenzo. 1990. *Madrid: bodegones, mesones, fondas y restaurantes: cocina y sociedad, 1412–1990*. Madrid: Espasa Calpe.

Domínguez Ortiz, Antonio. 1976. *Sociedad y Estado en el siglo XVIII español*. Ariel Historia 9. Barcelona: Ariel.

Dubet, Anne. 2008. *Un estadista francés en la España de los Borbones: Jean Orry y las Primeras reformas de Felipe V (1701–1706)*. Biblioteca Saavedra Fajardo de Pensamiento Político. Madrid: Biblioteca Nueva.

Dufour, Georges. 1996. "Lujo y pauperismo en Ramón de la Cruz." In *El teatro español del siglo XVIII*, edited by Josep María Sala Valldaura, 329–36. Lérida: Universitat de Lleida.

Egido López, Teófanes. 2002a. *Opinión Pública y Oposición al Poder en la España del Siglo XVIII (1713–1759)*. Historia y Sociedad 101. Valladolid: Universidad de Valladolid, Secretariado de Publicaciones e Intercambio Editorial.

Egido López, Teófanes. 2002b. *Prensa Clandestina Española del Siglo XVIII: "El Duende Crítico."* Estudios y Documentos (Departamento de Historia Moderna, Universidad de Valladolid) 24. Valladolid: Universidad de Valladolid, Secretariado de Publicaciones e Intercambio Editorial.

Egido López, Teófanes, ed. 1973. *Sátiras Políticas de la España Moderna*. El libro de bolsillo. Humanidades 473. Madrid: Alianza.

Escudero, José Antonio. 1979. *Los orígenes del Consejo de Ministros en España*. 2 vols. Madrid: Editora Nacional.

Fernández de Moratín, Leandro. 1982. *La comedia nueva. El sí de las niñas*. Ed. John Dowling and René Andioc. Clásicos Castalia 5. Madrid: Castalia.

Fernández Gómez, Juan F. 1996. "El humor y la crítica como elementos didácticos del sainete." In *El teatro español del siglo XVIII*, edited by Josep María Sala Valldaura, vol. 2, 363–75. Lleida: Universitat de Lleida.

García Cárcel, Ricardo. 2002a. *Felipe V y los españoles: Una visión periférica del problema de España*. Así fue. La historia rescatada 50. Barcelona: Plaza & Janés.

García Cárcel, Ricardo. 2002b. "Felipe V y su imagen histórica." In *Historia de España. Siglo XVIII: La España de los Borbones*, 27–40. Historia. Serie Mayor. Madrid: Cátedra.

García Cárcel, Ricardo. 2002c. Introducción. In *Historia de España. Siglo XVIII: La España de los Borbones*, 9–22. Historia. Serie Mayor. Madrid: Cátedra.

Giard, Luce. 1998. "Doing-Cooking." In *The Practice of Everyday Life. Volume 2: Living and Cooking*, edited by Michel de Certeau, Luce Giard, and Pierre Mayol; translated by Timothy H. Tomasik. Minneapolis and London: University of Minnesota Press.

González del Castillo, Juan Ignacio. 1914. *Obras completas*. Biblioteca selecta de autores clásicos españoles 13–15. 3 vols. Madrid: Librería de los Sucesores de Hernando.

Haidt, Rebecca. 1998. *Embodying Enlightenment: Knowing the Body in Eighteenth-Century Spanish Literature and Culture*. New York: St Martin's Press.

Haidt, Rebecca. 2011. "Los Majos, el 'españolísimo gremio' del teatro popular dieciochesco: sobre casticismo, inestabilidad y abyección." *Cuadernos de Historia Moderna* 10: 155–73. https://doi.org/10.5209/rev_CHMO.2011.38675.

Hargreaves-Mawdsley, W.N. 1973. *Spain under the Bourbons, 1700–1833: A Collection of Documents*. History in Depth. Columbia: University of South Carolina Press.

Hargreaves-Mawdsley, W.N. 1979. *Eighteenth-Century Spain, 1700–1788: A Political, Diplomatic and Institutional History*. Totowa, NJ: Rowman and Littlefield.

Hernández, Bernardo. 2002. "Economía y sociedad en el siglo XVIII." In *Historia de España. Siglo XVIII: La España de los Borbones*, 283–325. Historia. Serie Mayor. Madrid: Cátedra.

Jovellanos, Gaspar Melchor de. 2008. "Informe de ley agraria." In *Obras completas*, vol. 10, *Escritos económicos*, edited by Vicent Llombart i Rosa and Joaquín Ocampo Suárez-Valdés, 693–848. Oviedo and Gijón: Ayuntamiento de Gijón, Instituto Feijoo de Estudios del Siglo XVIII, KRK Ediciones.

Kamen, Henry. 1969. *The War of Succession in Spain, 1700–1715*. Bloomington: Indiana University Press.

Kamen, Henry. 2001. *Philip V of Spain: The King Who Reigned Twice*. New Haven: Yale University Press.

Lafarga, Francisco. 1990. Introducción. In *Sainetes*, by Ramón de la Cruz, 11–61. Letras Hispánicas 262. Madrid: Cátedra.

Lafarga, Francisco. 1996. "La lengua francesa en el teatro español del siglo XVIII." In *L'"universalité" du français et sa présence dans la péninsule ibérique: actes du Colloque de la SIHFLES tenu à Tarragone, Université Rovira i Virgili, du 28 au 30 septembre 1995*, edited by Juan García-Bascuñana, 461–73. Documents pour l'histoire du français langue étrangère ou seconde 18. Saint-Cloud: SIHFLES [Société Internationale pour l'Histoire du Français Langue Etrangère ou Seconde].

Latassa y Ortín, Félix de. 1798–1802. *Biblioteca nueva de los escritores aragoneses que florecieron desde el año 1500 hasta 1599*. 6 vols. Pamplona: Oficina de Joaquin de Domingo.

León Sanz, Virginia. 2002. "La llegada de los Borbones." In *Historia de España. Siglo XVIII: La España de los Borbones*, 41–111. Historia. Serie Mayor. Madrid: Cátedra.

Lynch, John. 1989. *Bourbon Spain 1700–1808*. A History of Spain. Oxford: Basil Blackwell.

Martín Gaite, Carmen. 1975. *Macanaz, otro paciente de la Inquisición*. Ensayistas 132. Madrid: Taurus.

Martín Gaite, Carmen. 1987. *Usos amorosos del dieciocho en España*. Colección Argumentos 86. Barcelona: Editorial Anagrama.

Martínez Llopis, Manuel M. 1989. *Historia de la gastronomía española*. El libro de bolsillo. Libros útiles 1378. Madrid: Alianza.

Mata, Juan de la. 1747. *Arte de reposteria, en que se contiene todo genero de hacer dulces secos, y en lìquido, vizcochos, turrones, y natas: bebidas heladas de todos generos, rosoli, misterlas, & c. Con una breve instruccion para conocer las frutas, y servirlas crudas, y diez mesas, con su explicacion.* Madrid: Antonio Marín.

Mauclair, Patricia. 1996. "La France dans les saynètes de Ramón de la Cruz." In *L'image de la France en Espagne pendant la seconde moitié du XVIIIe siècle/La imagen de Francia en España durante la segunda mitad del siglo XVIII*, edited by Jean-René Aymes, 155–64. Colección Ensayo e Investigación 61. Alicante: Instituto de Cultura "Juan Gil-Albert" and Paris: Presses de la Sorbonne Nouvelle.

Moorman, John. 1968. *A History of the Franciscan Order from Its Origins to the Year 1517.* Oxford: Oxford University Press.

Mor de Fuentes, José. 1981. *Bosquejillo de la vida y escritos de José Mor de Fuentes.* Edited by Manuel Alvar. Nueva Biblioteca de Autores Aragoneses. Zaragoza: Guara.

Orléans, Elisabeth Charlotte, Duchesse d' [Liselotte von der Pfalz]. 1984. *A Woman's Life in the Court of the Sun King: Letters of Liselotte von der Pfalz, 1652–1722.* Translated by Elborg Forster. Baltimore: Johns Hopkins University Press.

Palacio Atard, Vicente. 1998. *La alimentación de Madrid en el siglo XVIII y otros estudios madrileños.* Clave Historial 10. Madrid: Real Academia de la Historia.

Pérez Moreda, Vicente. 1980. *La crisis de mortalidad en la España interior.* Madrid: Siglo Veintiuno de España.

Pérez Samper, María de los Ángeles. 2000. "La mesa real en la corte borbónica española del siglo XVIII." In *España festejante: el siglo XVIII*, edited by Margarita Torrione, 205–18. Málaga: Servicio de Publicaciones, Centro de Ediciones de la Diputación de Málaga.

Pérez Samper, María de los Ángeles. 2003. "La alimentación en la corte española del siglo XVIII." *Cuadernos de Historia Moderna*, Anejo II: 153–97. https://core.ac.uk/download/pdf/38832082.pdf.

Pérez Samper, María de los Ángeles. 2004. "La alimentación en la corte de Felipe V." In *Felipe V y su tiempo: congreso internacional*, edited by Eliseo Serrano Martín, vol. 1, 529–84. 2 vols. Zaragoza: Institución Fernando el Católico (CSIC).

Pisa Villarroya, José M. 1994. Delantal. In *Nuevo arte de cocina*, by Juan Altamiras, 9–38. Colección Alifara. Huesca: La Val de Onsera.

Ramírez Aledón, Germán. 2005. "Penitencia para después de una guerra: las misiones populares jesuíticas en la Nueva Colonia San Felipe (1712)." In *Llibre Fira D'Agost*, 115–37. Xàtiva: Ajuntament de Xàtiva.

Ribot García, Luis Antonio. 2004. "La sucesión de Carlos II: diplomacia y lucha política a finales del siglo XVII." In *Estudios en homenaje el profesor Teófanes Egido*, edited by Máximo García Fernández and María de los

Ángeles Sobaler Seco, vol. 2, 63–99. 2 vols. Valladolid: Junta de Castilla y León, Consejería de Cultura y Turismo.

Rubí i Casals, Maria Gemma. 2009. "La supervivencia cotidiana durante la Guerra de la Independencia." In *La Guerra de la Independencia en España (1808–1814)*, edited by Antonio Moliner Prada, 299–324. Alella (Barcelona): Nabla Ediciones.

Saint-Simon, Louis de Rouvroy, duc de. 1968–72. *Historical Memoirs of the Duc de Saint-Simon: A Shortened Version*. Edited and translated by Lucy Norton. 3 vols. New York: McGraw-Hill.

San Felipe, Vicente Bacalar y Sanna, marqués de. 1957. *Comentarios de la Guerra de España e Historia de Su Rey Felipe V, el Animoso*. Edited by Carlos Seco Serrano. Biblioteca de Autores Españoles 99. Madrid: Atlas.

Sarrailh, Jean. 1957. *La España Ilustrada de la Segunda Mitad del Siglo XVIII*. Translated by Antonio Alatorre. Mexico City: Fondo de Cultura Económica.

Sempere y Guarinos, Juan. 2000. *Historia del lujo y de las leyes suntuarias en España*. Edited by Juan Rico Giménez. Estudi general, textos valencians 2. Valencia: Alfons el Magnànim.

Simón Palmer, María del Carmen. 1982. *La alimentación y sus circunstancias en el Real Alcázar de Madrid*. El Madrid de los Austrias. Serie Estudios 2. Madrid: Instituto de Estudios Madrileños.

Simón Palmer, María del Carmen. 1991. "Cocineros europeos en el Palacio Real." Ciclo de conferencias, Madrid, capital europea de la cultura 9. Madrid: Artes Gráficas Municipales.

Simón Palmer, María del Carmen. 1997. *La cocina de Palacio 1561–1931*. Madrid: Castalia.

Torrione, Margarita, Lucienne Domergue, and Reyes Escalera Pérez. 1998. *Crónica festiva de dos reinados en la* Gaceta de Madrid *(1700–1759)*. Editions Thématiques du CRIC [Centre des recherches sur la péninsule ibériques à l'époque contemporaines], Université Toulouse-Le Mirail. Toulouse-Le Mirail and Paris: CRIC, Université Toulouse-Le Mirail, and Ophrys.

Tortella, Jaime. 2002. "El legado cultural." In *Historia de España. Siglo XVIII: La España de los Borbones*, 329–90. Historia. Serie Mayor. Madrid: Cátedra.

Vázquez, Sebastián. 1792. "Paca la salada y merienda de horterillas." Madrid: Librería de Quiroga. http://www.memoriademadrid.es/buscador.php?accion=VerFicha&id=248617&num_id=28&num_total=36.

Voltes Bou, Pedro. 2008. *Felipe V: fundador de la España contemporánea*. Grandes Biografías de la Historia de España. Barcelona: Planeta DeAgostini.

Zavala, Iris M. 1978. *Clandestinidad y Libertinaje Erudito en los Albores del Siglo XVIII*. Letras e Ideas. Maior 12. Barcelona: Ariel.

8 The Representation of Gastronomy and Urbanity in the Journalistic Articles of Mariano José de Larra (1808–1837): Analysis of a Modern Perspective

ÍÑIGO SÁNCHEZ-LLAMA

I. Introduction

> Preciso es confesar que no es nuestra patria el país donde viven los hombres para comer: gracias, por el contrario, si se come para vivir: verdad es que no es éste el único punto en que manifestamos lo mal que nos queremos: no hay género de diversión que no nos falte; no hay especie de comodidad de que no carezcamos. (Larra 1960, vol. 1, 95)

> [We ought to confess that our homeland is not the country where men live to eat: be thankful, on the contrary, if one eats to live: it is true that this is not the only way in which we manifest how poorly we love ourselves: there is no type of diversion that we are not short of; there is no kind of comfort that we do lack.]

The future of the liberal project in Spain seemed dark and uncertain in the 1830s. Mariano José de Larra associates this problem with the absence of modern values similar to the ones developed in France or England. These moral deficiencies are evident in the "tristísimo cuadro de nuestras costumbres" [very sad status of our customs] (Larra 1986, 401). The uncritical devotion to the past, the neglect of etiquette, the lack of refinement, and the firm purpose to avoid any innovation limit the success of any modernizing enterprise. Other critics writing in the time of Larra emphasize the same problem. Manuel Pando Fernández de Pinedo, marqués de Miraflores, points this out in his *Apuntes histórico-críticos* [Historical and critical notes]: "las mágicas voces en otros países, de libertad y de igualdad, en España se oyen con desprecio y con desdén, y aún como grito de irreligión" [the magic voices in other countries, of liberty and equality, are heard in Spain with contempt and disdain, even as the cry of the unreligious] (Miraflores 1834, xii).

The peculiarity of Spain resided not so much in the notable popularity of the Old Regime's traditionalist values as in the marked social rejection of any reformist project that had been inspired abroad. Another impediment to liberal modernity had to do with its minor impact on the Spanish population. The social group that might be more receptive to this reformist project, the middle class, not only developed a defensive attitude against modernity but also felt constrained by an uneven modernization that explained, according to Larra, its reduced influence in Spanish society: "la pobre clase media, cuyos límites van perdiéndose y desvaneciéndose cada vez más, por arriba en la alta sociedad, en que hay de ella no pocos intrusos, y por abajo en la capa inferior del pueblo, que va conquistando sus usos" [the poor middle class, whose boundaries are progressively getting lost and disappearing upward into high society, in which are not a few intruders, and down into the lower class, which threatens to occupy its space] (Larra 1857, vol. 1, 96).

The Anglophile perspective maintained in the second decade of the nineteenth century by José María Blanco White[1] and, in the following decade, by the marqués de Miraflores and Larra, shows the difficulties of proposing a reformist project in Spain – nineteenth-century liberalism was associated by its detractors with foreign tendencies incompatible with the presumed Spanish idiosyncrasy.[2] This did not impede the gradual articulation of cosmopolitan values, whose development shows the complex thinking of modernity in the Spanish mode. Antonio Alcalá Galiano, in his translation of Samuel Dunham's *Historia de España y Portugal* [History of Spain and Portugal] (1832–3), indicates how since the "período corrido desde 1833 a 1843" [period between 1833 and 1843] in Spain there may be seen "contradicciones entre leyes, usos y costumbres, y aun entre pensamientos y afectos, cuales de fecha novísima, cuales de antiquísimo arraigo, cuales de naturaleza mixta; ya cediendo, ya resistiendo; ahora tirando a unirse, ahora manifestando repugnancia a amalgamarse, o disonando más por verse juntos" [contradictions among laws, practices, and customs, and even among thoughts and feelings, some new, some deep-rooted, some of a mixed nature; now giving way, now resisting; now drawing together, now showing disgust for combining, or disagreeing more because they see themselves together] (1844, vol. 7, 599). There is no incompatibility between the mournful criticisms of the marqués de Miraflores or Larra and the more enthusiastic view defended by Alcalá Galiano. The minority profiles of nineteenth-century Spanish liberalism in the 1830s, not all that different from that experienced by the Spanish Enlightenment during the last third of the eighteenth century,[3] also overlap with the significant appearance of liberal perspectives that propose to reconcile this political ideology (i.e., secularization, religious tolerance, cosmopolitanism, economic progress) with Spanish cultural heritage.[4] The tensions between "España antigua" [old Spain] and "España moderna" [modern Spain] (599), significant at least until the "glorious" Revolution of 1868,[5] overlap the emergence of a reformist discourse whose detailed articulation must confront the false dilemmas traced by the influential, traditionalist, Schlegelian romanticism.[6] Schlegelian detractors of liberalism in Spain question not so much its ideological background as its alleged incompatibility with the supposed medieval (not modern) and chivalric heart of the Spanish nation. Spanish liberals during the 1830s rejected this, highlighting the inevitable intellectual stagnation favoured by the Old Regime. Their criticism is continuous, both of its antiquated nature and of the useless moral emptiness inscribed in Spanish traditionalism. Their perspective is unifying to the extent to which they also reject the possibility of dispensing with the cultural values that make Spain unique in the European context. Larra vindicates, in 1834, the value of the "laureles ganados" [deserved laurels] by the Spanish "cisnes" [swans] during the sixteenth and seventeenth centuries: "hubo un tiempo feliz para nuestra patria, en que supo en armas, en política, en letras, dar ley al mundo. Cuando es llegada para una nación la hora de la gloria, parece que se complace el cielo en acumular lauros de todas especies sobre su generosa frente. Tocóle a España esta época y sublimóse a un grado de esplendor que difícilmente alcanzará ni ella ni pueblo alguno" [there was a happy time for our country, in which it was possible to influence the whole world in arms, politics, literature, and law. When a nation reaches its peak, it seems that heaven is pleased to grant all kinds of recognition. It was Spain's turn at this time and she submitted herself to a degree of splendour that neither she nor any other people will reach] (Larra 1857, vol. 1, 184). Larra also remembers, nevertheless, that the intellectual isolation of Spain during the second half of the seventeenth century favours a sterile literature governed by "una ridícula amalgama de conceptos sutiles, de metáforas metafísicas, de pedantismo escolar y de sentimentalismo" [a ridiculous combination of subtle notions, metaphysical metaphors, pedantic academicism, and sentimentalism] (Larra 1960, vol. 1, 206). To assume both of these hopes – to purify the irrational, anachronistic nostalgias of past ages and to maintain the autochthonous cultural legacy – defines the complex thinking of liberal perspectives held in Spain during the "Romantic Decade" (1833–43).[7] Liberal discontent with the sluggishness of Hispanic customs can be seen in Larra's observations about what he views as a non-existent Spanish gastronomic culture. He not only criticizes the total lack of aesthetics in the preparation of meals but also the problematic content of the product offered to the public: "Por lo que hace falta a adornos de mesa, sabido es que en España no somos fuertes; bien que falta lo principal, que es *qué comer*" [As for presentation at the table, it is known that in Spain we are not strong on that point; moreover our main problem is that we miss the basics, which has to do with *what to eat*] (Larra 1857, vol. 1, 220, original emphasis).

Lucid analyses by José Ortega y Gasset on the development of modernity in the West after the Renaissance are productive for understanding the force of liberal modernity in the Spanish mode during the 1830s. Ortega y Gasset identifies the modern conscience semantically with concepts of innovation, expectation, transformation, cosmopolitanism, the development of possibilities, universalism, reform, and the quality of being provisionary (1961–2, vol. 5, 505–7). Other works by this author emphasize the importance of the rationalist temperament[8] or the secular dimension – "intrahuman" in his terminology[9] – as the unique characteristics of modern mentality. A trait of greater interest for its application in Spain in the 1830s may be found in his observations on the duality between ideas of reform and the simultaneous illegitimacy that conditions the historical thinking of modernity:

> Modernidad es, pues, enriquecimiento y viceversa; pero esa vida moderna, que material y técnicamente es más eficaz que la antigua, ha sido creada fuera y aparte de la creencia firme, compacta, consagrada, en la cual se fundaba la pura legitimidad del pasado inmemorial, y es, por tanto, un vivir sin firme sacramento. Modernidad es enriquecimiento, pero es también por sí y sin más germen de ilegitimidad.
>
> Con toda modernidad empieza siempre – bien patente está ante nosotros – la lucha entre lo eficaz y lo legítimo. (1961–2, vol. 9, 137)

[Modernity is prosperity and vice versa; but that modern life, which materially and technologically is more effective than the ancient one, has been created outside of and apart from the firm, compact, consecrated belief in which the pure legitimacy of the immemorial past was founded, and it is, therefore, a life without stable sacrament. Modernity is prosperity, but it is also by itself and without further grounds of illegitimacy. With all modernity there always begins – as we see before us – the battle between what is effective and what is legitimate.]

The importance of these criticisms is enough to understand in their fitting terms the development of modern liberal tendencies in nineteenth-century Spain. One should note how modernity favours an inevitable epistemological transformation through the existence of a "teclado de múltiples posibilidades del pensamiento" [keyboard of multiple possibilities of thought] (Ortega y Gasset 1961–2, 136) whose application surpasses the static quality of non-modern societies. Such mutations generate expectations that permit the reform of beliefs associated with tradition. Initial resistance to the illegitimacy of the modern ends up being overcome once the benefits of the effective application of these beliefs become obvious. This was the horizon of expectation taken up by Spanish liberalism in the 1830s. The added difficulty was grounded in the fact that traditionalism of Schlegelian descent invalidated modern tendencies not only for the illegitimacy of their reformist aspirations but also for their presumed incompatibility with a supposed Spanish identity impermeable to any intent of intellectual transformation.

Mariano José de Larra was associated by his contemporaries with the genre of satire that in its detailed development could turn out excessively corrosive. Ramón de Mesonero Romanos emphasizes "aquel escepticismo que le dominaba" [that dominating scepticism] and "aquella sarcástica sonrisa que nunca pudo echar de sí" [that sarcastic smile that he could never cast off] (1967, vol. 5, 218). Alcalá Galiano connects him to that "acre malignidad" [acrid malignity] practised as "censor amargo y gracioso de las faltas de los personajes de nota, y de las ridiculeces de la vida en la gente de las clases superiores" [a bitter and amusing censor of the faults of notable people, of the ridiculous things of the life of the higher classes] (1844, 591–2). Antonio Ferrer del Río believes that his "obstinado escepticismo" [obstinate scepticism] and "índole viciosa" [vicious nature] (1846, 221) condition his propensity "a dudar de todo, a acibarar los más codiciados placeres, a ennegrecer toda esperanza de ventura y a presentar el suicidio como único remedio contra las dolencias del alma" [to doubt everything, to turn the most desired pleasures into bitterness, to darken every hope, and to present suicide as the only remedy for the pains of the soul] (233). Most recent analyses have highlighted, nevertheless, the genuine patriotism of a satirical perspective intimately linked to the ideology of liberalism: "Español del siglo XIX, Larra se dirige siempre a sus compatriotas: la realidad de España no le gusta y la describe crudamente, para transformarla" [A Spaniard of the nineteenth century, Larra always addresses his compatriots: he does not like Spain's reality, and he describes it crudely in order to transform it] (Goytisolo 1967, 12).

Larra straightforwardly acknowledges his interest in the genre of satire in the measure to which it does not cloak "una pasión dominante de criticarlo todo con razón o sin ella" [an overriding passion for criticizing everything, rightly or not] (1857, vol. 2, 74).[10] His *costumbrista* articles do not depart from the definitions of "satire" included in modern Spanish dictionaries of the time. The *Diccionario castellano con las voces de ciencias y artes* [Castilian dictionary of science and arts] (1786–8), by Esteban Terreros y Pando, defines satire as "especie de poema, inventada para reprender y corregir las costumbres y para criticar las obras" [a kind of poem, invented to reprove and correct customs and to criticize works and deeds] (1987, vol. 3, 444).[11] The first edition of the *Diccionario de la lengua castellana* [Dictionary of the Castilian language] (1780) insists on the pedagogical purposes of this literary genre: "la obra en que se motejan y censuran las costumbres y operaciones o del público o de algún particular" [the work in which customs and proceedings, either of the public or of an individual, are mocked with nicknames and denounced] (Real Academia Española 1991, 826). This usage would be maintained in later editions of the Academy's dictionary in 1832, 1837, and 1843. Larra's identification with liberalism's program during the 1830s justifies his implacable condemnation of its traditionalist detractors through satirical rhetorical means. The author is also conscious of the illegitimacy of the liberal project for Old Regime partisans. His aesthetic values are eclectic as he works to defend not only the artistic merits of the literature of the Golden Age (1857, vol. 1, 184–5), which had been reassessed by romantic criticism, but also those of the reviled eighteenth-century Spanish classicism (144–9).[12] Larra considers the reform of contemporary Spanish literature indispensable – an openly modern attitude – so long as the romantic creed does not become "la divisa exclusiva e intolerante de un partido literario que no quisiese capitular con el contrario" [the exclusive and intolerant emblem of a literary party that refuses to surrender to the enemy] (1960, vol. 1, 207). His criticism of the superficial pedantry and artistic inauthenticity of *culteranismo* is modern as well (206). His literary criticism marks the parallel between the decadence of Spain in the seventeenth century, the intellectual isolation of the country, and the development of the poor taste of *culteranismo* with its anti-modern affiliation (207). The modern transformation of Spanish letters is only considered plausible insofar as expressive simplicity is recovered, the "llamaradas deslumbradoras" [blinding flashes] and the "primor en el decir" [skill in speaking] practised by the writers of the sixteenth century (206).[13] It is not an unwarranted assertion to specify how he perceives what a genuine renaissance of Spanish letters should be. The fusion of tradition – in this case, the classicisms of the sixteenth and eighteenth centuries[14] – and romantic novelty allows him to introduce new expectations with respect to *culteranismo* while keeping, nevertheless, a genuine legitimacy assigned to Spanish classicism.[15] Mariano José de Larra embodies in a precise way the modern ideal of the "verdadero artista" [true artist] who, according to Azorín, is "un hombre que ha llegado a saber que el arte supremo es la sobriedad, la simplicidad y la claridad" [a man who has come to know that the supreme art is sobriety, simplicity, and clarity] (1915, 18).

The articles on gastronomy written by Mariano José de Larra indicate a discursive negotiation similar to the project of liberal modernity. His interest in culinary themes, inscribed as well in the sphere of urbanity, is not unwarranted in the Western Euro-American context. The transformations that occurred in the West after 1780 generate social circumstances in which "classes were defined not only, and perhaps not even largely, by relation to the means of production, but also by knowledge and taste" (Auslander 1996, 142). Pierre Bourdieu reminds us that the consolidation of a social class only occurs "cuando hay agentes capaces de imponerse a sí mismos, como autorizados a hablar y actuar oficialmente en su lugar y en su nombre" [when there are agents capable of being fashionable to themselves, as authorized to speak and act officially in their place and in their name] (2000, 126). The good taste of the emergent bourgeoisie – a social class identified in the Spain of 1830 with liberalism – is important in order to articulate a reformist project of cosmopolitan inspiration. Codes of etiquette or culinary habits, consequently, are relevant both for asserting the bourgeois distinction and for accentuating the parodic traits of its traditionalist detractors. Mariano José de Larra ridicules the culinary habits of social groups that propose an anachronistic anchor for Spain in the remote past. The author's satire signals the imperative necessity of introducing cosmopolitan gastronomic tendencies. Larra also affirms the lack of vital authenticity noticeable in social groups hostile to any transformation of good culinary taste. Cosmopolitan reform and genuine vitality define a perspective whose textual development associates liberalism with the practice of gastronomic habits in keeping with the exigencies of modern consciousness in the nineteenth century.

II. Larra's Gastronomic *Costumbrista* Articles: Liberalism, Modernity, and Good Taste

> Por lo que hace a adornos de mesa, sabido es que en España no somos fuertes; bien que falta lo principal, que es *qué comer*. (1857, vol. 1, 220, original emphasis)

[With regard to table decorations, it is well known that in Spain we are not strong; especially since the most important part is missing, that is, *what to eat*.]

The abundant criticism written after the second half of the nineteenth century on Mariano José de Larra's *costumbrista* articles offers a plurality of interpretations that include the study of his literary work's French affiliation,[16] his cosmopolitan orientation,[17] the artistic debts of his *costumbrista* articles to the tradition of Quevedo,[18] rationalist classicism,[19] and liberal romanticism,[20] or his brilliant anticipation of fin-de-siècle *regeneracionismo*.[21] There are also analyses that emphasize his exceptionalism in nineteenth-century Spanish letters[22] and even his connections to a certain kind of exquisite dandyism.[23] In the *costumbrista* articles that have culinary content, the interest of Hispanists in "El castellano viejo" [The old Castilian] (11 December 1832) and "La fonda nueva" [The new inn] (23 August 1833) stands out. The importance of etiquette in his gastronomic articles is not inconsequential. Susan Kirkpatrick reminds us that "en todos sus escritos sobre costumbres sociales, salvo en sus últimas producciones, se refleja una fuerte preocupación por el vestido elegante, la cortesía y la urbanidad" [in all his writings on social customs, except in his final pieces, there is a strong preoccupation with elegant dress, courtesy, and urbanity] (1977, 112). "El castellano viejo" presents a detailed X-ray of the cultural habits of an openly nationalist middle class resistant to the introduction of any foreignizing novelty. Larra offers criticism that transcends the format of a *costumbrista* article and even the specific gastronomic content of the text. The work constitutes, in a certain way, a moral disquisition, a political speech, a manual on the psychology of traditionalism, and a meditation on the dilemmas of liberal modernity in Spain during the 1830s. The author repeatedly insists on the pernicious effects of the purist nationalism taken up by the figure of the old Spaniard: "Es tal su patriotismo, que dará todas las lindezas del extranjero por un dedo de su país. Esta ceguedad le hace adoptar todas las responsabilidades de tan inconsiderado cariño" [His patriotism is such that he will give all the foreign beauties for a finger of his homeland. This blindness makes him adopt all the responsibility of such a thoughtless affection] (1857, vol. 1, 32). Braulio's character, the unyielding old Spaniard, organizes a banquet at his home whose chaotic unfolding permits Larra to effect an implacable satire of Spanish traditionalism. For the reader, Braulio's visceral rejection of any kind of conduct conditioned by etiquette is obvious: "Llama a la urbanidad hipocresía, y a la decencia monadas; a toda cosa buena le aplica un mal apodo; el lenguaje de la finura es para él poco más que griego" [He calls urbanity hypocrisy, and decency childish games; to every good thing he gives a nasty nickname; refined language is for him little more than Greek] (32). Larra situates this figure in the ambiguous middle class that, during the 1830s, began to have a certain visibility in the Spanish political sphere: "Braulio está muy lejos de pertenecer a lo que se llama hoy gran mundo y sociedad de buen tono; pero no es tampoco un hombre de la clase inferior, puesto que es un empleado de los de segundo orden" [Braulio is very far from belonging to what is today called the grand world and high society; but neither is he a man of low class, since he is a second-order employee] (31–2). The author's criticism emphasizes the fact that this social group, identified with anti-liberal traditionalism, refuses to adopt "una educación más escogida y modales más suaves e insinuantes" [better-chosen behaviour and smoother and more ingratiating manners] (32).

The obvious vulgarity of this middle class presents a certain semantic affinity with the concept of "grosero" included in the *Diccionario de la lengua castellana* of 1832: "el descortés que no observa decoro ni urbanidad" [a discourteous person who does not observe decorum or urbanity] (Real Academia Española 1991, 381). It is important to note that the absence of urbanity during the banquet organized by Braulio and the rustic presentation of the food offered in the meal reveal a mental predisposition that associates alleged Spanish purity with the manifestation of primitive instincts uncontaminated by any kind of artifice: "exijo la mayor franqueza; en mi casa no se usan cumplimientos" [I demand the greatest frankness; in my house, we do not use niceties] (Larra 1857, vol. 1, 34). The different events that transpire in the banquet reveal not so much the host's coarseness as the absence of a minimal, regularizing order in the process of this social act. The slowness in bringing out the food, the dirtiness of the tablecloths, the defective presentation of the food and other "negligencias [que] se repetían tan a menudo" [negligences repeated so often] (36) create a chaotic atmosphere articulated around the culinary disorder, the lack of urbanity, and the proud adoption of primitive instincts obstructed by an obstinate nature.[24]

Hispanists have privileged the aesthetic dimension of the problem presented by Larra in "El castellano viejo." Oliver's early analyses perceive that "no se trata, para él, de una mera depuración del gusto, de un simple problema retórico ... Larra perseguía una mutación de valores literarios: el valor mental presidiendo el valor gramatical y lingüístico" [for him, it is not a matter of mere purification of taste, of a simple rhetorical problem ... Larra pursues a change of literary values: the mental value taking precedence over the grammatical and linguistic value] (1918, 72–3). Nombela y Campos indicates the link that the *costumbrista* article establishes between bad manners, insipid vulgarity, and poorly understood patriotism (1906, 100).[25] It should be noted that both criticisms relate the absence of a refined etiquette in the Spanish middle class to a traditionalist nationalism hostile to liberal modernity. More recent studies praise the presentation of incompatible models of conduct in this *costumbrista* article, which occurs through the use of "dualismo perspectivista" [perspectivist dualism] (Baquero Goyanes 1963, 36–41) or "oposiciones binarias" [binary oppositions] (Kirkpatrick 1977, 222). Criticism also exists that focuses on Larra's use of rhetorical processes to ridicule the anachronistic world affiliated with the "old" etiquette of old Spaniards.[26] James Mandrell's detailed analysis points out the *costumbrista* article's clear textual dependence "point by point" on "Observaciones sobre la cortesanía" [Observations on courtesy] (1820) by José de Urcullu (Mandrell 2011, 79). It is interesting to remember the liberal affiliation of Urcullu, who emigrated to England and was an active collaborator in the literary undertakings of exiled Spanish romantics in that country (Llorens 2006, 249). The interest of liberal writers in etiquette or gastronomic topics shows the symbolic importance assigned to the rules of urbanity by the promoters of this political ideology in Spain. Sánchez Reboredo asserts that for Larra "la educación es la asunción de la vida en libertad ... El hombre no educado difícilmente sabrá vivir esa libertad" [manners are the act of taking up life in liberty ... The unmannered man will understand how to live that liberty only with great difficulty] (1967, 175). Such characteristics as lack of urbanity, the chaotic planning of a banquet at home, and the repeated failure to comply with the fundamental requirements of etiquette interfere with Braulio's behaviour in "El castellano viejo." Larra's satire links traditionalism with the dogmatic perceptions assigned to outdated traditionalism. The fact that these behaviours produce domestic disorder, culinary chaos, or a buried primitivism could show us the devastating effects that, for Larra, a traditionalist behaviour incompatible with liberal modernity generates.

Pierre Bourdieu's perspicacious reflections on the links that unite social class with gastronomic habits are productive for understanding the satire articulated in "El castellano viejo." Bourdieu points out the symbolic character of the norms of etiquette prescribed by the nineteenth-century bourgeoisie (1991, 194). Such codes are interpreted as a "juego de estilizaciones [que] tiende a desplazar el acento de la substancia y la función hacia la forma y la manera, y, con ello, a negar o, mejor, a rechazar la realidad groseramente material del acto de consumir" [a game of stylizations [that] tend to displace the stress of substance and function for form and manner, and, along with this, to deny, or better, to reject the grossly material reality of the act of eating] (195). An aesthetic refinement exists, even an artistic aspiration whose precise, ceremonious execution makes the bourgeois etiquette essentially different from the alimentary habits taken up by the more populous classes "que se abandonan a las satisfacciones inmediatas del consumo alimenticio" [who abandon themselves to the immediate satisfaction of consuming food] (195). Bourdieu's reference to the intimate relation between urbanity, social class, and refinement offers a suggestive interpretation of the significance inscribed in the codes of etiquette maintained during a gastronomic event. With regard to "El castellano viejo," it does not seem gratuitous that this article parodies the coarseness and lack of urbanity of a social group, the Spanish middle class, that in theory ought to have aspirations of refinement to distinguish their social status. What motives might explain the fact that these old Spaniards disdain "esa delicadeza de trato que establece entre los hombres una delicada armonía" [that delicacy of manners that establishes among men a delicate harmony] (Larra 1857, vol. 1, 32)? Larra's article believes that unyielding traditionalism and a nationalist sentiment resistant to any cosmopolitan tendencies stimulate a compulsive predisposition to dogmatism in Braulio: "es un hombre, en fin, que vive de las exclusivas" [in sum, he is a man who lives off what is exclusive] (32). Here might lie the roots of the principal problem that, for Larra, gives rise to the detractors of modernity in Spain. The intolerant rejection of any kind of nuance or the inability to interpret complex social relationships is not only anachronistic in the Western socio-historical coordinates of the nineteenth century dominated by Ortega y Gasset's "teclado de múltiples posibilidades del pensamiento." These behaviours also favour a moral disintegration visible in the grotesque banquet organized by Braulio. The burned chickens, the excessively smoke-flavoured stew, the rotting fish that was served, the low quality of the wine at the banquet, and "la lluvia maléfica de grasa" [maleficent rain of grease] poured on the diners (37) display to the reader not so much the obvious mediocrity championed by outdated Spanish traditionalism as its disturbing aesthetic lack. The satirical tone of this *costumbrista* painting, considered excessive, curiously, by traditionalist detractors of Larra,[27] shows how urbanity, gastronomy, and, in a general sense, the etiquette ascribed to bourgeois sociability may represent a profound symbolic dimension in Spanish letters in the first third of the nineteenth century.

Noël Valis observes the notable presence of the phenomenon of tastelessness in nineteenth-century Spanish culture. Tasteless perceptions reflect "the sense of inadequacy that a marginalized society in transition experiences when moving from a traditional economy to an industrialized, consumer-oriented economic organization" (2002, 32). "El castellano viejo" does not present, in an explicit way, a problematic of tastelessness. Nevertheless, moral attitudes exist that anticipate, within the proper limits, tendencies ascribed to tastelessness. What causes the failure of Braulio's homemade banquet? Dogmatic exclusivism or the absence of urbanity does not totally explain this circumstance. Larra also attributes it to the moral factors of "vanidad" [vanity] and "ceguedad" [blindness] (1857, vol. 1, 32). These references show perhaps one of the most important keys of the regenerative discourse taken up in "El castellano viejo" with regard to gastronomy or etiquette. The satire never employs the term "cursi" [tasteless] in its textual unfolding. It is evident, nevertheless, that Braulio's coarse, anachronistic conduct during the banquet anticipates the phenomenon of tastelessness in the measure that it represents the ridiculous character of behaviour not adapted to the expectations of nineteenth-century bourgeois etiquette. The unsuitability that, according to Valis, conditions tasteless behaviour may be seen not only in Braulio's exclusivist anachronisms. We may perceive as well a censure of pretensions to refinement or urbanity: "¿Hay nada más ridículo que estas gentes que quieren pasar por finas en medio de la más crasa ignorancia de los usos sociales?" [Is there anything more ridiculous than these people who want to pass for refined in the middle of the most crass ignorance of social customs?] (1857, vol. 1, 36). Different circumstances, in short, explain the chaotic sociability presented in "El castellano viejo": the antiquated determination to reject modern tendencies, obstinate dogmatisms about etiquette, pretensions to urbanity, awful manners, and, ultimately, the lack of economic resources that would justify bourgeois refinement. These factors allow Larra's mental deprecation of old Spaniards to satirize "estas casas en que es un convite un acontecimiento, en que sólo se pone la mesa decente para los invitados, en que creen hacer obsequios cuando dan mortificaciones" [these houses in which a banquet is a big deal, in which a decent table is only set for guests, in which they believe they give gifts when in reality they give torture and humiliation] (38). The author's perspective transcends the specific event of the banquet. Larra's criticism emphasizes the visible moral deficiencies in those who actively promote the anachronistic intellectual isolation of Spain in the name of a presumed uniqueness that is not modern. This is the quality of being static, rigid, and morally disordered, of social failure, and of a lack of vital authenticity. These factors, broadly documented in Larra's article, correspond exactly with the adverse judgments formulated by modern authors since the Renaissance against formalist mannerism or the artistic emptiness observed in medieval culture. The moral failure of the old Spaniards, in the end, is clearly set out through the skilful fusion of a satire of pretensions to urbanity and the criticism of culinary habits that fail as much for their chaotic arrangement as for their unsuitable artistic presentation. The gastronomic model prescribed in "El castellano viejo" privileges the merits of the "honradas casas donde un modesto cocido y un principio final constituyen la felicidad diaria de una familia" [honoured houses where a modest meal and a final principle constitute the daily happiness of a family] (37). Opposing food defined by its genuine simplicity to the failed pretensions of banquets organized without etiquette or exactness reveals, ultimately, not only the moral deficiencies that Mariano José de Larra detects in those who destroy the slightest trace of vitality or authenticity in the name of antiquated and insipid anti-modern prejudices. We also see the modern reclamation of gastronomic habits identified with simplicity and a renewed harmony marked by urbanity.

"La fonda nueva," considered by Azorín to be "uno de los más interesantes artículos del autor" [one of the author's most interesting articles] (1915, 79), offers the reader a detailed typology of the different inns[28] that existed in Madrid at the beginning of the 1830s. The critical studies that have been carried out on this work accentuate the symbolic content from a perspective that links the mediocrity of the restaurants with the failure of the Spanish progressive ideology.[29] Evaluations written by Larra's contemporaries also indicate the deficiencies of the inns of the period. Mesonero Romanos in the *Manual de Madrid* [Guide to Madrid] (1831) identifies the more refined character of these inns in contrast to "hosterías" [hostels] and "las tiendas de comestibles y figones, donde se sirven comidas y almuerzos a la clase menos acomodada, y con toda conveniencia" [cheap restaurants where they serve foods and meals to the less fortunate class, with every convenience] (1967, vol. 3, 27). The inns differentiated themselves by offering "en general mayor elegancia en el servicio … a pesar de que las fondas no están en Madrid tan brillantemente montadas como otros establecimientos" [in general, greater elegance in their service … in spite of the fact that the inns of Madrid are not as brilliantly put together as other establishments] (26).[30] Mesonero Romanos evokes with a certain nostalgia in the *Memorias de un setentón* [Memoirs of a Septuagenarian] (1880) the "opíparo festín" [sumptuous feast] that the literary and politically minded youth celebrated at the end of the 1820s in the Inns of Genieys, La Fontana de Oro, or the Inn of San Fernando (1975, 275). The overriding perspective, nevertheless, shows that the inns of Madrid did not have available the material resources, the refinement, and the gastronomic variety that could be enjoyed in similar establishments in other European countries.

Larra's sharp satire links the dirtiness of Madrid's inns with apathy, indifference, and the rejection of visible innovations in "el monótono y sepulcral silencio de nuestra existencia española" [the monotonous and sepulchral silence of our Spanish existence] (1857, vol. 1, 95). The different inns mentioned by the author share identical untidiness and lack of hygiene. In the Inn of Dos Amigos, "tendremos que salirnos a la calle a comer, o a la escalera, o llevar una cerilla en el bolsillo para vernos las caras en la sala larga" [we will have to go out to the street to eat, or to the stairs, or carry a candle in our pockets to see each other's faces in the long room] (97). The Inn of Comercio stands out for its mediocre distribution of decoration similar to other establishments where "no les da el naipe a los fondistas para escoger local; en cuanto al adorno, nos cogen acostumbrados a no pagarnos de apariencias" [the patrons of the inn are not lucky enough to choose their place; as for the decoration, they find us accustomed not to judge by appearances] (98). Even the prestige of the Inn of Genieys, evoked by Mesonero Romanos for its succulent delicacies, was considered unworthy. This establishment's deficiencies are seen as much in the rustic layout of its dining rooms as in the lack of foreign products. The author sets out in great detail the reasons for his thinking: "Las salas son feas; el adorno ninguno: ni una alfombra, ni un mueble elegante, ni un criado decente, ni un servicio de lujo, ni un espejo, ni una chimenea, ni una estufa en invierno, ni agua de nieve en verano, ni … ni Burdeos, ni Champagne … Porque no es de Burdeos el Valdepeñas, por más raíz de lirio que se le eche" [the rooms are ugly; there is no decoration: no carpet, no elegant furniture, no decent servants, no luxury service, no mirrors, no chimneys, no stoves in the winter, no ice-water in the summer, no … no Bordeaux, no Champagne … Because Valdepeñas is not from Bordeaux, no matter how many roots the lily puts down there] (97). The inns of Madrid, in short, reproduce the problems that the author observes in Spanish society of the time: excessive purity, the rejection of cosmopolitan innovations, the dogmatic defence of autochthonous tradition, a congenital inability to recognize complex social relations in modern life, the lack of vitality, and the absence of bourgeois refinements. Mariano José de Larra's final reflections do not contemplate improvement in the immediate future:

¿Quiere usted que le diga yo lo que nos darán en cualquier fonda adonde vayamos? Mire usted: nos darán en primer lugar mantel y servilletas puercas, vasos puercos, platos puercos y mozos puercos: sacarán las cucharas del bolsillo, donde están con las puntas de los cigarros; nos darán luego una sopa que llaman de yerbas, y que no podría acertar a tener nombre más alusivo; estofado de vaca a la italiana, que es cosa nueva; ternera mechada, que es cosa de todos los días; vino de la fuente; aceitunas magulladas; frito de sesos y manos de carnero, hechos aquéllos y éstos a fuerza de pan; una polla que se dejaron otros ayer, y unos postres que nos dejaremos nosotros para mañana. (97–8)

[Would you like me to tell you what they will give us in whatever inn we go to? Here we go: they will give us, first, the tablecloth and dirty napkins, dirty glasses, dirty plates, and dirty serving boys: they will pull the spoons out of their pockets, where they've been sitting with cigarette butts; they will then give us a soup that they say is herbs, and which couldn't have a more allusive name; beef stew à la italiana, which is a new thing; larded calf, which is an everyday thing; wine from the fountain; bruised olives; fried lamb brains and lamb feet, made with bread; a chicken that somebody abandoned yesterday, and desserts that we will abandon today.]

Larra's reasoning develops a strategy similar to that which is presented in "El castellano viejo." One may see how the lack of care for the food's presentation in the inn, the mediocre condition of what is offered to the public, and the nonexistent urbanity of the waiters reveal, to a greater or lesser degree, the aesthetic failure of a commercial project aimed at the Spanish middle class. The lack of vitality and the nonexistent authenticity of such businesses show the urgent cosmopolitan reformation that the author considers unavoidable in Spanish society. Not having available the bourgeois refinements, for Larra, leads to primitive behaviour that stimulates the lowest instincts. It is interesting that in the Inn of Comercio, frequented by the middle class and "algunos elegantes" [some elegant people], diners adopted a rebellious lack of manners: "¿De qué se ríen tanto? ¿Han dicho alguna gracia? No, señor; se ríen de que han comido, y la parte física del hombre triunfa de la moral, de la sublime, que no debiera estar alegre sólo por haber comido" [What are they laughing at so loudly? Have they said something funny? No, sir; they laugh because they have eaten, and the physical part of man triumphs over the moral, over the sublime, which must not be happy solely because it has eaten] (98). The artistic singularity that bourgeois etiquette prescribes for gastronomic events systematically fails to be fulfilled by these diners. The triumph of physical materiality over any aesthetic aspiration of sociability presents us with a dying social atmosphere whose moral insufficiencies reveal the vital impoverishment caused by purist traditionalism.

III. Conclusion

"… [las personas elegantes son] un muy reducido número de personas, las cuales, entre paréntesis, son siempre las mismas, y forman un pueblo chico de costumbres extranjeras, embutido dentro de otro grande de costumbres patrias, como un cucurucho menor metido en un cucurucho mayor (Larra 1857, vol. 1, 96)

[the number of elegant people is very reduced, in parentheses, they are always the same, and they form a small group of people with foreign customs, crammed inside another larger group of people with the customs of their homeland, like one ice-cream cone nested inside a larger one]

César Antonio Molina's recent analysis highlights the modern currency of critical patriotism noticeable in Larra's *costumbrista* articles: "¿Quiénes son más patriotas, los que aman a la patria porque no les gusta o los que aman a la patria porque les gusta? Los primeros son críticos, desean cambios, están molestos por el inmovilismo, son sinceros y dicen la dolorosa verdad … Larra pertenecía al primer grupo … Él fue acusado, por este motivo, de mal español, de renegado, de afrancesado" [Which are greater patriots, those who love their country because they do not like it or those who love their country because they do? The first are critics, they desire change, they are bothered by stagnation, they are sincere and tell the painful truth … Larra belonged to the first group … He was accused, for this reason, of being a bad Spaniard, of being a renegade, of being Frenchified] (2014, 126). Mariano José de Larra's gastronomic articles celebrate with enthusiasm the liberal reformist project, adopted by the author through satire. Different factors justify his parodic approach: the lack of manners and refinement in the Spanish middle class, the aesthetic deficiencies noted in gastronomic events, and the obvious moral disintegration displayed by traditionalist purity. Ridiculing these defects is important not only to show the wearing out of Spanish traditionalism but also to suggest to the reader a cultural alternative inspired in cosmopolitanism, tolerance, urbanity, refinement, aesthetic consciousness, and other values ascribed to the principles of liberal modernity.

NOTES

1 For a representative sample of the difficulties experienced by liberalism in Spain during the first decades of the nineteenth century, see Blanco White

(2005, 26, 72, 178; and 2007, 338–9). Unless otherwise noted, translations are by Gregory Baum.

2 For a historiographic analysis that emphasizes the disturbing effects of the tendentious association of political traditionalism and Spanish national identity during the first third of the nineteenth century, see Michelet (1843, 108).

3 For an analysis of the difficulties experienced by the Spanish Enlightenment in the last third of the eighteenth century, see Elorza (1986 and 1989). For a recent analysis that associates the work of Mariano José de Larra with the Enlightenment spirit of 1780–1808, see Mainer (2014, 144).

4 For a precedent of this perspective during the War of Independence (1808–14), see Martínez Marina (1988, 161–2). For an identical perspective formulated during the 1860s by progressive liberalism, see Fernández de los Ríos (1879, 1: 1–15).

5 For a historiographic interpretation that signals the irreversible (modern) secularization of Spanish culture since the "Sexenio," see Clarín (1891, 62–77); Croce (1996, 241); Zavala (1970, 293–310).

6 Schlegelian traditionalism challenges in a generic sense the modern values of cosmopolitan rationalism brought about by the Enlightenment and the French Revolution (1789). In the case of Spain, the proponents of this project question the artistic legitimacy of Renaissance and eighteenth-century classicisms. Genuine Spanish literature, in contrast, is associated with medieval literature and the *comedias* of Calderón. For an analysis of the influential impact this formulation had in nineteenth-century Spanish culture, see Carnero (1978, 247–98); Flitter (2006, 8–38); Flitter (1995, 148–81); Iarocci (2006, 23, 26, 41); Löwy and Sayre (2001, 22); Kagan (2002, 23); Tully (1997, 26, 56–7).

7 For a historiographic interpretation that draws attention to the identification of liberalism with romanticism during the decade of 1834–44, see Ginger (2012, 78); Llorens (2006, 683–8); Navas Ruiz (1982, 120–49); Ruiz Ramón (1981, vol. 1, 311–37); and Valis (2002, 33–5).

8 See Ortega y Gasset (1971, 17; 1963, 124–5).

9 See Ortega y Gasset (1961–2, vol. 9, 532, 570).

10 For an extensive reflection by Larra on satire, see Larra (1857, vol. 2, 68–74).

11 Dictionaries from the seventeenth century also record the didactic purpose assigned to the genre of satire: "es un género de verso picante, el cual reprehende los vicios y desórdenes de los hombres" [it is a genre of spicy verse, which reproaches the vices and excesses of men] (Covarrubias 1994, 886).

12 For an analysis of classicism's loss of academic prestige during the nineteenth century because of the influence of romantic criticism, see Sánchez-Llama (2014).

13 For an analysis of the importance of simplicity and purity in the configuration of values that contrapose the modern consciousness to the devalued mannerisms of medieval affiliation, see Huizinga (1946, 148).

14 For a suggestive literary periodization that observes the continuity of a certain Spanish classicism from the sixteenth century until the last third of the nineteenth century, see Sebold (2003, 117).

15 For an accurate summary of Larra's values, see the article "Literatura" (18 January 1836) (1857, vol. 2, 40–7).

16 See Blanco García (2007, vol. 1, 341); Caravaca (1963, 17); Hendrix (1979, 219); Lomba y Pedraja (1936, 65); Nombela (1906, 194).

17 See Marún (1981, 386); Torrecilla (1996b, 74).

18 See Baquero Goyanes (1949–50, 735); Escobar (1972, 12); Goytisolo (1967, 12); Mateo del Peral (1967, 186); Varela (1983, 232).

19 See Pérez Vidal (1997, 194).

20 For an analysis of Larra's liberalism, see Kercheville (1931, 199); Kirkpatrick (1977, 197); Salinas (1983, vol. 3, 186). For a different analysis that proposes an "equivocal political position" in Larra's work, see Tarr (1936, 107).

21 See Oliver (1918, 35 and 77); Azorín (1973, 105).

22 Azorín emphasizes precisely this aspect in *Rivas y Larra* (1916): "Larra es el hombre más moderno de su tiempo, *el único hombre moderno de su tiempo*, en España" [Larra is the most modern man of his time, the only modern man of his time, in Spain] (1973, 105, original emphasis). For a similar analysis of Larra's atypical literary work, see Peers 1973, vol. 2, 91); Romero Tobar (1994, 452); Oliver (1918, 29); and Torre (1979, 97).

23 Alborg (1982, 224); Barja (1933, 144–5); Umbral (1965, 22).

24 The detailed analysis of Nombela y Campos notes in "El castellano viejo" the presentation of a traditionalist social conduct that identifies primitive spontaneity with the authentic Spanish character: "Persiste en estos individuos [castellanos viejos] el recuerdo de una sociedad nimiamente ceremoniosa, recuerdo que ha venido a unirse a los instintos de una naturaleza cerril" [There persists in these individuals (old Castilians) the memory of a triflingly ceremonious society, a memory that has come to overlap with the instincts of their wild nature] (1906, 100). For a similar analysis of Larra's critique of traditionalism, see Torrecilla (1996a, 92).

25 For a similar analysis of Larra's criticism of the traditionalist sectors "que carecen del gusto, culinario y literario, que sólo la mejor sociedad puede dar" [that lack the taste, culinary and literary, that only the best society can provide], see Llorens (1979, 350).

26 For an analysis of the figurative language developed by Larra in "El castellano viejo," see Cabrera (1977, 14); Ilie (1974–5, 157); Ullman (1971, 399n10); Varela (1983, 100–18 and 167–8).

27 For a traditionalist analysis that censures the severe tone used in "El castellano viejo" against the partisans of anti-modern exclusivism, see Azorín (1942, 12); Blanco García (1891, vol. 1, 341); Lomba y Pedraja (1936, 65–8).

28 Throughout the remainder of the article, the word "fonda" is translated as "inn."

29 See Perry (1988, 99–100); Teichmann (1986, 116).

30 Identical observations are formulated two decades later by Mesonero
    Romanos in his *Nuevo manual histórico-topográfico-estadístico y descripción
    de Madrid* [New historic-topographic-statistical and descriptive manual
    of Madrid]: "Preciso es reconocer ... que la escasez de viajeros, propia-
    mente tales, hace que nuestra capital carezca de aquel refinamiento de
    comodidad y buen gusto que ofrecen al extranjero los *hoteles* de París,
    Londres, Bruselas y otras capitales extranjeras, llegando en este punto la
    desidia hasta el extremo de no haber uno solo construido expresamente
    para este objeto. Las pocas *fondas* y casas de comida suplen escasamente
    aquella falta, hospedando en ella a algunos forasteros" [It is necessary
    to recognize ... that the shortage of travellers as such means that our
    capital lacks the refinement of comfort and good taste offered by hotels
    in Paris, London, Brussels, and other foreign capitals. At this point lazi-
    ness reaches the extreme of not having built even one such structure ex-
    pressly for this purpose. The few inns and houses where food is served
    barely make up for that lack by hosting a few foreigners] (1854, 637, orig-
    inal emphasis).

WORKS CITED

Academia Española. 1832. *Diccionario de la lengua castellana*. 7th ed. Madrid:
    Imprenta Real.

Academia Española. 1837. *Diccionario de la lengua castellana*. 8th ed. Madrid:
    Imprenta Nacional.

Academia Española. 1843. *Diccionario de la lengua castellana*. 9th ed. Madrid:
    Imprenta de D. Francisco Marín Fernández.

Alcalá Galiano, Antonio. 1844. "Del reinado de Isabel II y del gobierno de la
    reina su madre hasta su renuncia en 1840." In *Historia de España y Portugal*,
    by Samuel Dunham, translated by Antonio Alcalá Galiano, vol. 7, 216–599.
    Madrid: Imprenta de la Sociedad Literaria y Tipográfica.

Alborg, Juan Luis. 1982. *Historia de la literatura española. El Romanticismo*. Vol. 4.
    Madrid: Gredos.

Auslander, Leora. 1996. *Taste and Power: Furnishing Modern France*. Berkeley:
    University of California Press.

Azorín [José Martínez Ruiz]. 1915. *Al margen de los clásicos*. Madrid:
    Publicaciones de la Residencia de Estudiantes.

Azorín, José Martínez Ruiz. 1942. "Comento a Larra." In *Artículos de costumbres*
    by Mariano José de Larra, edited by José Martínez Ruiz Azorín, 9–15.
    Buenos Aires: Espasa-Calpe.

Azorín, José Martínez Ruiz. 1973. *Rivas y Larra. Razón social del romanticismo en
    España*. Madrid: Espasa-Calpe.

Baquero Goyanes, Mariano. 1949–50. "Barroco y Romanticismo (dos ensayos)." *Anales de la Universidad de Murcia*, 725–70.

Baquero Goyanes, Mariano. 1963. *Perspectivismo y contraste (de Cadalso a Pérez de Ayala)*. Madrid: Gredos.

Barja, César. 1933. *Libros y autores modernos*. Los Angeles: Campbell's Bookstore.

Blanco García, Francisco. 1891. *La literatura española en el siglo XIX*. Vol. 1. Madrid: Sáenz de Jubera.

Blanco White, José María. 2005. *"Semanario Patriótico."* 1809. Edited by Antonio Garnica and Raquel Rico. Granada: Almed.

Blanco White, José María. 2007. *"El Español"*. 1810. Edited by Antonio Garnica, J.M. Portillo, and J. Vallejo. Granada: Almed.

Bourdieu, Pierre. 1991. *La distinción. Criterio y bases sociales del gusto*. Translated by María del Carmen Ruiz de Elvira. Madrid: Taurus.

Bourdieu, Pierre. 2000. *Poder, derecho y clases sociales*. Translated by Andrés García Inda et al. Bilbao: Desclée de Brouwer.

Cabrera, Vicente. 1977. "El arte satírico de Larra." *Hispanófila* 59: 9–17.

Caravaca, Francisco. 1963. "Notas sobre las fuentes literarias del costumbrismo de Larra." *Revista Hispánica Moderna* 29.1: 1–22.

Carnero, Guillermo. 1978. *Los orígenes del romanticismo reaccionario español. El matrimonio Böhl de Faber*. Valencia: Universidad.

Clarín [Leopoldo Alas]. 1891. *Solos*. Madrid: Librería de Fernando Fe.

Covarrubias Orozco, Sebastián. 1994. *Tesoro de la lengua castellana o española*. [1611]. Edited by Felipe C.R. Maldonado. Madrid: Castalia.

Croce, Benedetto. 1996. *Historia de Europa en el siglo XIX*. [1932]. Translated by Atilio Pentimalli Melacrino. Barcelona: Ariel.

Elorza, Antonio. 1986. "La excepción y la regla: reaccionarios y revolucionarios en torno a 1789." *Estudios de Historia Social* 36–7: 179–202.

Elorza, Antonio. 1989. "Ilustración en España a finales del siglo XVIII." *Anales de la Cátedra Francisco Suárez* 29: 141–58.

Escobar, José. 1972. "*El Pobrecito Hablador*, de Larra, y su intención satírica." *Papeles de Sons Armadans* 64: 5–44.

Ferrer del Río, Antonio. 1846. *Galería de la "literatura" española*. Madrid: Establecimiento Tipográfico de D.F. de P. Mellado.

Fernández de los Ríos, Ángel. 1879. *Estudio histórico de las luchas políticas en la España del siglo XIX* [1864]. 2 vols. Madrid: English y Gras.

Flitter, Derek. 1995. *Teoría y crítica del romanticismo español*. Translated by Benigno Fernández Salgado. Cambridge: Cambridge University Press.

Flitter, Derek. 2006. *Spanish Romanticism and the Uses of History: Ideology and the Historical Imagination*. London: Legenda.

Ginger, Andrew. 2012. *Liberalismo y Romanticismo. La reconstrucción del sujeto histórico*. Madrid: Biblioteca Nueva.

Goytisolo, Juan. 1967. *El furgón de cola*. Paris: Ruedo Ibérico.

Hendrix, William S. 1979. "Notas sobre la influencia de Jouy en Larra." In *Mariano José Larra*, translated by María Elena Francés and Rubén Benítez, 217–25. Madrid: Taurus.

Huizinga, Johan. 1946. *Erasmo* [1924]. Translated by J. Farrán y Mayoral and S. Olives Canals. Barcelona: Ediciones del Zodíaco.

Iarocci, Michael. 2006. *Properties of Modernity: Romantic Spain, Modern Europe, and the Legacies of Empire*. Nashville: Vanderbilt University Press.

Ilie, Paul. 1974–5. "Larra's Nightmare." *Revista Hispánica Moderna* 38.3: 153–66.

Kagan, Richard L. 2002. "U.S. Historical Scholarship on Spain." In *Spain in America: The Origins of Hispanism in the United States*, edited by Richard L. Kagan, 21–48. Urbana: University of Illinois Press.

Kercheville, F.M. 1931. "Larra and Liberal Thought in Spain." *Hispania* 14.3: 197–204. https://doi.org/10.2307/332128.

Kirkpatrick, Susan. 1977. *Larra: el laberinto inextricable de un romántico liberal*. Translated by Marta Eguía. Madrid: Gredos.

Larra, Mariano José de. 1857. *Colección de artículos dramáticos, literarios, políticos y de costumbres*. 2 vols. Barcelona: Imprenta de La Publicidad.

Larra, Mariano José de. 1960. *Obras*. Edited by Carlos Seco Serrano. 4 vols. Madrid: Atlas.

Larra, Mariano José de. 1986. *Artículos varios*. Edited by E. Correa Calderón. Madrid: Castalia.

Llorens, Vicente. 1979. *El Romanticismo español*. Madrid: Castalia.

Llorens, Vicente. 2006. *Liberales y románticos. Una emigración española en Inglaterra (1823–1834)* [1954]. Madrid: Castalia.

Lomba y Pedraja, José R. 1936. *Mariano José de Larra (Fígaro). Cuatro estudios que le abordan o le bordean*. Madrid: Tipografía de Archivos.

Löwy, Michael, and Robert Sayre. 2001. *Romanticism against the Tide of Modernity* [1992]. Translated by Catherine Porter. Durham, NC: Duke University Press.

Mainer, José-Carlos. 2014. *Historia mínima de la literatura española*. Madrid: Turner.

Mandrell, James. 2011. "Etiquette and Table Manners in Larra's *El castellano Viejo*: Another Point of View." *Forum for Modern Languages Studies* 22: 74–84. https://doi.org/10.1093/fmls/cqr041.

Martínez Marina, Francisco. 1988. *Discurso sobre el origen de la monarquía y sobre la naturaleza del gobierno español* [1813]. Edited by José Antonio Maravall, 79–169. Madrid: Instituto de Estudios Políticos.

Marún, Gioconda. 1981. "Apuntaciones sobre la influencia de Addison y Steele en Larra." *Hispania* 64.3: 382–7. https://doi.org/10.2307/342042.

Mateo del Peral, Diego Ignacio. 1967. "Larra y el presente." *Revista de Occidente* 50: 181–204.

Mesonero Romanos, Ramón de. 1854. *Nuevo manual histórico-topográfico-estadístico y descripción de Madrid*. Madrid: Carlos Bailly-Bailliere.

Mesonero Romanos, Ramón de. 1967. *Obras*. Edited by Carlos Seco Serrano. 5 vols. Madrid: Atlas.

Mesonero Romanos, Ramón de. 1975. *Memorias de un setentón* [1880]. Madrid: Tebas.

Michelet, Jules. 1843. *Introduction a l'histoire universelle* [1831]. Paris: Hachette.

Miraflores, Marqués de [Manuel Pando Fernández de Pinedo]. 1834. *Apuntes histórico-críticos para escribir la historia de España desde el año 1820 hasta 1823*. London: R. Taylor.

Molina, César Antonio. 2014. *La caza de los intelectuales. La cultura bajo sospecha*. Barcelona: Destino.

Navas Ruiz, Ricardo. 1982. *El romanticismo español*. Madrid: Cátedra.

Nombela y Campos, Julio. 1906. *Larra (Fígaro)*. Madrid: Imprenta de La Última Moda.

Oliver, Miguel de los Santos. 1918. *Hojas del sábado. Revisiones y centenarios*. Vol. 2. Barcelona: Gustavo Gili.

Ortega y Gasset, José. 1961–2. *Obras completas*. 5th ed. 9 vols. Madrid: *Revista de Occidente*.

Ortega y Gasset, José. 1963. *El tema de nuestro tiempo* [1923]. Madrid: *Revista de Occidente*.

Ortega y Gasset, José. 1971. *Historia como sistema* [1935]. Madrid: Espasa-Calpe.

Peers, E. Allison. 1973. *Historia del movimiento romántico español* [1940]. Translated by José María Gimeno. 2 vols. Madrid: Gredos.

Pérez Vidal, Alejandro. 1997. "La obra periodística de Mariano José de Larra." In *Historia de la literatura española. Siglo XIX (I)*, edited by Guillermo Carnero, vol. 8, 183–206. Madrid: Espasa Calpe.

Perry, Leonard T. 1988. "La presencia de lo extranjero en los artículos de Mariano José de Larra." In *Resonancias románticas: evocaciones del romanticismo hispánico*, edited by John R. Rosenberg, 93–102. Madrid: José Porrúa Turanzas.

Real Academia Española. 1991. *Diccionario de la lengua castellana* [1780]. 1st ed. Madrid: Real Academia Española.

Romero Tobar, Leonardo. 1994. *Panorama crítico del romanticismo español*. Madrid: Castalia.

Ruiz Ramón, Francisco. 1981. *Historia del teatro español*. 2 vols. Madrid: Cátedra.

Salinas, Pedro. 1983. *Ensayos completos*. Edited by Solita Salinas de Marichal. Vol. 3. Madrid: Taurus.

Sánchez-Llama, Íñigo. 2014. "La quiebra del clasicismo en la crítica moderna y contemporánea: análisis de la evaluación de la poesía de Juan Meléndez Valdés." *Dieciocho* 37.2: 1–30.

Sánchez Reboredo, José. 1967. "Larra y los seres irracionales." *Revista de Occidente* 50: 172–80.

Sebold, Russell P. 2003. *Lírica y poética en España, 1536–1870*. Madrid: Cátedra.

Simón Palmer, María del Carmen. 1982. *La alimentación y sus circunstancias en el Real Alcázar de Madrid*. Madrid: Instituto de Estudios Madrileños.

Simón Palmer, María del Carmen. 1991. *Cocineros europeos en el Palacio Real*. Madrid: Instituto de Estudios Madrileños.

Simón Palmer, María del Carmen. 1997. *La cocina de Palacio, 1561–1931*. Madrid: Castalia.

Tarr, F. Courtney. 1936. "More Light on Larra." *Hispanic Review* 4.2: 89–110. https://doi.org/10.2307/469478.

Teichmann, Reinhard. 1986. *Larra: sátira y ritual mágico*. Madrid: Playor.

Terreros y Pando, Esteban. 1987. *Diccionario castellano con las voces de ciencias y artes* [1786–8]. 3 vols. Madrid: Arco Libros.

Torre, Guillermo de. 1979. "Larra." In *Mariano José Larra*, edited by Rubén Benítez, 96–9. Madrid: Taurus.

Torrecilla, Jesús. 1996a. *La imitación colectiva. Modernidad vs. autenticidad en la literatura española*. Madrid: Gredos.

Torrecilla, Jesús. 1996b. *El tiempo y los márgenes. Europa como utopía y como amenaza en la literatura española*. Chapel Hill: University of North Carolina Press.

Tully, Carol Lisa. 1997. *Creating a National Identity*. Stuttgart: H.-D. Heinz.

Ullman, Pierre L. 1971. *Mariano de Larra and Spanish Political Rhetoric*. Madison: University of Wisconsin Press.

Umbral, Francisco. 1965. *Larra. Anatomía de un dandy*. Madrid: Alfaguara.

Valis, Noël. 2002. *The Culture of Cursilería: Bad Taste, Kitsch, and Class in Modern Spain*. Durham, NC: Duke University Press.

Varela, José Luis 1983. *Larra y España*. Madrid: Espasa-Calpe.

Zavala, Iris M. 1970. "La prensa ante la Revolución de 1868." In *La Revolución de 1868. Historia, pensamiento, literatura*, edited by Clara E. Lida and Iris M. Zavala, 293–310; foreword by Vicente Llorens. New York: Las Américas.

9 The Meaning of Meals in Benito Pérez Galdós's *El amigo Manso*

DOROTA HENEGHAN

Unlike *Fortunata y Jacinta* (1886–7), Benito Pérez Galdós's *El amigo Manso* [Friend Manso] (1882) received sparse critical attention with respect to the significance of meals.[1] While scholars mentioned Máximo Manso's predilection for simple food and drink (Gullón 1980, 66) and remarked on his student Manuel Peña's delight in candies (Castillo 1985, 51–3), they have not explored the symbolic value of culinary products in connection to Galdós's views of Restoration society. It is true that, as Jo Labanyi noted, *Fortunata y Jacinta* "has the most references to food" (1988, 56). Yet, considering that Galdós, as she also observed, "is of all contemporary Spanish writers … the one, who, after 1881, pays most attention to material detail — notably money and food" (Labanyi 1993, 13) and that he deployed the act of eating and food imagery in his fiction prior to *Fortunata y Jacinta*, the author's use of gastronomy in *El amigo Manso* is not surprising.[2]

In what follows, I examine the symbolic values of meals in *El amigo Manso* and the manner in which Galdós implicated them in his critique of the conservative and progressive sectors of Restoration society. Informed by the author's journalistic works on food, popular cookbooks, and culinary manuals that emerged from the writings of social hygienists and commentators in late nineteenth-century Spain, this study will explore the ways in which Galdós entwined references to meals and eating habits with his views on politics, education, and gender (particularly the bourgeois notion of masculinity) and, in doing so, conveyed his preoccupation with the impact of the status quo on the future of Spain.

Galdós's articles on contemporary eating customs, his contribution to Ángel Muro's *Diccionario de la cocina* [Kitchen dictionary] (1892), and his references to food in his narrative show that culinary art was a subject of interest to him (Esteban 1992). Admittedly, unlike Emilia Pardo

Bazán, who authored two cookbooks and openly admitted to her passion for culinary delights (Ingram 2009, 20; Sinovas Maté 2006, 285), Galdós wrote less on contemporary cuisine and insisted on his neutrality towards gastronomic pleasures: "Sepan que no soy glotón, ni siquiera goloso, y que poseo una dichosa indiferencia hacia lo que llamamos placeres de la mesa" [Let it be known that I am not a glutton, not even a gourmand, and that I am happily indifferent to what we call the pleasures of the table] (1923a, 64). Similarly to his colleagues, however, he was aware of eating habits as effective tools for marking his characters' identity and an important feature of Spain's cultural life.[3] As early as 1865, in his essay "Navidad – Glotonería universal – La Plaza Mayor – Nacimientos" [Christmas – Gluttony – Main Square – Births] the writer described, albeit ironically, food consumption as the lifeblood of the Christmas celebration in Spain:

> El hombre es el que come: su inteligencia se reconcentra en el estómago: su sentimiento se localiza en el paladar: su voluntad reside en la mandíbula: el alma está ocupada en la percepción de los olores suculentos, en el temple de los sabores ... El hombre come y pudiera decir, parodiando a Descartes: *yo como, luego existo* ... Nosotros vemos en esta comilona universal un objeto que no es la simple satisfacción de un apetito ... un símbolo de nuestra religión viene a mezclarse aquí con la perspectiva del comedor ... Los cristianos celebramos con frucciones estomacales la venida al mundo del Dios Redentor ... (Quoted in Shoemaker 1972, 247, original emphasis)[4]

> [Man is he who eats: his intelligence is concentrated in the stomach: his feelings are located in the palate: his will resides in the jaw: the soul is occupied in the perception of succulent smells, in the temper of flavours ... Man eats and could say, parodying Descartes: *I eat, therefore I am* ... We see in this universal feast an object that is not the simple satisfaction of an appetite ... A symbol of our religion is here mixed with the perspective of the dining room ... Christians celebrate the coming of the Redeemer with stomach fruitions ...]

Similarly, years later, in his social sketch "El mes de marzo" [The month of March], Galdós observed (again with irony) that even during Lent "la penitencia ... es poco más que un nombre vano" [penitence is little more than a name in vain] (1923b, 107), since "personas de mucha devoción no acaban de convencerse de que sea santidad comer langosta en vez de perdices, y de año en año se hace camino y lleva trazas de hacerse dogmático el dicho aquel de San Francisco de Sales, de que *lo que entra por la boca no daña al alma*" [devout people are not entirely convinced that it is saintly to eat lobster instead of quail, and from year to year the way is paved so that a saying by Saint Francis de Sales becomes more and more dogmatic: what enters through the mouth does not harm the soul] (107–8, original emphasis). Yet, indulgence was hardly the only aspect of food consumption that interested Galdós. In the opening passages of his essay "Madrid," in which he invited readers to "dar un paseo por los mercados de Madrid" [take a walk through the markets of Madrid] (1923a, 50) and proudly went over the breathtaking assortment of "lo variado … lo sabroso y abundante" [the varied … tasty and abundant] (51) imported to the capital from the diverse parts of Spain, Europe, and overseas, Galdós pointed to the shift in general attitude towards eating:

> Las materialidades de la vida … reciben hoy, de las personas más espirituales, homenaje de consideración … ya no se ve en el comer una función puramente orgánica, íntimamente emparentada con uno de los pecados capitales más feos; ya los principios de la educación física … han adquirido el imperio que merecen, y no nos parece extravagante el aplicar a los pueblos, como a los individuos, este aforismo: "Dime lo que comes y te diré quién eres." (50)

> [The materialities of life … receive today, from the most spiritual of people, a tribute of consideration … eating is no longer seen as a purely organic function, intimately related to one of the ugliest capital sins; and the principles of physical education … have acquired the exalted place they deserve, and it does not seem extravagant to apply to countries, as well as individuals, this aphorism: "Tell me what you eat and I will tell you who you are."]

Considering it unnecessary to convince anyone that food, as the author of *The Physiology of Taste* (1826), Anthelme Brillat-Savarin, claimed several decades earlier in France, should not "be confused with either a sin or a mere bodily function" (Parkhurst Ferguson 2001, 23), Galdós was amazed by the gastronomic diversity of Madrid. Although it might appear that the writer penned his essay to emphasize the high quality of Spanish products (since he dedicated lengthy paragraphs to praise local items and claimed that he hardly ever noticed a difference between domestic and foreign goods), it was the integration of national and imported food in late nineteenth-century Spanish culture and the ways in which the world of contemporary gastronomy reconciled tradition with innovation, regional with international, that fascinated Galdós. However, social sketches were not the only place where the author signalled his awareness of the ways in which food and eating habits reflected upon the evolving nature of bourgeois society in nineteenth-century Spain. As we shall see in *El amigo Manso*, years before marvelling at the variety of alimentary riches in his essay, Galdós used references to the culinary art to explore the complexities of contemporary life in his fiction. Set in Madrid in the late 1870s and early 1880s, *El amigo Manso* depicts the life of an educator and scholar of philosophy, Máximo Manso. Meek (as his last name *Manso* indicates), bookish, and lacking masculine vigour, the protagonist-narrator agrees to tutor his wealthy neighbour's son, Manuel Peña. Bound by a promise to his mother before she died, Manso also often financially helps the once affluent and now impoverished yet still pretentious widow, doña Cándida, and her orphaned niece, Irene. After Irene completes her education, she becomes a governess in the house of Manso's brother, José María, who has recently returned from Cuba. As such, the protagonist-narrator envisions her as a progressive woman and an ideal life companion. Manso confronts José María, who, to his wife's despair, makes advances towards Irene and conspires with her aunt to seduce the girl. While effective at defending her from his brother, Manso finds out that Irene not only lacks vocation as a teacher but also aspires to marry his protégé, Manuel Peña, who is young, charming, and wealthy. Although disillusioned with doña Cándida's niece as an ordinary woman, who like everyone else in the novel is concerned with satisfying her social ambition, Manso advocates on her behalf to Manuel's mother, doña Javiera, who opposes her son's marriage with an ex-governess. Manso succeeds and Manuel and Irene marry. Shortly after their wedding, the protagonist falls ill and dies. He is quickly forgotten by all.

Returning now to the topic of nourishment in the novel, it is important to note that descriptions of meals are neither frequent nor lavishly detailed in *El amigo Manso*. Aside from specifics of Máximo Manso's eating habits, readers find limited accounts of secondary characters' diets. Nevertheless, references to culinary products accompany depictions of all personages in the novel. In fact, it would not be an exaggeration to observe that through allusions to food, Galdós effectively reinforced images of his characters' personalities, their obsessions, and their ambitions: "doña Cándida … la rapiña; doña Javiera … la huida del pasado carniceril … Irene … el matrimonio de conveniencia" [doña Cándida … the predatory one; doña Javiera … the flight from a butchering past … Irene … the arranged marriage] (Caudet 2001, 82). The mention of birds in doña Cándida's menu in chapter 42, for example, "los pichones … un pavo trufado" [squabs … a truffled turkey] (Pérez

Galdós 2001, 386), in conjunction with the image of her as a vulture, accentuates her predatory nature. "No como más que alguna pechuguita de chocha" [I eat nothing more than a little partridge breast] (176), she tells us also in chapter 5. Similarly, in the case of doña Javiera, references to meat point not only to the source of her prosperity but also to her obsession with distancing her son from the family's butcher business to improve his social status. "Mi hijo ... tiene y tendrá siempre con qué vivir ... Pero no me gusta ... que ... sea carnicero, ni tratante en ganados, ni nada que se roce con el cuerno, la cerda y la tripa ... Yo quiero que sepa todo lo que debe saber un caballero que vive de sus rentas" [My son ... has and will always have the means to live ... But I don't like ... that ... he is a butcher, or cattle rancher, or anything that is in contact with horns, pigs, or tripes ... I want him to know everything that a gentleman who lives from his rents ought to know] (164–5), the aspiring widow informs Manso in chapter 3. Finally, the desire to eat and the food shortage explain to a large extent Irene's ambition to marry *"el hijo de la carnicera"* (190, original emphasis), the butcher's son. In addition to images of her as a child suffering from hunger,[5] the description of a meal comprised of "alimentos fríos y desabridos" [cold and tasteless foods] (387) in her aunt's house makes patent the driving force behind Irene's determination to escape poverty through marriage.

While effective in enhancing images of his characters, references to food and eating habits also allowed Galdós to voice his critique of the Restoration regime. Consider, for instance, the account of the new dining habits in José María's house in chapter 9.

Las relaciones de la familia aumentaban de día en día ... Al mes de instalación, mi hermano tenía la mesa puesta y la puerta abierta para todas las notabilidades ... Las visitas sucedían a las visitas ... No tardó en comprender el jefe de la familia que debía desarraigar ciertas prácticas muy nocivas a su buen crédito, y así, en la mesa, cuando había convidados, que era los más días del año, reinaba un orden perfecto, no turbado por las disputas sobre carne y vino, ni por las rarezas de la *niña Chucha* [original emphasis], ni por las libertades de los chicos. Tomaron un buen jefe, un maestresala o mozo de comedor, y aquello *parecía* [emphasis mine] otra cosa. (202)

[Family relationships increased day by day ... Within a month, my brother had the table set and the door open for all notables ... There were visits after visits ... The head of the family soon understood that certain harmful practices ought to be uprooted, and so, at the table, when there were guests, which was most days of the year, a perfect order reigned, undisturbed by disputes over meat and wine, or by the oddities of the *Chucha girl*, or the liberties from the boys. They took on a good boss, a steward or waiter, and that *seemed* something more.]

At first blush, there is nothing unusual about the improvements in the manner of serving and consuming food at José María's table. As Mariano Pardo de Figueroa (writing under the pseudonym of Dr Thebussem) indicated in his seminal culinary text, *La mesa moderna* [The modern table] (1888), carefully coordinated meals constituted an important site for social interaction among the nineteenth-century Spanish upper classes and for advancement of their political careers. "La mesa se ha transformado dos veces en poco tiempo. De la antigua, que estaba instituída sólo para comer … se pasó a la moderna … destinada … a tratar. Hoy en la mesa se trata y se come … pudiéndose observar que hasta en los palacios . . . los banquetes llevan por lo común un fin político … " [The table has been transformed twice in a short time. From the old one, which was instituted only to eat … we switched to the modern … destined … to treat. Today at the table one treats and eats … even in palaces … banquets usually carry a political purpose] (Pardo de Figueroa 1888, 93).

Thus, considering that Galdós's character represents "el paradigma del político que llega a los foros sin preparación … política alguna … producto … del ocio y de la necesidad de figurar como un personaje relevante dentro del espectro social" [the paradigm of the politician who arrives unprepared to forums … no policy … a product … of leisure and the need to appear as a relevant person within the social spectrum] (Quevedo García 1990, 481), the picture of well-served meals reflects fittingly, alongside the wealthy *indiano*'s endeavour to integrate his family into the highest social strata, his attempt to build a successful political career. And yet, reading this passage in a wider context, particularly the author's critique of the Restoration regime's discourse "de 'armonizar,' como sea, los contrarios de todo tipo" [of "harmonizing," in any way, the opposites of all types] (Blanco Aguinaga 1994–5, 15), it is evident that the depiction of José María's dinner table afforded Galdós the opportunity to speak to issues larger than his character's personal ambitions.

Critics have noticed the political subtext in *El amigo Manso* (Rodríguez Puértolas 1982, 59–61) and the writer's ironic allusion to the Restoration's discourse of unification of "los extremismos de todo tipo" [extremisms of all kinds] (Blanco Aguinaga 1994–5, 15) through the description of José María's "espíritu reconciliatorio" [conciliating spirit] (Pérez Galdós 2001, 246) and the *indiano*'s eagerness to "acoplar

y emparejar las cosas más heterogéneas ... el separatismo y la na-
cionalidad, la insurrección y el ejército, la monarquía y la república"
[couple and unite the most heterogeneous things ... separatism and
nationality, the insurrection and the army, the monarchy and the re-
public] (246). While providing examples of this concept in speeches
by leading politicians of the Restoration regime and even by progressive figures such as Gumersindo de Azcárate (one of the founders of
the Institución Libre de Enseñanza), Blanco Aguinaga observes with
reference to José María: "¿cómo extrañarse de que el ignorante indiano tenga en todo lo político 'ideales casamenteros' ... si Gumersindo
de Azcárate era capaz de escribir las tonterías citadas?" [why would
the ignorant *indiano*'s "marriageble ideals" in politics surprise us ... if
Gumersindo de Azcárate was capable of writing the nonsense above?]
(Blanco Aguinaga 1994–5, 17).

However, José María's ideas are not the only venues through which
Galdós criticized the above discourse. In recent studies on literary representations of food, scholars have demonstrated how everyday life
practices such as consuming, sharing, or serving meals have been utilized to circulate, reinforce as well as transgress dominant ideologies
(LeBesco and Naccarato 2008, 1–10). Annette Cozzi, for instance, in her
discussion on the role of nourishment in the construction of national
identity in nineteenth-century England, shows how writers availed
themselves of the familiar aspect of culinary habits and rituals to dis-
seminate, normalize, and ultimately sustain the ideology of cohesive,
homogeneous Englishness (2010, 5–12). It is the domestic and familiar
attribute of food, affirms Cozzi, that "allows for otherwise distasteful
ideologies to be swallowed whole, so that the individual not only in-
ternalizes them, but does so willingly" (4). Writing on the importance
of shared meals in creating the identity of an English gentleman, Gwen
Hyman, on the other hand, demonstrates how nineteenth-century British novelists drew on the association between the act of eating together
and the idea of union only to expose "the lack of such union ... at the
Victorian table" (2009, 245). Although both scholars' observations relate
to circumstances that are different from late nineteenth-century Spain,
they are illuminating, nevertheless, with respect to the use that Galdós
made of his description of meals in *El amigo Manso*.

Presented as an improvement over the time of eating together marked
by José María's never-ending disputes with his wife, Lica, over her
diet, his mother-in-law's "acerbas críticas a la cocina española" [harsh
criticisms of Spanish cuisine] (Pérez Galdós 2001, 198), and the wild
behaviour of his children in chapter 8, the picture of the family sharing meals in a harmonious manner only few pages later seems – like

the Restoration discourse of "convivencia, paz y orden interno" [coexistence, peace and internal order] (Martínez Cuadrado 1974, 26) after years of conflicts and chaos (Carr 2000, 207–21) – worthy of admiration. However, the place that Galdós assigned to the amended dinners in his novel, the presence of irony, and the selection of words already suggest that, although the author relied on the domestic aspect of a family's mealtime to convey (in recognizable terms) his thoughts on the aforementioned ideology, he did so not to feed his readers with it but to sharpen, through the scene of a feast, their awareness of its duplicity.

Indeed, by inserting the account of the family dining together in impeccable style already in chapter 9, that is, right after the main character describes meals at his brother's place as torture ["eating with the family … was cruel martyrdom for me" (Pérez Galdós 2001, 198)], Galdós skilfully puts a question mark over the feasibility of such a rapid and drastic change. Additionally, one can hardly ignore the irony underlying the protagonist's depiction of the refined dinner parties in José María's house, as he points out that the etiquette at the *indiano*'s table is in place only in the presence of guests. Like the "peaceful life after 'anarchy'" (Carr 1980, 6), which only in theory represented the integration of opposites, while, in reality, reflecting "la pretensión de haber logrado el difícil equilibrio (incluso 'el matrimonio') entre factores históricos hasta entonces antagónicos" [the pretence of having achieved the difficult balance (even "marriage") between hitherto antagonistic historical factors] and the efforts of conservative groups to "enmascarar los conflictos latentes y las nuevas formas de represión'" [mask latent conflicts and new forms of repression] (Blanco Aguinaga 1994–5, 15), the feasts in José María's house assume merely the appearance (as the choice of the verb *parecer* instead of *ser* at the end of the passage implies) of bond and reconciliation of differences.[6] As is patent in Manso's observations, José María achieves peace in his dining room primarily through the exclusion of his unruly children and the suppression of Lica's and her mother's natural eating habits and only in part through the assistance of his newly hired staff.

Significant in this context is also a lack of references to concrete dishes at the dinners mentioned in chapter 9 as well as at other meals in José María's house. Considering the *indiano*'s determination to climb high society's ladder and the culinary hegemony of France in Spain and in the rest of the nineteenth-century Western world (Vázquez Montalbán 2001, 60–81; Luján 1997, 193–9; Parkhurst Ferguson 2004, 49–82), it is safe to assume that, unlike guests in doña Cándida's house, invitees to José María's gatherings could actually enjoy elaborate French or French-inspired dishes. José Esteban, in his study of gastronomy in

Galdós's narrative, attributes the omission of *haute cuisine* in the author's works to his personal preference for Spanish food and the lack of close acquaintance with French delicacies. Based on Galdós's concluding remarks in his sketch "Madrid," in which the writer placed traditional Spanish dishes on equal footing with French specialties, Esteban infers that "el novelista prefería la cocina española a la sofisticada francesa, que empezaba a ponerse de moda entre las clases altas" [the novelist preferred Spanish cuisine to the sophistication of the French, which was becoming fashionable among the upper classes] (1992, 5). However, he adds, "Galdós no perteneció a esa clase ni supo contárnosla" [Galdós did not belong to that class nor did he know how to describe it] (5). It is true that Galdós did not belong to the highest echelons of Restoration society. But, at the same time, given his ability to compare French and Spanish dishes in the above essay and the fact that he could access information related to court menus and elite banquets,[7] one wonders whether Galdós indeed lacked the capacity to reproduce those details in his novels or whether he excluded them on purpose.[8]

In *El amigo Manso*, the omission of the particulars of José María's diet could be interpreted as the novelist's further critique of the Restoration regime. While perceptive and eager to share specifics of his brother's life style, Máximo Manso does not discuss concrete dishes (outside chapter 8) served at José María's table because neither the selection nor the quality of these aliments ultimately matters. Similar to the way in which the *indiano* absorbs trendy domestic and foreign political ideas – that is, quickly, in great quantities, and with no preparation or genuine interest in understanding them – José María eats, as the scene in chapter 15 illustrates, without knowing (or caring to know) what he ingests: "Almorzamos. Tan afanado estaba José María con … la política, que ni en la mesa descansaba, y apoyando el periódico en una copa, leía, como a bocados y a sorbos, la sesión del día anterior" [We had lunch. José María was so focused on politics that he didn't rest, not even at the table, and placing the newspaper against a glass, he read, in bites and slurps, the session from the day before] (Pérez Galdós 2001, 229).[9]

Equally telling are the accounts of Máximo Manso's eating habits and the descriptions of meals in his house. When considering Manso's status as a narrator and protagonist, as well as his place in the frame and within the story, it is tempting to assume that Galdós developed scenes of the main character eating or discussing culinary preferences to distance his readers from thinking of him as a dual creation. Indeed, references to meals in chapter 2, in which Manso enters the narrative as a full-fledged individual,[10] strengthen his image of a figure of flesh. But, at the same time, details related to his culinary choices and food consumption – in particular, his modest taste,[11] his predilection for a single dish,[12] and, as we learn later, his tendency to eat alone[13] – also function as a means for Galdós to comment on issues such as education, gender, and moral values that the protagonist represents.

As mentioned earlier, scholars have not elaborated on the significance of the main character's favourite dish. After all, since chickpeas with water fit so perfectly into the protagonist's self-portrait as a plain, orderly, and frugal man, their presence in the text does not seem to require further explanation. Yet *garbanzos*, like all comestibles in *El amigo Manso*, are charged with specific meaning. Foreign visitors to Spain observed that in the first part of the nineteenth century, chickpeas, considered an indispensable component of *cocido*, enjoyed popularity among Spaniards of all social classes (Díaz-Plaja 1969, 64; Díaz 2005, 120–5). In the last decades, however, they were customary mainly among the petty bourgeoisie and working masses (Díaz-Plaja 1969, 53–5). Thus, in line with the aphorism *dime lo que comes y te diré quién eres* [you are what you eat], which Galdós quotes in "Madrid," chickpeas aptly accentuate Manso's position in society. Unlike his brother, the protagonist does not aspire to join the upper classes that traded traditional Spanish cooking for elaborate French dishes. Instead, he finds himself more at home with those who still appreciate the flavour of chickpeas and other domestic specialties, "un sector de la clase media ilustrada, progresista" [a sector of the enlightened progressive middle class] (Caudet 2001, 60), who, like him, deposited their faith in education as an indispensable step towards Spain's modernization.[14]

And yet, contrary to appearances, Galdós did not deploy the images of the leading character regaling himself with his favourite meal to praise his virtues or to endorse uncritically his ideas or methods of operation. While commendable, the protagonist's efforts to share his beliefs with Peña do not bring the expected results because, like the chickpeas that Manso fails to make appealing for anyone else, he fails to convince his student of the value of his education. That Manso's teaching, similar to his plate with *garbanzos* and water, is too plain for his protégé to ingest is also evident during their time together when the young man literally sweetens his lessons with Manso by sucking on candies. In chapter 7, Manso recalls the following with respect to Peña's love for sweets: "Imposible me fue quitarle el vicio de fumar … pero triunfé contra la maldita maña suya de estar siempre chupando caramelos, de los cuales tenía lleno el bolsillo … y lo peor era que durante la lección me engolosinaba a mí" [It was impossible for me to make him quit the vice of smoking … but I succeeded against his damn habit of sucking on candies, of which his pockets were full … and the worst was that during the class, he enticed me] (Pérez Galdós 2001, 187). Manso's initial acceptance of candies from his student, and not the other way around, already implies his subordinate position in their relation and his lack of authority over Peña. More important, however, is Manso's elimination of Peña's candies at the end. By ignoring Manuel Peña's natural drive for sweets and suppressing his own craving for them,[15] Manso not only evinces his stubborn adherence to his belief in the superiority of reason over instinct but also makes patent his disregard for popular tastes. His encounter with Peña in the *buñolería* reinforces this notion. It is true that, as G.A. Davis observed, the *buñolería* scene marks the moment in the novel in which "not only are Manso's and Peña's attitudes to life juxtaposed, but their attitudes to politics are as well" (1962, 26). However, what is also true is that this passage prefigures and explains – via both men's gastronomic inclinations – the outcome of their respective speeches at the upcoming charity event. Already in 1865, in his essay for *Revista de la semana*, Galdós asserted that "el buñuelo ... no morirá mientras haya españoles sobre la tierra ... a pesar de su insípido sabor, de su aceite hirviente, no será destronado por el elegante Savary, ni por el Chantilly, ni por todas esas almibaradas especies de la familia repostera que ostenta en su escaparate la Pastelería Suiza" [The *buñuelo* ... will not die while there are Spaniards on earth ... despite its insipid taste, its boiling-hot oil, it will not be dethroned by the elegant Savary, nor by the Chantilly, nor by all those syrupy species of the pastry family showcased at the Swiss Pastry Shop window] (quoted in Shoemaker 1972, 86–7). Thus, it is precisely the seductive flavour of Peña's discourse that, like *el buñuelo* and brandy, devoid of alimentary value but tasty, accounts for the young man's success. In contrast, when Manso describes his talk as "severo, correcto" [severe, rightful] but bereft of "brillantez oratoria" [oratorical radiance] (Pérez Galdós 2001, 293), it is hardly surprising that his speech bored the audience. For the tastes of the shallow elites and ignorant masses, his reasons, like his beloved meal, offered too much healthy nourishment and not enough spice.

While Manso's overly modest taste and his continuous predilection for a single meal allowed Galdós to underscore the main character's inflexibility in his beliefs and pedagogical methods, references to such elements as meat in his diet enabled the novelist to touch on another subject, namely the protagonist's masculinity. Judging by the use that Galdós made of Juanito Santa Cruz's appetite for *carne* in *Fortunata y Jacinta* (King 1983; Chamberlin 1985; Goldman 1985), it is obvious that the author was well aware of the prevalent image in Spain and the rest of the nineteenth-century Western world of a bourgeois meat eater as an affluent, sexually active male.[16] But years before he composed his masterpiece, already in *El amigo Manso*, the author pointed to one's access to meat and the privilege of consuming it as markers of successful virility. In chapter 8, for instance, José María's insistence that Lica includes *carne* in her diet attests to the *indiano*'s wealth in the sense that meat abounds at his table to share. Additionally, given José María's engagement in political life and his wife's fourth pregnancy at that time, the *indiano*'s own intake of animal products strengthens his image as a prominent and sexually potent male. Equally, doña Javiera's late husband, a prosperous owner of a butcher shop, is remembered as a paradigm of a robust masculinity: "hombre de gran probidad, muy entendido en cuerno y cerda, sagaz negociante, castellano rancio, buen bebedor" [a man of great probity, very knowledgeable in horn and sow, a sagacious businessman, an old Castilian, a good drinker] (Pérez Galdós 2001, 166). And as well, his son is portrayed as a successful, physically attractive man: "un hombre ... alto ... de partes, calidades y preeminencias físicas superiores ... a las mías" [a man ... tall ... with qualities and physical pre-eminences superior ... to mine] (354), Manso tells us in chapter 37.

As for the main character, he too is granted access to meat thanks to doña Javiera's generosity. "No me faltaba ... el regalito de chacina, jamón u otros artículos apetitosos de lo mucho y bueno que en la tienda había" [I was never missing ... presents of sausages, ham, or other tasty products among all the abundant and good ones there were at the store] (160), the protagonist recalls in chapter 3. But meat, as Manso's accounts of his eating habits reveal, lags secondary to vegetables in his meals. The opening paragraph in chapter 39 provides a suitable example: "Y vi desfilar en ordenado tropel, por delante de mí, los garbanzos redondos con su nariz de pico, y *después* una olorosa carne estofada, a quien siguieron pasa de Málaga, bollo ... mostillo" [And I saw parading, as an orderly troop in front of me, round chickpeas with their beak nose, and *then* a fragrant meat stew, which was followed by Málaga raisins, bun ... *mostillo*] (361, emphasis mine). Given that consuming vegetables was deemed a feminine attribute in nineteenth-century Spain and the rest of Western culture (Adams 1990, 30–7), this excerpt, in conjunction with Manso's recurrent declarations of his fondness for *garbanzos*, clearly allowed Galdós to accentuate one more way in which Manso deviates from the conventions of normative masculinity.[17] And yet, the protagonist's unmanly preference for eating chickpeas over meat carries a deeper meaning. Consider the passage from *La fisiología y patología de la mujer* [Female physiology and pathology] (1827), in which the medical doctor Baltasar de Viguera explained the feminine inclination towards a plant-oriented diet:

> Su paladar es ... mucho más fino y delicado, mientras que la excitabilidad de su estómago está en contradicción con la voracidad del hombre. Así es, que por su impulso natural son ... inclinadas a las frutas, ensaladas y demás alimentos sencillos. Sobre todo miran con repugnancia y aun hastío los manjares muy suculentos, y los licores fuertes que tanto lisonjean el apetito de los hombres. (Quoted in Jagoe, Blanco, and Enríquez de Salamanca 1998, 372)

> [Their palate is ... much finer and more delicate, while the excitability of their stomach is in contradiction with the voracity of men. This is, because by natural impulse they are ... inclined to fruits, salads, and other simple foods. Above all they look with disgust and even weariness on the very succulent delicacies, and the strong liquors that so flatter the appetite of men.]

The above text is helpful to our understanding of Manso's problematic masculinity: Viguera's differentiation between feminine and masculine culinary choices sheds light on Galdós's character's inappropriate predilection (for a male) for vegetables. But even more telling is the doctor's comment about women's distaste for men's food, as it makes it possible to observe that Galdós's protagonist does not display a particular aversion towards it. In fact, judging by Manso's remark on the inviting aroma of the meat that he is about to consume in chapter 39, i.e., *olorosa carne*, it appears that he will devour it with gusto. Thus, it is not as much Manso's appetite for chickpeas per se as the voluntary choice that he makes between animal and plant products that is of importance here. If food in truth "demarcates power relationships," as the twentieth-century critic Mervyn Nicholson contended (1987, 38), albeit in a different literary context, Manso's conscious determination to place himself in the role of an inoffensive plant eater (even though his diet does include other substances, i.e., meat) could be understood as Galdós's critique of the progressive sectors of the Restoration era. Like the main character, these sectors accepted too readily a marginal position in society and politics and lacked, or seemed to have underestimated the importance of, physical and emotional strength to actively pursue their goal of modernizing Spain by diffusing their ideas with vigour and conviction.[18] Manso's discourse does not reach most listeners at the charity event. And this happens not only because of the content of his talk, but also because of the deficiency in his mental and bodily fortitude to overcome his timidity and to deliver his speech using a strong voice. As doña Javiera affirms: "desde arriba no se oyó nada de lo que usted dijo, porque como habla usted tan bajito … Es el caso que como oía tan mal me iba quedando dormida" [from above we heard nothing of what you said, because you speak so quietly … As I heard so badly I was falling asleep] (Pérez Galdós 2001, 305).

Lastly, the language of meals equipped Galdós with a creative method to address moral values and ideas of conduct that his character claims to represent. Scholars detected the lack of correlation between the virtues that Manso believes himself to embody and his actions later on in the novel. The protagonist's self-description as an individual "de … espíritu observador y práctico" [with an observant and practical spirit] (Pérez Galdós 2001, 156) who never errs in judging "las cosas como son realmente" [things as they really are] (156) is, as Linda Willem remarked, "the most ironic statement in the novel" (1998, 154), as Manso's views of Irene turn out to be a fiction. Likewise, the protagonist's feelings for the young governess and his dealings with his brother's family hardly attest to his image as a man who is "in control of his emotions and actions at all times" (Copeland 2007, 113). These instances make painfully obvious, in fact, the opposite, that is, as Copeland showed, Manso's submissive, reliant nature (114–16). Whereas interactions with others provided Galdós with the opportunity to highlight the main character's self-deception and detachment from reality, the protagonist's eating habits offered the writer an effective way to comment on Manso's exaggerated notion of self-restraint in the area of sexual intimacy. Consider the scene of Manso's making up for depriving himself of his beloved *garbanzos* in chapter 21:

> Concluí por echar de menos mi habitual mesa humilde y el manjar preferente de ella, los garbanzos, que para mí, como he dicho antes, no tienen sustitución posible. *El apetito* de aquella legumbre me fue ganando, y *llegó a ser irresistible*. Estaba yo como el fumador vicioso, cuando por mucho tiempo se ve privado de tabaco. Siempre que pasaba … por la tienda … *se me iban los ojos* al gran saco de garbanzos colocado en la puerta … *No pudiendo refrenar más mi deseo … me desquité bárbaramente* de la privación que había sufrido. (Pérez Galdós 2001, 261, emphasis mine)

> [I finally started to miss my habitually humble fare, and my favourite dish, chickpeas, for which in my view there is, as I have said, no possible substitute. My *appetite* for that legume grew and grew, and *became irrepressible*. I had become like the habitual smoker who is deprived of tobacco over a long stretch of time. Whenever I went … [by] a store … my eyes were

drawn to the great sack of chickpeas placed right at the door … *Unable any longer to restrain my appetite … I took barbarous revenge* upon the privation I had suffered.]

The inability to curb his cravings for chickpeas places Manso at odds with his previous declarations of self-control[19] and adherence to sobriety. But, judging by the choice of vocabulary and the intensity with which he describes his desire for the beloved meal, his exasperation with its temporary unavailability, and, ultimately, his savage satisfaction of his appetite, the protagonist's gastronomic hunger is not all what Galdós refers to here. By having the main character depict his urge to consume his favourite dish in words that could also delineate one's need for physical love ["el apetito … llegó ser irresistible; no pudiendo refrenar más mi deseo"] and by infusing Manso's description with tension that recaptures feelings akin to sexual excitement and gratification ["se me iban los ojos; me desquité bárbaramente"], the author effectively foregrounded the analogy between gastronomic and sexual appetites to address Manso's celibacy.

Of course, Galdós was not the only late nineteenth-century Spanish novelist who resorted to alimentary metaphors to outline his characters' sexuality in his works (King 1983, 81–2; Chamberlin 1985; Urey 1986, 40–2). Clarín and Picón, to name only two of his colleagues, proved to be equally skilful in deploying the language of meals to comment on their protagonists' engagement in sexual intimacy.[20] However, if the use of the association between gastronomic and sexual appetites in novels about free love or adultery seems self-explanatory, the employment of such connections in *El amigo Manso* might appear hardly fitting, as the lead character opts for celibacy. And yet, drawing attention to sexual needs via gastronomic hunger was a way for Galdós to question Manso's commitment to sexual abstinence. For if the protagonist proves unable to resist his gastronomic urge after being deprived for a short time of his beloved meal and when presented with the opportunity for gratification, should we indeed believe, Galdós seems to ask via the aforementioned passage, in his resolve to remain above basic human needs through his adherence to chastity? Manso's interest in Irene already demonstrates abundantly that, if offered the chance to build a relationship with her (that is, if she reciprocated his feelings), the confirmed bachelor would only be too happy to give up his celibacy.

This is not to say, of course, that by casting doubt on Manso's ability to keep up with his line of conduct, Galdós was disappointed with his protagonist's less than solid pledge to refrain from sexual activities. In fact, judging by examples in which Manso replaces physical love with food – as in chapter 21 where he resorts to eating as one does to sexual intimacy to release stress, and in chapter 39 where he consoles himself with a large meal after his amorous disillusionment with Irene – the novelist did not view Manso's observance of celibacy in a positive light. Described in the writings of most Spanish nineteenth-century hygienists and social moralists as behaviour that was unhealthy for men and detrimental for the well-being of the nation (Copeland 2007, 114–16), lifelong chastity was considered one of the causes of the country's incipient degeneration (Clemenson and Vázquez García 2007, 202–15). As the century drew to its end, the link between men's sexual restraint and the nation's decline became even more explicit in discourses of Spanish regenerationists (Clemenson and Vázquez García 2007, 175–98). Although Galdós did not blame the shortcomings of Restoration society on Manso's celibacy, the protagonist's sterility and ultimate death suggest the author's scepticism about Spain's ability to integrate the progressive thoughts that Manso incarnates under the current political system. Like the wine-water ["el agua del Lozoya, que es mi vino" (Pérez Galdós 2001, 150)] that the character drinks with his meals – refreshing but inconsequential in contrast to wine, which implies transformation, melting boundaries, and creating community (Hyman 2009, 180–2) – men like Manso, while able to offer stimulating ideas, could not alone make a significant impact on the status quo and affect the future of Spain in tangible ways.

Further examination of the scenes in which the novelist outlined his characters' attitudes towards food and eating habits, such as doña Cándida's obsession with adopting a French menu, Lica's fondness for sweets and coffee, or her mother's shallow adherence to a Spanish diet, would reveal a great deal more with respect to Galdós's views of Restoration society's superficial zeal for modernization and Spain's increasingly problematic relation with Cuba (Heneghan 2016, 97–9, Coffey 2020, 243–7). They would also demonstrate, as do the aforementioned excerpts, that meals in *El amigo Manso* are often not about food per se but about ways in which they are consumed or places where they are served. The fact that Manso, for instance, participates frequently in feasts at others' tables, while hardly anyone shares meals at his home, points as effectively to his weak position in the society as to the symbolic value of the food that he takes in. Equally telling is the protagonist's seemingly trivial comment in the concluding part of the novel: "Estaba escrito que todo lo malo y desagradable de aquellos días me pasara al tiempo de comer en mesa ajena" [It was written that everything bad and unpleasant during those days happened to me while eating at another's table] (Pérez Galdós 2001, 390). While Manso

avoids taking responsibility for his actions, i.e., "estaba escrito que …
me pasara," by accepting nourishment from others, he agrees to a relation with them in which he places himself in the role of the one who is
not the feeder but the one being fed, not the one who imposes his will
but the one who cedes to others' demands. Thus, much more could be
inferred from Galdós's depictions of meals here. Since throughout his
career, food and eating habits fascinated the author as faithful reflections of cultural values, fears, and preoccupations, it is hardly surprising that he employed them as a means to confront in *El amigo Manso* the
current political and social situation and to voice his concerns with the
impact of the status quo on the future of Spain.

NOTES

1 For studies on culinary art in *Fortunata y Jacinta*, see King (1983), Chamberlin (1985), Goldman (1985), Gold (1986), Labanyi (1988), and Vilarós (1991).
   Unless otherwise noted, translations are by the author.
2 On food imagery and cannibalism in *Lo prohibido* (1885), consult Courtad
   (2005).
3 For the importance of gastronomy in works by Galdós's contemporaries,
   e.g., Pardo Bazán, Clarín, and Valera, see Gold (2009), Charnon-Deutsch
   (2010), Sinclair (1992), Suárez Solis (1994), and Yáñez (1998) respectively.
4 Also in his essay "Fiesta de San Eugenio – Las bellotas del Pardo –
   Orígen de esta costumbre – El pueblo de Madrid en el Pardo – Bailes de
   Capellanes – Paralelo," published in the same year in *La Nación*, Galdós
   provided a similar description of Spaniards' gluttony. "El día de San
   Eugenio no se trata de formar alegres grupos a las orillas del viejo canal … desdoblar una servilleta y regalarse … un plato de callos, un par
   de chuletas … El placer de comer carne de cerdo durante esta temporada
   del chorizo y de la salchicha … A esto se reduce la fiesta … de San Eugenio" (quoted in Shoemaker 1972, 210–11). For more examples of Galdós's
   accounts in *La Nación* of the importance of food and eating habits in late
   nineteenth-century Spanish culture, consult Shoemaker (1972, 86–7, 462–3
   and 525).
5 "La pobrecita parecía que había estado un mes privada de todo alimento,
   según honraba los platos" [Judging by the honours she paid to the dishes,
   the poor thing seemed as if she had been deprived of food for a month]
   (Pérez Galdós 2001, 182).
6 The political compromise as a farce and the methods of repression under
   Cánovas del Castillo and since 1881 under Sagasta are discussed at length
   in Martínez Cuadrado (1974, 12–34).

7 *La mesa moderna*, for instance, which appeared first in 1876 in *La Ilustración Española y Americana* as a series of letters, abounds in such details.

8 Also prior to 1876, texts such as the 1835 translation from French by Rementería y Fica, *Manual del concinero, cocinera, repostero, pastelero, confitero y botillero, con el método para trinchar y servir toda clase de viandas, y la cortesía y la urbanidad que se deben usar en la mesa,* and Mariano Muñoz's *La cocina moderna, según la escuela francesa y española. Estudios prácticos de este arte, según los adelantos de la época,* published in 1857–8, offered a wealth of data on preparation of French delicacies and manners of serving them in affluent households. For more examples of similar writings, consult Simón Palmer (2003, 108–210) and Martínez LIopis (1989, 341–8).

9 The method of blending food with politics is not unique to *El amigo Manso.* For comments on similar scenes in *Fortunata y Jacinata* and *Episodios nacionales,* see Labanyi (1988, 57) and Urey (1986, 37–42), respectively.

10 "Soy bien nutrido, fuerte … no recuerdo haber comido nunca sin apetito" [I am well nourished, strong … I don't remember having ever eaten without appetite] (Pérez Galdós 2001, 148–9).

11 "No soy gastrónomo; no entiendo palotada de refinados manjares" [I am no gourmet; I understand nothing of refined delicacies] (Pérez Galdós 2001, 149).

12 "en punto de preferencias, sólo tengo una … que en romance llamamos garbanzo" [as of preferences, I only have one … that in Spanish we call chickpea] (Pérez Galdós 2001, 149).

13 "Quedéme solo delante de mi sopa" [I was left alone in front of my soup] (Pérez Galdós 2001, 361).

14 The role of education in *El amigo Manso* has attracted a great deal of attention from scholars. The pedagogical aspect of the novel has been discussed in studies by Davis (1962), Lida (1967), and Castillo (1985), among others.

15 "el día en que … faltaron los caramelos, los echó mi lengua de menos, y casi casi me mortificó aquella falta" [on the day there was no candy, my tongue missed them, and that lack almost mortified me] (Pérez Galdós 2001, 187).

16 On consumption of meat as a male prerogative and a sign of power in nineteenth-century culture and the contemporary Western world, see Adams (1990, 23–9).

17 For more examples of Manso's failing to adhere to the qualities of normative bourgeois masculinity, consult Krauel (2004) and Copeland (2007).

18 I agree with Ricardo Krauel's view that one ought not to be too hasty to accuse Manso of having an effeminate spirit, but instead, as Eva Copeland has argued, should consider him as an embodiment of an alternative model of masculinity (2007, 119–21).

19 "he sabido sofocar pasioncillas … apetitos … vicios nacientes" [I have succeeded in suffocating little passions, appetites, nascent vices] (Pérez Galdós 2001, 156).

20 For an extensive discussion on connection between gastronomic and sex-
    ual appetites in Clarín's *La Regenta* (1885), see, for instance, Valis (1981,
    65–71) and Sinclair (1992). On the use of metaphors that link food with sex
    in Picón's *Dulce y sabrosa* (1891), consult Mandrell (1992, 184–7).

WORKS CITED

Adams, Carole J. 1990. *The Sexual Politics of Meat: A Feminist-Vegetarian Critical Theory*. New York: Continuum Publishing Company.

Blanco Aguinaga, Carlos. 1994–5. "De vencedores y vencidos en la Restauración, según las Novelas Contemporáneas de Galdós." *Anales Galdosianos* 29–30: 13–49.

Carr, Raymond. 1980. *Modern Spain 1875–1980*. Oxford: Oxford University Press.

Carr, Raymond. 2000. "Liberalism and Reaction, 1833–1931." In *Spain: A History*, edited by Raymond Carr, 205–42. Oxford: Oxford University Press.

Castillo, Debra A. 1985. "The Problematics of Teaching in *El amigo Manso*." *Revista de Estudios Hispánicos* 19: 37–55.

Caudet, Francisco, 2001. "Introducción." In *El amigo Manso* by Benito Pérez Galdós, edited by Francisco Caudet, 9–140. Madrid: Cátedra.

Charnon-Deutsch, Lou. 2010. "A Gourmand at the Foot of the Eiffel Tower: Emilia Pardo Bazán at the 1889 Paris Exposition." *Siglo Diecinueve* 16: 119–36. https://doi.org/10.37677/sigloxix.vi16.175.

Chamberlin, Vernon A. 1985. "A Further Consideration of Carnal Appetites in *Fortunata y Jacinta*." *Anales Galdosianos* 20: 51–9.

Clemison, Richard, and Francisco Vázquez García. 2007. *"Los Invisibles": A History of Male Homosexuality in Spain, 1850–1939*. Cardiff: University of Wales Press.

Coffey, Mary L. 2020. *Ghosts of Colonies Past and Present: Spanish Imperialism in the Fiction of Benito Pérez Galdós*. Liverpool: Liverpool University Press.

Copeland, Eva M. 2007. "Galdós's *El amigo Manso*: Masculinity, Respectability, and Bourgeois Culture." *Romance Quarterly* 54.2: 109–23. https://doi.org/10.3200/RQTR.54.2.109-123.

Courtad, James C. 2005. "Cannibal Imagery in Galdós: Bourgeois Efforts at Social Dominance." *Monographic Review/Revista Monográfica* 21: 63–78.

Cozzi, Annette. 2010. *The Discourses of Food in Nineteenth-Century British Fiction*. New York: Palgrave Macmillan.

Davis, G.A. 1962. "Galdós' *El amigo Manso*: An Experiment in Didactic Method." *Bulletin of Hispanic Studies* 39: 16–30. https://doi.org/10.3828/bhs.39.1.16.

Díaz, Lorenzo. 2005. *Ilustrados y románticos. Cocina y sociedad en España [siglos XVIII y XIX]*. Madrid: Alianza.

Díaz-Plaja, Fernando. 1969. *La vida española en el siglo XIX*. Madrid: Prensa española.

Estebán, José. 1992. *La cocina en Galdós y otras noticias literario-gastronómicas*. Madrid: El Museo Universal.

Gold, Hazel. 1986. "Problems of Closure in *Fortunata y Jacinta*: Of Narrators, Readers and Their Just Deserts/Desserts." *Neophilologus* 70: 228–38. https:// doi.org/10.1007/BF00553317.

Gold, Hazel. 2009. "Del foro al fogón: Narrativas culturales en el discurso culinario de Emilia Pardo Bazán." In *La literatura de Emilia Pardo Bazán*, edited by José Manuel González Herrán, Cristina Patiño Eirín, and Ermitas Penas Valera, 313–23. Coruña: Fundación Caixa Galicia.

Goldman, Peter B. 1985. "Juanito's 'chuletas': Realism and Worldly Philosophy in in Galdós's *Fortunata y Jacinta*." *Journal of the Midwest Modern Language Association* 18.1: 81–101. https://doi.org/10.2307/1315105.

Gullón, Ricardo. 1980. *Técnicas de Galdós*. Madrid: Taurus.

Heneghan, Dorota K. 2016. "The Indiano's Marriage and the Crisis of Imperial Modernity in Galdós' *El amigo Manso*." Siglo diecinueve. *Literatura hispánica* 22: 91–108.

Hyman, Gwen. 2009. *Making Man: Gentlemanly Appetites in the Nineteenth-Century British Novel*. Athens: Ohio University Press.

Ingram, Rebecca Elizabeth. 2009. "Spain on the Table: Cookbooks, Women, and Modernization, 1905–1933." PhD diss., Duke University.

Jagoe, Catherine, Alda Blanco, and Cristina Enríquez de Salamanca. 1998. *La mujer en los discursos de género. Textos y contextos en el siglo XIX*. Barcelona: Icaria Antrazyt.

King, Sarah E. 1983. "Food Imagery in *Fortunata y Jacinta*." *Anales Galdosianos* 18: 79–88.

Krauel, Ricardo. 2004. "El epónimo de un rebaño: crisis de masculinidad en *El amigo Manso*, de Benito Pérez Galdós." *Letras peninsulares* 17.2–3: 335–43.

Labanyi, Jo. 1988. "The Raw, the Cooked and the Indigestible in Galdós's *Fortunata y Jacinta*." *Romance Studies* 13: 55–66. https://doi.org/10.1179/026399089786621112.

Labanyi, Jo, ed. 1993. *Galdós*. London: Longman Group.

LeBesco, Kathleen, and Peter Naccarato, eds. 2008. *Edible Ideologies: Representing Food and Meaning*. Albany: State University of New York Press.

Lida, Denah. 1967. "Sobre el krausismo de Galdós." *Anales Galdosianos* 2: 1–27.

Luján, Nestor. 1997. *Historia de la gastronomía*. Barcelona: Folio.

Mandrell, James. 1992. *Don Juan and the Point of Honor: Seduction, Patriarchal Society, and Literary Tradition*. University Park: Penn State University Press.

Martínez Cuadrado, Miguel. 1974. *La burguesía conservadora (1874–1931)*. Madrid: Alianza.

Martínez Llopis, Manuel M. 1989. *Historia de la gastronomía española*. Madrid: Alianza.

Nicholson, Mervyn. 1987. "Food and Power: Homer, Carroll, Atwood and Others." *Mosaic* 20.3: 37–55.

Pardo de Figueroa, Mariano ["Thebussem"]. 1888. *La mesa moderna: Cartas sobre el comedor y la cocina cambiadas entre el doctor Thebussem y un cocinero de S.M.* Madrid: Librerías de Fernando Fe.

Parkhurst Ferguson, Priscilla. 2001. "A Cultural Field in the Making: Gastronomy in Nineteenth-Century France." In *French Food on the Table, on the Page, and in French Culture*, edited by Lawrence R. Schehr and Allen S. Weiss, 5–50. New York and London: Routledge.

Parkhurst Ferguson, Priscilla. 2004. *Accounting for Taste: The Triumph of French Cuisine*. Chicago: University of Chicago Press.

Pérez Galdós, Benito. 1923a [1883?]. "Madrid." In *Fisionomías sociales. Obras inéditas*, vol. 1, 50–65. Madrid: Renacimiento.

Pérez Galdós, Benito. 1923b [1883?]. "El mes de marzo." In *Fisionomías sociales. Obras inéditas*, vol. 1, 106–12. Madrid: Renacimiento.

Pérez Galdós, Benito. 2001 [1882]. *El amigo Manso*. Edited by Francisco Caudet. Madrid: Cátedra.

Quevedo García, Francisco Juan. 1990. "Tres indianos en la novela galdosiana: Agustín Caballero, Teodoro Golfín y José María Manso." In *Actas del Cuarto Congreso Internacional de Estudios Galdosianos*, vol. 1, 479–95. Las Palmas de Gran Canaria: Cabildo Insular de Gran Canaria.

Rodríguez Puértolas, Julio. 1982. "*El amigo Manso*, novela política. Galdós y la tercera vía." *Nuevo Hispanismo* 2: 57–71.

Shoemaker, William H. 1972. *Los artículos de Galdós en La Nación*. Madrid: Ínsula.

Simón Palmer, María del Carmen. 2003. *Bibliografía de la gastronomía y la alimentación en España*. Gijón: Ediciones Trea.

Sinclair, Alison. 1992. "The Consuming Passion: Appetite and Hunger in *La Regenta*." *Bulletin of Hispanic Studies* 69.3: 245–61. https://doi.org/10.1080/1475382922000369245.

Sinovas Maté, Juliana. 2006. *Emilia Pardo Bazán. Cartas de La Condesa en el Diario de la Marina de La Habana, Cuba (1909–1921)*. Newark: Juan de la Cuesta.

Suárez Solis, Sara. 1994. "Gastronomía en *La Regenta*." *Boletín del Instituto de Estudios Asturianos* 144: 701–9.

Urey, Diane F. 1986. "Names for Things: The Discourse of History in Galdós' O'Donnell." *Bulletin of Hispanic Studies* 63.1: 33–46. https://doi.org/10.3828/bhs.63.1.33.

Yáñez, María-Paz. 1998. "Las enumeraciones alimentarias en la obra de Juan Valera." In *Fictio Poetica. Studi italiani e ispanici in onore di Georges Güntert*, edited by Katharina Maier-Troxler and Constantino Maeder, 265–78. Florence: Cesati.

Valis, Noël. 1981. *The Decadent Vision in Leopoldo Alas: A Study of "La Regenta" and "Su único hijo."* Baton Rouge and London: Louisiana State University Press.

Vázquez Montalbán, Manuel. 2001. *Contra los gourmets.* Barcelona: Mondadori.

Vilarós, Teresa M. 1991. "Ingestión, digestión y eliminación: Jacinta, Fortunata y la avidez masculina." *Crítica Hispánica* 13.1–2: 111–25.

Willem, Linda. 1998. *Galdós's Segunda Manera: Rhetorical Strategies and Affective Response.* North Carolina Studies in the Romance Languages and Literatures. Chapel Hill: University of North Carolina Press.

10 The Palate of Memory: Gastronomy and Cultural Critique in Manuel Vázquez Montalbán

JOSÉ COLMEIRO

El hecho cultural más importante de los últimos treinta años en España es lo que ha pasado en la cocina española.

[The most important cultural fact of the last thirty years in Spain is what has happened in Spanish cuisine]

Cuando se come se convoca la memoria del paladar, y en cierto sentido es el territorio más firme de la gastronomía, donde hemos refugiado las pasadas experiencias y el patrimonio de los sabores

[When we eat we summon the palate of memory, and in a sense, it is the firmest territory of gastronomy, where we shelter our past experiences and the patrimony of flavours]

Manuel Vázquez Montalbán

There is no doubt that Manuel Vázquez Montalbán occupies a central and pioneering role in social discourses about gastronomy in the last fifty years in Spain, as much in the intellectual arena as in popular culture.[1] The gastronomic reflections of this Catalan author and journalist have accompanied the long political, economic, and social transitions from the postwar period to the globalization of contemporary Spanish culture, and they have taken a leading role in the parallel and meteoric transformation of Spanish gastronomy, one of the most visible manifestations of Spain's material culture. As in other aspects of Spanish popular culture, traditionally undervalued by intellectual elites, Vázquez Montalbán was a pioneer in recognizing the importance of gastronomy as a form of culture, collective memory, and identity.

Throughout the second half of the twentieth century, Spanish gastronomy underwent a profound and accelerated transformation, moving from traditional cuisine rooted in local and regional elements – and therefore greatly varied, fundamentally artisanal, and basically self-sufficient – to experiencing a double process of rapid and polarized modernization. This modernization signified the qualitative devaluation of traditional cuisine, owing to the accelerated technological and economic industrialization, as well as the homogenization of local consumer habits with international culinary trends throughout the 1960s, with the added imposition of normative, dietetic-cultural discourses. At the same time, Spain suffered an exorbitant intensification and important massification of its network of restaurants because of the enormous consumer pressure brought by tourism. Vázquez Montalbán's position with regard to this transformation was always in defence of the popular nature of Spain's traditional cuisines, considering them a fundamental part of its culture, history, and identity, and a form of resistance in the face of impositions of economic power, as much from above as from outside. In a second instance, and in a contrary way, the process of modernization also signified a qualitative reevaluation, with the creation of an image of Spanish cuisine as innovative, modern, and fresh; particularly with the global explosion of *tapas* culture, the reclamation of the Mediterranean diet, and the entrance of Spanish cuisine into the pantheon of gourmets. Through these processes, gastronomy came to occupy a prominent place in the international promotion of the "Spanish brand," which is evident, for example, in the rise of Spanish chefs and their presence in media and cinema.[2] Vázquez Montalbán's position in the face of this new gastronomic wave is more ambivalent. Even if he values innovation, good gastronomic practice, and the defence of local, autochthonous roots, he criticizes both the snobbishness constructed around gastronomy by elites as a new form of classism and dietetic discourses as the dogma of a new sectarian religion.

Vázquez Montalbán was as much a privileged witness as he was a principal actor of this manifold gastronomic transformation in his varied roles as critical analyst, editorialist, encyclopedic disseminator, and author of essays, cookbooks, short stories, and columns that positioned him as a fundamental cultural critic in the area of gastronomy. One may say without exaggeration that the general interest in gastronomy and the subsequent food craze in Spain, awakened only after the years of the Transition, found in Vázquez Montalbán both their great champion and their great critic. His work consists of thousands of pages dedicated to gastronomy, including innumerable articles and columns, and some twenty-three volumes wholly dedicated to culinary practice and knowledge.[3] Among the latter are numerous cookbooks on both traditional and regional Spanish gastronomy[4] – as well as on modern and cosmopolitan gastronomy, on the most heterogeneous and innovative side of the gastronomic genre, such as the celebratory erotic-culinary humorous recipe book *Las recetas inmorales* [Immoral recipes] (1981), the literary pseudo-anthology *Las recetas de Carvalho* [Carvalho's recipes] (1989), and the culinary *summa* of nine volumes titled *Carvalho Gastronómico* [Gastronomic Carvalho]. Likewise, his essays on gastronomic reflections stand out, in particular the intellectual pamphlet *Contra los gourmets* [Against gourmets] (1985) – which constitutes his work most critical of culinary snobbishness – and *La Boquería: la catedral dels sentits* [La Boquería: Cathedral of the senses] (2001), a defence of popular gastronomy and of Barcelona's cultural memory, and his around-the-table conversations with leading figures of the Transition, *Mis almuerzos con gente inquietante* [My lunches with unsettling people] (1984), a title that parodies the book of *franquista* writer José María Pemán, *Mis almuerzos con gente importante* [My luncheons with important people] (1970). His fiction with gastronomic themes also holds a place of greatest importance, such as the heterogeneous book of essay-fiction *La gula* [Gluttony] and *Reflexiones de Robinson frente a un bacalao* [Robinson's reflections before a cod] (1995), or the novels and stories from the Pepe Carvalho series, which add another twenty-two volumes to his work. In its entirety, Vázquez Montalbán's vast and continued dedication to the subject of gastronomy through various decades comes together in an overflowing textual archive of truly monumental proportions, richly nuanced and, therefore, difficult to summarize. I will attempt, in the following pages, to sketch the general lines of his gastronomic thought.

I. The Palate of Memory

Gastronomy in the life and work of Vázquez Montalbán is inseparable from personal and collective memory, as well as from his practice of cultural critique, since it emerges from the same position of social conscience. Born at the end of the Civil War in an occupied Barcelona, he grew up in the marginal neighbourhood District V (later called the Raval) at the heart of a Republican family. After his father was imprisoned by Franco's police within a few days of the author's birth, Vázquez Montalbán spent his childhood in great adversity during the period commonly referred to as the "years of hunger." Without a doubt, these difficult circumstances explain in good measure his peculiar obsession with food since his youth.[5] The Raval, a neighbourhood of proletariat workers and immigrants, adjacent to the red light district, was characterized by a subsistence and exploitation economy that was subject to the conditions of the postwar black market. Rationing of foodstuffs, which originated in the Civil War, continued until 1951, but the material and psychological conditions of poverty lasted much longer. This explains Carpanta's longevity as a character – the miserable, ragged, starving character of picaresque lineage in the popular children's comics created by José Escobar. The experience of scarcity, but also resilience and resistance in the face of adversity, both personal and collective, marked Vázquez Montalbán's consciousness from his earliest years.[6]

Of clear autobiographical reminiscences, his first story, entitled "1945" – written in 1965, published in *Recordando a Dardé y otros relatos* (1969) and later republished in *Pigmalión* (1987) – sketches his childhood memories in the Raval. Here, the connection between memory and the palate, which will be repeated obsessively in his later writings, appears for the first time: the essential and plentiful image of bread and black olives from the postwar years, associated with the protective figure of the mother. In the story, the mother is transformed into the character of the female coal seller, which increases the synthetic contrast of colours and senses concentrated in the bread and olives brought from the deepest part of the memory's palate: "La carbonera me dio pan recién comprado, crujiente, negro, caliente, y un puñado de aceitunas negras de las llamadas 'de Aragón'" [The coal seller gave me bread she had recently purchased, crunchy, black, hot, and a handful of black olives, the kind that are said to be from Aragon] (Vázquez Montalbán 1987b, 12).[7]

This powerful image of simultaneous material poverty and abundance is the original *Rosebud* in Vázquez Montalbán´s writing, a seed of identity and of the formation of memory and desire. As the author would remark many years later to Georges Tyras, that *Rosebud* represents "un instante de plenitud," "la clave para definirnos o para explicarnos a nosotros mismos" [an instant of fullness, the key to defining ourselves or to explaining ourselves] (Tyras 2003, 84). In what follows, we will return to this persistent multisensorial image from the palate of memory, the postwar black and white *Rosebud*, which reappears as the Proustian madeleine in the author's work.

In the sociohistorical context of the postwar period, for Vázquez Montalbán food is a basic act of defence and survival in the face of a cruel and repressive reality, while at the same time, the search for pleasure in food can also be an antidote against this mean material reality. Thus, food can function in a similar way to other postwar cultural forms like cinema and literature, serving both as sources of oppositional collective identity and as places of refuge.[8] The double attitude towards gastronomy, both as an act of resistance in the realm of popular culture and as a search for escape, would continue throughout his life.

Likewise, during his university years, gastronomy would become an act of resistance to and subversion of Franco's dictatorship, particularly throughout Vázquez Montalbán's imprisonment in Lérida between 1962 and 1963, where he would spend a year and a half sharing a cell with three other political prisoners (Salvador Clotas, Ferran Fullà, and Martí Capdevila). While in prison, Vázquez Montalbán built a makeshift stove with a large tin can for a pot and a smaller can for a stove. The stove was filled with alcohol-soaked cotton stolen from the prison infirmary where he worked, an anecdote that was frequently fictionalized in the Carvalho series. This improvised stove allowed him to experiment with cooking for his fellow prisoners, a small cell of intellectual resistance to the regime. The need to overcome their present circumstances was transcended by a mixture of subversion and surrealist acts of imagination. Thinking back on his time in prison, the author commented in the dedication to *Cuestiones marxistas*, "cuando fuimos en cierta manera los hermanos Marx" [when we were, in a way, the Marx brothers] (Vázquez Montalbán 1974a, 7), referring to the surrealist reunion of Carlos [Karl], Groucho, and Harpo Marx.[9] It was also in prison where he would meet a young car thief who, years later, became Biscuter, Pepe Carvalho's faithful helper in his investigations, as well as his makeshift cook. Paradoxically, prison, like his neighbourhood, becomes a refuge, a space of guarded freedom, of learning and intellectual dialogue. Here, he writes his first book of essays, *Informe sobre la información* [Report on information], his first stories, and his first books of poems.[10] Food, imagination, and creativity go together as cooking becomes a celebration of freedom and authentic imagination. In this small detail we can see the author's early outline, closer perhaps to the surrealist revolution than to orthodox Marxism, which connected with his vision of the permanent need to find a balance between the impulses to change history (Marx) and to change life (Rimbaud), frequently formulated in the generational dichotomy "Marat-Sade" that pervades all his work.[11]

II. Against the Theology of Food

Vázquez Montalbán's heterodox attitude towards gastronomy represents a position of dissidence towards hegemonic thought. His stance originates in a revolutionary way of conceiving culture, in a defence of gastronomy as a form of culture and identity, like other marginal or repressed cultural forms – such as popular songs, mass culture, or sexuality. At the same time, he opposes all the gastronomic and medical-cultural catechisms and any form of orthodoxy, straightforwardly confronting the "theology of food."

In fact, Vázquez Montalbán dedicates his attention to a subject that, with very few exceptions, had not been an object of serious reflection for Spanish writers and intellectuals.[12] Vázquez Montalbán's approach towards gastronomy conflicted with the neglect and abandonment of gastronomic culture at the time by leftist intellectuals, who regarded it as a reactionary and bourgeois idea. Precisely because of the ideological polarization of the time, the most important writings on gastronomy in the period came from the conservative or moderate political wings – as well as from the periphery of the state, where regional cuisines have always had greater force and have created a tradition of gastronomic writing.[13]

Vázquez Montalbán's appearance in Spanish letters would radically change this tendency, adding sociocultural, historical, and political depth to gastronomic literature in Spain. Indeed, Vázquez Montalbán brought gastronomic discourse to a position of maximum visibility, legitimizing it in the ideological context of anti-Franco (post)resistance that had previously considered it a bourgeois legacy, unworthy of the attention of a committed intellectual or leftist writer. The author justified his position in a playful, double front against the moderation and austerity of leftist hegemonic thought, which in a sense was nothing more than a variation of the morality of suffering and bodily repression typical of Falangist and Catholic Francoist thought. Thus, in the late 1960s, Vázquez Montalbán introduced the topic of gastronomy and sexuality as conscious antidotes and forms of provocation in the face of both Francoism and the antiludic cultural austerity of Marxism.

It is important to note as well that Vázquez Montalbán's break coincides with the new tendencies towards gastronomic reform – both in theoretical approaches and in culinary practices – that rose internationally during the 1960s and 1970s, and were later developed with the great experimental and innovative explosion at the end of the millennium. Such is the case with the boom of French *nouvelle cuisine* and the parallel "California cuisine" of Alice Waters (with her temple Chez-Panisse in Berkeley) that originated in the countercultural effervescence of those decades. With its discourse of ecology and healthy nutrition, this new "cuisine" modernized traditional gastronomic approaches and established a different conceptualization and practice at the international level. Thus, a new appreciation of fresh and natural cooking, with local and traditional roots, emerged in parallel with countercultural movements, vegetarianism, macrobiotics, and ecological agriculture.

The establishment of Vázquez Montalbán's gastronomic discourse also coincides with the first phase of culinary globalization in Spain during the 1970s and 1980s, after the successful process of *cocalización* or "Coca-Colification." Gastronomic consumption is rapidly transformed by the offerings of a plural marketplace with the sudden arrival of McDonald's, Burger King, Pizza Hut, and other multinational corporations; the palate is "industrialized" and the diet of the Spanish population changes radically, consequently eroding the foundations of the traditional Mediterranean diet. All of these factors produce a gastronomic discourse "of resistance." This period is also marked by the progressive cultural opening towards other international gastronomies after the Transition; timidly at first, limited to Italian and Chinese restaurants, but later opening to the exoticism of other, more remote and lesser-known cuisines, and finally to the experimentalism of *haute cuisine.*

In this sense, Vázquez Montalbán's position towards the process of gastronomic changes is complex and diverse. On the one hand, the author understands gastronomy as a form of memory and identity, and of resistance to the introduction of new culinary and consumption habits from abroad, especially to multinational agro-industrial corporations, which are iconic in their economic and cultural penetration, such as Coca-Cola or McDonald's.[14] Therefore, it constitutes a defence of tradition and cultural memory, which curiously coincides with the physicians who defend the health benefits of the Mediterranean diet. At the same time, he makes a bid for freedom and gastronomic fusion, experimentation, and a life-affirming defence of bodily pleasure – a certain hedonistic practice that is reflected throughout the author's work – in defiance of austerity, repression, and the mortification of flesh, both in sexuality and in other areas of corporal gratifications. The author situates himself in a position of political incorrectness, by running counter to the dietetic-medical discourses that proclaim the doctrine of diets, moderation, and the principle of health before pleasure. Thus, using political and legal terms, he has referred to "la dictadura de la cocina dietética" [the dictatorship of dietetic cuisine] and to the "almuerzos bajo libertad condicional" [luncheons under probation], in reference to dietetic prescriptions for diners (Vázquez Montalbán 1984, 11).

In this respect, *Contra los gourmets* constitutes his most elaborate, anti-theological critical manifesto with regard to these dietetic approaches, although this attitude appears in his earliest gastronomic writings. Already in *L'art del menjar* [The art of eating] (1977) he criticized indoctrination by deconstructing the rational, prescriptive bases of diets, doing it in his typically satirical, irrefutable manner (44–5). His corrosive satire of weight-loss clinics is the central subject of his 1986 novel *El balneario* [The spa], a symbolic *roman à clef* with clear political intentions, as he makes the spa a metaphor of the closed-off, privileged social club of the rich nations of the North.[15] Inspired by the author's stay at the famous Buchinger Clinic in Marbella, an elite oasis frequented by the rich and famous, the novel is another clear display of his sharp pen and anti-conventional point of view. Through caricature, the author disassembles the rhetoric of detoxification cures and liquid diets, which are exposed as false and useless like any other dispensable object of consumption promoted by the marketing of consumer society.[16] The contradictory personality of his fictional detective Pepe Carvalho stands out in this respect, since he is known for his alcoholic and culinary excesses, at times perpetrating borderline desperate and pathological acts that suggest the characteristics of a psychotic personality. On the other side of the coin of excess are the cures of fasting and weight-loss regimens in *El balneario*, with cures and obesity both presented as syndromes of cultures of abundance, before returning to "sinful" behaviours.[17]

Through a heavily political voice, the author clearly expressed his rejection of the morals of suffering, fasting, and restraint, legitimized by redemptive theological doctrines: "Para los moralistas, sólo el sufrimiento es moral. En las religiones hay ayunos, cuaresmas y ramadanes. Estoy en contra de todas ellas – la católica, la islámica y la neoliberal – porque, al defender valores absolutos, acaban siendo totalitarias" [For moralists, only suffering is moral. In religions there are fasts, Lents, Ramadans. I am against all of these – the Catholic, the Muslim, the neoliberal – because, by defending absolute values, they end up being totalitarian] (quoted in Preciado 1996). In Vázquez Montalbán's work on gastronomy, there is a sense of excess – as in many other senses of his copious work – that, paradoxically, is both vitally affirming and self-destructive.[18] It is an excess that manifests itself, as in the gastronomic field, in the sphere of the erotic, of the politically incorrect and unrestrained, and in that of the purely literary: in the overflow of generic limits, in encyclopedic erudition, in his condition as a multifaceted writer, and in his legendary prolific creative output.

Vázquez Montalbán understood gastronomy as a metaphor of culture and of knowledge, following Feuerbach's view that "el hombre es lo que come" [man is what he eats] (or what he reads). He considered gastronomy as a repository of cultural tradition and knowledge, but also as a form of social stratification and cultural difference.[19] Vázquez Montalbán always positioned himself against gastronomic theology, against culinary elitism, and when he wrote on gastronomy he tried to do it "sin caer en la dictadura del gourmet que suele convertirse en un teólogo poseedor de la verdad revelada desde los sabores" [without falling into the dictatorship of the gourmand, who often becomes a theologian possessing the truth revealed through flavours] (2002b, 10). The author himself described his book *Contra los gourmets* as the "inicio de su cruzada contra la teología de la alimentación" [beginning of his crusade against the theology of food] (1990a, 52). It consisted of a reasoned protest against the hegemonic discourses of gastronomic wizards and priests who proclaimed themselves spiritual leaders of the tribe, exercising a form of domination based on controlling the language that sustained their power. Vázquez Montalbán positions himself in opposition to this "theology of food," to the cultural elitism of the ruling class, criticizing the gourmands as "aprendices de teólogo" [theologian's apprentices] and the gastronome as a "sacerdote ensimismado" [self-absorbed priest] (1990a, 16). In that sense, his position is one of subversion of the language of power, in a similar vein to the recurring metaphor in his work of the myth of Prometheus, who stole fire from the gods in order to give it to men; that is to say, appropriating the power of language to give it to those without a voice.

Vázquez Montalbán understands his gastronomic project as a defence of a certain sense of life and collective history. On the one hand, gastronomy constitutes for him a reflection and a metaphor of culture. As he indicates in *Contra los gourmets*, "la gastronomía tiene una lógica histórica, y una estructura sociológica que refleja la sociedad que la contempla" [gastronomy has a historical logic and a sociological structure that reflects the society that contemplates it] (1990a, 17).[20] As I have set out previously in an essay on the role of food in the Pepe Carvalho novels, the gastronomic discourse of the series

> ... cumple primeramente una función referencial doble como reflejo del mundo real que ayuda a la construcción del mundo novelesco representado, proporcionando un detalle de color local pintoresco a la manera costumbrista, y literalmente como receta culinaria cuya lectura es degustada con placer en anticipación de su degustación real ... A su vez lo gastronómico sirve como radiografía analítica de la variada cultura popular de una sociedad determinada ... A través de la gastronomía se emprende la crónica antropológica de la sociedad española contemporánea. (Colmeiro 1994, 186)

> [... fulfils firstly a double referential role as reflection of the real world that helps with the construction of the fictional world, offering a detail of local colour in the *costumbrista* style, and literally as a cooking recipe whose reading is savoured with pleasure in anticipation of tasting the real thing

> … In turn, gastronomic elements serve as analytic tools for a radiography
> of the varied popular culture of a given society … Through gastronomy,
> an anthropological chronicle of contemporary Spanish society is carried
> out.]

On the other hand, this gastronomic discourse functions simultaneously as a political instrument for the reconstruction of the signs of cultural identity against the erosion provoked by hegemonic powers. Already in *Los mares del Sur* [Southern seas], the sybarite Marquis de Munt emphasizes that "últimamente la izquierda está empeñada en recuperar las famosas 'señas de identidad popular', y la cocina popular es una de ellas" [lately, the Left is insisting in recuperating the so-called "signs of popular identity," and popular cuisine is one of them] (1979b, 67). In that sense, Vázquez Montalbán proposed a defence of traditional cuisine in the face of economic and cultural neocolonialism (internal and external), the rhetoric of innovation for innovation's sake, and gastronomic snobbery:

> La gastronomía sirve también como vía de recuperación de las señas de
> identidad colectivas en medio de la desnaturalización general de la so-
> ciedad de consumo y la uniformidad masiva del neocolonialismo de las
> multinacionales. En una sociedad obsesionada por la pérdida de la iden-
> tidad cultural y entregada a la operación reivindicativa de la idiosincrasia
> autonómica, la búsqueda de las auténticas raíces culturales pasa por la
> recuperación de la cocina tradicional de la región. (Colmeiro 1994, 187)

> [Gastronomy also serves as a way of recovering the collective signs of
> identity in the midst of the general denaturalizing of consumer society
> and the massive uniformity of neocolonialism imposed by multinational
> corporations. In a society obsessed with the loss of cultural identity and
> dedicated to the defence of autonomous idiosyncrasy, the search for au-
> thentic cultural roots involves the recovery of regional traditional cuisine.]

Thus, from a position of raising political awareness, Vázquez Montalbán proposes a vindication of popular traditional gastronomy, with deep roots in people of the land and the sea, collected in the proverbial recipes of grandmothers, and the great variety and diversity of regional cuisines of Spain.[21] In that sense, Vázquez Montalbán, and his fictional alter ego Pepe Carvalho have always chosen to refer to Spanish gastronomy in the plural: "Carvalho es contrario a aceptar la existencia de cocinas nacional-estatales justificadas por el escaparate de la restauración capitalina. Las cocinas son zonales y modificadas por la evolución de los mercados, de ahí que sea más ilustrativo hablar de *cocinas de España* que de *Cocina Española*" [Carvalho is opposed to accepting the existence of national cuisines justified by the showcase of the capital's restaurants. Cuisines are region-based and are modified by the evolution of markets, and for this reason it makes more sense to speak of *Spain's cuisines* rather than of *Spanish cuisine*] (Vázquez Montalbán 2002b, 47, original emphasis). The author coincides with a rebirth of the national consciousness of peripheral gastronomies, with the open processes of political devolution and cultural decentralization of post-Francoism, with the search for and defence of autochthonous cultural roots, and with the new appreciation of collections of regional cuisine. As the author indicated, gastronomy functions as a reflection and metaphor of political changes in the national map: "Las en otro tiempo llamadas cocinas regionales españolas que cuentan con más bibliografía son la vasca, la catalana y la gallega, porque también en los fogones se cocieron los llamados hechos diferenciales" [The cuisines, which in other times were called regional Spanish cuisines, that have the most bibliography are the Basque, the Catalan, and the Galician, because in stoves too were cooked what we call the differential facts"] (2000b). The author argued for the defence of popular gastronomy (local, regional, and national) as a sign of cultural identity, at the same time that he denounced the gastronomic colonialism of the state and multinational corporations, particularly in the case of Catalonia.[22] In that sense, it is important to note that the original subtitle of his *L'art del menjar* was *Crónica de la resistència dels senyals d'identitat gastronòmica catalana* [Chronicle of the resistance of the signs of Catalan gastronomic identity], a book reedited in 1979 as *El llibre roig de la identitat gastronòmica catalana* [The red book of Catalan gastronomic identity], with the political and cultural undertones of Catalan gastronomy already clearly showcased in their titles. In the note to the second edition, the author evidences the important advance of Catalan gastronomy in the crucial years of the Transition, partly a result of his own intervention.[23]

The author marked the tight relationship between gastronomy and cultural and political-economic imperialism in a highly perspicacious way, highlighting the double meaning of "lengua" [tongue/language] in relation to imperialism: "Fue Nebrija quien dijo: 'Siempre fue la lengua compañera del Imperio', y nadie tiene porque interpretar la palabra lengua en una sola significación" [It was Nebrija who said: "Language was always the companion of Empire," and no one has reason to interpret the word "language" in only one way] (Vázquez Montalbán 1977, 23). Likewise, a casual commentary on gastronomy may serve to bring about a corrosive reflection on cultural globalization, forced homogeneity, and the erosion of difference:

> A mí me sacan de la hamburguesa, y me pierdo. Y eso que aún no estamos en la OTAN, pensó Carvalho. En cuanto nos metan en la OTAN lo primero que van a instalar van a ser oleoductos de catsup y de mostaza. (Vázquez Montalbán 1986b, 7)

> [If they take away my hamburger, I'm lost. And that's without us even being in NATO, thought Carvalho. As soon as they put us in NATO, the first thing they'll install is pipelines of ketchup and mustard.]

A central idea about gastronomy that runs through all of Vázquez Montalbán's thought is the artificiality and the double standard of culture, with gastronomy seen as a metaphor of power relations, domination, and cruelty on which the social framework is built. Basing his thought on Lévi Strauss's theory about the difference between culture and nature, the raw and the cooked, Vázquez Montalbán offers examples of the reversibility of the concepts of civilization and barbarism, culture and savagery, knowledge and cannibalism, order and crime:

> La cocina es una metáfora ejemplar de la hipocresía de la cultura. El llamado arte culinario se basa en un asesinato previo, con toda clase de alevosías. Si ese mal salvaje que es el hombre civilizado arrebatara la vida de un animal o de una planta y se comiera los cadáveres crudos, sería señalado con el dedo como un monstruo capaz de bestialidades estremecedoras. Pero si ese mal salvaje trocea el cadáver, lo marina, lo adereza, lo guisa y se lo come, su crimen se convierte en cultura y merece memoria, libros, disquisiciones, teoría, casi una ciencia de la conducta alimentaria. No hay vida sin crueldad. No hay historia sin dolor. (1990a, 9–10)

> [Cooking is an exemplary metaphor of the hypocrisy of culture. What we call the culinary art is based on a previous murder, with all kinds of malice. If that evil savage that is the civilized man snatched away the life of a plant or animal and ate the cadaver raw, he would be pointed at as a monster capable of horrifying bestialities. But if that evil savage chops up the cadaver, marinates it, seasons it, cooks it, and eats it, his crime becomes culture and deserves remembering, books, disquisitions, theory, almost a science of alimentary conduct. There is no life without cruelty. There is no history without pain.]

This idea that interconnects crime and culture is implicitly present through the whole Carvalho series, and Vázquez Montalbán developed it more explicitly in *Las recetas de Carvalho* [Carvalho's recipes], exposing gastronomy as a symbolic act that hides some fundamental violence:

Yo suelo plantear la cocina como una metáfora de la cultura. Comer significa matar y engullir a un ser que ha estado vivo, sea animal o planta. Si devoramos directamente al animal muerto o a la lechuga arrancada, se diría que somos unos salvajes. Ahora bien, si marinamos a la bestia para cocinarla posteriormente con la ayuda de hierbas aromáticas de Provenza y un vaso de vino rancio, entonces hemos realizado una exquisita operación cultural, igualmente fundamentada en la brutalidad y la muerte. Cocinar es una metáfora de la cultura y su contenido hipócrita, y en la serie Carvalho forma parte del tríptico de reflexiones sobre el papel de la cultura. Las otras dos serían esa quema de libros a la que Carvalho es tan aficionado y la misma concepción de la novela como vehículo de conocimiento de la realidad, desde el mestizaje de cultura y subcultura que encarna la serie Carvalho. (1989, 7)[24]

[I often suggest cooking as a metaphor for culture. Eating means killing and devouring a being that has been alive, whether animal or plant. If we devour a dead animal directly, or a lettuce freshly ripped from the ground, people would say we are savages. Now, if we marinate the beast in order to cook it later with the help of aromatic herbs de Provence and a glass of wine, then we have brought about an exquisite cultural operation, equally founded in brutality and death. Cooking is a metaphor for culture and its hypocritical content, and in the Carvalho series it constitutes one part of the triptych of reflections on the role of culture. The other two would be the book burning of which Carvalho is so fond and the concept itself of the novel as a vehicle for understanding reality, out of the fusion of culture and subculture that embodies the Carvalho series.]

Through the complex narrative instrument that is Pepe Carvalho, Vázquez Montalbán explores the contradictions, phobias, pleasures, violence, and emotions of gastronomy. Gastronomy forms an unmistakable part of Carvalho's characterization, accompanies his vital and psychological processes, is part of his memory and identity. As the author tells us, "Carvalho cocina por un impulso neurótico, cuando está deprimido o crispado" [Carvalho cooks because of a neurotic impulse when he is depressed or tense], the product of a "filosofía compulsiva y devoradora" [compulsive and devouring philosophy] (1989, 8).

Oftentimes, the processes of culinary preparation serve as deep immersions in the psychology and memory of the character.[25]

For Vázquez Montalbán, gastronomy is a fundamental part of individual and cultural experience, since his own identity is marked by the structure of the "palate of memory." His character Pepe Carvalho, like the author himself, identifies with the gastronomy of his memory, popular and familiar cuisine: "La base de sus gustos la forma una materia esencial: el paladar de la memoria, la patria sensorial de la infancia. Por eso sus gustos fundamentales proceden de la cocina popular, pobre e imaginativa de España, la cocina de su abuela, doña Francisca Pérez Larios, a la que dedica el nombre de un bocadillo notable, recogido en este recetario" [The base of his tastes is formed by an essential material: the palate of memory, the sensory homeland of childhood. For that reason, his fundamental tastes originate in the popular, poor, and imaginative cuisine of Spain, the cuisine of his grandmother, doña Francisca Pérez Larios, to whom he dedicates the name of a notable sandwich, collected in this cookbook] (1989, 8). A memorable scene, in that regard, is his remembrance of the "arroces individuales de su abuela" [individual rice dishes from his grandmother], an homage to the memory of the family and neighbourhood of his childhood in the context of the erosion of sites of memory after the "Olympification" of Barcelona. As a result of the political and economic conditions of the postwar period, food was poor, rationed for many years, and therefore always counted in the singular: "con una alcachofa sólo una, con un calamar sólo uno, un tomate, un pimiento, como si el uno fuera la expresión misma de su soledad y de la impotencia de comunicarse o simplemente de lo miserable de la pensión que cobraba" [with an artichoke, just one, with a squid, just one, one tomato, one pepper, as if one were the very expression of her loneliness and of her impotence of communicating or simply of how miserable the pension she received was] (2000a, 50–1).

Carvalho neither follows ideological or preconceived guidelines nor has any nationalist leanings. Nevertheless, he identifies gastronomically with the palate of his memory, in the end, his only homeland:

> Sus pocas creencias e ideales le alejan del chauvinismo patriótico o ideológico, de cualquier forma de nacionalismo, y le hacen español más por defecto y circunstancia que por convicción personal, como irónicamente comenta el narrador: "si la guerra de los Treinta Años no hubiera sentenciado la hegemonía de Francia en Europa, la cocina francesa a estas horas padecería la hegemonía de las cocinas de España. Su único patriotismo era gastronómico." (Colmeiro 2014, 161)

[His few beliefs and ideals distance him from patriotic or ideological chauvinism, from any form of nationalism, and they make him Spanish more by default and by circumstance than from any personal conviction, as the narrator ironically comments: "if the Thirty Years' War had not determined France's hegemony in Europe, French cuisine at this time would suffer the hegemony of Spain's cuisines. His only patriotism was gastronomic."]

It is others who try to describe him by nationality, since Carvalho always sees himself as a cultural hybrid on the border whose only homeland is his childhood. In the memorable scene of the murder in the Gourmet's Club in *Quinteto de Buenos Aires*, Carvalho is presented publicly as Spanish/Galician, that typical transatlantic confusion of Spanish identity resulting from the great Galician diaspora: "Os presento a un gran *gourmet* español: el señor Carvalho: Hoy representará entre nosotros la memoria del paladar español que es en buena parte nuestra propia memoria, bueno, la de los que somos de origen gallego" [I give you a great Spanish gourmet: mister Carvalho: today he will stand in, among us, for the memory of the Spanish palate that is in good part our own memory, that is, the memory of those of us who are of Spanish/Galician origin] (Vázquez Montalbán 1997, 436). But, as a sign of the times, Carvalho is also open to experimentation, improvisation, and fusion. He is therefore "eclectic" and "postmodern" in everything pertaining to the culinary arts: "Carvalho es gastronómicamente ecléctico. He aquí su única connotación posmoderna" [Carvalho is gastronomically eclectic. Behold his unique postmodern connotation]; "Nuestro hombre integra cocina catalana, cocina de autor de distintos restauradores de España y de diferentes extranjerías gastronómicas" [our man integrates Catalan cuisine, *haute cuisine* from various chefs of Spain and from different foreign gastronomies] (Vázquez Montalbán 1989, 8).

Carvalho's devotion to culinary and alcoholic pleasure is in inverse proportion to his antagonism for any cultural artifice and ideological baggage. The exaggerated anti-culturalism of the main character, who insists on bodily pleasures above artistic or literary pleasures, is present from the beginning of the series. His radical anti-culturalism and political incorrectness appear in his repeated remarks: "El sexo y la gastronomía son las cosas más serias que hay" [Sex and gastronomy are the most serious things there are] (1987c, 194); "Cambiaba a todo Rembrandt por un culo femenino hermoso o un plato de spaghetti a la carbonara" [He would exchange every Rembrandt for a woman's pretty ass or a plate of spaghetti à la carbonara] (1987c, 98); "Carvalho tiene el paladar en la memoria como algunas mujeres tienen el sexo en la garganta" [Carvalho has his palate in his memory the way some women have sex in their throat] (Vázquez Montalbán 1987a, 9).

In this sense, for Vázquez Montalbán, the relationship between gastronomy and sexuality is underlined as a form of opposition to hegemonic thought. In the editorial of the special issue of *Camp de l'arpa* on "Literatura y Gastronomía" coordinated by Vázquez Montalbán in 1979, the writer already realized that "La escritura sobre la mesa y cama es una escritura judaico-calvinista, culpable y culpabilizadora, tanto más culpable y culpabilizadora cuanto más excelso y pretencioso pretende ser el autor" [Writings on matters of the table and bed are Judeo-Calvinist writings, full of guilt and blame, and the more guilty and blaming they are, the more splendid and pretentious the author pretends to be] (1979a, 5). Precisely because he understands gastronomy as a metaphor of culture and society, it is very difficult to separate gastronomic discourse from that of sex or politics, other ingredients that reappear as thematic obsessions in all of his work:

Es bastante frecuente comprobar que la cultura literaria española desdeña hablar del sexo y la comida desde un extraño pudor sólo explicable por la vigilancia de la Iglesia, especialmente aplicada a los excesos del sexo y la pitanza, y cuántos pocos escritores insumisos han pecado en nuestra cultura de un exceso de austeridad y autoflagelamiento o complejo de culpa que les ha impedido valorar el prodigio de que un mercado pueda representar a una ciudad, como gran escenario de la tragicomedia de la cultura material alimentaria. (Vázquez Montalbán 2001, 199)

[Frequently enough one can prove that Spanish literary culture disdains to speak of sex and food out of a strange modesty that can only be explained by the Church's vigilance, especially when applied to excesses of sex and the daily ration of food, and how many rebellious writers have sinned in our culture out of an excess of austerity and self-flagellation or a guilt-complex that has kept them from valuing this wondrous fact that a food market can represent a city, like the great stage of the tragicomedy of material food culture.]

In this way, Vázquez Montalbán articulates the relationship between sexuality and gastronomy – what are called the innocent pleasures – which have traditionally been the object of demonization, considered as something low and sinful, immoral, by a self-righteous society:

Los placeres normalmente se convierten en material literario para estigmatizarlos, y no sólo la lujuria, que ha llevado al infierno de las escrituras

a buena parte de los mejores personajes, sino también a la comida, uti-
lizada sólo como paisaje por los grandes escritores o a lo sumo como dato
naturalista." (2002b, 6)

[Pleasures normally become literary material in order to stigmatize them,
not only lust, which has carried off to the scriptures' hell a good number
of the best characters, but also food, used only as a background by the
greatest writers, or at most as a naturalist datum.]

The author indicates an anti-theological alternative, a defence of
pleasure and even of excess in an effort to recover "una antigua y olvi-
dada alianza entre el hombre y el instinto de la felicidad" [an old and
forgotten alliance between man and the instinct of happiness] (1990a,
178). Likewise, in *Las recetas inmorales*, he defended an alternative morality, in regard to both food and love: "Cada una de estas recetas es
una apuesta por otra posible moral, por una moral hedonista al alcance
de los partidarios de la felicidad inmediata, basada en el uso e incluso
abuso de sabidurías inocentes: saber guisar, saber comer, intentar
aprender a amar" [Each of these recipes is a bid for another possible
morals, for a hedonist morals within reach of the partisans of immediate happiness, based on the use and even the abuse of innocent wis-
doms: knowing how to cook, knowing how to eat, trying to learn to
love] (1981b, 4).[26]

III. Globalization and Anti-Globalization: Super-Chefs and Slow Food

The tension observed between tradition and modernity in gastronomy,
between its attachment to roots and innovation, the defence of signs of
identity and homogeneity, resistance and cultural domination, takes on
new intensity because of the currents of globalization and the resistance movements of anti-globalization. In this new panorama of global
gastronomic consumption, Spain would enjoy a privileged position,
which translated into the ascendance of Spanish food in the international hierarchy, with the worldwide success of the concept of *tapas* and
the use of gastronomy as a distinctive element of the Spanish brand. In
this panorama, what stands out is the appearance of new superstars of
world gastronomy with new and heterodox approaches, with Spanish
chefs praised by Michelin guides, the *Restaurant* magazine rankings bestowed on Spanish restaurateurs, and the *New York Times* announcing
with fanfare that Spain, gastronomically, was "the new France." The
transformation of chefs into a media spectacle for global consumption,
as in the case of Ferran Adrià, Juan Mari Arzak, or José Andrés – like

stadium arena rock superstars, brand-name postmodern super-architects like Frank Gehry, Norman Foster, and Santiago Calatrava, or *supervedette* judges in the style of Baltasar Garzón within the new universal jurisdiction – follows the same planetary new order and logic. Gastronomy now functions as a reflection and metaphor of this new phase of globalized culture and the logic of capitalist transnational consumption.

The experimental gastronomic revolution of Spanish superstar chefs was captained by Ferran Adrià and his mythical restaurant El Bulli. Vázquez Montalbán was a travelling companion in this exploration of new culinary frontiers led by Adrià. Long before the unbounded success of the Catalan chef, Vázquez Montalbán spent periods of time resting on the Costa Brava, and from the mid-1980s on he was in the habit of visiting El Bulli's cove in his boat, when the chef's leap to international glory was still far off. Vázquez Montalbán established a relationship of friendship, understanding, and mutual devotion with Adrià, and he became the great intellectual force behind Adrià's gastronomic project. In this sense, too, the author went countercurrent, and it has taken a long time for his visionary position to be universally accepted, as his son recalled after his death: "Lo que realmente molestaba a estos ortodoxos es que tú, que habías escrito *L'art del menjar a Catalunya* y defendido la cocina de la memoria ... hubieras sido capaz de percibir el potencial de quienes iban a liderar una nueva generación de la cocina catalana, llamada a revolucionar la cocina mundial" [What really bothered those orthodox people is that you, who had written *L'art del menjar a Catalunya* and defended the cuisine of memory ... were capable of perceiving the potential of those who would lead a new generation of Catalan cuisine, called to revolutionize world cuisine] (Vázquez Sallés 2013, 121).[27]

Vázquez Montalbán also outlines an ideological resistance against the concept and practice of fast food imposed by multinational food corporations, mainly from the United States, as a new form of economic and cultural colonization, a metaphor of the new neoliberal global order:

Otros instrumentos de penetración cultural son perfectamente discutibles, especialmente los que giran en torno al *fast food* y sus dos elementos fetiches: la hamburguesa y la salsa *ketchup*. Ese tumor carnal y esa sanguinolenta salsa se suman a la conjura de la verdad única, el mercado único, el discurso único y el ejército galáctico único. (Vázquez Montalbán 2002b, 73)

[Other instruments of cultural penetration are perfectly arguable, especially those related to fast food and its two fetishes: the hamburger and ketchup. That carnal tumour and that bloody sauce make up the conspiracy of the sole truth, the sole market, the sole discourse, and the sole galactic army.]

Likewise, he criticizes the "*fast food* colonizador" [colonizing fast food] and "la barbarie de la cocina rápida" [the barbarism of fast food] (2002b, 73–4), proposing as an antidote the new, anti-globalization gastronomic movement that arose in Italy and that spread globally under the name Slow Food, in response to the shock wave of fast and junk food:

Frente a la cultura de la prisa hay que valorar empeños como el de Slow Food dentro del movimiento italiano de Archigola [*sic*], que reivindica un tiempo para cocinar, otro para comer y la salvación de aquellos productos y hábitos alimentarios amenazados por las pulsiones del mercado y la prisa. (2002b, 74)

[In the face of a culture of haste, one must value efforts like that of Slow Food within the Italian movement Archigola [*sic*], which defends time for cooking, time for eating, and the rescue of those alimentary products and habits threatened by the pressures of the market and of haste.]

In the last long journey of Carvalho and Biscuter in *Milenio* [Millennium], while passing through Italy they attend a dinner held by an alternative gastronomic group, which a waiter ironically describes as a "sect," surrounded by posters of Slow Food:

Se trata de una secta de gastrósofos, así me lo ha dicho un camarero, que se originó en la izquierda italiana, sobre todo en el PCI, y ha acabado convirtiéndose en un importante movimiento reformador del gusto y protector de variedades autóctonas frente a las incomprensivas normativas agrícola ganaderas del Mercado Común. Están en la fase de defensa de algo que llaman la Biodiversidad. (2007, 27)

[It's a sect of gastrosophers, that's how a waiter put it, that was organized among the Italian left, especially in the PCI, and that has ended up becoming an important movement for the reform of tastes and the protection of autochthonous varieties in the face of the thoughtless, agricultural-ranching regulations of the Common Market. They are in the defence-phase of something that they call Biodiversity.]

The narrator takes the opportunity to introduce a programmatic manifesto of the Slow Food movement, as a gastronomic critique from an ecological perspective of the political, economic, and cultural disorder of the global era:

> Lo cierto es que, en la parte del globo terráqueo que solemos habitar los lectores y escritores de Slow Food, la selección de las especies está condicionada por la lógica interna biológica de cada especie y la lógica del mercado, y sólo la inteligencia humana condicionada por la curiosidad o la compasión puede enfrentarse a tal fatalidad. Frente a la especulación inmobiliaria o industrial, hay que salvar un bosque o un río, y frente al juego de la vida o la muerte de las especies a veces hay que salvar la supervivencia de alguna de ellas especialmente amenazada por su fragilidad o por el mercado de todas las verdades, desde la científica a la alimentaria. (2007, 28–9)

> [What is certain is that, in that part of the globe that we, the writers and readers of Slow Food, tend to inhabit, the selection of species is conditioned by the internal biological logic of each species and by the logic of the market, and only human intelligence conditioned by curiosity or compassion can confront such a misfortune. In the face of real estate or industrial speculation, we must save a forest or a river, and in the face of the game of the life or death of species at times we must ensure the survival of some of those especially threatened by their fragility or by the market of all truths, from the scientific to the alimentary.]

From the perspective of this new anti-globalization revolution, respecting the "memoria del paladar," and one's own cultural identity, runs parallel to respecting biodiversity and nature:

> Slow Food es una apuesta por el saber como principal condicionante de la necesidad alimentaria. Salvar especies no sólo es un ejercicio lúdico o una operación más o menos narcisista del respeto a la propia memoria del paladar, sino también una filosofía de vida, porque conservar la supervivencia de una especie contribuye a la cultura de la vida en su totalidad. (2007, 30–1)[28]

> [Slow Food is a bid for knowledge as the principal determining factor of nutritional need. Saving species is not only a playful exercise or a more or less narcissistic operation with respect to the memory of the palate, but it is also a philosophy of life, because ensuring the survival of a species contributes to the culture of life in its totality.]

The vindicatory, pamphleteering tone of these statements collides with Carvalho's disillusioned scepticism, which shades the theoretical approaches, distancing himself from the temptation of a theology of food, from any sole and final truth:

> Me falta fe. En el fondo, estos gastrónomos ecólogos militan en una religión. Son optimistas, tienen el futuro como religión, aunque sean materialistas. Se creen capaces de salvar a la vaca chianina de la indiferencia de millones de tragones de proteínas, vengan de donde vengan, incluso de las hamburgueserías de McDonald's. Frente a ese optimismo sostengo mi pesimismo original. Mi total desacuerdo con la Creación tal como la entienden todas las religiones, es decir, como un acto mayestático y generoso de un Dios bueno o de una ignorada inteligencia superior y urdidora. La Creación es una chapuza impresentable que no resiste el más mínimo análisis ético porque se basa en la necesidad de matar para comer, convirtiendo así a todo ser vivo en un asesino directo o indirecto. (2007, 32)

> [I lack faith. At bottom, these ecologist-gastronomes serve in a religion. They are optimists, they have the future as their religion, although they are materialists. They believe themselves capable of saving the Chianina cow from the indifference of millions of protein gluttons, wherever they come from, even the hamburger stands of McDonald's. In the face of this optimism, I sustain my original pessimism. My total disagreement is with Creation as religions understand it, that is to say, as a majestic and generous act of a good God or of an unknown superior, designing intelligence. Creation is a disgraceful piece of shoddy work that does not hold up to the most minimal ethical analysis because it is based on the necessity of killing in order to eat, in this way making every living being a direct or indirect murderer.]

IV. Coda: Return to the Seed

As we have seen, for Vázquez Montalbán, the memory of the palate represents a return to the seed, to childhood, and therefore to a commitment to memory, the true homeland of the writer. In spite of his extensive knowledge as a well-travelled and encyclopedic gastronome and gourmet, in spite of his fame as a sybarite hedonist, in spite of his culinary and alcoholic excesses, in reality Vázquez Montalbán did not need much to reconcile with himself and his memory, so long as it was authentic and genuine. For Rafael Chirbes, "la vivencia de la felicidad montalbanesca no necesita de rotundas experiencias pantagruélicas" [the lived experience of Vázquez Montalbán's happiness does not need elaborate pantagruelian experiences] (cited in Alonso 2013, 15). It could simply be a "Señora Paca" sandwich, the individual rice dishes of his grandmother, or even a loaf of bread and some black olives, the multisensorial image of the palate of memory that runs through Vázquez Montalbán's work from beginning to end.

When Vázquez Montalbán was asked for a New Year's Eve sample menu for the magazine *Sobremesa*, the author sent them an autobiographical story, in which the protagonist, Manuel, waits in a ration line outside a bakery, as Luis Alonso recounted:

> De pronto tengo delante a mi madre, que me tiende pan caliente y una bolsita de papel de estraza llena de aceitunas negras, de las llamadas de Aragón, sin duda de allí venían, porque entonces se respetaba el turno de las estaciones y los mercados. Pan y aceitunas. Un título de película neorrealista, pero en el alma la saciedad de todos los deseos y el 31 de diciembre, después de las doce uvas, me tomaré furtivamente un pedazo de pan y un puñado de aceitunas negras. (Quoted in Alonso 2013, 15)

> [Suddenly I have my mother in front of me, holding out hot bread and a brown paper sack full of black olives, the kind they say are from Aragon, and there is no doubt they came from there because back then people respected the changing seasons and one's turn in the food markets. Bread and olives. A title for a neorealist film, but in my soul the satisfaction of all desires and on the 31st of December, after eating the twelve grapes at midnight, I will furtively eat a piece of bread and a handful of black olives.]

It is the same feeling of nostalgia noted in the early story "1945" and experienced by Carvalho in *Quinteto de Buenos Aires* when he remembers the country of his childhood:

> … era la posguerra en Barcelona y circulaban leyendas sobre hombres vampiros tuberculosos que les chupaban la sangre a los niños. Una mañana mi madre me dio un pedazo de pan que parecía recién hecho y un puñado de aceitunas negras que se llaman de Aragón. Recuerdo aquellos sabores, la alegría de la libertad de la calle. La mirada protectora de mi madre. Si pudiera volver a aquella mañana. Ésa sería mi verdadera patria. Mi Rosebud. ¿Recordáis *Citizen Kane*? – El país de la infancia. (Vázquez Montalbán 1997, 390)

> [… it was after the war in Barcelona, and stories were circulating about tuberculous vampire men that sucked children's blood. One morning, my mother gave me a piece of bread that looked freshly baked and a handful of black olives that they say are from Aragon. I remember those flavours, the happiness of the freedom of the street. My mother's protective gaze.

If I could return to that morning. That would be my true homeland. My *Rosebud*. Do you remember *Citizen Kane*? – The country of childhood.]

For Vázquez Montalbán, the bread and black olives, like the postwar period, were similar to Orson Welles's childhood *Rosebud*, a mixture of memory and desire. They represent that place from which one would never wish to return, and to which unfailingly one wishes to go back, as one desires the return to the seed, that pleasing location of the placenta (Tyras 2003, 84–5). That *Rosebud* is the authentic vertex of memory, the button that holds the memory of the palate and the formation of identity, as the author confessed in an interview:

... en la vida de todo escritor hay un *Rosebud* como el de *Ciudadano Kane*. Recuerdo un día que estaba sentado en el portal de mi casa, frente a la panadería, y vi salir a mi madre con un pan caliente y un cucurucho de aceitunas negras. Me dio un trozo de aquel pan con aceitunas. Eran los años cuarenta. Asocio el placer con el pan caliente y las aceitunas negras; es mi *Rosebud*. (Preciado 1996)

[in the life of every writer there is a *Rosebud* like that of *Citizen Kane*. I remember a day when I was sitting by the entrance to my house, in front of a bakery, and I saw my mother come out with hot bread and a cone of black olives. She gave me a slice of that bread with olives. It was the 1940s. I associate pleasure with hot bread and black olives; it is my *Rosebud*.]

In the television special *Epílogo* that Vázquez Montalbán recorded for Canal+, intended to be broadcast posthumously, when asked for a phrase to say goodbye to the world, the author chooses a culinary image that returns to his earliest history. The last reference is precisely to that particular *Rosebud* from the palate of his memory: "un puñado de aceitunas negras y un pedazo de pan caliente, que forma parte de una vivencia de infancia" [a handful of black olives and a piece of hot bread, which forms part of the lived experience of childhood] (Canal+ España 2003).

NOTES

1 See, for example, the work of Roser i Puig, Pérez Escohotado, Rodríguez Abella, Saval, Sánchez Gómez, Rodríguez-Morán, and Martínez Iturrioz. Unless otherwise noted, translations are by Gregory Baum.
2 In a parallel way, gastronomic subcultures have experienced the same process of identity reaffirmation and international recognition that would also

fit within the concept of a national brand. For an analysis of gastronomy's importance for Spain's brand, see the work of Alfredo Martínez Expósito and the webpage: http://marcaespana.es/es/educacion-cultura -sociedad/gastronomia.

3 For an analysis of Vázquez Montalbán's gastronomic journalism, see Sánchez Gómez (2007).

4 Most prominently, his cookbooks on Catalan gastronomy, *L'art del menjar a Catalunya* [The art of eating in Catalonia] (1977), its updated version (1979), and *Les meves recetes de cuina catalana* [My recipes of Catalan cuisine] (1995), his series on *Las Cocinas de España* [The cuisines of Spain] in four volumes dedicated to the traditional cuisines of Catalonia, Galicia, Valencia, and Extremadura (1980–1), and the cookbook *Tiempo para la mesa* (1986).

5 The construction of memory for Vázquez Montalbán is tied to certain gastronomic experiences from his early childhood on. Thus, his obsession with bread comes from the time of rationing and scarcity and from the experience of postwar imprisonment, as much his father's as his own. In this way, his son Daniel Vázquez Sallés remembers him posthumously: "Eras flaco como el alambre. Luego tu padre salió de la cárcel, y su obsesión por borrar las huellas del hambre canina acumulada en una celda acondicionada para los condenados a la pena capital te rompió el metaboslismo. '¡Come pan, come pan!', te gritaba el abuelo. Nunca culpaste a Evaristo de tus problemas de peso, y jamás le culparás por una compasión agridulce" [You were as skinny as a wire. Then your father came out of prison, and his obsession with erasing the traces of canine hunger, accumulated in a cell destined for those condemned to capital punishment, broke your metabolism. 'Eat bread, eat bread', my grandfather shouted at you. You never blamed Evaristo for your weight problems, and you will never blame him thanks to a bittersweet compassion] (2013, 17). In a rare Italian interview, Vázquez Montalbán confessed that his love for cooking went back to his oldest childhood memories, when he would cook for his mother, who worked all day outside the home. This dedication would continue when he was an adult and married, since his wife did not know how to cook (2006, 106).

6 As the author acknowledged in his monumental exercise of collective postwar memory, *Crónica sentimental de España*, when he talks about "los párvulos roedores de pan negro" [primary school children gnawing on black bread] (1986c, 43): "Esta crónica sentimental se escribe desde la perspectiva del pueblo ... que sustituía la mitología personal heredada de la guerra civil por una mitología de las cosas: el pan blanco, el aceite de oliva, el bistec de cien gramos ... La mitología del racionamiento y de las restricciones está presente de una manera obsesiva en los años cuarenta" [This sentimental chronicle is written from the perspective of the people ...

that replaced the personal mythology inherited from the Civil War with a mythology of things: white bread, olive oil, hundred-grams of beef ... The mythology of rationing and restriction is obsessively present during the 1940s] (35).

7 For an analysis of the story as a sentimental chronicle of childhood, see Parellada (2010), who describes this significant fragment as an "auténtico collage de los sentidos" [an authentic collage of the senses].

8 With regard to this, the author has indicated that in the postwar years of his childhood, he and his mother, "una desafecta de la realidad" [disaffected with reality], would escape to the theatre whenever they could and would spend the whole afternoon "mamando tecnicolor" [sucking technicolour] (Colmeiro 2013, 96).

9 As it may be obvious, this prison experience was of enormous importance both in his personal development and in confirming his identity as an intellectual. Commenting on the significance of a few lines of Cesare Pavese, whose reading accompanied him in prison, Vázquez Montalbán pointed out that "el pan es la *madalena* de Proust del encarcelado" [bread is the prisoner's Proustian madeleine] (Lyria 2004, 36). In his case, personal memory and the historical memory of that period go hand in hand with gastronomic reflection.

10 This autobiographical episode was going to be precisely the point of view of the chronicle-novel that Vázquez Montalbán intended to write before his death, *Memorias de la cárcel de Aridel* [Memoirs of the Prison of Aridel], as he indicated in one of his last interviews in Italy (Vázquez Montalbán 2006, 98–9). See also the Catalan TV documentary "Barcelona 1962. L'ombra dels Creix" (2014), "Barcelona 1962. L'ombra dels Creix," in which his three cellmates share detailed memories of those experiences.

11 See Colmeiro (2014, 39–42).

12 The case of Emilia Pardo Bazán is exceptional, who in this aspect, as in other areas of culture and knowledge, was ahead of her time. The writer understood gastronomy as an ethnographic document, both in her fiction and in her cookbooks.

13 Such as Josep Plà, Néstor Luján, Joan Perucho, and Xavier Domingo in Catalonia, or Manuel María Puga y Parga "Picadillo," Julio Camba, José María Castroviejo, and Álvaro Cunqueiro in Galicia. See in this regard Luján (1979).

14 Vázquez Montalbán used this sexual metaphor of penetration expressively, always influenced by the dialectic of master and slave, in his essay *La penetración americana en España* [The American penetration in Spain] (1974b).

15 The satiric view of the Buchinger Clinic appeared early in *Los mares del Sur* [Southern seas] (1979b, 51), and he also refers to his own experience in this

"Germanic and rational" clinic in *Mis almuerzos* (1984, 129). On the gastronomic lack of restraint in the Carvalho series, see Rodríguez Morán (2007).

16 See Vargas Llosa (1999), where the Peruvian author, a veteran visitor to the Buchinger Clinic, shows his worry about the possibility that writers will be prohibited from entering after the scandal of the "case" of Vázquez Montalbán's time in the clinic and his literary portrait of it.

17 As on other occasions, Vázquez Montalbán settles the score with his phobias and his adversaries through the characters of his fiction. He did this with the assassination of the leader of the Communist Party in Spain in *Asesinato en el Comité Central* [Murder in the Central Committee], and in a metafictional way with the director Aristarain (director of the first and infamous television series on Carvalho) in *Asesinato en Prado del Rey* [Murder at the Prado del Rey], with the editorial world in *El premio* [The prize], with the neoliberal hero in *El hombre de mi vida* [The man of my life], and with the medical, legal, and academic establishment in *El estrangulador* [The strangler].

18 See his speech "El corazón como fruto amargo" [The heart as bitter fruit] (2002a), given to the Association of Spanish Cardiologists, written from his condition as a gastronomic hedonist and a sufferer of cardiopathy, where he reiterates his conviction that "la cocina es la gran máscara de la operación de matar para comer" [gastronomy is the great mask of the operation of killing to eat] (1169).

19 In this regard, see Saval (1995).

20 This aspect of Vázquez Montalbán's novels, so rich in autochthonous cultural references, makes them a challenge to transfer and translate into other languages. See, for example, Rodríguez Abella (2008 and 2012) for an analysis of the idiosyncratic linguistic-cultural culturemes from gastronomy used in the Pepe Carvalho novels, and the difficulties of translating them into Italian.

21 At the same time, he affirms the cultural identity of gastronomy from the conviction that "todas las cocinas son mestizas. Sólo el crudívoro puede presumir de conservar, si quiere, una cocina tan original que se remonta al instinto depredatorio" [all cuisines are *mestizas*. Only the crudivorous can brag about conserving, if he will, a cuisine so original that it dates back to the depredatory instinct] (Vázquez Montalbán 2003e, 9).

22 For a general analysis of gastronomy in Catalonia, see Roser i Puig (2011).

23 See the prologue to the second edition of the book: http://www.vespito. net/mvm/intmenj.html. The author was fully conscious of his role in the great transformation of gastronomy within the cultural Spanish and Catalan map; for example, on a macro scale, the literary mythologizing of emblematic places in Barcelona of the palate of memory – restaurants like Casa Leopoldo or Quo Vadis, or markets like La Boquería – of its

transformation into a place of identity and memory, and of its central role in that process. Thus, in one of his last books, he reflected on the role of the Carvalho series as a vehicle for discovering reality and affirming identity and memory, individual and collective, for themselves and for foreigners, in relation to food: "Debo haber sido yo y muy especialmente mi personaje Pepe Carvalho el que haya contribuido a literaturizar la relación espacio, tiempo y memoria que propicia un mercado que has intentado leer, es decir, descodificar. Y como eco de este Carvalho que compra en la Boquería, me he encontrado a veces con lectores extranjeros que aprovechan su visita a Barcelona para descubrir la verdad o la mentira de un mercado ya mítico, vinculado al detective" [It must have been me, and especially my character Pepe Carvalho, who contributed to turning into literature the relation between space, time, and memory generated by the market you have tried to read, that is, to decodify. And as an echo of the Carvalho who shops at the Boquería market, I have found foreign readers who, in their visits to Barcelona, seize the opportunity to discover the truth or lie of an already mythical market connected to the detective] (Vázquez Montalbán 2001, 204). On the recovery of traditional markets in Catalonia, see García-Fuentes et al. (2014).

24 See also Vázquez Montalbán (1990b). Montalbán has also frequently used the parable of Robinson/Ciro Smith to express the mastery of knowledge over nature. He does this in *Reflexiones de Robinson ante un bacalao*, relating gastronomic, theological, and political discourses through the allegory of a cookbook written by a shipwrecked old bishop based on the manna sent by Providence in the form of a cod fish, all seen from the Marxist point of view of using and transforming material culture. Here Vázquez Montalbán proposes multiple ways of cooking the cod fish as an ironic *summa theologica*, possibly inspired by the classic book of the Galician gastronome Picadillo, *36 maneras de guisar el bacalao* [36 ways of cooking cod] (1901).

25 On the multiple roles of gastronomic discourse in the Carvalho series, see Colmeiro (2013, 64). Aranda has shown the importance of the gastronomic drifts in the Carvalho series and its provocative attitude towards the rigid norms of the detective genre. From a technical viewpoint, they are also literary instruments used as a way of creating suspense and narrative rhythm. See Colmeiro (2013, 186–7).

26 With regard to this, see Preciado (1996), an interview with Vázquez Montalbán on the subjects of cuisine, sex, and politics.

27 On the wars between traditional and experimental restaurateurs and the gastronomic polemic around Vázquez Montalbán's position with regard to this, see Vázquez Sallés (2013, 121–3). Symbolically, the writer's ashes were spread on the waters of Cala Montjoi, in front of the restaurant El Bulli, in consideration of "un lugar en que hubieras disfrutado mucho …

con El Bulli resguardando tus espaldas" [a place you would have enjoyed very much ... with El Bulli guarding your back] (Vázquez Sallés 2013, 77).

28 Elsewhere, Vázquez Montalbán makes reference to this same dialogue, recognizing explicitly how much tied him to these approaches, beyond the possible theological sectarianism: "[un texto] que utilizo para hablar de esta complicidad indiscutible que me ata al Slow Food, un frente filosófico bionaturista y materialista, en el sentido más elevado del materialismo, el materialismo subliminal más conectado con la teoría de las necesidades que con la de la resurrección de la carne" [(a text) I use to talk about this unquestionable complicity that ties me to the Slow Food movement, a philosophical bio-naturist and materialist front, in the highest sense of materialism, the subliminal materialism more connected to the theory of needs than to the resurrection of the flesh] (Lyria 2004, 39).

WORKS CITED

Adrià, Ferrán. "Un intelectual de la cocina." *El País*. 20 October 2003: 40.

Alonso, Luis M. "La memoria del paladar." *Faro de Vigo*. 17 November 2013: 15.

Aranda, Quim. 1997. "Carvalho y la cocina." Epilogue to *El balneario*. Barcelona: Planeta.

"Barcelona 1962. L'ombra dels Creix." 2014. *Senseficció*. 28 October. TV-3.

Canal+ España. 2003. *Epílogo: Manuel Vázquez Montalbán*. 21 October. https://www.youtube.com/watch?v=SRwqP3lpTI0

Colmeiro, José. 1994. *La novela policiaca española: teoría e historia crítica*. Barcelona: Anthropos.

Colmeiro, José. 2013. *El ruido y la furia: Conversaciones con Manuel Vázquez Montalbán, desde el planeta de los simios*. Madrid and Frankfurt: Editorial Iberoamericana and Vervuet.

Colmeiro, José. 2014. *Crónica general del desencanto: Vázquez Montalbán – Historia y ficción*. Barcelona: Anthropos.

García-Fuentes, Josep-María, Manel Guàrdia Bassols, and José Luis Oyón Bañales. 2014. "Reinventing Edible Identities: Catalan Cuisine and Barcelona's Market Halls." In *Heritage, Culture and Identity: Edible Identities: Food as Cultural Heritage*, edited by Ronds Brulotte and Michael Di Giovine, 159–74. Farnham: Ashgate Publishing.

Luján, Néstor. 1979. "De la literatura del hambre a los deleites del paladar." *Camp de l'arpa* 70: 7–9.

Lyria, Hado, ed. 2004. *Il viaggio in Italia. Omaggio del Premio Grinzane a Manuel Vázquez Montalbán*. Piacenza: Frassinelli.

Martínez Expósito, Alfredo. 2015. "Tapas, dietas y chefs: La Marca España en el nuevo cine gastronómico español." In *Encrucijadas globales: Redefinir*

España en el Siglo XXI, edited by José Colmeiro, 285–310. Madrid: Editorial Iberoamericana-Vervuert.

Martínez Iturrioz, María Teresa. 1992. "Hay que beber para recordar y comer para olvidar: Pepe Carvalho." In *Codici del gusto*, edited by Maria Grazia Profeti, 45–51. Milan: Francoangeli.

Parellada, Joaquín. 2010. "'1945': Crónica sentimental de la infancia." In *Manuel Vázquez Montalbán desde la memoria. Ensayos sobre su obra*, edited by José Manuel López de Abiada et al., 410–31. Madrid: Verbum.

Pérez Escohotado, Javier. 2010. "El pensamiento gastronómico de Manuel Vázquez Montalbán." In *Manuel Vázquez Montalbán desde la memoria. Ensayos sobre su obra*, edited by José Manuel López de Abiada et al., 432–51. Madrid: Verbum.

Preciado, Nativel. "Hay una relación directa entre comer, beber y amar." *Tiempo*. 4 November 1996. Vespito.net.

Puga y Parga, Manuel María. 1901. *36 maneras de guisar el bacalao*. La Coruña: Imp. Roel.

Rodríguez Abella, Rosa María. 2008. "El hombre de mi vida: Análisis de la traducción de los culturemas del ámbito gastronómico." In *La comunicación especializada*, edited by Carmen Navarro et al., 319–55. Bern: Peter Lang.

Rodríguez Abella, Rosa María. 2012. "La traducción de los elementos culturales en una novela de Vázquez Montalbán." In *Atti del XXIV Congresso AISPI*, 709–33. Padua: AISPI.

Rodríguez-Morán, Gustavo. 2007. "Del bien comer y del bien escribir: Desestabilizando cánones culturales en la Serie Carvalho." In *Manuel Vázquez Montalbán: El compromiso con la memoria*, edited by José F. Colmeiro, 91–102. Woodbridge: Tamesis.

Roser i Puig, Montserrat. 2011. "What's Cooking in Catalonia?" In *A Companion to Catalan Culture*, edited by Dominic Keown, 229–52. Woodbridge: Tamesis.

Sánchez Gómez, Fernando. 2007. "La columna gastronómica de Manuel Vázquez Montalbán." *Tonos. Revista electrónica de estudios filológicos* 14. http://www.um.es/tonosdigital/znum14/secciones/estudios-24-Gastronomia.htm.

Saval, José Vicente. 1995. "La lucha de clases se sienta a la mesa en *Los mares del sur* de Manuel Vázquez Montalbán." *Revista Hispánica Moderna* 48: 389–400.

Tyras, Georges. 2003. *Geometrías de la memoria. Conversaciones con Manuel Vázquez Montalbán*. Granada: Zoela Ediciones.

Vargas Llosa, Mario. "Agua sin pan." *El País*, 22 August 1999. https://elpais.com/diario/1999/08/22/opinion/935272807_850215.html.

Vázquez Montalbán, Manuel. 1974a. *Cuestiones marxistas*. Barcelona: Anagrama.

Vázquez Montalbán, Manuel. 1974b. *La penetración americana en España*. Madrid: Cuadernos para el diálogo.

Vázquez Montalbán, Manuel. 1977. *L'art del menjar a Catalunya. Crònica de la resistència dels senyals d'identitat gastronòmica catalana*. Barcelona: Edicions 62.

Vázquez Montalbán, Manuel. 1979a. "Contra la tuberculosis y la esquizofrenia." *Camp de l'arpa* 70: 5–6.

Vázquez Montalbán, Manuel. 1979b. *Los mares del Sur*. Barcelona: Planeta.

Vázquez Montalbán, Manuel. 1980a. *Las Cocinas de España: Cataluña*. Madrid: Sedmay.

Vázquez Montalbán, Manuel. 1980b. *Las Cocinas de España: Extremadura*. Madrid: Sedmay.

Vázquez Montalbán, Manuel. 1980c. *Las Cocinas de España: Galicia*. Madrid: Sedmay.

Vázquez Montalbán, Manuel. 1981a. *Las Cocinas de España: Valencia*. Madrid: Sedmay.

Vázquez Montalbán, Manuel. 1981b. *Las recetas inmorales*. Barcelona: Oh, Sauce.

Vázquez Montalbán, Manuel. 1984. *Mis almuerzos con gente inquietante*. Barcelona: Planeta.

Vázquez Montalbán, Manuel. 1986a. *Tiempo para la mesa*. Barcelona: Difusora Internacional.

Vázquez Montalbán, Manuel. 1986b. "El barco fantasma." In *Historias de fantasmas*. Barcelona: Planeta.

Vázquez Montalbán, Manuel. 1986c. *Crónica sentimental de España* [1971]. Madrid: Espasa-Calpe.

Vázquez Montalbán, Manuel. 1987a. "Federico III de Castilla y León." *Historias de política ficción*. Barcelona: Planeta.

Vázquez Montalbán, Manuel. 1987b. *Pigmalión y otros relatos*. Barcelona: Seix Barral.

Vázquez Montalbán, Manuel. 1987c. *Tatuaje* [1974]. Barcelona: Planeta.

Vázquez Montalbán, Manuel. 1989. *Las recetas de Carvalho*. Barcelona: Planeta.

Vázquez Montalbán, Manuel. 1990a. *Contra los gourmets* [1985]. Barcelona: Difusora Internacional and Muchnick.

Vázquez Montalbán, Manuel. 1990b. "Entre el canibalismo y la gastronomía." *El País*, 27 April: 18.

Vázquez Montalbán, Manuel. 1995a. *Les meves receptes de cuina catalana*. Barcelona: Edicions 62.

Vázquez Montalbán, Manuel. 1995b. *La gula. Reflexiones de Robinsón ante un bacalao*. Barcelona: Lumen.

Vázquez Montalbán, Manuel. 1997. *Quinteto de Buenos Aires*. Barcelona: Plenta.

Vázquez Montalbán, Manuel. 2000a. *El hombre de mi vida*. Barcelona: Planeta.

Vázquez Montalbán, Manuel. 2000b. "Una nación gastronómica." *El País*, 27 August.

Vázquez Montalbán, Manuel. 2000c. "Las angulas y la bondad de la creación." *El País*, 30 August.

Vázquez Montalbán, Manuel. 2001. *La Boquería: la catedral dels sentits*. Barcelona: Ajuntament de Barcelona.

Vázquez Montalbán, Manuel. 2002a. "El corazón como fruto amargo o como cazador solitario." *Revista Española de Cardiología* 55: 1169–72. https://doi.org/10.1016/S0300-8932(02)76780-8.

Vázquez Montalbán, Manuel. 2002b. *Saber o no saber*. Colección Carvalho gastronómico 1. Barcelona: Ediciones B.

Vázquez Montalbán, Manuel. 2002c. *La cocina de autor en España*. Colección Carvalho gastronómico 2. Barcelona: Ediciones B.

Vázquez Montalbán, Manuel. 2003a. *La cocina del Mediterráneo y la mediterraneidad*. Colección Carvalho gastronómico 3. Barcelona: Ediciones B.

Vázquez Montalbán, Manuel. 2003b. *Beber o no beber*. Colección Carvalho gastronómico 4. Barcelona: Ediciones B.

Vázquez Montalbán, Manuel. 2003c. *Guía de restaurantes obligatorios*. Colección Carvalho gastronómico 5. Barcelona: Ediciones B.

Vázquez Montalbán, Manuel. 2003d. *La cocina de la harina y el cordero*. Colección Carvalho gastronómico 6. Barcelona: Ediciones B.

Vázquez Montalbán, Manuel. 2003e. *La cocina del mestizaje*. Colección Carvalho gastronómico 7. Barcelona: Ediciones B.

Vázquez Montalbán, Manuel. 2003f. *La cocina de los finisterres*. Colección Carvalho gastronómico 8. Barcelona: Ediciones B.

Vázquez Montalbán, Manuel. 2003g. *Diccionario indispensable para la supervivencia*. Colección Carvalho gastronómico 9. Barcelona: Ediciones B.

Vázquez Montalbán, Manuel. 2003h. *El otro recetario*. Colección Carvalho gastronómico 10. Barcelona: Ediciones B.

Vázquez Montalbán, Manuel. 2006. *L'Utopia di Pepe Carvalho. Racconti e interviste*. Roma: Datanews.

Vázquez Montalbán, Manuel. 2007. *Milenio Carvalho*. Barcelona: Planeta.

Vázquez Sallés, Daniel. 2013. *Recuerdos sin retorno (Para Manuel Vázquez Montalbán)*. Barcelona: Península.

Contributors

José Colmeiro (PhD, UC-Berkeley) has held the Príncipe de Asturias Chair in Spanish Studies at the University of Auckland since 2010. He has published widely on Spanish, Galician, and Hispanic transatlantic cultural studies. Major recent publications include *Peripheral Visions/ Global Sounds: From Galicia to the World* (2017); *Crónica general del desencanto: Vázquez Montalbán – Historia y ficción* (2014); *Galeg@s sen fronteiras* (2013); *El ruido y la furia: Conversaciones con Manuel Vázquez Montalbán* (2013); and *Memoria histórica e identidad cultural* (2005). Recent edited work includes the volumes *Repensar los estudios ibéricos desde la periferia* (2019); *Encrucijadas globales: Redefinir España en el siglo XXI* (2015); and *Manuel Vázquez Montalbán: El compromiso con la memoria* (2007). He has also authored critical editions of Vázquez Montalbán's *El pianista* (2017) and Silvia Mistral's *Éxodo: Diario de una refugiada española* (2009). As a fiction writer, he is the author of the forthcoming novel *Cambios de piel* (2021).

Frederick A. de Armas is Andrew W. Mellon Distinguished Service Professor in the Department of Romance Languages and Literatures at the University of Chicago, where he has also served as Chair of the Department and Director of Graduate Studies. He has been President of the Cervantes Society of America and President of AISO. He received his PhD from the University of North Carolina, Chapel Hill (1969) and has been honoured with a doctorate *honoris causa* from the University of Neuchâtel (Switzerland) in 2018. His more recent books and collections include *Cervantes, Raphael and the Classics* (1998); *Writing for the Eyes in the Spanish Golden Age* (2004); *Quixotic Frescoes: Cervantes and Italian Renaissance Art* (2006); *Ovid in the Age of Cervantes* (2010); *Objects of Culture in the Literature of Imperial Spain* (2013); and *El retorno de Astrea: astrología, mito e imperio en Calderón* (2016). He has also authored two novels set in Cuba in the late 1950s: *El abra del Yumurí* (2016) and *Sinfonía salvaje* (2019).

Ryan D. Giles is Professor in the Department of Spanish and Portuguese at Indiana University, Bloomington. His research centres on medieval and early modern Iberian works – in particular parody and satire, picaresque writing, and expressions of sanctity and popular devotion. He is the author of *The Laughter of the Saints: Parodies of Holiness in Late Medieval and Renaissance Spain* (2009) and *Inscribed Power: Amulets and Magic in Early Spanish Literature* (2017). He co-edited (with Matthew Bailey) *Charlemagne and His Legend in Early Spanish Literature and Historiography* (2016); (with Steven Wagschal) *Beyond Sight: Engaging the Senses in Iberian Literatures and Cultures, 1200–1700* (2018); and (with José Manuel Hidalgo) *A New Companion to the "Libro de buen amor"* (2021). He won the John K. Walsh Prize for an outstanding essay in 2008 and 2016.

Dorota Heneghan is an Associate Professor of Spanish at Louisiana State University. She is the author of *Striking Their Modern Pose: Fashion, Gender, and Modernity in Galdós, Pardo Bazán, and Picón* (2015). She received her PhD in Spanish from Yale University and specializes in nineteenth- and twentieth-century Spanish peninsular literature and culture, gender studies, comparative literature, and transatlantic studies. Her work has appeared in *Anales Galdosianos, Hispanic Review, Bulletin of Hispanic Studies, Siglo Diecinueve,* and *Revista de Estudios Hispánicos.* She is currently working on a book-length project tentatively entitled *Gender Relations and Nation in Sofía Casanova's Writings from Poland (1913–1933).*

James Mandrell teaches Hispanic studies at Brandeis University, where he also participates in the programs in American Studies and Film Studies and directs the University Writing Program. He is the author of *Don Juan and the Point of Honor: Seduction, Patriarchal Society, and Literary Tradition* (1992) and has published on Spanish literature and culture, as well as Latin American and comparative literature, and US popular culture.

Carolyn Nadeau is the Byron S. Tucci Professor of Spanish and teaches medieval and early modern Spanish literature and culture classes at Illinois Wesleyan University. Her research focuses primarily on food representation in early modern Spain. *Food Matters: Alonso Quijano's Diet and the Discourse of Early Modern Food in Spain* was published in

2016. Other recent publications include articles on images of taste on the early modern Spanish stage, sensory ailments in early modern domestic literature, peppers and basil as Old World–New World markers in the writing of Cervantes, a gastronomic map of *Don Quixote*, the role of wine in the formation of Morisco identity, and contributions of medieval food manuals to Spain's culinary heritage. With the support of an NEH fellowship, she is currently finishing a critical edition and translation of Francisco Martínez Montiño's *Arte de cocina, pastelería, vizcochería y conservería* [The art of cooking, pie making, pastry making and preserving] (1611).

Íñigo Sánchez-Llama is Professor of Modern Spanish Literature and Culture at Purdue University. He is the Series Editor of Purdue Studies in Romance Literatures and Cultures (PSRL) and member of the editorial board of *Siglo Diecinueve* and *Anales Galdosianos*. He is the author of a monograph on Isabelline women writers and has prepared critical editions of Isabelline women's journalism, Benito Pérez Galdós's novels, and Emilia Pardo Bazán's essays. He has published refereed articles in *Hispanic Review*, *Revista Hispánica Moderna*, *Romance Quarterly*, *Dieciocho*, *Siglo Diecinueve*, *Hispanófila*, *Hispania*, *Letras Peninsulares*, *Boletín Galego de Literatura*, *La Tribuna*, and *Studi Ispanici*. He is currently working on a book on representations of Spanish modernity in Spanish essays written between the 1850s and the 1930s.

Fernando Serrano Larráyoz is Professor in the Departamento de Cirugía, Ciencias Sanitarias y Sociales in the Facultad de Medicina y Ciencias de la Salud at the Universidad de Alcalá. His research pertains to food, medicine, and pharmacy in the kingdoms of Navarra and Castile during the late Middle Ages and the Renaissance, and food and medical lexicography in the kingdom of Navarra during the same period. He has published several studies on these topics, including *La mesa del rey: cocina y régimen alimentario en la corte de Carlos III "el Noble" de Navarra (1411–1425)* (2002); *Medicina y enfermedad en la corte de Carlos III "el Noble" de Navarra (1387–1425)* (2004); and *Léxico médico y farmacológico en lengua vulgar y latina de la documentación cortesana navarra (siglos XIV–XV)* (2015). He has also authored a study and prepared a two-volume facsimile edition of Juan Vallés's *Regalo de la vida humana* (2008).

John Slater is the author of *Todos son hojas: Literatura e historia natural en el barroco español* (2010), as well as co-editor of *Medical Cultures of the Early Modern Spanish Empire* (2014) and Calderón de la Barca's *En la vida* *todo es verdad y todo mentira* and *Sueños hay que verdad son* (2016). His research examines the ways that competing regimes of representation – primarily literature, sacred oratory, and science – organize human beings' understanding of the natural world in seventeenth-century Spain. He is the author of over fifty publications, and his articles and reviews have appeared in journals such as *Isis, MLN, Renaissance Quarterly*, and *Social History of Medicine*. He has taught at Indiana University, the University of Colorado, and the University of California, Davis; he joined the faculty of Colorado State University in 2020.

Julio Vélez-Sainz received his PhD in Romance Languages from the University of Chicago (2002) and in Hispanic Philology from the University of Salamanca (2008). He is Catedrático (Professor) of Literature at the Universidad Complutense de Madrid, where he directs the Theatre Research Institute and two group research projects: one on classical drama (ucm.es/PTCE) and one on the contemporary stage (teatrero. com). He has been Assistant Professor at the University of Massachusetts–Amherst and Ramón y Cajal fellow at the Complutense. He has also been invited to teach at Brown University, the University of Georgia, and the University of Chicago as well as the Université de Toulouse-Jean-Jaurès and the Université de Neuchâtel. He has published over one hundred articles and book chapters, seven monographs, nine critical editions, and thirteen edited volumes. He blogs on theatre and culture on the Huffington Post, Spain https://www.huffington-post.es/author/julio-velez-sainz.

Index

Acosta, Cristóbal, 4
adafina, 6, 52
Adrià, Ferran, 3, 263–4, 273–4n27
Alarcón, Juan de, 16, 98, 105–9, 110,
    113–14, 117n9, 118n26
Alba, Dukes of, 116n6, 130, 134n7
Alba, first Duke of (García Álvarez
    de Toledo), 116–17n6
Alcalá Galiano, Antonio, 203, 206, 220
Alfonso X, 30, 34, 36, 39–41, 42n4
alimentación, 4
Altamiras, Juan, 185–7, 194; *Nuevo
    arte de cocina*, 185–7
Álvarez de Toledo, García. *See* Alba,
    first Duke of
Ambrose of Milan, 34–5
Andrés, José, 263
Anthony of Padua, 35–6
Antidotarium Nicolai, 117n8
appetite, 18, 140, 155, 178, 183, 184,
    187, 191, 193, 194, 235, 237, 238–9,
    242nn10, 19, 243n20
Apuleius, 141–50, 164, 166nn13, 15
Arellano, Ignacio, 152, 166n13
Aristotle, 123
arroz. See rice
Arzak, Juan Mari, 263
Astraea, 19, 157
Augustine of Hippo, 8, 35

Avicenna, 105
Azorín (José Martínez Ruiz), 214, 220

Badius Ascensius, 123
banquet of sense, 15, 17–18, 140, 144,
    150, 152, 158–62, 163, 164
Banquete de nobles caballeros, 100, 124,
    132–3n2
Barbiere, Domenico del, 160–1
Barthes, Roland, 10–12
Bartolo de Saxoferrato, 133n3
Baum, Gregory, 20, 114n1, 132n1,
    218n1, 269n1
Bavarian cuisine, 69
Bible, 8, 34–6, 40–1, 75
Blanco White, José María, 203
bodegones. See still lifes
Bonaventure, St, 35–6, 40
Boschetti, Isabella, 141, 165n4
Bourbons, Bourbon dynasty, 177,
    179–80, 182, 194–5n1
Bourdieu, Pierre, 132, 208, 211, 212
Bouza, Fernando, 123
Brillat-Savarin, Anthelme, 227
Bryson, Norman, 14

Calderón de la Barca, Pedro, 17, 51,
    139, 144, 145–54, 162, 164; *La cena
    del rey Baltasar*, 150–4, 167nn20, 25;

Toronto Iberic

CO-EDITORS: Robert Davidson (Toronto) and Frederick A. de Armas (Chicago)

EDITORIAL BOARD: Josiah Blackmore (Harvard); Marina Brownlee (Princeton); Anthony J. Cascardi (Berkeley); Justin Crumbaugh (Mt Holyoke); Emily Francomano (Georgetown); Jordana Mendelson (NYU); Joan Ramon Resina (Stanford); Enrique García Santo-Tomás (U Michigan); H. Rosi Song (Durham); Kathleen Vernon (SUNY Stony Brook)